D1615768

DEMOCRATIC
THEORY
AND
TECHNOLOGICAL
SOCIETY

DEMOCRATIC THEORY AND TECHNOLOGICAL SOCIETY

Edited by

Richard B. Day
Ronald Beiner
Joseph Masciulli

M. E. Sharpe, Inc.
Armonk, New York, and London, England

Library of Congress Cataloging-in-Publication Data

Democratic theory and technological society.

    1. Democracy.   2. Technocracy.   3. Technology and civilization—
Political aspects.   I. Day, Richard B.   II. Beiner, Ronald, 1953–
III. Masciulli, Joseph, 1947–
JC 423.D444   1988   321.8   88-4442
ISBN 0-87332-448-X

Printed in the United States of America.

MA   10 9 8 7 6 5 4 3 2

In Memory of

Crawford Brough Macpherson

1911 - 1987

CONTENTS

INTRODUCTION

Political deliberation and political action require, at the very minimum, a sense of efficacy, the possibility of controlling human affairs. Aristotle remarks in the *Nicomachean Ethics*: "Practical wisdom [is concerned with] matters about which deliberation is possible ... no one deliberates about things that cannot be other than they are, nor about things that are not directed to some end, an end that is a good attainable by action" (1141b8-12). That is, to the extent that we are confronted, in our lives, with a feeling of inexorable fatality, political deliberation is meaningless. Politics can only address itself to *contingencies*, things that could be otherwise; to conceive of ourselves as enmeshed in necessary and irreversible processes is to assume that politics is obsolete, no longer relevant to the direction of human affairs. Yet it is just this sense of contingency highlighted by Aristotle that we today can no longer count upon. Technology promises efficacy, promises to give us control over our own affairs. But its effect upon us, as social and political beings, is the very opposite. It removes not only the sense of efficacy but real efficacy, not efficacy as technological beings to be sure (beings who shape and reshape nature), but our efficacy as social and political beings (that is, beings who try to shape and define our own purposes). We are debarred from the exercise of Aristotelian *phronesis*, the practical wisdom by which we discern worthy ends of human life, because the commitment to technological goals is so deeply entrenched that the question of the good has become a closed question. As Hans Jonas writes, "science, with its application governed solely by its own logic, does not really leave the meaning of happiness open: it has prejudged the issue, in spite of its own value-freedom. The automatism of its use ... has set the goal of happiness in principle: indulgence in the use of things. [Hence] the direction of all effort and thereby the issue of the good tends to be predecided." In this sense, technology disempowers us at the very core of our nature as purposive beings - not as beings who endlessly manipulate *means*, but in Aristotle's sense, as beings who strive to determine proper *ends*.

Allied to this is the question of the present and future meaning of democracy. Strictly speaking, it would be more accurate (simply on grounds of linguistic precision) to describe contemporary societies, including liberal societies, as technocracies, ruled by experts in possession of a *techne*, than to describe them as democracies, ruled by the people's representatives, let alone by the people themselves. The challenge posed to democratic theory by contemporary technology is expressed most sharply by H.D. Forbes, in his essay on Dahl:

> effective debate is confined to a narrow circle of specialists; the ordinary citizen is bewildered; he takes little or no part in the discussion; and his cogitations have virtually no effect on the outcome. Consider some of the issues governments face today: recombinant DNA research, nuclear reactor safety, clean air, ozone depletion, government debt, and the cost of medical care. "What problems like these have in common is that they have enormously important consequence for a vast number of people, they seem to require government decisions of some kind, and in order to make wise decisions, decision-makers need specialized knowledge that most citizens do not possess." The control of nuclear weapons is thus an extreme but not misleading example of a much deeper problem in contemporary democracy. The democratic process as we know it today - the institutions of liberal, representative democracy - seem incapable of achieving democratic control of the "crucially important and inordinately complex" issues of modern technological society.

One way of characterizing the basic dilemma is as follows: Without an extremely sophisticated specialized knowledge, one can scarcely even join in the debate with respect to the major issues, from nuclear weapons to biotechnology, that dominate the political world of today. On the other hand, specialized knowledge of this kind does not seem adequate to the unique moral-political dimensions of these issues. As matters stand, the vast majority of us are simply incompetent. But even the most technically competent members of the technocratic elites who monopolize political deliberation appear unequipped for the present tasks of practical judgment. Forbes, following Dahl, considers, and rejects, four possible strategies of democratic theory:

> more participation in politics by all citizens (more participation by incompetent citizens will only increase the weight of incompetence in

decision-making); more conventional education for all citizens (at best the result would be a larger supply of specialists demanding coordination, and we would be no closer to solving our political problem); better public officials (a good thing in itself, of course, but not a step towards real democracy); and, finally, the fuller development of modern policy science (counterproductive, since ... it perfects the instruments of rule without considering the ends for which these instruments should be used).

Locked within this impasse, it is unclear whether democratic theory has anything very substantial to say in the face of technological society; or rather, the possibility looms that technological society makes a nonsense of democratic theory. We are mocked by our own technical powers, while the very idea of democracy lingers on only as an embarrassing recollection.

One might say that, in our present straits, the relation between *phronesis* and *techne* described by Aristotle has been transformed by the imperatives of technology so that those who might offer practical wisdom are excluded by deficiencies of technical expertise, whereas those schooled in technical knowledge are the most improbable sources of practical wisdom. In other words, it is as if prudence and *techne* serve merely to disqualify each other from supplying the needed political wisdom. How are we to redeem *phronesis* under these circumstances? Our destiny as technological creatures conspires to deny to us a ready answer.

Similar concerns are voiced by Hans Jonas, who captures better than any other contemporary author the enormity of our present undertakings in a technological civilization. According to Jonas, the problems of modern technology are *so* urgent that they threaten to eclipse the priority of democratic ideals: with democracy "the interests of the day necessarily hold the stage," whereas "the coming severity of a politics of responsible abnegation" requires sight of long-range horizons. Democratic politics tends to focus on what is local and immediate, whereas the really pressing concerns of contemporary politics demand that we attend to what is global and remote. (What Jonas objects to in existing socialist societies is not so much their authoritarianism, which may even offer a kind of advantage in our current grim circumstances, but rather their unbridled enthusiasm for technological mastery.) The challenge for democratic theory is to show that democracy *can* be given a meaningful content in an age where technological imperatives dominate the political agenda.

The dimensions of this challenge can hardly be overstated. The historical record of Marxist practice in this century does not exhibit any inclination to restrain the dominance of technological imperatives, nor to strengthen democracy. Liberalism as an ideology is virtually defined by the impulse to exploit technology to the utmost, and this is visible even in the case of as thoughtful and perceptive a thinker as John Dewey. The anarchist tradition, by contrast, offers glowing visions of efforts to reassume control over technology, but nothing in modern experience encourages us to think that these dreams can become realities. The disturbing but unavoidable question is: Can liberal democracy summon up the will and vigor to contend with the formidable challenges that now govern modern societies? Democratic theory can no doubt give voice to the question, but not necessarily formulate a coherent answer. For the rest, what remains are the voices of protest, muted or strident, despairing or resigned, whether of Heidegger, Ellul, Walter Benjamin and the Frankfurt School, or Hannah Arendt.

The problem, as we have stated it, is that technological progress renders the prospect of real democracy more, not less, remote. Indeed, as the grip of technocracy closes in all modern societies, liberal and socialist, this distant prospect recedes to infinity. It is not fully clear that these challenges and predicaments are amenable to theoretical resolution. But this in itself should not necessarily constitute grounds for despair. It may be that only in the concreteness of democratic *praxis* can one locate political possibilities that remain unforeseeable within democratic theory. It is a common error of intellectuals to assume that practical dilemmas must be submitted to an *intellectual* solution (must be solved in theory), rather than grappled with on the basis of skills and aptitudes immanent to the sphere of practice itself (debate, consensus, compromise, common-sense deliberation). Theorists cope with grim realities by theorizing; only citizens, acting, can actually bring about change.

Ronald Beiner

Acknowledgements

The editors would like to acknowledge financial assistance from the Connaught Program in Legal Theory and Public Policy at the University of Toronto, as well as from the Social Sciences and Humanities Research Council of Canada. We also wish to record our deep gratitude to Anna Apuzzo, Fjola Burke, Lyn Gladman, Mary Pacy and Brenda Samuels for their invaluable work in preparing the text for publication. Lastly, our thanks go to Leonard Brooks, Vice-Principal of Erindale College, for his indispensable help and support in the consummation of this project.

PART I

THE REIGN OF *TECHNE*

POLITICAL IMAGINATION
IN A TECHNICAL AGE*

Willem H. Vanderburg

If the roles modern science and technology play in shaping our modern world are both fundamental and decisive, I would expect them to be the focus of a great deal of political imagination. Yet this does not appear to be the case. Despite the fact that science and technology are human creations, their development is typically treated as something close to an independent variable in present-day human and social evolution. Whether this situation results from a profound belief that this strategy will usher in a better world for us all, create a true socialism, lead to a revitalization of democracy, or whether it is considered the only "realistic" option (because if we do not take advantage of this or that new technical possibility the Russians or Japanese will, and ...) makes no real difference. The result in each case is that political creativity and imagination is withdrawn from modern science and technology.[1]

I am not denying that problems and issues related to the influence science and technology have on society receive considerable attention. Individuals and groups constantly demand that governments take action, but at the same time there is a profound skepticism that much will come of it. The fact that so many human activities today are directly or indirectly regulated and controlled by the state and other large institutions, the influence of power elites, and the ideological implications of modern science and technology, unquestionably make genuine democratic political action difficult. This is all the more reason, however, to treat the widespread skepticism about the possibility of genuinely effective political activity as a phenomenon of great significance. Governments come and go, and with them hopes wax and wane, public opinion oscillates, but there is a sense that underneath it all flows a fundamental current that keeps moving in the same direction.

Political life today may perhaps be regarded as an ocean on whose surface things change constantly. From time to time storms may whip up large waves and create a great deal of turbulence while at other times there may be a great calm. One hundred feet below the surface everything remains much calmer and stable, while at the very bottom things proceed largely undisturbed by events at the surface. Similarly, few of the political events reported by the media appear to have a decisive and long-lasting effect. Much in the political life of the community changes while its deep structures appear to change much less rapidly. If this analogy has any merit, it would suggest that modern political life must be regarded in its complete sociocultural setting. This is particularly true if the political state of affairs in a society is to be understood "as if people mattered"[2] and as if democracy is a goal worth striving for. The macro-level analyses of a society's political framework, institutions and processes must include the broad cultural forces which shape the political will, imagination, determination, and action present in the daily lives of its people.

Although democracy is an "essentially contested concept,"[3] I shall assume that a genuine democracy permits the members of a community to exercise political imagination and creativity in both thought and action when making choices between viable options they recognize as having a significant and lasting effect on their community, so as to pursue their aspirations and traditions according to values freely arrived at. They thus exercise power to create, maintain and expand a sphere of public freedom in the face of determinisms and constraints. While this state of affairs may never be achieved by any one society, democracy may be seen as an ongoing process whereby a community accepts the constraints under which its members live as a challenge to be overcome by creating a sphere of freedom through political thought and action.[4]

The social sciences and humanities have revealed the extent to which the individual and collective life of a community is determined by internal and external factors. When a society accepts these constraints as a destiny, its ability to develop freely its way of life in the face of these constraints will decline, causing its mechanistic aspects to grow as its vitality diminishes.[5] True democratic politics therefore excludes any decision which merely recognizes a constraint or necessity such as administrative expediency or economic efficiency. In the face of such constraints, democracy gives the members of a society at least some control over their lives and an opportunity to renew, redirect or modify the social order in some way. It is an expression of what it is to be alive in a world of determinisms. It struggles against the constraints imposed by scientific and technical development and refuses to accept that human life and social change are little more than dependent variables in a world where other forces and phenomena constitute the independent variables.

What concerns me in this article is what I perceive as a lack of effective political imagination and action throughout the world to match the power and effectiveness of the development of science and technology. I shall attempt to analyze the cultural deep structures which are blocking this political imagination and action in order to come to some understanding of what might be done to weaken these constraints. By shedding some light on the constraints and determinisms related to modern political life, I hope to make a contribution to stimulating democratic political imagination and action, which are vital if humanity is to transcend the many problems it now faces.

Technology and Politics

The division of intellectual labor currently found in the university makes it difficult to obtain a comprehensive understanding of the roles science and technology play in human life and society in general and the political sphere in particular. The social sciences and humanities on the one hand, and the professional applied sciences and engineering on the other, evolve with minimal reference to and dependence on each other. When surveying the textbooks introducing students to the former, one has the impression that an understanding of a particular sphere of human life can be obtained without giving the phenomena of science and technology a central place. Textbooks related to the professional applied sciences likewise make minimal reference to the human and social context. If the pictures drawn of these different spheres of human activities are accurate, then either our daily life experience of the transforming roles of science and technology must be an illusion or the pictures are fundamentally inadequate.

The recognition that the traditional conceptual frameworks such as liberal capitalism and state socialism were created for a radically different context from the present one, does more than simply invite the research hypothesis that their relevance for the present situation has progressively been eroded, particularly during the past fifty years. The extent of the discussions about the nature of modern societies and human life within them might be taken as support for such a research hypothesis. This is equally true for a particular sphere of human activities such as politics. Researchers have noted complex and fundamental changes in the political sphere resulting from the widespread application of modern science and technology, but these are not easily integrated into the traditional frameworks of interpretation.

It might be objected that I am implying too great a role for modern technology. This indeed would be the case if we continued to think about technology in ways that were quite adequate for the nineteenth and first half of the twentieth century. Max Weber, however, already alerted us to a fundamental transformation when he wrote:

The term "technology" applied to an action refers to the totality of means employed as opposed to the meaning or end to which the action is, in the last analysis, oriented. Rational technique is a choice of means which is consciously and systematically oriented to the experience and reflection of the actor, which consists, at the highest level of rationality, in scientific knowledge. What is concretely to be treated as a "technology" is thus variable. The ultimate significance of a concrete act may, seen in the context of the total system of action, be of a "technical" order; that is, it may be significant only as a means in this broader context. Then concretely the meaning of the particular act lies in its technical result; and conversely, the means which are applied in order to accomplish this are its "techniques". In this sense there are techniques of every conceivable type of action, techniques of prayer, of asceticism, of thought and research, of memorizing, of education, of exercising political or religious control, of administration, of making love, of making war, of musical performances, of sculpture and painting, of arriving at legal decisions.[6]

Weber goes on to state that:

The presence of a "technical question" always means that there is some doubt over the choice of the most efficient means to an end. Among others, the standard of efficiency for a technique may be the famous principle of "least action", the achievement of the *optimum* result with the least expenditure of resources, not the achievement of a result regardless of its quality, with the absolute minimum of expenditure.[7]

In other words, techniques have increasingly displaced the customs and traditions of a society's culture to the point (as we shall see later) of fundamentally affecting the role of a society's culture as its socio-ecology. Several decades later, the French sociologist Jacques Ellul concluded that the phenomenon of technique had become the most decisive one in western civilization at this point in its history. He defined technique as "the totality of methods rationally arrived at and having absolute efficiency (for a given stage of development) in every field of human activity."[8] In other words, Ellul's concept of technique includes but is not limited to machines or a specific procedure for obtaining an end. Because of the widespread misinterpretation of Ellul's work, I shall begin by outlining the significance of the phenomenon of technique for human life and society in general and politics in particular, by making use of my theory of culture cited earlier.

It would appear that in the debate over the nature of modern society (whether it is postcapitalist, postindustrial, technological or other) the declining role of culture has been overlooked. Surely one of the things that sets these societies apart from all others is that a wide range of activities is no longer based on custom or tradition grounded in a culture. These societies systematically investigate virtually every sphere of human activity in order to render it more effective, rational and efficient or to eliminate certain problems. They do this on the assumption (and this is one of the implicit cultural hypotheses that underlies modern societies) that the quality of life can be improved by rendering the means of our existence more efficient. These investigations take the form of what I shall call the technical operation, constituted by four stages.

The first stage comprises the study of some area of human life for a particular purpose. The results of the study are used in the next stage to build some kind of model that can range from a precise mathematical theory to one that is largely qualitative. In the third stage the model is examined to determine what happens when its parameters are altered in order to discover when it functions optimally. The technical operation concludes with the reorganization of the area of human life studied originally, to achieve the highest efficiency and rationality demonstrated possible by the model. It is by means of this pattern of events that modern societies seek to improve the productivity of a plant, the running of a large office or hospital, the effectiveness of classroom instruction, the performance of a professional athlete or hockey team, the functioning of a group and even the satisfaction derived from a sexual relationship. As a result, the technical operation deeply permeates the fabric of individual and collective life. Its application has produced a wide range of technologies or techniques.

Modern societies are not so much characterized by their industrial and machine-related technologies as by the fact that almost every aspect of these societies is organized and reorganized on the basis of a variety of techniques that together have helped to constitute a knowledge base that is drawn on to ensure that everything is done as effectively as possible. Technology is only one part of the larger phenomenon of technique.

The reason why the so-called industrially advanced nations began to generate a mass of information at a certain point is now evident. When techniques increasingly replaced tradition as the basis for a sphere of activities, a great deal of information about that sphere was generated as a result of the pattern of events that we have called the technical operation. As these developments gained momentum, bottlenecks occurred which necessitated new technologies or techniques to deal with the mass of information. The computer and associated techniques were developed to meet this challenge, and as a result immediately found a wide range of applications. This in turn greatly accelerated the patterns of development described above.

The development of a so-called information economy, the proliferation of theoretical services, the rise of new intellectual techniques, the emergence of a new class of technical experts, the growth of the service sector in the economy and other phenomena taken to be signs of a new "postindustrial age" are therefore simply the result of the proliferation of techniques in society and the accompanying decline of the role of culture.

When we reflect on the above description of the technical operation, it is immediately evident that techniques are not culturally neutral. We shall discuss four of the many implications and briefly indicate their political significance. An area of human life is studied not holistically but rather for a specific purpose. As a result certain aspects of the situation will be externalized in the technical operation as being of little or no relevance to achievement of the goals. While a greater efficiency will be achieved in some domain, some externalities will inevitably result. These often yield serious negative effects which are passed on to the social and natural context in which the particular technical operation takes place. The state is increasingly obliged to step in, and this continues to be a major factor explaining the growth of the state which accompanies the proliferation of the technical phenomenon in society.[9]

A second implication flows from the fact that whatever the technical operation is applied to, is separated from its social and natural contexts. It is then improved on the basis of criteria which make little or no reference to the way it fitted into and will fit into these environments. Efficiency, cost-effectiveness or cost-benefit measures are all ratios which compare outputs with inputs without any reference to how any improvements are going to fit into the socio-cultural matrix of a society or into the ecosystem. (This came as an afterthought in the forms of techniques such as technology assessment and environmental assessment.) The same problems occur to varying degrees in the rational allocation of resources by means of cost-benefit analysis, risk-benefit methods, input-output analysis, environmental assessment, social indicators and technology assessment. The technical way of life, therefore, produces a variety of tensions within the socio-cultural fabric of a society as well as straining the balance found within the ecosystem. The technical way of life is in sharp contrast to the way traditional societies developed on the basis of custom and tradition, which embodied a variety of values able to adapt the socio-cultural matrix to new circumstances without losing sight of the integrity of the whole.

It is difficult to imagine how a technical approach to politics, based on techniques for developing and implementing public policies, could bring the role of ideology to an end.[10] A society does not have the structure of a mechanical system in which the subsystems are typically connected in such a way that the greatest efficiency of each tends to improve the efficiency of the whole. In a society, as in all living systems, there are no parts with a distinct existence prior to the whole. Elsewhere I have shown that the members of a society are *enfolded* into a dialectical whole when they are socialized into its culture.[11] Also, a society's institutions are not substructures because they too are enfolded into its way of life. Rather, they constitute dimensions of the way a culture mediates its existence in the world. I shall return to the significance of the role of culture as social ecology later, but for now it is important to stress that in an enfolded system the striving for micro-level rationality produces nonrationality on the level of the whole. A technical approach is likely to aggravate incoherence, tensions and conflict - hardly a climate in which ideology is likely to wither away.

A third implication of the widespread application of the technical operation derives from the way it separates knowing from doing as well as the knowers from the doers, thus requiring external control over a technicized activity.[12]   Assembly-line work is an obvious case in point. As the diversity and interdependency of technicized activities grow in the cultural fabric of a society, control over the networks of these activities tends to be centralized in large institutions such as the transnational corporation and the modern state. The latter must also control the many externalities referred to above, which may occur in areas of society other than the ones which produced them. The rise of the technical phenomenon creates the need for separate management and regulation of a growing range of activities. Separation of regulatory and control functions from the activities themselves makes this regulatory apparatus much less effective than the traditional ones, which were largely built into these activities themselves. It is also much more costly to run and maintain.

There is an additional problem as well. Since the combined effects of the many technical undertakings in a society cannot be derived from the specific impact of individual undertakings, a piecemeal regulation tends not to be very effective. Consider, for example, the area of chemical technology. There are some 65,000 chemicals in current use. Estimates of the number of new chemicals that are added each year range from about 500 to 1,000. Some of these are tested by exposing animals to large dosages of these chemicals. No testing occurs for low-dosage, long-term exposure, nor are there any methods for assessing the overall impact on our health of the many chemicals in our environment to which we are exposed every day. Yet their overall effect cannot be deduced from the specific effects taken one at a time. Therefore, it is their overall effect which should be regulated, because it is only on this level that we can assess the true and long-term implications for human health. This is probably scientifically impossible, however.

Society continues to act as though our striving for micro-level rationality and efficiency will translate into improvements on the level of the whole. We have already noted that in living systems this is not necessarily the case. Many of our advances on the micro-level are undercut by massive problems on the macro-level. We can observe this in the fabric of society, the ecosystem, human health, the arms race, automation and the depletion of natural resources.

The separation of the knowers from the doers and the externalization of control has many politically significant consequences. Human life in a technicized society is made up of some activities in which a person is the "knower" and a great many others where he or she is a "doer," largely controlled by others. To some extent this has always been the case, but the rise of the technical phenomenon has massively tipped the balance against self-regulated activities. The result has been a fundamental insecurity about activities that people have successfully engaged in for tens of thousands of years. One is not to rely on one's own experience but on expert knowers, to a degree detrimental to the human individual. There is an excessive dependence on the "how to" books in bringing up children, communicating with one another, making love and a host of other activities.[13] Too many of these are regulated and interconnected by complex policies of large institutions, policies that are neither intelligible nor accessible to a great many people. The result is an erosion of meaning, the displacement of a traditional by a technical morality and a sense of no one being morally responsible. When people face problems such as a complex set of allergies, the inability to find work, a vague sense of being depressed most of the time, a drug problem or a tendency to resort to violence, they often have difficulty finding the source of their problem and the responsible party. The result is a sense of helplessness, anxiety, frustration or discontent. The political consequences of this reification of human life are immense, undermining the very possibility of a genuine democracy.[14]

A fourth implication of the widespread use of the technical operation is that a society's culture is profoundly affected by the proliferation of techniques in society. What we call the process of industrialization should, in fact, be conceptualized as follows. An area in the socio-cultural matrix is rationalized by a power elite, causing the dynamic equilibrium that exists between it and adjacent areas to be disturbed. The resulting tensions within the socio-cultural fabric create problems. If a technical orientation is present in the culture of that society, the problem will be resolved by means of the technical operation, thus creating tensions in other areas of the socio-cultural fabric of the society, and so on. Gradually, the integrity of the traditional socio-cultural fabric is replaced by a system of interdependent techniques forming the new framework for society. This new framework gradually produces a new urban-technical information milieu in which new generations grow up. Since their minds are in part shaped by this milieu, a process of retroaction of these technical developments on the culture of the society is established. This is manifested in the emergence of a new morality, a shift in artistic expression, new religious tendencies and other developments we shall examine shortly. The political implications are considerable, and much of the latter part of this paper will be devoted to their analysis.

Culture and Politics

Regardless of their political beliefs, the members of a society interpret their experience and structure their relationships with one another and the world into a coherent way of life on the basis of a shared culture. This symbolization of, and acting on, reality, constitutes a society as a social ecology based on its culture. It is this culture which determines the benchmarks by which the people of a society judge what is acceptable and what is not, what makes sense and what does not, what they will tolerate and for what purpose they will take to the streets. In other words, in the long run governments, multinationals and vested interest groups can exercise power in a society only within a domain set out by the cultural ground of a society's way of life. There are many examples of this. When a law does not sufficiently embody the values of a culture, it risks being spontaneously and massively disobeyed. It then becomes inapplicable without the use of force. An oppressive government may, sooner or later, have to face a population which has taken to the streets. A similar process occurred toward the end of the Middle Ages: when the cultural ground of West-European societies began to crumble, the power structures built on it were never the same again.

Some key questions that should be asked are the following. How well have the cultures of the industrially advanced nations conceptualized the complex changes that have occurred particularly since the Second World War, given the separation of knowing, doing and control resulting from a technical way of life? How adequate is the current political and ideological spectrum with regard to the phenomenon of technique and the modern state? An exploration of the deep cultural structures that underlie politics might be useful here.

Using a theory of culture, I have argued that human life becomes coherent and integral to the extent that internalized experiences are interrelated into patterns and structures grafted into the genetically established organization of the brain. These patterns constitute mental images of society, the world, human life and one's own self. These images and their collective structure of experience, enfolded into the organization of the brain, constitute a cultural paradigm of sorts by which people relate to each other and the world in culturally unique ways. In other words, metaconscious "knowledge" is derived from the interrelation of specific experiences into patterns to which human beings have no direct access. I am thus drawing a distinction between the subconscious (repressed experiences and the "knowledge" implied in the genetically determined organization of the brain) and the metaconscious (the "knowledge" implied in the structure of experience constituting the mind). The latter plays a central role in the way a culture structures individual and collective existence. Babies and children develop by creating metaconscious "knowledge" of the way their culture structures conversation distance, eye etiquette, body language, conceptions of time, space and matter, an image of onseself, the social selves of significant others, social roles, values and their society's way of life.

I shall give two examples of metaconscious knowledge. We have probably all at some time remarked about a good friend, "I never thought she would do such a thing." Our surprise is not based on a one-by-one recall of all our experiences with the friend to discover typical patterns of behavior. It simply reflects the fact that the experience in question cannot easily be related to the metaconscious patterns in our structure of experience derived from the many previous encounters with the friend. Similarly, a child's experiences related to eating will metaconsciously imply the norm that food is not to be spilled, long before he can explicitly articulate this.

A great deal about human cultures can now be explained. Memory contains a systematic panorama of a person's past as lived in a particular social stratum of a society. It is individually unique in its specific memories and microstructures but culturally typical, particularly in its macrostructure. The more people come from a similar position in the social hierarchy, the more the intermediary structures will also be similar. Memory is thus a kind of mental map of a person's life as lived in his or her culture, which permits orientation in a social and physical environment by using prior experiences as models. Thus, by growing up in a society, people acquire and learn to use mental maps constituted by the structure of internalized experiences that the mind enfolds into the whole of their lives. These maps include our hopes, fears, convictions and beliefs. Much of life can be made routine, permitting critical intervention by thought, creativity and imagination at any time. Socialization transforms us from natural into cultural beings belonging to a social system based on a unique culture.

No understanding of a social system is adequate, however, if only its individuals' relations with reality are described. The characteristics of the whole cannot be derived from its members. To understand the role of culture as the social foundation of a society we also need to recognize that if the relationship between human beings and their environment is not entirely genetically determined, the structure of a society and its relationships with reality are not fixed either. In other words, they too must be structured by a society's culture. The scientific, technological, economic, social, political, legal, moral and religious institutions and structures are probably better conceptualized as *dimensions* of a way of life by which a culture symbolically mediates the relationships of a society with reality.

From the perspective of a society, the similarity of the mental maps created by the process of socialization functions as a kind of social gyroscope, allowing the system to evolve by keeping its members oriented in the same direction. It cannot, however, explain the extraordinary stability of cultural systems. Such processes as creativity, imagination, thought and exploration, and events like natural disasters, religious conversions or wars could cause the diversity within a culture to increase to the point where the system would disintegrate. There must be a cultural unity that goes deeper than the similarities in the mental maps of its members described thus far.

When we make a distinction between reality as it is known by a society and the reality that lies beyond, it is clear that existentially the members of a culture act as if their knowledge of reality and their lives within it are reliable and will not be called into question by the unknown. Yet in the natural sciences such experiences are not uncommon during a paradigm shift. Einstein, for example, recalled such an experience when new discoveries called into question the established models and images of physical reality: "It was as if the ground had been pulled out from under one with no firm foundation to be seen anywhere upon which one could have built."[15] Niels Bohr suggested that "we are suspended in language in such a way that we cannot say what is up and what is down."[16]

These kinds of experiences do not occur in the daily life of a society. The closest phenomenon is severe anomie experienced by some individuals, typically when a society is in a state of profound and massive change. The reasons for the difference are several. Not the least of these is the fact that the members of a culture metaconsciously absolutize reality as they know it, by converting the unknown into missing details and direct extensions of the Gestalt of reality as it is known. This involves an operation of a religious kind, as first described by Feuerbach. Yet generations later, this known reality typically turned out to be fundamentally incorrect because it implied a set of implicit cultural assumptions and models about human life and the world that proved untenable. Yet at the time these models and assumptions were so self-evident that any alternative was simply unimaginable and unthinkable.

These deeply metaconscious myths contribute substantially to the stability of a culture. They emerge, evolve and disappear only in the course of many generations. This happens when one historical epoch of a society draws to a close to make room for another, based on a new way of life and a new set of myths. On these myths rest the patterns of metaconscious images, values and commonplaces that structure thought, communication and social behavior. They help make the social order self-evident and "natural." Myths provide the most fundamental models for responding to new situations in ways that are compatible with the cultural order and way of life. Myths are not directly experienced by the members of a culture because it is through myths that the world is experienced.

The religious operation which I noted above involves a great deal more than the creation of metaconscious myths. A limited but absolutized knowledge of reality is not sufficient to delimit the range of possible relations into which the members of a society can enter, nor does it leave open only one way of life. Within the realm of possibilities everything would be equally good or bad, useful or useless, beautiful or ugly and so on. In other words, life would be a meaningless random sequence of events. Every culture evaluates all its experiences by paradigmatically expanding innate structures of the brain, emotions and feelings. These values are the result of the metaconscious patterning of experiences.

The values of a society reflect the basic vitality of a culture because they participate in the religious operations referred to above. Generally speaking, the metaconscious structure of experience tends to identify one or more phenomena in the life of a community which so permeate it that its very existence and thus the lives of its members also become inconceivable without them. For the prehistoric group such a phenomenon is what we would call nature, and for the societies that began to emerge at the dawn of history it became society itself.

The metaconscious recognition of these kinds of phenomena places a community before a dilemma. It could decide that such a phenomenon is so all-determining that the community has little or no control in the face of this fate. On the other hand, and this is in fact what happens, it could sacralize the phenomenon by metaconsciously bestowing an ultimate value upon it. Necessity is thereby transformed into the "good," and the social order is the expression of the community's members freely striving for that good. The freedom and cultural vitality thus metaconsciously created eventually permit the sacred to be transcended as an all-determining force and make human history possible while exacting a heavy price. At the dawn of history natural determinisms were slowly transcended, although social ones eventually took their place.

The bestowing of an ultimate value upon whatever is most central and determining in the life of a community, metaconsciously orders all other values in the structures of experience of the members. Thus this religious operation creates a sacred, a system of myths and a hierarchy of values which together constitute the basis for cultural unity. Because it is profoundly metaconscious, this unity gives a great deal of stability to a culture as well as giving it a history distinct from natural evolution.

There are three interpenetrating yet relatively distinct phases in the evolution of a culture's unity during an epoch of its history. Each one provides a unique cultural basis for a society's political life. The first begins when an emerging power elite in society organizes a new way of life while the rest continue to live as before. If the new way of life continues to develop, it increasingly threatens the old one, creating tensions and conflict.

During the second phase, the new way of life is sufficiently developed so as to reveal clearly its possibilities, and its benefits reach a growing portion of society. New generations begin to know the old way of life only in a state of serious decay and thus no longer as a viable alternative. They identify with the new way of life as the only viable one they know. In the course of generations the locus of conflict now gradually shifts from a dispute over the kind of society people wish to have toward tensions over a more adequate and just participation in the new way of life for everyone. The process is reinforced by the retroaction of the new way of life on the minds of the generations growing up within it and thus on the culture. A new cultural unity, comprising a sacred, a system of myths and a hierarchy of values, is formed by metaconsciously extrapolating and interpolating the tendencies of the new way of life. New metaconscious images and models of the present, past and future are created.

The necessities imposed by the new way of life tend to be sacralized as they permeate the community, creating a new cultural vitality derived from the gradual metaconscious establishment of the new unity. Once this happens, society again constitutes a cultural whole, which characterizes the third phase. It ends when the society withdraws its allegiance via a process of desacralization. A transition to a new historical epoch will then emerge, or a process of cultural disintegration will begin.

The locus of political activity shifts as one phase follows another. At first there is a struggle between the old and new "societies" incarnated by two or more groups which have the characteristics of social classes as Marx described them. Assuming that the classes pioneering the new way of life continue to be successful in imposing the new way of life (and only the myth of progress can make this self-evident), the gradual establishment of the new cultural unity tends to shift the locus of political debate and conflict to one over how the benefits and costs of the new way of life are to be shared. The power structure is challenged in a less radical way as groups struggle over participation in it. Any fundamental calling into question is pushed to the fringes of what constitutes acceptable political debate, where it remains until the cultural unity begins to break down.

I shall attempt briefly to reinterpret some aspects of the modern political stage as it was being set in the nineteenth century. By introducing the cultural context I shall challenge the rational view of politics, human life, society and the dawning of the secular age.[17] From the present-day transfer of technology to the Third World we are increasingly learning that industrialization of a traditional society is not merely a matter of affecting some sectors but constitutes a radical transformation of all the structures of society. The name Industrial Revolution is misleading because industrialization is a transformation of the entire way of life of a society. Underneath the individual technological, economic, social, legal, political, moral and religious changes, lies a larger pattern of change of which these specific changes are an integral part.

The nineteenth century saw the establishment of what is generally called capitalism, which designates a historically unique structure and organization of the industrial societies of that time. Capital became the life-blood of society. Everything was organized for the accumulation and growth of capital. Everything happened by means of money, not only in the economy but also in the other spheres of life, and everything could be expressed in terms of it. Society was temporarily divided into at least two "societies," each with its own culture of sorts: one constituted by those who developed the new way of life and reaped most of the riches that it produced, and the other by those who increasingly had to submit to the new order created by capital and many of whom sold their labor for money, with everything that implied. Capital became the first secular sacred in human history, by which and through which almost all new socio-cultural structures were created in the emerging industrial societies.

Along with the sacred of capital, a new system of myths evolved. At its center we find the myths of happiness and progress. Happiness became the motivating central image. Earthly happiness could be achieved by hard work rewarded with the ownership of things produced by the system. By constantly raising the level of production, the poor would also eventually be made happy. The myth of happiness identified general well-being with material well-being. People could not accept that all the energies and resources being poured into production would yield only things and nothing else. Only by means of a myth could something more be achieved. Prestige and social status were based on the things one owned, and everything could be bought with money. Through myths, being became having. The myth of happiness was supported by other myths. Comfort, for example, was transformed into its material dimension.[18] Comfort relaxed the hard-working person who became happy by possessing material objects. It excluded all physical effort.

The world was made for humanity and for its happiness. But this could only happen by means of action and hard work. The limits traditional societies had placed on action fell by the wayside. This led to the myth of progress. No longer was progress limited in scale or to a particular sphere, and no longer did this progress have positive and negative aspects. Progress became good in itself, and this could happen only by linking experience to a sacred. History became the progress of humanity through economic development. Civilizations could be classified simply on the basis of their materials and tools. Progress was obvious everywhere. Abundance would replace poverty, science would replace religion and democracy would replace oppressive regimes. All this could be achieved simply by means of economic development. Poverty resulted from not contributing to progress and work. Everything was assimilated by the myths of progress and happiness.

It is noteworthy that possibly the most brilliant observer of what was happening in the nineteenth century, namely Karl Marx, was totally in the grip of the most fundamental myths of his time even though he exposed so many of the hidden assumptions made by those who had views different from his own. Marx took it to be self-evident that each stage of human history constitutes progress over the previous one. He also uncritically accepted the view that human beings were decisively characterized by the phenomenon of work, and thus he regarded society as having an economic base on which rests its superstructure. These are, as I have indicated, part of the system of myths of the nineteenth century. The result was that Marx was not sufficiently critical of technology, which he regarded as a neutral means whose influence on society was essentially determined by the use to which it was put by its owners. He thus contributed greatly to the elimination of the most fundamental questions about technology from the political arena. These have remained on the fringes of left and right orthodoxy to this day. He unintentionally created an ideology which, like liberal capitalism, did not question the emerging cultural unity.

With regard to the newly emerging secular sacred, neither Marx nor his opponents appear to have demystified it. The only difference is that Marx regarded capitalism as a *necessary* stage on the way to socialism, while his opponents bestowed an ultimate value on the system and put their faith in it. Both responses to the determinisms faced by society as a result of the new social order thus escaped the kind of fundamental critique necessary to create an iconoclasm toward the new cultural foundation. Alienation prevented real progress toward true democracy and socialism.

Whatever is sacralized is withdrawn from public criticism, political debate and conflict. The same is true for whatever is believed necessary, realistic or inevitable. As a result, a genuine political imagination with regard to capital, science and technology has been pushed to the fringes for the past hundred years and been banished from the central political arena. I am suggesting that the problem of idolatry takes on a new reality in what we hoped would be a secular age.

The Modern Sacred and Secular Political Religions

It is customary to think of technology and technique solely in terms of means with which to accomplish human ends.[19] This is true of course, but it is only a part of the picture. Technology and techniques also mediate relationships, thus constituting an intermediary between human beings and between them and their environment. This perspective is analogous to the one I used for culture and thus helps to illuminate the cultural role of technique.

A great many relationships today are technically mediated. Telephones mediate between many people who may never meet face to face. Television mediates between producers and consumers, politicians and voters, religious leaders and followers, and between viewers and events in their community and around the world. This would be a trivial observation, were it not for the fact that these relations are transformed in a consistent way. In a telephone conversation the non-verbal aspects of communicating (conversation distance, eye etiquette and body language)[20] are eliminated. A politician may come across well in person but may have to rely on a media consultant to ensure that he or she projects the right image. This image can be dissociated from policies.[21] Advertising, by associating products or politicians with symbols in people's minds, interferes with the way they would make decisions in the absence of the metaconscious influence of symbols. The media help induce public opinions about current events which are fundamentally different from private opinions arrived at by experience or by critical reading and reflection.[22] In each instance an aspect of someone's being is externalized.

A relationship can be technically mediated with little or no intervention of devices. Techniques of organization, group dynamics, human relations or operations research can mediate in ways that transform the way people would deal with one another on the basis of their structures of experience as, for example, the studies of bureaucracy by Max Weber and others have shown. I am not suggesting that mediation on the basis of culture as social ecology is totally eliminated in a modern society, but that there exist both culturally and technically mediated relationships and that the latter kind predominates. If the cultural mediation were entirely to disappear, we would find the human and social transformation described by A. Huxley in *Brave New World*[23] or what L. Mumford calls the megamachine society.[24] This would be a transformation whereby human beings would be completely adapted to society as mere pieces in a social mechanism. Such a transformation is far more radical than the one we are describing, and there is little sociological evidence of that situation coming about.

Many techniques respond to various necessities created by other techniques. No large office, factory, school, hospital, service agency, government, television or radio network, newspaper or transportation system can do without them. But to act out of technical necessity is contrary to the goals and aspirations with which we veil the situation.

A society undergoes a fundamental transformation once most of the relationships in which its members are engaged are technically mediated. Technique interposes itself between people and society and between them and nature. It has become a primary milieu in relation to which human life evolves, just as society became the primary milieu at the dawn of history, when it interposed itself between the group and nature (within which prehistoric life was immersed). Because today people relate to the *secondary* milieu (society) and the *tertiary* milieu (nature) via the *technical* milieu, the latter provides everything necessary for human life as well as the most significant threats to human existence.[25] This ambivalent relationship is reflected in the deepest metaconscious patterns within which the sacred itself and the sacred of transgression are embedded. Each primary milieu thus fundamentally permeates most individual experiences, metaconscious patterns, human consciousness and the culture of a society in ways no power elite can control or directly manipulate.

It is generally accepted that the sacred, the system of myths and the hierarchy of values were largely related to nature in prehistoric cultures, and to nature and society in the cultures of societies in history. Since the dominant religious forms tend to spring up around the sacred of a culture, a correspondence between the milieu of technique and the dominant religious tendencies might be expected to emerge. Thus the metaconscious patterns resulting from the technical way of life should imply the decisive roles played by technique and the nation-state. This should, then, be manifested in the thought and behavior of the members of such a society. If they treat these phenomena as all-determining forces undermining human freedom, they would exhibit a "realistic" attitude toward them. After all, without them their lives would be inconceivable and hence without any meaning, purpose or coherence. They would see their lives as being possessed body and soul the way a slave is possessed by a master. To put it in modern terms, they would feel alienated. This is the secular version of what once was a central problem in the Judeo-Christian tradition.

If, however, technique and the nation-state are metaconsciously sacralized to help constitute the cultural unity of society, the obedience of necessity is transformed into an act of responsible human freedom and a striving for human well-being. A sense of alienation is then avoided, at least for the majority of society, particularly during the third phase in the development of a cultural unity.

The myths of the nineteenth century have helped to create the belief that the members of the most evolved societies have come of age. In fact, a great deal of evidence can be cited to show that traditional religious attitudes have simply been replaced by secular ones. Neither technique nor the nation-state are treated the way other phenomena in daily life are. When someone suggests, for example, that a particular technique is not all it is made out to be or that it might possibly do more harm than good, reactions tend to be completely out of proportion and the critical person is treated the way a heretic might be in a traditional society. Retorts like, "Do you want to go back to the Dark Ages?" or "Be realistic. If we do not make these sacrifices we will be left behind and may even become an underdeveloped nation," are not uncommon. It is as if history has only one pathway left, namely that of technique, to be advanced and coordinated by the nation-state. When faced with considerable problems, many of which are directly or indirectly related to the growth of technique, virtually the only response recognized as being

viable is to resolve these problems by accelerating technical development.
The question is rarely asked whether it is realistic to expect that these
problems can be solved by doing more of the kinds of things that helped
produce them in the first place. Only the process of sacralization can
withdraw the most vital forces in a society's development from widespread
critical scrutiny and attempts to assess their implications on the basis of
values independent from them.

It is not a question of being opposed to technique or to the nation-state.
It is clear that the current world population cannot be supported without
technique. The primary milieu in relation to which human life evolves most
directly produces what is vitally necessary as well as what is life-threatening.
If people in prehistory had responded to the threats of the natural milieu by
burning it, they might have perished with it. What concerns me is the typically religious all-or-nothing kind of attitudes, betrayed by terms such as
"pessimist" in discussions about technique and the nation-state in the academic literature. Why should a researcher be branded a "pessimist" when he
or she comes to the conclusion that the problems humanity faces today may
require a different approach? Surely it is much more constructive to engage
in a critical analysis of the research in order to point out any weaknesses or
errors. I am suggesting that the sacralization of technique and the nation-
state and the emergence of secular religious attitudes toward them divide the
world into believers and unbelievers. We must break through this religious
polarization and recognize what is happening to us. If we do, new roads to
peace and effective solutions to our problems will open up.

Western civilization overcame many difficulties and improved life in a
variety of ways by means of technique. The retroaction of events during the
past two hundred years on the human mind and culture have led to the indis-
criminate use of technique. It has become difficult to recognize any clear
limits. Everything increasingly appeared to have a technical solution, and
human life became a series of problems requiring techniques of all sorts.
Yet it is obvious that technique is useful in some situations and useless in
others. Only the process of sacralization can create phenomena whose abilities have no limits. The situation is somewhat analogous to that of a car-
penter who finds his hammer so effective for nailing that he also tries to do
everything else with it. As a result, the realm of political options related to
the shaping and reshaping of the roles of technique and the nation-state in
human life and society has been narrowed greatly.

A number of researchers have found evidence for the sacralization of
technique and the nation-state in the technically advanced societies. Particularly in his book *The New Demons*, Jacques Ellul has analyzed the sacralization of technique and the nation-state.[26] He argues that the modern
sacred is dialectically structured, with sex and revolution being the modern
sacred of transgression, corresponding to the sacred of technique and the

nation-state respectively. He has analyzed in considerable detail the modern secular religions built on the modern sacred, and argued that their sociological role is identical to those of the traditional religions. Marxism, Leninism, Nazism and Maoism in their sacred writings, secular theologies or theories, party structures and functions, are readily recognized as secular religions because of the role they have played and continue to play in various societies.

Ellul also shows how in the liberal-democratic nation-states politics is taking on a religious character, causing these societies to become less liberal. The technicization of life necessarily causes this stage to become more and more totalitarian in the way it is forced into regulating a growing number of activities and dealing with increasingly complex problems stemming from the technical way of life. The technical means required need to be increasingly more powerful and hence totalitarian. This is particularly true with regard to the modern megaprojects related to defense, space and energy. Such a state cannot justify itself except on the basis of a secular political religion. Political choices are translated into choices between good and evil, and a religious intolerance develops toward other viewpoints. The growing control that the state must exercise over society as a result of the technical way of life can be tolerated only through the politicization of human life. Politics appears no longer to have any limits.

Modern politics has become the locus of ultimate seriousness. It creates some of the most radical divisions within humanity. It separates good from evil, and trivializes many of the past divisions within and between traditional religions by politicizing or spiritualizing them. Politics appears to be worth the sacrifice of everything, including the survival of humanity. This can only happen in the presence of a sacred related to the conditions under which human life is lived. Such a sacred springs from profound existential and spiritual human needs, which can be illuminated only through a comprehensive analysis. Ellul's argument that the religious tendencies in modern life have been hidden by the pretense of our having become rational, secular and of age must be taken seriously. An important part of Ellul's analysis deals with the influence the establishment of a secular sacred has had on Christianity, including its political implications.[27] It has tranformed faith into religion. An important extension of Ellul's analysis to American society has been undertaken by R. Stivers.[28] All these analyses build on the research of the roles of the sacred and myths in a society by other investigators.[29]

I shall conclude this section by briefly mentioning similar research findings. Cassirer was concerned about the rise of mythical thought in the twentieth century.[30] He analyzed the new political myths that accompanied the rise of national socialism and the associated rituals. For him, the combination of the rational and the magical in modern politics should not surprise us.

He warns that humanity should not underestimate the strength of a political myth, lest we repeat the errors of the past. The relationship between spirituality and fascism has also been studied by others.[31]

The political control exercised by a culture's myths and rituals has also been analyzed.[32] As the basic models of a society, myths express themselves in social routines called rituals. Political myths and rituals largely determine what the members of a society can accept as politically realistic, plausible and reassuring. Public opinion mediates between specific events and the deep structures of a culture. Whatever cannot be assimilated into the cultural unity of a society constitutes a threat, which may be met with powerful defense mechanisms such as massive intolerance if a power elite exploits the sacred. From this perspective, a radical political alternative may be rejected by a society, not so much because it is unworkable, not because it would not enhance the quality of life or the public good, but because it cannot be integrated into the system of myths. Power elites can manipulate symbols, which play on a culture's myths, in order to advance their interests. However, since the deep metaconscious structures of the members of a society are changed only in the course of many generations, these myths can neither be created nor directly manipulated by a power elite. Since any elite depends on its culture for mediating their relationship with reality, they cannot escape the retroaction of the patterns of development of their society on their minds and thus avoid being alienated by them, particularly during the third phase of the establishment of a new cultural unity. Marx clearly recognized this danger for the power elite of his time.

If one accepts the importance of the metaconscious in shaping the way of life of a society as I have outlined it above, it is not possible to analyze the mythical and ritual dimensions of political phenomena by means of the traditional behaviorist or statistical approaches. A conceptual framework like the one developed in this paper might serve to develop such methods, but this falls beyond the scope of this chapter. When an observer is a member of the society being observed and is thus largely unaware of the deep metaconscious patterns implicit in his or her structure of experience, this involves a difficult but not impossible theoretical challenge.

According to this perspective, political policies are much more than mere responses to societal challenges designed to solve them as if they were mere technical problems. It is not unusual for policies to remain popular even though they fail to bring about any results. Their role is in part to reinforce the images of a society which serve to perpetuate its way of life and power relations. In other words, their function in a good many cases must be regarded more in terms of social control by affecting public opinion according to a culture's myths, even when that goes against the well-being of the community. A good example is furnished by many antipoverty programs.[33] In the same vein, elections, regardless of their political impact, are the most important rituals in modern societies. They cannot become policy-making forums nor can they be a vehicle for serious ideological debates. The political process rests too heavily on myths in a mass society. When political candidates propose a policy incompatible with prevailing myths, they tend to be overwhelmingly defeated. A successful campaign translates the concerns of citizens into public images linked to myth-symbols. The most powerful political candidates typically embody these symbols, and their struggle becomes one between good and evil. The election ritual delimits possible outcomes while reinforcing the vital images of the society.

The retroaction on the human mind of technique, as the primary milieu, creates a technical consciousness and a culture permeated by technique. By means of the process of sacralization, a community gives its ultimate commitment to mere human activities. As a result, the phenomenon of technique takes on a measure of autonomy for as long as this commitment remains in place.[34] This socio-cultural basis of an autonomous technique has not been well understood by many readers of Ellul. As a sociologist, Ellul observes that people's minds and the cultures of the so-called industrially advanced nations have been so influenced by the accomplishments of technique that they have become spontaneously oriented in a technical direction. As a result, values independent of technique for guiding human decisions, political decisions free from technical necessity, and an autonomous politics have all but disappeared. Without question, technique has permeated our culture, with the result that science and technology have become much more than an ideology. Neither can it be questioned that this is to the benefit of a power elite. But it does not follow that Marx's theoretical framework can be extended to the twentieth century. Technique is not a neutral tool, producing very different results depending on how it is controlled and owned.[35]

The rituals that spring up around the sacred of transgression, such as the sexualization of technical objects and the anticipation of a revolution, provide meaning and hope to many who are alienated by the modern sacred. The very nature of a sacred of transgression is to provide the illusion of an escape hatch in the system, thus reinforcing it. If my analysis is correct, political revolutions based on the modern sacred of transgression cannot deal with the fundamental problems created by the sacralization of technique and the nation-state.[36]

The Political Revised Sequence

With very few exceptions,[37] the political implications of a (socio-culturally) autonomous technique, as originally formulated by Jacques Ellul, have been largely misunderstood. Sociologists have observed that the human mind is profoundly influenced by the primary milieu in relation to which human life is lived, with the result that during certain times in the history of a society the thought and actions of its members are spontaneously oriented in a certain direction. Such an observation does not exclude or deny the influence power elites have in a society, but the limits of their influence and the degree to which their power is accepted as "natural" are largely determined by deeper cultural developments over which these power elites have no direct control. The question then needs to be asked: Does the social system of a society serve the aspirations and values its members freely impose on it or do the people serve the system they created to serve them? Galbraith[38] has argued that it can no longer be assumed that consumers are autonomous in making economic choices with regard to the large producers. The consequence is a revised sequence, wherein producers no longer respond to demand but instead first develop their product and then create a demand through advertising. Ellul sees a similar process in politics: societies which sacralize technique and the nation-state deprive citizens of the autonomy they are presumed to possess in democratic theory.

A major factor contributing to this situation in liberal-democratic societies is the rise of what Ellul calls integration propaganda.[39] The concept has its basis in the sociological observation of the change in the relationship between the individual and society that comes about when the social structure of a traditional society disintegrates as the technical way of life establishes itself. In a traditional society, the individual was well-integrated into the group through strong personal relationships which formed the context for most daily life activities. The individual was, therefore, largely determined by local influences, customs and traditions. The more macro-level changes in the society were mediated by the local group and thus had little direct influence on the individual. For example, the propaganda of a totalitarian state tends to have little effect on a traditional peasant community, with the result that some regimes deliberately sought to break down these traditional communities.

The disintegration of the traditional social structure of a society under the influence of technique greatly weakened the constraints imposed on the individual by the traditional groups. These groups were gradually replaced by crowds of people encountered in a great many activities in the industrial urban environment. Crowds impose new pressures on increasingly vulnerable individuals. By no longer being firmly integrated into society via traditional groups the individual became the measure of all things, having to make daily life decisions without the guidance of customs and traditions which increasingly lost their relevance in a technical way of life. The resulting uncertainty, coupled with the absence of sociological protection from the pressure of the crowd and the lack of traditional frames of reference, created a social milieu which had to be fed information from the outside if it was to cohere. Broad ideological currents began to have an influence in the nineteenth-century industrial societies. Thus, a mass society is not a disintegrating traditional society but one which integrates the individual into society by mass sociological currents. It is well known that crowds are easily manipulated by outside influences and that their members are inhibited in the use of their critical faculties. The result is a certain psychological unity. Beliefs and opinions are widely shared despite the fact that many members of a mass society may not have any direct experience or personal knowledge of what they have opinions about. Constant exposure to the crowd modifies the individual's psyche, making him or her more credulous, more excitable and thus susceptible to currents of public opinion.

All of this is well known but the political implications are rarely drawn. In a detailed analysis of the psychological and sociological condition of the individual in a mass society, Ellul demonstrates the necessity of integration propaganda which he distinguishes from totalitarian propaganda. A public opinion on a variety of issues is created primarily via the media, the newspapers and the movies. They portray the life-styles that become the norms sociologically equivalent to customs and traditions in earlier societies. These images of society and life within it, typically laden with stereotypes and myth-symbols, are the primary means of social integration in a society based on the technical way of life. I have already shown that the structures of such a society separate knowing from doing, the knowers from the doers, and externalize control from the activities. The result is the reification of the individual living in a network of largely impersonal relationships. Effective participation in them can be achieved only when individuals are convinced of the value of these technical structures and the purpose of their participation in them, which can no longer be derived from strong personal relationships. Individuals thus come to depend on a whole range of human techniques such as human relations, public relations, group dynamics and advertising, be it economic or political. Together these techniques constitute the phenomenon of integration propaganda. To raise productivity, for example, one needs to motivate the worker through a variety of technical means which create the psychological climate for improving production.

Integration propaganda would not be effective if it were simply imposed from the outside without meeting deep psychological and social needs in the community. Take the relationship between the modern state and the citizen as an example. In a traditional society a political elite could make decisions in relative isolation. Their decisions simply did not have the far-reaching effects they do today because they lacked the means at the disposal of the modern state. Nor did they have to deal with public opinion, which did not form in such societies. Today the population expects to have a political say in things. There are good historical reasons for this. If there is a war, everyone may become a soldier, and hence everyone wishes to have a say in war and peace. Taxes have increased enormously over the past two hundred years, and one might expect, therefore, that those who pay them will have a greater interest in how the money is spent. We have already shown how the modern state needs to get involved in almost every activity as a result of the technical way of life. Consequently, the state can no longer govern without public support.

In a democracy the actions of government are supposed to be based on popular opinion, which expresses itself in the form of public opinion in a mass society. The problem is that public opinion is not based on the experience and personal knowledge of the individual who holds it; it is nonrational, and on any specific issue it emerges, develops and vanishes much like the wind. It is impossible for any democratic government to act on public opinion which is generally unable to anticipate problems far enough in advance, incapable of sustaining government action for the length of time it takes to plan and implement policies, and tends to lead to extremes in times of crisis. The rise of the phenomenon of public opinion is coupled with a growing inability of the citizen to participate meaningfully in society, because the technical way of life has largely destroyed the self-regulating character of the socio-cultural fabric of society rooted in individual and group action by externalizing control and concentrating it in large institutions.

Under these conditions, no government can legitimate itself if it constantly ignores and goes against public opinion. Even the greatest dictators pay lip-service to the will of the people. A government must, therefore, explain the emergence of a new problem and show how the action it proposes is exactly what the public would have wanted. If any resistance is encountered, public relations techniques are drawn on to transform a government's decision into the will of the people. If such techniques are used effectively, the public will demand that the action be taken with greater speed, more resources, or that its scope be broadened. On the international scene, psychological warfare by means of propaganda is equally necessary to deal with international public opinion. Governments can defend their people from this psychological warfare only by their own propaganda. An important component of modern education prepares the citizens of a modern state to be able to participate in and fulfill the need they have for integration propaganda.

The political component of integration propaganda meets an essential need of the citizen in a modern state. The individual is incapable of understanding the many complex issues dealt with in the political process, such as economic, social, defense or foreign policies. Yet no one would readily admit that he or she is unable to form a genuine opinion about these complex issues, with which we are confronted every day. Thus citizens are ready to receive the explanations offered by integration propaganda. Information by itself is not enough. Preconceived positions and value judgments must accompany the information. In this way citizens can feel a little more effective and secure in face of the complex forces and issues shaping their lives. This is in sharp contrast with a traditional society, in which most of the important events are local and thus more accessible. As a result of the media, the individual is confronted with an image of what is happening in the world that is extraordinarily fragmented, discontinuous and piecemeal, singling out the events that disturb the order in the world. It is existentially impossible for people to live in such a world. They attempt to make sense of it by means of their culture, which distorts and stereotypes much of what happens in other parts of the world. Again integration propaganda comes to the rescue. It provides an ideological map on which all these events can find a meaningful place. Loneliness in the crowd and the absence of strong personal relations further adds to the need to find some personal meaning in this world of images. In a world of experts it is difficult for individuals to act on their own authority.   Integration propaganda increasingly provides the collective signal for their actions.

Ellul has also shown how technique has transformed the modern state, how this change inevitably reduces the control politicians have over it, and how the role of the political party is altered by it.[40] The reduction of political sovereignty of the citizens and politicians with regard to the modern technicized state creates a political revised sequence,[41] in which technique creates imperatives to which political life responds.   A critical re-examination of the political frameworks of interpretation largely inherited from the nineteenth century would expose what Ellul has called the political illusion. It is the widespread belief in liberal democracies that people continue to control their lives as well as or better than in any other society past or present. In reality, political control is constantly diminishing despite the fact that life has become politicized. For Ellul, the political illusion is one of the most devastating consequences of the sacralization of technique.

The usual critique of Ellul's analysis is that it is so general that it leads to withdrawal from political life. His own life is hardly one of an ivory-tower academic critic.   His extensive concrete and practical efforts for reform make him a deeply committed activist. His approach is quite concrete:

> We are therefore in the presence of the following dilemma: either we must continue to believe that the road to solving our problems is the traditional road of politics, with all sorts of constitutional reforms and "revolutions" ... or we turn away from the illusory debate, and ... admit that for man "to exist is to resist", and that ... it is important above all never to permit oneself to ask the state to help us. This means that we must try to create positions in which we reject and struggle with the state, *not* in order to modify some element of the regime or force it to make some decision, but, much more fundamentally, in order to permit the emergence of social, political, intellectual, or artistic bodies,

associations, interest groups, or economic or Christian groups totally independent of the state, yet capable of opposing it, able to reject its pressures as well as its controls, and even its gifts. These organizations must be completely independent, not only materially but also intellectually and morally, i.e., able to deny that the nation is the supreme value and that the state is the incarnation of the nation. The idea should be opposed that because a group is *inside* a nation ... the state, representing the nation, can therefore control it and dictate to it....What is needed is groups capable of extreme diversification of the entire society's fundamental tendencies, capable of escaping our unitary structure and of presenting themselves not as negations of the state ... but as *something else*, not under the state's tutelage but equally important, as solid and valuable as the state.42

What Ellul is prescribing here is a desacralization of the state and modern politics. As John Schaar has put it so well:

He is recommending not that we abandon the public realm, but that we come to it by another route. Nor is he recommending that we turn our backs on technology - which is impossible anyway - but that we reconstruct society so that there are genuine alternatives to life lived under the determination of technique and in servitude to the state. He is urging us to repudiate the mentality of the passive and the colonized, the mentality that says, "someone else is in charge and I just live here, doing what I must, getting what I can." He is proposing social action and social institutions that can nurture integral persons and encourage them on the path of public liberty.43

The sacralization of the nation-state, as argued by Jacques Ellul, is able to explain one of the great contradictions of our time. On the one hand, this secular sacred draws in and permeates all aspects of individual and collective human life just as any traditional sacred. Thus, human life has been politicized and politics appears to have no limits today. On the other hand, the secular political religions reinforce a religious attitude toward the state with the result that a large proportion of the citizens have no participation in politics other than their participation in public opinion. When they protest against the state, their action is little different from the traditional responses to the gods who have not replied to human wishes expressed in prayers and rituals. In neither situation do these dissatisfactions lead to a critical examination of the *ability* of the gods to deliver what is asked of them, which would lead to an iconoclastic attitude, resulting in a process of desacralization. Ellul thus argues that in the modern state, power elites both manipulate and are dominated by the modern sacred, much as Marx claimed that the bourgeoisie both owned and was owned by capital in the nineteenth century. Thus, the ability of a power elite to exploit the sacred and lean on it to maintain a position of privilege is rooted in and dependent on the cultural unity of a society. A political revolution can change the power elite, but to transform the cultural unity requires a much more complex and time-consuming process. The sacralization process makes it extremely difficult for the majority of a society to see certain key phenomena for what they are. By myths, the things that these phenomena are fundamentally incapable of achieving are converted into what can reasonably be expected and hoped for.

A Political Imagination for Our Time

In the presence of the massive problems humanity faces today, essentially two kinds of responses are encountered. Both recognize that these problems are intimately related to the technical way of life. In the one case, however, they are interpreted as signs that further technical development is urgently required to eliminate them, while in the other they indicate that something is fundamentally wrong. In other words, in the one case these problems reaffirm a profound belief in the present system, while in the other they affirm the belief that society must and can alter its present course of development. The fact that the former belief tends to dominate in the so-called industrially advanced societies reflects the basis for cultural unity.

I have argued that by growing up in a society permeated by technique and the nation-state, the members of society lack effective external points of reference for thinking and acting. Anything not permeated by the sacred tends to become a threatening unknown. The members of a society find themselves symbolically so encapsulated in a "system" that they have as much difficulty critically assessing things as if they were trying to judge the speed of a train from which they could not see out. The technical consciousness makes it difficult to know when a problem can appropriately be addressed through the application of technique and when such an approach would amount to doing more of the kinds of things that helped produce the problem in the first place. If we can admit that no human being with or without power, rich or poor, is exempt from these difficulties, discussions and disagreements might gradually translate into a more iconoclastic attitude toward technique and the nation-state. It would be a very slow and difficult process, but if the religious attitudes towards technique and the nation-state were gradually undermined, political imagination and creativity could be freed from a technical consciousness to take on a new vitality. A civilization might eventually be created which includes technique but whose culture is not permeated by it. Once again technique and government would become the object of a realistic and critical attitude which would restore them to their proper places. A political imagination and creativity would call on them insofar as they could contribute to the goals and aspirations of society. Their use would have clearly established limits resulting from their desacralization.

While on the fringes of society a more critical attitude toward technique and the nation-state is beginning to develop, there is no sociological evidence as to whether this will or will not spread to the mainstream of society. In the unlikely event of this happening in the future, the present cultural unity of society would gradually disintegrate to make room for a new one. The intervention of human freedom with regard to technique as milieu and system would make the corresponding concepts less and less relevant for the emerging historical epoch.

Once again the thought of Jacques Ellul is highly informative on these matters. Following a detailed analysis of why the enormous technical progress in the twentieth century has not brought us much closer to realizing the aspirations and values embodied in a striving for a genuine democracy or socialism, Ellul explains why the new generation of techniques associated with the computer will not bring about a more decentralized society where many things would be on a scale more appropriate to human life.[44] The hopes generated by these new techniques are misplaced and have an air of *déjà vu*. When people dreamt about the possibilities of electricity, they also thought that this power, once distributed to everyone, would lead to a greater autonomy for the individual and the small group. People forgot about the electrical networks which required one of the most centralized and powerful organizations ever conceived. The average person, when equipped with an "intelligent" terminal, may have access to a variety of large data banks, but remains dependent on the large and very powerful institutions that will be required to build and control them. There is also the hope that ongoing automation, made possible by computer-aided design and manufacturing techniques, would soon reduce the length of the workweek so that the growing leisure time could permit the development of a new human-centered culture. These hopes as well do not reckon with almost everything we have been able to observe thus far; on the contrary, as people have acquired more free time, what has proliferated are the mass media, video games and other such developments which extend rather than mutate the technical way of life characterized by individual passivity and lack of initiative.

Ellul argues that these new techniques and technical possibilities launched in the present context tend to end up further reinforcing the milieu and system created by technique. He denies that this is inevitable. He shows how these new techniques could in fact be used to begin a transition toward a very different kind of civilization which includes technique but whose culture is able to impose human values and standards for its development. What will have to happen first is a great deal of "reality testing" in the mainstream of society to see whether there is evidence for the claims made for technique and the state (whether democratic or socialist). The extensive work of Jacques Ellul[45] (most of which many of his critics appear to be unaware of) is one of the most systematic reality-testing efforts of our time; and his suggestion for a strategy for dealing with humanity's challenges is one of the few taking the cultural-religious dimensions of the present situation into account.[46] The last time Western Civilization did extensive reality testing was at the end of the Middle Ages, when the claims of the clergy and the church were found wanting. I have argued that it can and must happen again.[47]

Notes

*Research for this essay was supported by a grant from the Social Sciences and Humanities Research Council of Canada.

1. I am in agreement with Langdon Winner's argument that those who criticize authors such as Mumford and Ellul for their analyses of technology are often the real determinists by refusing to acknowledge that these criticisms of technology are intended as invigorating challenges. By writing off such critics as excessively pessimistic these authors reveal their willingness to take technology as the independent variable, thus exposing themselves as the real prophets of technological determinism. (See L. Winner, "On Criticizing Technology" in *Public Policy*, Vol. 20, 1972.)

2. This expression is taken from the subtitle of F. Schumacher's book: *Small is Beautiful: Economics as if People Matter* (New York: Harper and Row, 1973).

3. W. Connolly, *The Terms of Political Discourse* (Oxford: Robertson, 1983), chapter 1: "Essentially Contested Concepts."

4. C.D. Lummis,"The Radicalism of Democracy," *Democracy*, 2, No. 4 (Fall 1982), 9-16. See also S.S. Wolin, "What Revolutionary Action Means Today," *Democracy*, 2, No. 4 (Fall 1982), 17-28.

5. See W.H. Vanderburg, *Technique and Culture*, Vol. 1, *The Growth of Minds and Cultures: A Unified Theory of the Structure of Human Experience* (Toronto: University of Toronto Press, 1985).

6. Max Weber, *The Theory of Social and Economic Organization*, ed. T. Parsons (New York: Oxford University Press, 1947), pp. 160-161.

7. *Ibid.*, p. 161.

8. J. Ellul, *The Technological Society* (New York: Alfred Knopf, 1964), p.xxv. For an overview of Ellul's theory of contemporary society see W.H. Vanderburg, ed., *Perspectives on Our Age: Jacques Ellul Speaks of His Life and Work* (Toronto: CBC Enterprises, 1981, 1986). For further details see J. Ellul, *The Technological Society*, and J. Ellul, *The*

32   Willem H. Vanderburg

Technological System (New York: Continuum, 1980). The reader should be aware that some translators have rendered the French word "technique" as technology. This is erroneous since there is no term equivalent to technology in the French language. The French "technologie" refers to the thinking about or philosophy of technique.

9. It should be remembered that this growth of the state was at one time regarded by Christianity and Marxism as harmful to human life. The Biblical images of Egyptian, Babylonian and Roman empires symbolize bondage and slavery. It is instructive to read the warning received by Israel when it wants to become a kingdom in the book of Samuel. The only exception is, of course, the famous text of Paul in Romans, which when taken out of context has been used for the contrary argument. Marx also firmly believed that in a genuine socialist society the state would wither away. It is remarkable that both traditions so fundamental to Western Civilization have largely found peace with the large modern state, contrary to the teachings of their sources.

10. For a critique of technicized politics and the technicized state, see for example: B.Wynne, "The Rhetoric of Consensus Politics: A Critique of Technology Assessment," *Research Policy*, 4, No. 2 (May 1975), 108-158; L.H. Tribe, "Policy Science: Analysis or Ideology?", *Philosophy and Public Affairs*, 2, No. 1 (1972), 66-110; A. Feenburg, "The Idea of Progress and the Politics of Technology," *Research in Philosophy and Technology*, 5 (1982), 15-21; Edwin Black, "Politics on a Microchip," *Canadian Journal of Political Science*, XVI, No. 4 (1983), 675-690; L. Winner, "Techne and Politeia: The Technical Constitution of Society," in *Philosophy and Technology*, eds. P.T. Durbin and F. Rapp (Boston: D. Reidel, 1983); Volkmar Lauber, "Efficiency and After: The Dilemma of the Technicized State," *Alternative Futures*, 2, No. 4 (Fall 1979), 47-65.

11. I have analyzed the enfolded nature of a society in my work, *The Growth of Minds and Cultures*.

12. James R. Beniger, *The Control Revolution* (Cambridge: Harvard University Press, 1986).

13. E. Bittner, "Technique and the Conduct of Life," *Social Problems*, 30, No. 3 (Feb. 1983), 249-261.

14. The reification of modern life as a barrier to genuine democratic politics has been studied by authors such as Jacques Ellul, Ivan Illich, Herbert Marcuse, C. Wright Mills, and Lewis Mumford.

15. P.A. Schilpp, ed., "Autobiographical Note," *Albert Einstein: Philosopher-Scientist* (Evanston: Library of Living Philosophers, 1949).

16. A. Peterson, "The Philosophy of Niels Bohr," *Bulletin of the Atomic Scientists*, 19 (Sept. 1963), 8-14, and *Quantum Physics and the Philosophical Tradition* (Cambridge: MIT Press), p. 188.

17. The discussion that follows is based on W.H. Vanderburg, "Society as the Socio-Cultural Milieu of Traditional Technologies," in *Man-Environment Systems*, 16, Nos. 2 & 3 (1986), 76-82.

18. Giedion has given some interesting illustrations of what constituted medieval comfort. See S. Giedion, *Mechanization Takes Command* (New York: Norton, 1969), pp. 258-304.

19. The discussion that follows is in part based on W.H. Vanderburg, "The Human Implications of the Universalization of Modern Technology," in *Man-Environment Systems*, 16, Nos. 2 & 3 (1986), 93-102.

20. For numerous examples see E.T. Hall, *Beyond Culture* (Garden City, New York: Anchor Books, 1976). His interpretation of culture is in many respects different from mine.

21. See, for example, R. Dallek, *Ronald Reagan: The Politics of Symbolism* (Cambridge, Mass.: Harvard University Press, 1984).

22. See especially J. Ellul, *Propaganda* (New York: Knopf, 1965), especially chapters 2, 3 and 4, and D. Riesman, *The Lonely Crowd* (New Haven: Yale University Press, 1964).

23. A. Huxley, *Brave New World* (London: Chatto & Windus, 1932).

24. L. Mumford, *The Pentagon of Power* (New York: Harcourt, Brace, Jovanovich, 1970).

25. I am extending the theory of the three milieus proposed by Jacques Ellul in W. H. Vanderburg, ed., *Perspectives on Our Age*.

26. Jacques Ellul, *The New Demons* (New York: Seabury, 1975).

27. Jacques Ellul, *The False Presence of the Kingdom* (New York: Seabury, 1972). See also the following works by Ellul: *Betrayal of the West* (New York: Seabury, 1978); *The Subversion of Christianity* (Grand Rapids, Mich.: William B. Eerdmans, 1986); *L'Ideologie Marxist-Chretien* (Paris: Le Centurion, 1979); *Metamorphose du Bourgeois* (Paris: Calmann-Levy, 1967); *Changer de Revolution: L'Ineluctable Proletariat* (Paris: Seuil, 1982); *The Politics of God and the Politics of Man* (Grand Rapids, Mich.: William B. Eerdmans, 1972); "Anarchism and Christianity," *Katallagete*, 7, No. 3 (Fall 1980), 14-24.

28. R. Stivers, *Evil in Modern Myth & Ritual* (Athens, Ga.: University of Georgia Press, 1982).

29. See, for example: R. Caillois, *Man and the Sacred*, trans. M. Barash (New York: Free Press, 1959); M. Douglas, *Purity and Danger* (London: Routledge & Kegan Paul, 1966); M. Eliade, *The Sacred and the Profane*, trans. W. Trask (New York: Harper and Row, 1961); M. Eliade, *Patterns in Comparative Religion*, trans. R. Sheed (Cleveland: World, 1970); C. Levi-Strauss, *The Raw and the Cooked*, trans. J. and D. Weightman (New York: Harper and Row, 1969); P. Ricoeur, *The Symbolism of Evil*, trans. E. Buchanan (New York: Harper and Row, 1967).

30. E. Cassirer, "The Technique of our Modern Political Myths," in *Symbol, Myth and Culture: Essays and Lectures of Ernst Cassirer 1939-1945*, ed. D.P. Verene (New Haven: Yale, 1979).

31. Joe Hunt, "Spirituality and Fascism," *New Age Journal*, pp. 33-37.

32. W.L. Bennett, "Myth, Ritual and Political Control," *Journal of Communication*, 30, No. 4 (Autumn 1980), 166-179.

33. *Ibid.*

34. For an excellent discussion see D. Menninger, "Politics or Technique: A Defence of Jacques Ellul," *Polity*, 14, No. 1 (Fall 1981), 110-127; see also Menninger, "Political Dislocation in a Technical Universe," *The Review of Politics*, 42, No. 1 (1980), 73-91.

35. See, for example: Norman Balabian, "The Presumed Neutrality of Technology," *Society*, 17, No. 3 (1980), 7-14; L. Winner, "Do Artifacts Have Politics?", *Daedalus*, 109, No. 1 (Winter 1980), 121-136; D. Noble, "Present Tense Technology," *Democracy*, 3, No. 2 (Spring 1983), 8-24; Marilyn Fischer, "Tensions from Technology in Marx's Communist Society," *Journal of Value Inquiry*, 16 (1982), 117-129.

36. Jacques Ellul has sought to demonstrate this in his work. See especially: *Autopsy of Revolution* (New York: Knopf, 1971), *De La Revolution Aux Revoltes* (Paris: Calmann-Levy, 1972), and *Changer de Revolution*.

37. For excellent discussions of the political aspects of the work of Jacques Ellul, see: J.H. Schaar, "Jacques Ellul: Between Babylon and the New Jerusalem," *Democracy*, 2, No. 4 (Fall 1982), 102-118; J.H. Schaar, "The Possibility of Freedom in a Technological Society," *The Center Magazine*, XVI, No. 3 (1983), 51-64. See also David Menninger's works cited previously.

38. J.K. Galbraith, *The New Industrial State*, 3rd ed. (New York: Mentor, 1978).

39. J. Ellul, *Propaganda*.

40. J. Ellul, *The Political Illusion* (New York: Knopf, 1967).

41. Important aspects of the political revised sequence have been examined by many authors. I will give a few examples: Volkmar Lauber, "Efficiency and After: The Dilemma of the Technicized State," *Alternative Futures*, 2, No. 4 (Fall 1979), 47-65; B. de Jouvenel, "The Political Consequences of the Rise of Science," *Bulletin of the Atomic Scientists*, 19 (1963), 2-8; P.R. Moody Jr., "The Erosion of the Function of Political Parties in the Post-liberal State," *The Review of Politics*, 45, No. 2 (Spring 1983), 254-279; J.P. Young, "Intimate Allies in Migration: Education and Propaganda in a Philippine Village," *Comparative Education Review*, 26, No. 2, 1982, 218-234; D. Lovekin, "Artifacts, Politics and Imagination: From Marx to Vico," *Research in Philosophy & Technology*, 5 (1982), 65-75; E. Byrne, "Can Government Regulate Technology?", *Philosophy and Technology* (1983), 17-33; L.R. Beres, "Embracing Omnicide: President

Reagan and the Strategic Mythmakers," *Hudson Review*, XXXVI, No. 1 (1983), 17-29; Y. Hitoshi, "Science and Technology at the Turning Point: Founding the Technological State," *Canadian Journal of Political & Social Theory*, 8, No. 3 (Fall 1984); D. Noble, "Present Tense Technology."

42. Jacques Ellul, *The Political Illusion*, pp. 221, 222.

43. John H. Schaar, "Jacques Ellul: Between Babylon and the New Jerusalem," 118.

44. Jacques Ellul, *Changer de Revolution.*

45. A bibliography of his work has been published as: "Jacques Ellul: A comprehensive bibliography," *Research in Philosophy & Technology*, Supplement 1 (1984). It is remarkable how many of his critics appear to be largely ignorant of the scope of Ellul's analysis.

46. Ellul, *Changer de Revolution.*

47. For some reality testing of science and technology, see D. Shapley and R. Roy, *Lost at the Frontier: U.S. Science and Technology Policy Adrift* (Philadelphia: ISI Press, 1985).

MARX AND LUKACS ON TECHNOLOGY AND THE "VALUE" OF FREEDOM

Richard B. Day

In the *Grundrisse* Karl Marx portrays the development of human society as a movement from primitive tribal *unity*, through the *division* of labor, to restored *communality* at the higher level of socialized humanity. In the earliest tribal or clan communities, the individual is said to be born into a natural unity which mediates between him and nature as the objective condition of his existence. In capitalist society, by contrast, the individual becomes himself an object, labor power for sale in the market, and social integration must now occur objectively. The movement of commodities is governed not by consciously determined social values, but rather by pursuit of private profit in compliance with the capitalist "law of value." In this context "value" denotes the labor embodied in commodities; and "surplus value," or profit, arises from unpaid labor time in the service of capital. For the capitalist, "value" represents dehumanized wealth accumulated in the form of things. Communism, Marx argues, will redefine the purpose of production in terms of "communal needs and purposes."[1] "Real wealth," as distinct from private profit, will be understood in terms of *human* values as the "developed productive powers of all individuals." The presupposition of all wealth will become "disposable time" for the free development of each individual's universal skills.[2]

With the purpose of labor defined as "disposable time," Marx saw the transcendent goal of economic planning as a dramatic shortening of the working day through increases of labor productivity. In *Capital* he wrote that the "freely associated" producers would organize their activity "in accordance with a settled plan."[3] Marx considered it redundant to reflect upon *how* the priorities of the plan would be settled, for this was a technical and not a philosophical question: the overriding rationale of scientific planning was to reduce "necessary" labor time to a minimum and to replace it with embodied labor and embodied scientific knowledge. Marx believed that the technical conditions for rational planning could be established by reference to the objective need for "economy of time," for maintenance of technically given proportions between the various branches of production, and for "continuous relative overproduction" in order to ensure reserves against unanticipated disproportions.

In this paper I shall argue that there is a serious problem with Marx's reasoning in the sense that it leaves the content of "disposable time" indeterminate, with the consequence that production activity appears once more, as in capitalism, to be determined by objective necessity. By subsuming all needs under one universal need, abstractly defined as the need for free time, Marx provides a merely formal view of freedom. His treatment of planning excludes the possibility that particular groups of producers might disagree over relative planning priorities or that the technically "necessary" might conflict with the socially acceptable. The result of viewing the associated producers as an *immediate* unity is that Marx sees no need for an organization of *freedom*, or for social institutions which might mediate between particulars in the determination of "communal needs and purposes," only for the organization of *production*, which is said to be the precondition for actual freedom. In other words, Marx does not recognize the need for *choice* between technical alternatives or for a social determination of the "values" in accordance with which such choices might be made.

In his effort to reinterpret Marxism in terms of social ontology, Georg Lukács is one Marxist who has been sensitive to these difficulties. Alert to the manipulative implications of theories of technological determinism, Lukács believes that human freedom must be understood in terms of an ontological necessity for choice between competing alternatives:

> alternatives are possible within the concrete space of action which the major laws of development prescribe....Freedom exists ... in the sense that life provides men with concrete alternatives....Man is a responding being, and his freedom consists in his having a choice to make between the possibilities of a particular space of action.[4]

For Lukács the individual act of labor is "the atom from which society is built up."[5] Every act of labor presupposes the activity of consciousness in the sense that through labor "a teleological positing is realized within material being, as the rise of a new objectivity."[6] From its simplest to its most complex forms, labor involves the ontological coexistence of teleology and (natural) causality, the result of which is both "a retreat of the natural boundary" and the simultaneous emergence of a new (humanly altered) objectivity, which in turn imposes a new need for choice. Thus the labor process is structured ontologically as "a chain of alternatives"[7] through which human society strives for "free movement in the material" as "the predominant moment for freedom."[8]

Lukács views freedom as forever elusive, however, for "the teleological project involved in labor can never take account of the entire set of conditions of the causal series set in motion, so that something must necessarily emerge in the labor process other than what the laborer set himself as his aim."[9] The elusiveness of freedom is an "insuperable aspect of objectivity and lawfulness in social existence."[10] A teleological project "can only be present in a causally determined world."[11] In this manner Lukács asserts the objectivity of consciousness while at the same time upholding Marx's dictum that men make their own history - but not in circumstances of their own choosing.[12] For Lukács freedom means the need and the opportunity to choose within circumstances which cannot be chosen.

Having established the ontological necessity of choice, in his later work Lukács often appears to be aware that human choices must involve both technical and ethical dimensions. Because the end which ultimately governs all choice is the human end of freedom in community, he remarks that technology and technical reason are but the *means* to this end and that choices cannot be made on technical grounds alone: "no matter how high the level of development of technology (its support by a whole series of sciences), this cannot be the sole ground for decision between alternatives."[13] The most that technical reason can establish is an "if ... then" sequence; it cannot define "the 'ought' of the goal."[14] "No values are known in nature, but only causal connections and the transformations and changes in things and complexes that these bring about."[15] This line of argument implies, says Lukács, the "ontological reality of ethical ... behaviour."[16] To ignore this aspect of social being would merely be to "arrive at the kind of irrationality that indelibly marks all forms of ... 'Realpolitik'."[17]

Emphasizing the growing role of subjective choice, Lukács suggests that the actuality of social freedom also presupposes "secondary goal positing," the object of which is no longer nature but "the consciousness of a human group."[18] The purpose of these secondary positings is to "influence the consciousness of other people so as to bring about the desired teleological positings on their part."[19] Once the goal becomes that of influencing the positings of others, then "the development of human relations eventually leads to the self-transformation of the subject becoming the direct object of teleological positings of an 'ought' character. These positings, of course, are ... qualitatively distinguished ... from those forms of the 'ought' that we have discovered in the labour process."[20] Whereas the "ought" of the labor process is a "valuable" object, or a "being-for-us of the product of labour," at a higher level of social development the objects of human practice include both a "meaningful" life and determination of the conditions of social obligation: "Obligation implies those human attitudes that are determined through social ends (and not only through mere natural or spontaneous human inclinations)."[21]

Lukács recognizes that to speak of social obligation is to posit the need for certain "rules" of social practice as "forms of mediation." "We can refer here to the sphere of law in the broadest sense of the term (*Recht*)."[22] The argument appears to be that technical choices require knowledge of what is *correct* in terms of efficiency; law defines what is *right* and socially desirable; and the mediating function of law "must receive a constitution independent from the economy." For Lukács, "It is precisely the objective social independence of the realm of law from the economy, combined with the ensuing heterogeneity, that in their dialectical simultaneity determine both the specificity of value and its social objectivity." In other words, the purpose of law is to subsume technological "necessity" under the moral values of society, whose validity lies in their importance "for the objective development of the human species," meaning the awakening and development of "human capabilities."[23] These social commitments, Lukács comments, require "an institutional apparatus, which may of course assume very different forms ... (law, the state, religion, etc.)."[24]

Although Lukács ranges far beyond classical Marxism in his references to the distinction between natural necessity and social obligation, the foundations of his theoretical edifice do not always sustain the conclusions he wishes to draw. He sees an ontological "distancing" of man from nature which enables consciousness to fashion its own objectivity; yet at the same time he insists upon a "materialist" approach and continues to speak of the means and objects of labor as "in themselves natural things."[25] A similar "distancing" between human beings underlies the "ontological reality of ethical ... behaviour"; yet in this case too Lukács remains convinced that there exists "a closed system of the economic, with its own immanent basis, in which real practice is possible only through an orientation to immanently economic goals and the search for means to achieve them."[26] Economic acts are said to possess "an ontologically immanent intention towards the humanization of man in the broadest sense."[27] But this reassurance only provokes further uncertainty as to how this "immanent intention" can guarantee that economic acts are *right*, as opposed to *useful*.

The tension in Lukács' argument arises from the fact that he sees the most complex forms of social practice being modelled upon the simplest act of individual labor, without contemplating the alternative possibility that labor, even in its most primitive form, presupposes cultural meaning. He writes that social relations constitute a "totality," or a "dynamically contradictory interaction among individual actors" which possesses "a being *sui generis*."[28] But this assertion omits the question of how such a "totality" can be articulated without presupposing shared symbolic and linguistic meanings. These and other problems in Lukács' work have been the subject of critical review by his former students of the "Budapest school" of Marxism.

It is the opinion of these authors (Ferenc Fehér, Agnes Heller, György Márkus and Mihály Vajda) that in his final work, *Toward the Ontology of Social Being*, Lukács failed to establish in his own mind "a truly consistent conception of value" and remained undecided as to "whether to regard value as *only an economic category* or also a 'moral' one."[29] The inevitable consequence is that Lukács' *Ontology* shares the same weakness as we have referred to previously in Marx's *Grundrisse*: "The problem of value conflicts remains unresolved."[30] In some instances Lukács refers to value as objective "being-in-itself," while in other parts of the work "all values are transferred to ethics."[31]   At one time the need for law (as *Recht*) is emphasized; elsewhere law is portrayed in "completely negative terms" and regarded "purely as a means of class oppression."[32] The need for law as the articulation of ethical commitments suggests the need for politics in the determination of the law; but Lukács believed that politics is not a part of social ontology and belongs to the phenomenal sphere.[33]

Perhaps the real origin of Lukács' inconsistencies can be found in his ambivalence towards Hegel. The *Ontology*, as Ernest Joos contends, was Lukács' "last autocriticism," his final effort to repudiate his own early attempt to "out-Hegel Hegel" in *History and Class Consciousness*.[34] Hegel had treated Reason as both the form and content of world history; Lukács replaced Reason with conscious labor and made the proletariat into the *immediate* universal, the identical subject-object, with the implication that nature was but a "social category."[35] The *Ontology* is more faithful to Marx in restoring the category of natural objectivity, although Lukács still redeems the role of consciousness by saying that it is precisely the ontological "distancing" between man and nature which imposes the possibility and need for choice in the teleological projects of labor.

If the *Ontology* defers to Marx in one sense, it is equally true that the Hegelian influence remains unmistakable in another. For Hegel the identical subject-object was a *concrete* universal, or the *mediated* totality of ethical life as a socially self-imposed system of rights and duties. In Hegel's *Philosophy of Right* the ethical values of society are determined through discourse, and the need for politics results from the need to mediate particular interests (economic or otherwise) into the universal community of the state. Hegel differentiated between the *understanding* of the positive sciences and *reason*, or philosophical science, whose purpose was to explain the becoming of freedom through the laws.[36] To sublate particular interests, in Hegel's usage, means "to preserve, to maintain, and equally it also means to cause to cease, to put an end to....Thus what is sublated [or dialectically overcome] is at the same time preserved, it has lost its immediacy but it is not on that account annihilated."[37] Social integrity, for Hegel, presupposes the mediation of particulars, and the human potential for freedom is realized in and through this process alone. It is this process of social mediation which Lukács appears to have in mind when he refers to *Recht*, "secondary goal positing" and the social objectivity of values. The result is that the *Ontology* is pulled in two directions and ultimately fails to settle accounts either with Marx or with Hegel. For all of its weaknesses, however, it does sensitize the reader to the relation between technical reason and the problem of social emancipation. In this way it facilitates critical insight into the logic of Marx's *Grundrisse*.

The Movement from Communal Mediation to Commodity Mediation

Marx begins his analysis of social history in the *Grundrisse* with a discussion of early communal life. In the first human communities the process of cultural individuation has yet to begin: the naturally arisen clan community is an undifferentiated unity, a "communality [*Gemeinschaftlichkeit*] of blood, language, customs," and is not of human design. Rather it exists in-itself, with the earth as its "base" and "great workshop." Like the human community, the earth too exists initially in-itself: it is not a *product* of labor but simply *nature*, the objective condition of human life, to which members of the tribe or clan "relate naively ... as the *property of the community*." Humankind, in this natural state, "grazes off what it finds"; "the *clan community*, the natural community, appears not as a *result* of, but as a *presupposition for the communal appropriation* (temporary) *of the land*."[38] Rather than occurring *through* labor, appropriation is presupposed to labor: nature is "a presupposition of [man's] activity just like his skin, his sense organs"; and the individual relates to his surroundings "as the inorganic nature of his subjectivity, in which the latter realizes itself."[39]

In the absence of social individuation, Marx attaches little significance to the secondary positings of which Lukács writes. The original community is presented as lacking in self-reflective thought, attributing its unity to nature or to divinity, with the result that Marx concentrates instead on the mediation between man and his natural environment. The relation of each member of the community to the earth is said to be "mediated through his presence as a member of the commune";[40] this mediation occurs "instantly" through the fact of birth into "*a naturally arisen, spontaneous society*, clan etc.";[41] "property" means "no more than a human being's relation to the natural conditions of production as belonging to him, as *presupposed* along with his *own being*."[42] By virtue of his birth into the clan, he lives a mediated unity with nature and achieves his "subjective-objective existence" as a commune-being.[43]

Although this original membership in the natural community posited the human being's relation to the natural conditions of existence as his own, Marx observes that this relation could only be "realized by production itself," or by "really" positing the conditions of production as an "active relation."[44] The necessary result is that even in these still primitive communities property will come to "have different forms depending on the conditions of this production," both natural and man-made.[45] But whatever the forms in which property mediated by communal membership might appear - whether it be directly communal property, the dual existence of public and private property, or communal property as an adjunct to private property[46] - all types of early communal life presuppose an *immediate* and spontaneous community, and must therefore reproduce their members strictly within the established physical and cultural conditions.

These original limits to human existence are eventually suspended, however, through population growth and development of production, which together signify the "decay, decline and fall" of communal existence.[47] But the atrophy of the commune is not simply the loss of "species-being"; it is also the precondition for higher social development beyond the "clan being" and "herd animal."[48] Growth of exchange, the chief form of human individuation, makes the previous "herd-like existence superfluous and dissolves it."[49] Exchange is movement beyond the confines of communal specificity toward human universalization, a movement which occurs precisely through the proliferation of new specificities. Through development of particular skills, humanity begins to live the prehistory of the social individual, who will eventually emerge in communism as the universal man in restored unity with his world.

If the naturally arisen human community is "historic stage No. 1," Marx refers to the guild-corporation system as the archetype of "historic stage No. 2."[50] Here the raw material object of labor comes to be mediated no longer through natural membership in a natural community, but as the particular property of the craftsman through his work and his ownership of the means of production. In this context Marx acknowledges that particular properties imply particular communities as the constituent elements of the larger society. "Since the instrument itself is already the product of labour, [and] thus the element which constitutes property already exists as posited by labour, the community can no longer appear here in a ... spontaneous form ... but rather as itself already a produced, made, derived and secondary community, produced by the worker himself."[51] Further dissolution of the guild-corporate communities and of small landed property finally results in the total alienation of man from nature, in the appearance of the "free labourer," or the "objectless, purely subjective labour capacity, confronting the objective conditions of property as his not-property, as alien property, as *value* for-itself, as capital."[52]

This historic process of dissolving the original, communally mediated unity of man and nature is "the divorce of elements which ... were bound together; its result is ... not that one of the elements disappears, but that each of them appears in a negative relation to the other."[53] Original nature is transformed into a second (humanized) nature through the labor of the human species; but when the collectively produced world, the embodied labor of all the generations, is privately appropriated, it becomes alien to its human creators. With full development of the capitalist division of labor, the individual's labor becomes externally determined abstract labor, labor as a commodity alienated in the market, and all particular labors are mediated *post festum* through the movement of commodities rather than through any conscious human community. The objective laws of commodity circulation relate each worker both to the world and to his fellows through the movement of things. Commodity circulation is "the movement in which general alienation appears as general appropriation and general appropriation as general alienation." While it remains true that in the first instance this movement presupposes Lukács' "teleological positings" - in Marx's words, it arises from "the conscious will and particular purposes of individuals" - it is not consciously integrated by way of "secondary positings" and mediation through *Recht*. That is to say, the purposes of labor have lost all social objectivity and been reduced to the physiological needs of each individual. As a totality, the market and the division of labor are mediated objectively. Relations between individuals are "neither located in their consciousness, nor subsumed under them as a whole. Their own collisions with one another produce an *alien* social power standing over them, produce their mutual interaction as a process and power independent of them."[54]

In the absence of a plan, jointly "settled" by the workers themselves, capital and labor become abstractions which oppose one another in an objective antithesis. As embodied labor, capital seeks to overcome its abstraction through self-universalization, or through displacing "necessary" living labor with further accumulations of fixed capital: "Machinery appears, then, as the most adequate form of *fixed capital*, and fixed capital, in so far as capital's relations with itself are concerned, appears as *the most adequate form of capital as such*."[55] The overall movement of capitalist industrial production points in the direction of "an automatic system of machinery ... set in motion by an automaton, a moving power that moves itself."[56]

Capital strives for its own universality, as the self-constituted value which evaluates all things, but Marx argues that this ambition can never be realized. Not only is living labor the source of capital, but capital is also internally divided through competition in accordance with the laws of the market: "Capital exists and can only exist as many capitals, and its self-determination therefore appears as their reciprocal interaction with one another."[57] "A universal capital, one without alien capitals confronting it, ... is ... a non-thing."[58] Capital pursues its self-expansion through accumulation of surplus value; but each increment to production capacity, being uncoordinated with the actions of other capitals, suspends the relations of "proportionate production." Lack of *ex ante* integration means that "departure from the given proportions in one branch of production drives all of them out of [proportionality], and in unequal proportions."[59] In its limitless drive for self-expansion, capital creates the "unevenness" of its own development: periodic crises devalue and destroy parts of the existing capital, and capital therefore appears as its own self-limitation. It is precisely through its striving for universality that "capital ... works towards its own dissolution as the form dominating production."[60] Capital posits the universality of its own self-relation, but it remains a "moving contradiction."[61]

Labor too, like capital, is compelled to lead a double and self-contradictory existence. The material unity of combined labor is required by and subordinated to the machine, the objectification both of past labor and of the "scientific idea," of which living labor appears merely to be the "accessory." In its combination the total labor represents a combination of labors objectively related, yet its "individual component parts are alien to one another" and the overall process of production is not the product of the producer. This combination is not self-organization. It exists in-itself as an "alien combination," which both negates the labor of "*the particular, isolated worker*" and at the same time posits the return to "*communal or combined labour*" as social self-determination.[62] The return from isolated particularity to community is a necessary consequence of this "most extreme form of alienation," which creates "the full conditions for the total, universal development of the productive forces of the individual."[63] The self-expansion of capital leads to the negation of capital through creation of a need for the universal producer.

**The Movement from Particular Labor
to Universal Producer**

In Marx's *Grundrisse* developments at the level of the human community are expressed through the fate of the worker, both as an individual and collectively. The original natural community, as we have seen, was characterized by "the *reproduction of presupposed* relations ... of the individual to his commune, together with a *specific, objective* existence, predetermined for the individual."[64] Capitalism, in contrast, posits the "*production of wealth itself* and hence the universal development of the productive forces, the constant overthrow of its prevailing presuppositions as the presupposition of its reproduction."[65] In its ceaseless drive to expand relative surplus value, which can take the form of new fixed capital, capital creates both "new consumption" and "new needs." "This creation of new branches of production ... is not merely the division of labour, but is rather the creation ... of labour with a new use value ... of different kinds of labour, different kinds of production, to which a constantly expanding and constantly enriched system of need corresponds."[66] The objective totality of combined labor, performed within the division of labor, is therefore a process of universalizing labor through the multiplication of individual specificities. By universalizing both social and individual needs, capitalism points beyond the division of labor itself to a condition wherein each individual fully works out his "creative potentialities" and "does not reproduce himself in one specificity, but produces his totality."[67]

Capitalism creates wealth through impoverishment, which is at the same time the necessary condition for human enrichment. Each extension of the division of labor creates both a specific new skill and an added dimension of human interdependence through exchange. As individual labor becomes increasingly abstract, "the product ceases to be the product of isolated direct labour, and the *combination* of social activity appears, rather, as the producer." The labor of the individual is increasingly "*posited as suspended individual*, i.e., *as social labour*."[68] Capitalism tends to create the universal worker, from this perspective, as an identity in difference, wherein the concrete must become the communal worker, or the social individual. In other words, capitalism posits the return out of individual abstraction to the species-being and the species-life.

The concrete existence of the individual is only realized in the totality, through the proliferation of individual specificities; and at the same time the capitalist proliferation of needs, the "universality of individual needs" perfected through the division of labor, also posits the personal cultural enrichment of each member of society.[69] To move towards universality is to appropriate the world in a growing multiplicity of ways: it requires the production of man himself as "the most total and universal possible social product, for, in order to take gratification in a many-sided way, he must be capable of many pleasures [*genussfähig*], hence cultured to a high degree."[70] The capitalist universalization of commodity production therefore creates the potential and the need for universal culture. For this potential to be realized, however, the essential precondition is "disposable time."

Within capitalist society the potential for disposable time appears in the contradictory form of unemployment, or enforced idleness. It involves "the development of the workers' productive power, *as the reduction of the necessary labour time relative to the working day*, and *as the reduction of*

the necessary labouring population relative to the population."71   As Marx
would later argue in *Capital*, the accumulation of capital presupposes
production of a "relative surplus population" in the form of the "industrial
reserve army."72 Capital periodically re-creates the "surplus" population, as
a reserve necessitated by its own disproportionate (cyclical) movement,
while at the same time setting in motion the scientific forces of production
which promise to satisfy universal needs, including the need for disposable
time for purposes of human self-development. Production appears increasingly "as not subsumed under the direct skilfulness of the worker, but rather
as the technological application of science."73   Merely individual labor is
thus reduced to "pure abstraction" in a double sense. On the one hand,
technological application of the natural sciences presupposes growth of
"general scientific labour,"74 in which production becomes dependent upon
"the general state of science and on the progress of technology."75 Yet on
the other hand, in order to "work" with the sophisticated instruments of
embodied knowledge, the "worker" himself must possess universal skills
which will enable him to superintend the sequential activities of the
machines which labor has created. The worker, in other words, can and
must increasingly step to the side of the direct production process as a
universal superintendent. In Marx's words:

> In this transformation, it is neither the direct human labour he performs,
> nor the time during which he works, but rather the appropriation of his
> own general productive power, his understanding of nature and his
> mastery over it by virtue of his presence as a social body - it is, in a
> word, the development of the social individual which appears as the great
> foundation-stone of production and of wealth.76

In its striving to minimize "necessary" labor and expand production of
surplus value, capital seeks to reduce living labor to machine-like activity;
but in making direct labor relatively superfluous, capital both re-creates the
need for cultured "regulators" of the production process and at the same time
renders itself superfluous as the alienated "other" of the worker. Capital
posits the objective need for social appropriation of the forces of production
by the social individual, and in this way it likewise posits a redefinition of
wealth in social rather than in private terms. For capital, wealth is measured
through exchange value and surplus value, with "value" being ultimately
rooted in the labor time embodied in the resulting commodity. The secular
replacement of living labor by embodied labor, and increasingly by
embodied "scientific labour," negates this specific rationality of capitalism,
progressively removes living labor as the source of surplus value, and in this
way demands a new rationality to inform the production process. Labor
time continues to be the basis of this new rationality, but its meaning is now

redefined in terms of a new purpose - the production of human freedom. Marx summarizes this process in the *Grundrisse* as follows:

> As soon as labour in the direct form has ceased to be the great well-spring of wealth, labour time ceases and must cease to be its measure, and hence exchange value [must cease to be the measure] of use value. The *surplus labour of the mass* has ceased to be the condition for the development of general wealth, just as the *non-labour of the few* for the development of the powers of the human head. With that, production based on exchange value breaks down, and the direct, material production process is stripped of the form of penury and antithesis. The free development of individualities ... then corresponds to the artistic, scientific, etc. development of the individuals in the time set free, and with the means created, for all of them ... real wealth [is] '... *disposable time* outside that needed in direct production, for *every individual* and the whole of society.'[77]

The "value" of production must now be measured not in terms of embodied labor, but rather in terms of its opposite, the "disposable time" which, through the satisfaction of needs, any production process can create. With social appropriation of the forces of production, "real economy" ceases to be the saving of "necessary" labor time in capitalist terms - or the reduction of wage expenditures - and becomes the saving of labor time as "an increase of free time, i.e., time for the full development of the individual, which in turn reacts back upon the productive power of labour as itself the greatest productive power. From the standpoint of the direct production process it can be regarded as the production of *fixed capital*, this fixed capital being man himself."[78] The final return out of a rigid division of labor into restored "communality" requires that the social individual produce his own totality and thus find himself in "the absolute movement of becoming."[79] This process of becoming, as truly human history, is endless, for the "human being who has become" would be one "in whose head exists the accumulated knowledge of society."[80]

Scientific Planning and
the Problem of "Value"

By redefining surplus labor time in terms of the potential for human freedom, Marx hoped to transcend the objective technical rationality of capitalism by subsuming it under a higher subjective purpose. For Marx the emergence of social subjectivity is demanded by the movement of the universal in order to superintend the world of embodied labor and embodied knowledge which living labor has "worked out" of itself. To the degree, however, that communal production is the dialectical overcoming of capitalism, as a specific mode of production, Marx also believed the higher universal must preserve certain of capitalism's objective laws of movement by raising them to a subjective level. The realm of freedom, we are told in *Capital*, continues to presuppose the realm of necessity as its basis. Within the direct process of production, freedom

> can only exist in socialized man, the associated producers, rationally regulating their interchange with Nature, bringing it under their common control, instead of being ruled by it as by the blind forces of Nature.... But it nonetheless still remains a realm of necessity. Beyond it begins that development of human energy which is an end in itself, the true realm of freedom....The shortening of the working day is its basic prerequisite.[81]

In terms of Lukács' *Ontology*, what this means is that freely associated producers can "distance" themselves from the objective world and understand it conceptually, although both the means and the objects of labor remain "in themselves natural things, subject to natural causality."[82] This applies both to the raw material of nature and to the second nature created by man, for the latter (as Marx argued) represents only the transformation of original nature through the conscious application of the *natural sciences*. The sciences of Hegel's *understanding*, in other words, remain the foundation of positive knowledge of things. They establish the "if ... then" sequence; they do not address the "ought," of which nature knows nothing. To understand the natural sciences is to achieve what Lukács calls "free movement in the material." But as Lukács also points out, such understanding tells us nothing about the "ontological reality" of ethical behavior or the social objectivity of "values."

It is important to return to this distinction, for when Marx considers the question of social mediation in communal production he does so explicitly and exclusively in terms of law-governed economic planning, beginning with "the law of the rising productivity of labour time."[83] Marx's most concise formulation of this law reads as follows:

> On the basis of communal production, the determination of time remains, of course, essential. The less time society requires to produce wheat, cattle, etc., the more time it wins for other production, material or mental. Just as in the case of an individual, the multiplicity of its development, its enjoyment and its activity depends on economization of time. Economy of time, to this all economy reduces itself. Society likewise has to distribute its time in a purposeful way, in order to achieve a production adequate to its needs; just as the individual has to distribute

his time correctly in order to achieve knowledge in proper proportions or in order to satisfy the various demands on his activity. Thus economy of time, along with the planned distribution of labour time among the various branches of production, remains the first economic law on the basis of communal production. It becomes law, there, to an even higher degree.[84]

The problem with this law, if one considers it closely, is that it is a tautology. The planned "economization of time" is required in order to produce in the "proper proportions." The "proper proportions" are those which, through planning, economize on time. The most fundamental question which Marx leaves unanswered is the meaning of "proper." If, for example, one process of production maximizes "disposable time" but has other indirect and undesirable social consequences, how will relative social needs be ascertained? How, in other words, will *choices* be made between alternatives? Without moving from the organization of *production* to the organization of *freedom*, or the institutions through which the associated producers might themselves articulate their needs in terms of jointly defined social purposes, Marx cannot begin to answer this question.

Instead, both in *Capital* and in *Theories of Surplus Value* he takes the existing proportions of production as presupposed and speaks of the need to preserve proportionality through "continuous relative overproduction."[85] In capitalist society *periodic* relative overproduction is shown to be an element of anarchy, causing the destruction of capital and finished goods in accordance with the market "law of value." The way in which to overcome these crises is through planned investments and conscious maintenance of inventories with which to redress disproportions between the branches of industry. The law of "continuous relative overproduction" will guarantee smooth expansion in all branches of the economy and thus establish "conscious control by society over the material means of its own reproduction."[86]

These laws of scientific planning provide some insight into what Lukács calls "free movement in the material." However, they are flawed in principle in the sense that they do not begin to consider the ethical presuppositions of human cooperation. A simple (although admittedly extreme) example will illustrate the point. The logic of Marx's presentation suggests that the proper proportions of production can be statistically established. Past experience in the satisfaction of needs - for food, clothing, housing, etc. - will provide a reasonable projection of future demand, providing such goods were originally available in abundance and therefore demand can be assumed to be relatively constant. But let us now consider the demand for another natural human need, sexual satisfaction. Here a statistical projection might indicate that in order to minimize the frequency of rapes, society must each year devote a certain "proportion" of resources to the production of prostitutes. If "economy of time" is the issue, then appropriate means might be devised to make prostitutes more productive. If the worry is possible "disproportions," then a reserve" of prostitutes might be maintained through "continuous relative overproduction." In this way the laws of scientific planning would provide a technically efficient and correct solution to the problem of rape in the same way as they might technically determine society's need for cabbages. Provision of abortion services poses a similar ethical question, as does satisfaction of countless other perceived needs which may be transparently destructive of physical or mental health or may ignore the obligation of one generation to make life possible for the next. But whatever the specific example chosen, the real issue is that technical laws, to paraphrase Lukács, tell us if X_1 then Y_1, if X_2 then Y_2, if X_3 then Y_3, etc.; such laws tell us nothing of the ethical dimension of choice between the alternatives Y_1, Y_2 and Y_3. They do not elucidate why one alternative "ought" to be selected over the others.

Nowhere in Marx's scattered remarks on communist society is there a clear awareness of the fact that the "proper proportions" of production must be concretely determined by society. Communist society is to be a community for-itself, but before it can be for-itself it must first decide what it is "for." As Lukács argues, intersubjective human cooperation presupposes replacement of the "purely natural," as the object of teleological positings, with "the consciousness of a human group."[87] Social behavior governed by a posited future is "behaviour governed by the 'ought' of the goal."[88] The "'place' and organ" of decisions regarding the "ought" is "human consciousness."[89] Technical reason is instrumental reason, the *means* to the "ought." The objectivity of social values requires more than suspension of the capitalist "law of value," or replacement of surplus labor time with "disposable time"; it requires both knowledge of the *means* and social self-determination of the *right* and *legitimate*. "Freedom," writes Lukács, is "that act of consciousness which has as its result a new being posited by itself."[90] The realm of freedom cannot, as Marx would say, lie "beyond" the realm of necessity; instead, the realm of necessity must be subsumed under concrete social definitions of purpose.

Economic acts, which are not consciously informed by higher values, are and must remain the compulsive acts of "economic man," who in Lukács' words is driven by "immediately necessary behaviour in a world where production has become social."[91] Acts of this kind express no practical reason, only the randomness of perceived needs, whether these be the physiological needs of the alienated proletarian or the technical needs which Stalin had in mind when he "rationalized" terrorism by reference to the "law of planned, proportionate development." The historical experience of Stalinism convincingly demonstrates that without democractic institutions and law as *Recht*, a technically determined plan can never be more than a rationalization of irrationality and an exercise in willfulness on the part of a bureaucratic particular.

The necessary conclusion to which this essay points is that economic planning cannot be a mere "administration of things," as Engels would have it in *Socialism, Utopian and Scientific*,[92] or as Lenin similarly argued in *State and Revolution*. In Lenin's view "accounting and control" were "the *main* thing"; and capitalist culture had reduced control "to the extraordinarily simple operations ... of supervising and recording, knowledge of the four rules of arithmetic, and issuing appropriate receipts."[93] Nearly two decades later Leon Trotsky surveyed the results of this thinking in *The Revolution Betrayed*. Socialism, he observed, clearly required society "to subject nature to technique and technique to plan."[94] But socialism also presupposed "a free conflict of ideas"[95] and "spiritual creativeness"[96] in order that bureaucratic control might be replaced by "self-imposed cultural discipline," growing out of "education, habit and social opinion."[97] A socialist society must awaken human personality "in the realm of spiritual culture," including "critical views, the development of one's own opinion, the cultivation of personal dignity."[98]   In *The Revolution Betrayed* Trotsky's historical analysis led to the same conclusion as Lukacs' *Ontology*. Society might agree upon socialism as its goal, but it cannot thereby renounce the obligation to make further choices between humanly created alternatives: "The choice of the road," Trotsky declared, "is no less important than the choice of the goal. Who is going to choose the road?"[99]

Notes

1. Karl Marx, *Grundrisse: Foundations of the Critique of Political Economy* (New York: Vintage, 1973), pp. 171-2.
2. *Ibid.*, p. 708.
3. Marx, *Capital* (Moscow: Foreign Languages Publishing House, 1961), I, 80.
4. Theo Pinkus, ed., *Conversations with Lukács* (London: Merlin, 1974), p. 129.
5. *Ibid.*, p. 76.
6. Georg Lukács, *Labour* (London: Merlin, 1980), p. 3.
7. *Ibid.*, p. 33.
8. *Ibid.*, p. 118.
9. Pinkus, *Conversations*, p. 18.
10. *Ibid.*, pp. 76-7.
11. *Ibid.*, p. 77.

12. *Ibid.*, p. 131.
13. Lukács, *Labour*, p. 36.
14. *Ibid.*, p. 66.
15. *Ibid.*, p. 89.
16. *Ibid.*, p. 133.
17. *Ibid.*
18. *Ibid.*, p. 47.
19. *Ibid.*, p. 89.
20. *Ibid.*, p. 73.
21. Lukács, "The Vienna Paper," in Ernest Joos, *Lukács's Last Autocriticism: The Ontology* (Atlantic Highlands, N.J.: Humanities Press, 1983), p. 140.
22. Lukács, *Labour*, pp. 89-90.
23. *Ibid.*, p. 90.
24. *Ibid.*, p. 99.
25. *Ibid.*, p. 33.
26. *Ibid.*, p. 87.
27. *Ibid.*
28. Lukács, *Zur Ontologie des gesellschaftlichen Seins, Hegel's falsche und echte Ontologie*, Neuwied, 1971, p. 31.
29. Agnes Heller, ed., *Lukács Revalued* (Oxford: Blackwell, 1983), p. 134.
30. *Ibid.*, p. 143.
31. *Ibid.*, p. 146.
32. *Ibid.*, pp. 146-7.
33. *Ibid.*, p. 145 and p. 150.
34. See Ernest Joos, *op.cit.*; cf. Lukács, *History and Class Consciousness* (London: Merlin, 1971), p. xxiii.
35. Lukács, *History and Class Consciousness*, p. 130.
36. T.M. Knox, ed., *Hegel's Philosophy of Right* (London: Oxford University Press, 1967), p. 20.
37. H. Glockner, ed., *Sämtliche Werke*, Stuttgart, 1927-30, Vol. IV, p. 120, cited by Raymond Plant, *Hegel: An Introduction*, 2d ed. (Oxford: Blackwell, 1983), p. 14.
38. Marx, *Grundrisse*, p. 472.
39. *Ibid.*, p. 485.
40. *Ibid.*, p. 486.
41. *Ibid.*, p. 492.
42. *Ibid.*, p. 491.
43. *Ibid.*, p. 492.
44. *Ibid.*, p. 493.
45. *Ibid.*, p. 495.
46. *Ibid.*, p. 486.

47. *Ibid.*
48. *Ibid.*, p. 496.
49. *Ibid.*
50. *Ibid.*, p. 499.
51. *Ibid.*
52. *Ibid.*, p. 498.
53. *Ibid.*, p. 501.
54. *Ibid.*, pp. 196-7.
55. *Ibid.*, p. 694.
56. *Ibid.*, p. 692.
57. *Ibid.*, p. 414.
58. *Ibid.*, p. 421.
59. *Ibid.*, p. 414.
60. *Ibid.*, p. 700.
61. *Ibid.*, p. 706.
62. *Ibid.*, p. 470.
63. *Ibid.*, p. 515.
64. *Ibid.*, p. 486.
65. *Ibid.*, p. 541.
66. *Ibid.*, p. 408.
67. *Ibid.*, p. 488.
68. *Ibid.*, p. 709.
69. *Ibid.*, p. 488.
70. *Ibid.*, p. 409.
71. *Ibid.*, p. 769.
72. Marx, *Capital*, I, 628-40.
73. Marx, *Grundrisse*, p. 699.
74. *Ibid.*, p. 700.
75. *Ibid.*, p. 705.
76. *Ibid.*
77. *Ibid.*, pp. 705-6; cf. 708.
78. *Ibid.*, p. 711.
79. *Ibid.*, p. 488.
80. *Ibid.*, p. 712.
81. Marx, *Capital*, III, 800.
82. Lukács, *Labour*, p. 33.
83. Marx, *Grundrisse*, p. 139.
84. *Ibid.*, pp. 172-3.
85. Marx, *Capital*, II, 469; *Theories of Surplus Value* (London: Lawrence and Wishart, 1951), pp. 359-60.
86. Marx, *Capital*, II, 469.
87. Lukács, *Labour*, p. 47.
88. *Ibid.*, p. 66.

89. *Ibid.*, p. 39.

90. *Ibid.*, p. 114.

91. *Ibid.*, p. 87.

92. Robert C. Tucker, ed., *The Marx-Engels Reader*, 2d. ed. (New York: Norton, 1978), p. 713.

93. V.I. Lenin, *Selected Works* (Moscow: Foreign Languages Publishing House, 1960-61), II, 383.

94. Leon Trotsky, *The Revolution Betrayed* (New York: Pioneer, 1945), p. 180.

95. *Ibid.*, p. 276.

96. *Ibid.*, p. 180.

97. *Ibid.*, p. 46.

98. *Ibid.*, p. 176.

99. *Ibid.*, p. 268.

LANGUAGES, TECHNIQUES, RATIONALITIES

Dusan Pokorny

1. Modern tools and machines, which include information processors and servo-mechanisms of various kinds, may be, as to their design and the rules of operation directly following from it, described as the products of *ad hoc* integrations of elements of scientific knowledge. If we look at machinery from this point of view - from the inside, so to speak - then the human and social problems associated with its productive employment can result either from the occasional character of the integration or from the nature of scientific knowledge itself. One way or another, the investigation of these links leads to the realization that what is in fact at stake is the relation between objectivity of knowledge and subjectivity in history.

Questions of this kind touch, of course, upon the very core of the "world" in which we are, as actors, immersed. A reflection on it is always self-reflection, and the latter is best served by placing a distance between us and us. This is, in its turn, done most easily by contrasting our culture and civilization with those of others. In what follows, cast for the role of the "others" are two non-European groups: a primitive community in Melanesia (see section 2 below) and a large tribe in East Africa (section 4). While in the first case the traditional culture is still almost intact, in the second it is already under siege from Europe-originating values and attitudes. We cannot, therefore, proceed from one directly to the other: it is necessary to mention at least briefly, and, so to speak, in brackets (i.e., as a mediating link known to us, but extraneous to non-European civilizations) the historical presence of ancient Greece as a cofounder (with the Judaic-Christian traditions) of the cultural West (section 3).

Each of these three historical situations is looked at from the point of view of (1) the role of ordinary language in the constitution of the "worlds" in which people actually live; (2) the degree of recognition of the fundamental interest structures underlying all search for knowledge, including the scientific one; (3) the interrelation between the striving for universality of knowledge and its practicality (i.e., its being directed towards man's attempts at gaining mastery over his destiny); (4) the extent to which the techniques of material production (or knowledge-based patterns of man's action on nature) are in fact appropriated for this practical end; and (5) the concepts of rationality employed in the sphere of man-to-man relations. "Rational" will be understood in terms of two meanings: rational as "right" (presupposing substantively formulated norms and further to be designated rational$_1$), and rational as "correct" (based on formal rules and named rational$_2$).

The historical discussion conducted on these lines serves a dual purpose. In the first place, it enables us to take a brief look at Heidegger's contention that man's "point of view" dominates only modern science and at Gadamer's drawing a parallel between the historicity of Heidegger's Being (a quality said to be acquired precisely in the course of the latter's discussion of technology) and that of Hegel's Absolute (section 5). As with the earlier discussion of the Greeks, however, this can be, in the present study, only an interlude, for its main purpose is to look at science from a different vantage point. In traditional societies and modern ones alike, practical reason determines *how* the available production techniques will be used. The more these techniques themselves rely on scientific knowledge, the more evident it is that concepts of rationality will determine also *what* techniques will be available for productive employment. In this way, the attention turns to rationality in the scientific work itself, and we proceed to Lakatos (section 6). In short, the question to be asked is this: Can a formally defined concept of rationality in the acceptance (i.e., in the choice) of research programs serve also as the only code of honor to guide the actions of the scientist *qua* scientist?

While Lakatos is concerned only with *intra*disciplinary knowledge, the next part (section 7) looks into the concept of rationality in the context of *inter*disciplinary research. In the course of this discussion it is also shown that the scientists' decision to constrain or preclude the development of certain technologies would have to be seen as a prototype of institutional change. And this is an occasion to suggest some points of departure for the concept of rationality in this sphere of changes in norms and forms of social behavior. The conclusion of the essay (section 8) is that a modern society, in trying to master the tools and machines employed in it, is in effect attempting to attain in reality what the primitive society (section 2) started from in imagination. The purpose is again to employ techniques of material production that are "internal" to the world uniquely shared by "us." Only the word refers not to those united by a particular culture, whose function it is to include as well as exclude, but to "us" as the bearers of the "point of view of man," a point of view inherently aiming at emancipation.

The Trobrianders of Melanesia

2. In the language of a traditional community which has received much attention from anthropologists, there is no word for "to be" or "to become": being is still identical with the object itself, and is changeless. It is also self-contained in the sense of being both discrete and whole: it is seen and evaluated as itself, not typically in relation to, or in comparison with, something else. In fact, the word denoting an object or act is understood to include in its meaning all the qualities of the object or act.[1] In other words, there are no adjectives; the "thing" cannot change an attribute and still remain the same thing. Even one's childhood is not a previous phase of a continuous ("this") time: it is a different (kind of) time, that of (being) "in-child-his." There are no words for "because," "cause," "reason," "effect," "purpose," "why"; only the purposive "for" makes a rare appearance. (The word originally means "to jump.")[2] Things, or states of affairs, are, of course, changed (say, a canoe is built from the wood of a tree). But the project is still a *picture* of the final product - again, a static, self-contained whole - rather than a *purpose*, i.e., that for which means are used along a chainline of causation.

The individual (I or he or she) is still in the process of emerging from the continuous stream of life (started somewhere in the past by the group's ancestors, whether mythical or real) and from its present cross-section (we; they). He becomes himself primarily for the purpose, and to the extent, that he may assume moral responsibilities: to perform actions (such as gift-giving between kinship-related persons) which are "good" in the sense of conforming to a "pattern" (a set of interrelated, substantively defined forms of behavior),[3] characteristic of "us." This "giving-in-itself, that is, non-purposive giving" outside the sphere of the "freedom of choice" associated with individual ends, is sharply distinguished from barter which is seen as "purposive" and, for this very reason, is "despised."[4]

What we learn, for the present purpose, from this "original" state of affairs may be summed up as follows:

2.1. The range of what can be experienced as "real" is circumscribed by the ordinary language. Its grammar serves at the same time as a pretheory of "all that is." The "worlds" in which people live - the only worlds that there are for them - are constituted[5] by them and for them: the elements of myth are signs whose representative capability is rather narrowly limited by the fact that their sense is always *special* to the culture concerned.[6]

2.2. The core of the prescientific knowledge laid down in, and passed on through, the language reflects a point of view. The selection of what is to become "real" - or is to have a chance of becoming so - is guided by interests which are not merely individual, and possibly arbitrary, but universal, or fundamental to man as an historically evolved entity. One such orientation, from the very start guiding the search for knowledge, may be termed "work." But the word does not designate merely an activity of producing things which are useful, whether materially or symbolically: it is also, and indeed more importantly, an activity transforming the projects of the self (that is, self-projects) into an object (which is thus, and to that extent, appropriated by the subject and helps to form it). The other interest has to do with the basic fact that people live in groups which are, again from the very beginning, formed with the help of symbolically mediated (not simply "natural" or "physical") ties.[7] And the cultural identity of the group not only determines which things are useful and which projects are legitimate, but calls also for the expansion of the knowledge of "who we are" and what it is that is not "we."

2.3. Man's point of view, while particular to him (there is nothing inconsistent in the thought of other rational beings), at the same time inherently aims at universality, transcendence, infinity. The mythical theory of the world must be all-encompassing, even if it can be so only in a sketchy and frequently incoherent manner. For it is self-evident that only if it encompasses all there is, and can be, will mythology be capable of serving the eminently practical purpose for which it was created: to help those sharing this "world" to gain control over their destinies.[8]

2.4. This is also where the projects of material production and their implementations are still firmly anchored. The regularities and necessities upon which labor depends are internal to "our" world. Therefore, the techniques of production based on these "laws" are also endogenous: they are directly dependent upon, and derive their legitimacy from, their place in the universe uniquely shared by "us." In this sense, they are "proper"; and they are also "appropriated" in that they help to produce, and reproduce, "this" community (rather than a different, and perhaps alien one).

2.5. Obligatory gifts are intended to establish, give effect to, and strengthen social relations.[9] They require reciprocity which is understood as adequacy of response,[10] always relative to the norms of *this* community, not as quantitative equality. (The latter rule, which would in due course regulate market exchanges, is, at least in its pure form, culturally invariant.) Barter is a consequence of a naturally, rather than socially, induced division of labor and represents a deviant behavior. It is despised precisely because it is purposive, i.e., not good in itself (and for that reason, is sometimes disguised as gift-giving).[11]

Although the word is not yet coined, the difference is that between two concepts of practical reason. The type of obligatory gift-giving obtaining in this community is governed by a special case of "rational" as right, or of that concept of practical reason according to which an act is rational[1] only if it is in accordance with the community's sense of justice, as represented by (i) its norms, in their turn giving an "operational" expression to the universal

purpose of the community (to continue the life-stream begun by the ancestors of the group and to do so at the level of culture developed by the group
in the course of its history) and (ii) the norms' interpretation, expected or
actual, by the consensus of the group.[12] Barter, although at this stage still
influenced by the personal relations between the two parties, points in the
direction of "rational" as correct, i.e., to the idea that an act is rational$_2$ only
if the means are appropriate for the end sought - an end that is not subject to
a criterion of rationality - and just sufficient for attaining it, given the kind
and amount of knowledge available to the actor.[13]

Ancient Greece

3.   Although the Melanesian tribesmen were almost our contemporaries,
their "world" was of a kind that underlies ours only by way of countless
historical mediations.   From our point of view, the key transmitters-
transformers were the ancient Greeks, who altered for us the very conception
of what it is to know and to reason. An assessment of their contribution and
influence is, of course, far beyond the intent and scope of this essay. We can
only point briefly to a few momentous changes that are of immediate interest
in the present context.

3.1.   When we meet them (in the shape of, say, Homer or Hesiod), their
language includes the kind of linguistic sign which has "unlimited" power of
reference, so that signs with a limited range of representation are by and
large relegated to the role of intermediaries between unique images and
general concepts. Concomitantly, the mythological "world"-kaleidoscope,
whose elements are always culture-bound, is added to, and to a substantial
extent replaced by, theories and philosophies phrased in terms of concepts
that aim at being wholly transparent with respect to reality, i.e., that aim at
being, as to their contents, independent of a particular culture.

3.2.   The search for essences behind the observed phenomena leads to
the perception of science as a kind of knowledge whose nature it is to reveal
the inadequacy, and in this sense to deny the validity, of our day-to-day
experience. This impression is greatly enhanced when the phenomena inves-
tigated cease to be describable in ordinary language, and especially when
science starts to look into the behavior of "objects" of its own creation.[14] In
these and other similar ways, the awareness of the dependence of scientific
knowledge on the prescientific one, of theory on pretheory, tends to
diminish.

3.3.   The result is a substantial weakening, if not severance, of the link
between the universality and practicality of knowledge.   All scientific
"disciplines" depend on philosophy, which "investigates being *qua* being and
what belongs essentially to it," that is, on fundamental concepts such as
substance and attribute, unity and plurality, contradiction and contrariety.[15]

Contemplation, associated with philosophy, is the highest form of activity because (among other things) it is "the only activity that is appreciated for its own sake."[16] By contrast, "practical" is that which is directed towards "some other end"; and the province of "practicality" includes ethics and politics. It is true that contemplation itself is allowed to change the individual and to form his identity; it is practical in the sense of the individual's self-formation.[17] But the fact remains that, in the mainstream of the argument, philosophy, as the "science of the world as a whole,"[18] appears to be divorced from any "outside" interest structure.

3.4. The move from signs to concepts, from *bricolage*[19] to labor proper, constitutes the first technological revolution, a fundamental change in the *logos* of material production. Its techniques are no longer "internal" to a particular culture: having been secularized, they are felt to depend for their effectiveness on what is "external" to man himself. However, this is not tantamount to saying that techniques are treated as a kind of autonomous force. Implied in the classical argument are at least two fundamental constraints on this first revolution in material production. First, arts are seen as operating in the area of what can also be otherwise (and is indeed capable of non-being, depending on the producer's intent and ability) and therefore (at least in part) in the sphere of chance.[20] Second, even if techniques are recognized to depend in part on the knowledge gained in the specialized "disciplines" whose subject is necessity, it is also repeatedly stressed that these sciences themselves are in need of a philosophical basis for their self-understanding: without that, it is possible only to "add up" different items of partial knowledge, but not to integrate them.

3.5. Kinship cedes to politics the pride of place in the organization of the human group. While the kinship ties provided a safe, but basically static, *ex ante* type of the individual's identification in the community's whole, the *polis* offers to him security of a new, dynamic, "razor-edge" type: it is to be found in his identity being formed conjointly with that of the *polis* itself. (As Aristotle puts it, its members are many and different, and "there is a point at which a *polis*, by advancing in unity, will cease to be a *polis*.")[21] In this community, practical reason remains the faculty of discovering and directing one's action in accordance with what is right.[22] That is, in the sphere of man-to-man relations, "rational" is still rational$_1$ - except that, of course, there is a clear distinction between the norm and its consensual interpretation, and that the contents of "culture," for each generation of the tribal community given by the inherited myths and customs, is now subject to reflection and analysis.

This concept of rationality is also the point of departure for the discussion of "just price": for the result of the market transaction to be just, it must contribute to keeping the community together. Aristotle speaks here of grace and gratitude, of the initiation of benefaction, of good and evil; the presupposition of culturally distinct and substantively formulated norms is quite clear, and so is the qualitativeness of the "reciprocity" invoked.[23] However, when the argument proceeds to giving "just price" an economic, rather than primarily political meaning, the same "proportional requital" becomes a quantitative concept, whether the adjective "just" refers to the long-term cost-of-production price or to the short-term demand-based price.[24] These determinations point in the direction of rational as "correct," even if it took another two thousand years for this orientation to receive its ultimate expression in modern economics.   Retrospectively, therefore, Aristotle's difficulty with the concept of "just price" appears to have had its roots in the substantive norm-based framework of rationality$_1$ not being unambiguously translatable into that of the formal rules underlying rationality$_2$.

The Sukuma of East Africa

4.   The traditional group we started from in section 2 was a closely knit community, permeated by the integrative powers of one all-encompassing world-view and one set of ever-present customs. The Greek society was, of course, immeasurably more differentiated and much more exposed to outside influences; but it shared a culture that had for centuries no serious competitor. By contrast, the community to which we now turn is in a state of conflict between its own traditional way of life and the "other," represented mostly by the pressures and influences emanating from the market and the modern state. They are the Sukuma of East Africa, the largest tribe in Tanzania.[25]

In its attempt to undertake one of the first integrated long-term programs of agricultural development in Africa - implemented in 1948-1955 throughout Sukumaland at the cost of some two million pounds sterling - the Labour Government in Westminister authorized in 1950 its representatives in Dar es Salaam to issue a number of directives intended to increase the output of cotton, mainly by the use of more intensive cultivation methods, and at the same time to decrease the stock of cattle, which was felt to be far out of proportion to the size and quality of the available pastures.[26] The two goals were interconnected - although not positively, as the government appears to have thought.   In any case, the nature of the thinking behind both the aims can be illustrated by the substantiation of the second, a formula which was not only the guiding principle of the whole enterprise, but also the banner under which it sailed, and became therefore known as the Sukumaland Equation:

In ONE HOMESTEAD there are on the average TWO TAX-PAYERS or SEVEN PEOPLE with an average FOURTEEN CATTLE and TEN SMALL STOCK (at 5 small stock equalling one stock unit) equals SIXTEEN STOCK UNITS which produce altogether SIXTEEN TONS OF MANURE per annum. This manure is enough to manure EIGHT ACRES EVERY OTHER YEAR which is one acre more than the average acreage of arable land for Sukumaland but the stock requires TWO ACRES EACH OF PASTURE   (the average for Sukumaland is 2 1/2 acres) equals THIRTY-TWO ACRES PLUS EIGHT OF ARABLE LAND equals FORTY ACRES equals SIXTEEN HOMESTEADS PER SQUARE MILE equals 112 PEOPLE PER SQUARE MILE, SAY ONE HUNDRED. Three miles to walk to water is about THIRTY SQUARE MILES equals FIVE HUNDRED HOMESTEADS equals EIGHT THOUSAND STOCK.   FIVE GALLONS OF WATER x 120 DAYS (August to November) equals FIVE MILLION GALLONS equals 10,000 GALLONS (to allow for evaporation) PER 500 HOMES AND THIRTY SQUARE MILES.27

In short, the Equation required that, in the newly settled areas, the population density should be such as to allow each family to hold forty acres of land.28   Elsewhere, especially in the already congested areas where the holdings were much smaller, the formula called for higher yields per acre, or destocking - or emigration (i.e., leaving the ancestral land for settlement in other areas).   In the end, it became clear that either of the last two options was possible only as a police operation.29   In order to understand the result and see its implications, we shall turn to the frame of reference developed in the preceding parts of the study (sections 2 and 3).

4.1.   The formula is phrased in a language which is completely free from the social context in which the action called for would take place.30   The proponents of the scheme evidently believed that the message would be understood precisely because the medium of communication was, in this sense, "neutral." Put another way, the thought would be accessible and acceptable because it owed nothing, so to speak, to the culture-bound word. But that is an illusion. The thought is never independent of the word,31 and in this case, the thought was rightly felt to be one of a culture, only a *different* one. More precisely (we might add) it was the thought of a culture whose peculiarity it has become to express *itself* in noncultural (technical) terms where other cultures do not.

4.2. Although the Equation was a call for a definite action, it was phrased in the neutral language of description, the idea being that the objectivity of the latter would present the former as self-evident. To further this end, the description expressed, and appealed to, an "objectivity" understood as that which is beyond the confines, and therefore *outside*, the culture of the people to whom the directive was addressed. The point of view behind it was presented as no point of view, as if the action was what the *physis* itself demanded. However, the Africans are still keenly aware that "nature" is also a point of view. And this is so not only because of the long tradition of the mythical "appropriation" of nature, but also because their "life-worlds" are based on a language whose chief characteristic is the vividness and omnipresence of a complex classificatory apparatus.[32] Instead of the two or three genders of European languages, there are eight noun-classes which distinguish (with some overlaps) things without life *from* organic entities like trees and other plants *from* animals *from* persons *from* qualities and states of the preceding entities *from* infinitives of all verbs and *from* "places" (a class with one word).[33] To "distinguish from" is to "identify the place in the whole of," and the "whole" is clearly a selective one: a nonselective whole would be empty. From this point of view, the Equation is patently subjective: it results from an *arbitrary* selection of what will, and will not, have a chance of becoming "real." At this level of discourse, objective is that which has a definite place *within* a "world" that is "subjective," in the sense of being constituted with a view to *fundamental* (nonarbitrary) human interests.

4.3. Land is related *via* manure to cattle and *via* acres to the taxpayer's homestead, and there is no escaping the actuality of these relations. Through one's ancestors buried in it, however, land is also related to the tribe's myths, and by way of customs to certain culturally approved, and required, uses of it. Similarly cattle are a zoological species with certain physiological properties which make them productively useful. But the beasts also have several man-given properties, such as being a prime means of attaining socially generated security.[34] This is how the knowledge laid down in myths and customs - a knowledge encompassing the "whole," even if in a sketchy manner - shows itself to be directly aimed at attaining a measure of the group's control over its destiny. By contrast, the Equation represents partial knowledge that is no doubt more tightly knit, but aims only at technical success, or at enhancing the value-in-use of the beasts *qua* physiological entities: the link to a joint purposeful formation of social reality is lost. It is true that we have encountered the Sukuma in a period of transition, when some of them are wealthy enough to seek security in the sphere of market relations; for many more, however, dependence upon the market spells uncertainty. In their eyes, then, the Equation is a deliberately *fractional* knowledge attacking the *totality* of their life-style, a knowledge which is impractical in that it is unconcerned about, and indeed threatens, the fragile hold the community may feel itself to have, or to be able to attain, over its fate.

4.4. The starting point of the Equation was an extrascientific goal with a view to which various theorems (from zoology, botany, geology, meteorology etc.) were applied to the situation at hand; and the results were then combined to form a "whole," an internally consistent technique of action. The formula eschewed the kind of knowledge that one finds in anthropology, sociology, economics etc. And had one asked why it was so, the answer would probably have been that, given the purpose of the exercise, the presence in the Equation of the cultural elements of the scenery was unnecessary and in fact might have been counterproductive. This conforms to the rule of thumb according to which the upper limit on the bank of (scientific) knowledge employed for deciding on a course of action is determined by the (extrascientific) goal to be accomplished. There is, of course, also a lower limit; and in cases like the present, it appears at first to be given by the notion of "good practices" in the use of scientific knowledge for consultative purposes. But the content of this normative notion depends to a substantial degree on the state of the scientific knowledge itself, including the degree of its specialization and (re)integration. Production activities, which always occur in a social context, can never be adequately described in terms of "people" *sans phrase*, and the authors of the Equation would have found it the more difficult to reconcile this usage with their professional ethics - especially in a public document of that importance - the clearer, more structured would be the contents of, say, "physiology *and* psychology *and* sociology *and* economics *and* political science" not only in a mutually exclusive sense (determining what each is not), but also in an inclusive one: what they all are, taken together, each not only taking over from the other at a well-defined boundary, but also establishing jointly with the others a *communauté* of understandings about methods, fundamental concepts, and crucial theorems, as the basis for a dense network of linkages that could then be ignored only on pain of nonscientific arbitrariness.[35]

Since the Equation is phrased in terms of land and manure, cattle and water, one may be tempted to say that it conceives of production in purely physical terms. In fact, however, there is in it no production at all. We have inputs and outputs, but no link between them: neither labor (except for carrying water) nor material production tools are allowed to make an appearance. It is, of course, well known that in an underdeveloped economy of the Sukumaland type it is the size of land that is *the* limiting factor of agricultural production; and this is even more true of animal husbandry taken by itself. In addition, the labor-leisure division is still by and large regulated by custom, while the simple agricultural tools, the most important of which continues to be the hoe, are a constant which many calculations are free to leave out. Even when all this is taken into account, however, this feature of the Equation still deserves attention from at least two points of view.

4.4.1. In terms of the individual labor process itself, the hoe is a means, not a master.[36] But the producers have already lost the social control over that part of their product which is used for market transactions.[37] By reducing labor to an unseen, automatic, infinitely adjustable component of all production, the bureaucratic rule eliminates, by implication at least, the producer's mastery even over that part of his activity which is directed towards the satisfaction of his own needs.

4.4.2. At some long-forgotten time, the "first" hoe was incorporated into the previous, still more primitive production techniques employed by the (extended) family unit serving as a social basis of both human reproduction and material production. Since then, there has been no indigenous invention to demand a new, kinship-transcending type of "social relations of production." Even the plow, not to speak of the tractor, is introduced from the outside; the external is in this case not only, as it had been for the manual laborers in nineteenth-century Europe and North America, the scientific knowledge separated from their own "world" by the social division of labor, but a quite different culture, detached from their own by centuries of separate and distinct historical development. The alien culture affects then *first* the *social* relations, values and attitudes, and the notion of practical reason associated with them: new tools and machines usually come afterwards, at least in the sense that their widespread use is already the product of these changes in the group's social psyche. The "hardware" is brought in by the "software" - rather than the other way round - and the Equation is an attempt to extend this change-pattern to another part of agricultural production.

4.5. As an individual, occasional, exceptional transaction, barter seems to have been "always" there. It originated in the need of a famine-stricken community, or a member of it, to obtain food from "abroad": from a group, or an individual, residing both outside the area visited by the disaster and beyond the effective reach of the kinship ties to which the needy could appeal.[38] (Thus the starting point is not the social division of labor leading to increases in labor productivity. The use-values redistributed in this manner - i.e., as values-in-exchange - are seen as a bounty of nature or fate.) When barter becomes institutionalized, it is primarily in the form of the imposition of "conventional" (not supply-demand determined) exchange ratios. Then money in the modern sense of the word appears on the scene - mainly owing to the interventions of colonial governments - but the quasi-traditional barter is carefully separated from the money-mediated transfers: both "markets" operate side by side on the basis of quite different exchange ratios.[39] Finally, cotton comes in to enable the peasant to obtain money in amounts unknown before; but cash cropping, too, starts to become "traditionalized," even if in a more complex and subtle manner. For the peasant it is self-evident that "shillings do not breed"; their effectiveness as a means of obtaining foodstuffs in an emergency is doubtful;[40] and their use for the purpose of establishing long-term relations with others - the main source of one's security - is very limited. By contrast, cattle do breed; they can always be relied upon as an exchange-value of last resort; they are the main, the most reliable, and the most respectable material means of establishing a wealth of ties with other members of the community. Cattle are the proper "currency" of bridewealth payments as well as of other major traditional gifts; and even when only given in trusteeship to somebody else, they establish, or strengthen, a relation of friendship, or clientship, that can be relied upon in the future.[41] Evidently, the logical thing to do is to use cotton to obtain cash and *convert the unreliable money into "sterling" cattle.* This chain of reasoning leads to continuous increases in the output of cotton, but not necessarily by means of more intensive cultivation methods. For income expectations are still fairly stable, and the extensive type of cultivation allows more room for choices regarding how much labor to add (mainly during seasonal peaks) to what the traditional labor-leisure allocation provides for. In due course, to be sure, the market will change the expectations and the role of cattle will tend to diminish. But at the time of the Equation, and indeed for at least another two decades, attempts to reduce the stock of cattle were destined to fail.

The conclusions may be summed up as follows:

4.5.1. The peasants' refusal to destock was not necessarily an irrational response. For "cattle," as physiological objects, are not the same thing as "cattle," a means of attaining a socially generated sense of security. And the difference is the wider and sharper, the more the experience of "self-certainty" depends on the formation of extended and dense nets of social relations entered into in accordance with the community's norms and customs. In this case, even gifts of considerable value-in-use, such as cattle, are, in the last analysis, still a *symbolic* means of redistribution, if need be, of a wider (or more generally, to start with, indeterminate) range of the community's wealth. Put another way, the utility of an object or service is always a pure quality, and the "proper" response by the recipient of it must be governed by some objective "measure." In the market it is the competitive price which is "objective," in the sense of corresponding to the individual purposes of none of the anonymous buyers and sellers. In the traditional group, the word "objective" refers to what is established by social consensus. Therefore, the measure of "proper" response is, ultimately at least, the identity of the group. In this sense, the "objective" is an expression of the "subjective." This is then the context in which an action could be said to be rational$_1$. What the Equation did was to demand that this concept of rationality be replaced by rational$_2$.

4.5.2. In transforming the money earned by cash cropping into cattle as a source of security of the traditional type, the Africans have, in effect, confined the market to the sphere of the short run and retained the long run as the sphere to be governed by extramarket ties, primarily those of kinship and politics. Surprisingly enough, this intuitive assessment of the market's range of jurisdiction is quite close to that of some modern economists whose point of departure is the marginal utility theory.

> The amount of savings any one household undertakes ... will depend upon the goods and services it expects those savings will be able to purchase in future years - upon the expected level of prices....But the prices which will actually prevail in the future depend upon the savings decisions of other households, now and in the future....[As far as the market is concerned] No one household has any way of knowing what other households intend to do. The market does not provide it with the information it requires to make a rational decision. This is perhaps one of the more important senses in which the rate of saving (and investment) is unavoidably 'political'. The ordinary mechanism of the market cannot handle it. The ballot-box, or something else, must be substituted for the price system.[42]

In brief, the monological type of decision-making characteristic of the market cannot be a source of security in the long run. That task must be ceded to some form of joint "charting" of the future by the actors concerned.

4.5.3. Each of the string of attempts to subject the market to the code of the traditional way of life was an endeavor to reconstitute its identity by appropriating the "other." The Equation was also an "other," but of a special kind: it claimed to be objective knowledge and, as such, to be superior both to the historically developed "self" of the group and to the right to subjectivity, inherent in its being a "self" and extending also into the future. But to say that the "self" is historically developed is also to say that the community is in fact transparent to itself only to a limited degree. Its self-knowledge is in part false; in protecting its perceived identity, it also protects a partially distorted picture of its future self. So it needs "objectivity" - but of what kind? The search for socially generated security is a cultural matter; and as an appeal to a transcultural notion of rational behavior, the Equation could not provide the husbandmen with a basis for the comprehension of the problem they were faced with: how to reconcile their tradition-based dependence on cattle with the fact that land was no longer plentiful? Or more precisely: how to deal with a situation which has brought to a head the latent tension between the symbolic role of the beasts (cattle as proxy for the interpersonal relations developed, or developable, by means of them) and their material role (cattle as things dependent on other things and an object of productive as well as unproductive consumption)? In this regard, the Sukuma experience shows that a community's efforts to discard the false, dogmatic part of its identity cannot be helped by knowledge which is "objective" in the sense of being completely outside the group as a culturally constituted entity.

Heidegger

5. In the above discussion (3), ancient Greece was treated as a part of a continuum: a model "life-world," forming a necessary link between two twentieth-century non-European communities, one still untouched by the West, the other already under its influence. There is, however, a view according to which the Greek perception of the world - or more specifically, that of the pre-Socratics - has been lost to us almost completely, so that it cannot be recaptured without a radical "turnabout" of our present position. In this view - which is that of Heidegger - modern technology is assigned the role of precipitating that turnabout. Within the space allotted to this essay, it is impossible to do justice to this argument which is both subtle and forceful. Nor is it possible to ignore it, for no alternative conception of technology and science can be complete without coming to grips with Heidegger's. So let us take a brief look at a few areas where our argument is most obviously in conflict with his views.

5.1. Heidegger's discussion of modern science and technology may be said to begin with Parmenides' statement that "thought and being *are* the same thing." The identity claim is then rephrased to read: the "apprehending of what is *belongs* to Being because it is demanded and determined by Being."[43] (In this connection, "Being" is perhaps best understood as the manner in which everything that is encounters man and is revealed through him.)[44] Clearly, the active ("subjective") role is reserved for what is: *it* brings *itself* into appearance. Man "opens himself to what presences in that he apprehends it": he is passive (appears in a role usually associated with an object), or if he is active, he is so merely as *included* in that which is, in that which "presences" through him. It is only in the modern age that this original, proper relationship between man and what is, is said to be reversed. Today, it is the man who, as it were, causes that which is to parade in front of him: he is said to "bring what is present at hand before [him]self" and "to force it back into this relation to [him]self as the normative realm." That is, he takes his own "position"[45] vis-à-vis what is and sets himself up - at least in part arbitrarily - as the measure of all things.[46] On this view, it is not as if "subject" and "object" were always there as constitutive parts of the "worlds" in which we live: the joint emergence of the two is due only to modern science, seen as taking its cue from Descartes' interpretation of man as *subiectum*.[47] We have seen, however, that man takes a "position" towards what is already in the primitive community we have started from (in section 2). For instance, he gives a ripe yam-like fruit the name of *taytu* and the overripe stage of (what we would now see as) the same fruit the name of *yowana*.[48] For the plant itself, the change is immanent and continuous. It is because *for man* ripeness is one thing and overripeness quite another that in *his* "view" the change is discrete and transcendent.

5.2. In line with his understanding of the subject-object relationship, Heidegger conceives of *techne* as a species of "bringing-forth" (*Her-vor-bringen*), or *poiesis*, whose *highest* form is "*physis* [as] the arising of something from out of itself,"[49] i.e., *without* the help of man and his projects. Modern technology is then a particular kind of "revealing" (*Entbergen*), namely, one characterized by the shift from object (*Gegenstand*) to "standing reserve" (*Bestand*), or to that which is "ordered to stand by."[50] One might expect that this is where the autonomy of man's projects vis-à-vis what is becomes recognized. However, the argument unfolds in exactly the opposite direction. Man is *gathered* to "order the *self*-revealing [of "the real" in this special form of] standing reserve."[51] And in "open[ing] itself to the essence of technology," "man's essence" opens itself to that "whose essence is Being itself."[52] This is how modern techniques are expected to bring about - even if at some future, unspecified time - the turnabout already alluded to: they should make man realize that the passivity of "opening himself" to Being, or (which is the same thing) the activity of turning "away from himself,"[53] is his true vocation.

Within this frame of reference, there is obviously no meaning to the distinction between the "practical" and the "technical": there are no genuine, autonomous human projects; and contemporary techniques, no matter what their form, are (at least in principle) legitimized as Being which has made itself more cunningly dynamic than ever before; having brought about a radical absence of Being, *they* force us to recognize the imperativeness of its presence. Yet when the African peasant says that "cattle are our banks, our stores, our fields, our wives, our families,"[54] he does not mean that he and his fellow men have included themselves in, and entrusted themselves to, a great stream of all that just is, a stream which originally produced these animal machines without any help from man and now calls for real, metallic machines that require from him a sort of midwifery, but really nothing beyond that, no independent design to be found fit or unfit for the humans themselves, given *their* interests and aspirations.

No, in saying what he says, the African may be understood to make three points of a quite different kind. First, he says that in the market all transactions are between strangers ("at arm's length"), and technical success has no existential import (cannot deal with the problem of uncertainty in respect of the future). Second, he says that, by contrast, *in his community* cattle became at one time the *material* symbol of *socially* generated security (a role which is no part of their zoological description and does not even become theirs in each and every human group). And finally, he says that no matter how sophisticated, effective and powerful future machines may become, they could replace the animals in this role only if the former in their turn and at their time were actually experienced to have been truly appropriated by the group as a crucial means of removing extraneous constraints from the ongoing joint formation of the identity of the individuals and their social whole.

5.3. To say that Being at one point demands a form of "revealing" different from that required in the past is to treat Being as having a history of its own. That finding has been interpreted to mean that a new assessment of the relation between Hegel and Heidegger is in order: "One must allow that such an historical self-consciousness as this is no less all-inclusive than Hegel's philosophy of the Absolute."[55]

At the same time, however, it must also be allowed that the structure of the two "absolutes" is radically different. First, prominent in the argument for reassessment is the idea that Hegel's *Logic* itself should be properly interpreted as extending the power of the *logos* to the realm of human history.[56] To that, it seems necessary to add that the *Logic* can depict the self-development of the *thought* which thinks itself only because, in the *Phenomenology*, the evolution of *human* consciousness and self-consciousness has already culminated in the overcoming of the division between subject and object. Second, turning to the *Phenomenology* we find that the discussion of self-consciousness starts with man's "desire" to attain the "self-certainty" endangered by his body's finitude, and that the next step is to inquire into the meaning of labor for relations among men themselves.[57] In Heidegger, the discussion of technology has its root in the return to the *poiesis* of *physis* as the "*self*-bringing-forth"; labor is treated as just the second best, as the "bursting open ... in *another*," namely, the craftsman.[58] Finally, the turning-about in Heidegger is a response to a call addressed to man by Being, where the "speaker" and the man who "hears"[59] are equally stripped of social identity. For Hegel, however, the nature of the "turning point" is quite different: "this" thinker incarnating "this" moment of history hears in this town of Jena Napoleon's guns and is thus confronted with the French revolution and the collapse of the absolute but as yet insufficiently mediated freedom into absolute terror.[60]

Clearly, the two structures differ in the most sensitive sphere of all; that is, in the role attributed to man in the respective "histories."

A Game of Science

6. Heidegger disapproves of the calculative attitude characteristic of modern science,[61] but does not suggest an alternative criterion of rationality for the scientist's work. Contemporary analytical philosophy, however, has to face the problem directly and without fail: if a theory is accepted as scientific while being erroneous (as many have been shown in due course to be), and if theories have indeed been known to be upheld in the face of important "anomalies" (and even by the most reputable of scientists), then the dividing line between "science" and "fiction" cannot be based on a

criterion of rationality which is reducible to that of veracity. And if so, what precisely is the rule to be followed?

One of the recent attempts to answer this question, and to do so within the philosophical framework in which it had been posed, is that of Imre Lakatos, whose results may be summed up as follows. (i) The "basic unit of appraisal" - i.e., the unit in terms of which the rationality criterion is defined - is "research program," not theory. (ii) The program consists of a "hard core" and a "positive heuristic." The core is allowed to include what more strict logical positivists would have called metaphysical beliefs and is accepted by convention (in other words, is provisionally irrefutable). The "positive heuristic" is, in substance, the sum of approaches to, and ways of, the construction of theories proper. (iii) The only rational basis for the abandonment of a program is its "stagnation," i.e., its failure to generate theories which predict "novel facts with some success" (or at any rate perform in this respect better than a rival program). (iv) The rule defined in (iii) is understood also as the "code of scientific honesty." (v) The adherence to rule (iii) guarantees only that the "game" of science is "fair," which does not necessarily mean that its results contribute to "approximating the Truth about the Universe." For the game-rational to become epistemologically rational, one must posit "some extra-methodological inductive principle."[62]

6.1. When it is said that it is rational (irrational) for the scientist to do this or that, the statement may have two different meanings.

6.1.1. The criterion of rationality - in its operational form defined in (iii) - is used by the historian to appraise a scientist's acts *ex post*, evidently on the strength of his (the historian's) conviction that this concept of rationality is born out by the entire course of the development of science. Lakatos concedes that, at the time of action, the scientist himself may have had a quite different perception of what it was "rational" for him to do. And if the scientist's own "theory of ... rational behaviour" is declared by the historian to be "false,"[63] the norm clearly serves as a *meta*criterion of rationality imposed upon the scientists retrospectively. In this case, obviously, "rationality" means only the internal consistency of an *impersonal* flow of knowledge.

6.1.2. If the theory of rationality is to serve also as the scientist's code of honor (see iv), then the norm must be understood as applying to the decisions of the individual scientist and to be operative in an *ex ante* fashion. This presupposes that the criterion is (or can be and should be) present in his mind when he makes the decision and that he is actually in a position to act on the basis of the norm. But Lakatos admits that neither of these conditions is necessarily satisfied. The scientist need not always know *whether* his program is advancing or declining (keeping its momentum or losing it), and he may not even be aware of *what* in fact the program *is*. For the "objectivity" of the development of knowledge is understood to require that even "facts" will on occasion be allowed to appear in the "object's" flow only in "their radically improved form,"[64] i.e., in a form reconstructed by the historian but unavailable to the practitioner at the time his decision is made. Under these conditions, obviously, the norm (iii) is in its function as the individual scientist's code of honor (iv), empty. To say the least, it is not applicable in all cases: it lacks universality.

6.1.3.   The distinction between *ex post* (6.1.1) and *ex ante* (6.1.2) can be looked upon also from another angle.   In its historiographical use, the normative theory of the scientist's rational behavior serves to extract from the whole of the development of science the movement which is "rational," that is, "internal."   The remainder is then designated "external," meaning "irrational."   Since the latter is that which is not the former, the "internal" enjoys logical priority over the "external."[65]   In the actual historical development, however, it is the other way round.   As we have seen in section (1), the point of departure is a prescientific constitution of the "world"; "science" emerges as a distinct flow in the stream of knowledge only in the course of a protracted (and in fact never-ending) process of self-identification, or separation from influences that are, at various stages, disowned as exogenous.   To be sure, "science" is always a normative concept.   But there is still a world of difference between an *ex post* norm in the form of a today's philosophy of science and a succession of *contemporary* ("this day's") norms, each dependent on the historically attained degree of the science's self-formation under the social conditions in which the scientists actually live and work.

6.2.   When explaining the contents of his rationality concept by the development of spacio-temporal theories, Lakatos turns almost invariably to physics.   In its modern form this is, in part, a science that dissolves the objects of everyday experience into the tiniest of particles and reassembles them again into theory-bound wholes.   In terms of its molecular composition, say, marble can be given a longish name which may be represented here by "Y"; and it is at least in principle possible to teach kindergarten children, and perhaps already senior toddlers, to use "Y" for what their parents used to know as marble.   In this way, the word "marble" would gradually become redundant and disappear from use.[66]   However, "marble" originally meant "shining or sparkling stone," so that the thing was distinguished from others in terms of its daily experienced properties - qualities and possible employments relevant to actors in the context of work (and games) and interaction (for instance, in paying respect to the deities and the dead).   By contrast, "Y" is phrased in terms of ideal, explanatory entities constructed by observers - or by actors operating within a very specialized sphere long ago separated from the original unity of day-to-day life - and existing beyond "this" world and all its interest structures, those inherent in being "man" as a distinct species.

The same procedure could be repeated with many other words; but, as far as can be seen now, words like "intent," "subordination," "good," "contradiction" would not be treatable in this manner. These words would remain linked to the "subjective" understanding of the world through the ordinary language and the fundamental interest structure. There would then be a sharp split between this sphere of the ordinary language in the original meaning of the word and the science-based language of daily life, reflecting and demanding "objectivity" in the sense of independence of any (substantive) interest.

Of course nobody is embarking upon such a language revolution just yet. But what is, in an historical sense, regarded as "scientific knowledge" *is* already normatively divided into "scientific" and "nonscientific," and the boundary line *is*, in substance, drawn in accordance with the above, imaginary partitioning of the ordinary language. For Lakatos, physics, chemistry and related disciplines are on the right side of the railway track; and psychology, sociology, and their "kin" are on the wrong side. Economics, or parts of it, seem acceptable; but aside from that, "science" is *outside* the sphere of knowledge capable of contributing to the individual's and the society's self-understanding and self-formation, that is, the sphere most directly related to the practical (as distinct from the technical) purposes of the human group.

6.3.   Gaining scientific knowledge is a purpose-oriented activity, but the word "purpose" may be understood in various ways.

6.3.1.   In Lakatos' case, most of the discussion centers on what is the rational thing for the scientist to do when playing the "game" of science, and his purpose is, of course, to "win" (which word need not be taken in a vulgar or otherwise pejorative sense). For Lakatos, methodology does not propose "rules for solving problems" or for the *formation* of theories: it is concerned with the "*appraisal* of ready, articulated theories."[67]   The rationality criterion does not guide the scientist's "work": it governs his choices, albeit those which he makes *qua* scientist. Provisions (i) through (iv) are rules for a kind of preference ordering and may be legitimately compared with other rules in the sphere of rationality$_2$. It is easy to see that they are distinct from those discussed earlier in that the choice criterion is objective ("inherent" in the nature of scientific reason), rather than subjective (reflecting a person's individual preferences). Yet there is one important similarity: if knowledge is seen as growing along an imaginary curve, Lakatos' rationality criterion is *formal* in the sense that it is always defined in terms of the *slope* of the curve at a point, never in terms of the point itself. Decisive is the rate of the growth of knowledge, not its content.

6.3.2.   But gaining scientific knowledge may be purposive also in a quite different meaning of the word. Even within logical positivism itself, there is a school of thought which argues that "it is the task of the scientist as such to accept and reject hypotheses in such a way as to maximize the expectation of *good* for, say, a community for which he is acting."[68] The possibility, and indeed necessity, of this approach is explained as follows:

> [Since] no scientific hypothesis is ever completely verified, in accepting a hypothesis the scientist must make the decision that the evidence is *sufficiently* strong or that the probability is *sufficiently* high to warrant the acceptance of the hypothesis. Obviously, our decision regarding the evidence and respecting how strong is 'strong enough' is going to be a function of the *importance*, in the typically ethical sense, of making a mistake in accepting or rejecting the hypothesis.[69]

To cite a case in point, the degree of confidence in the hypothesis that the first atomic bomb would not start an uncontrollable chain reaction destroying the planet should have been higher than that of a hypothesis that a certain lot of machines would stamp nondefective buttons.

6.3.3. Having replaced the testing of hypotheses by the appraisal of "programs," Lakatos placed himself outside this version of rational as "ethical." The only nonformal principle to appear in his scheme is the "inductive principle" which is appealed to for the purpose of making the operative rules (iii, iv) epistemologically relevant (v). The substantively formulated principle is, however, introduced without any further justification or elucidation. Lakatos would probably reply that this is in the nature of things: we cannot go much beyond saying that any attempt to decipher a cryptogram is nonsensical, unless we believe - *prior* to the establishment of *any* meaning - that it has *some* meaning. True; but one has to add that our "prior" belief that the world has "some" sense appears to be connected with man's innate need to live in a "world" that is ordered, so that he can act on nature through labor and enjoy a measure of security in the sphere of interactions among men themselves. But Lakatos makes no such connection. In his scheme, "subjectivity," in the sense of the scientist's personal likes and dislikes, is eliminated only at the cost of excluding "subjectivity" in the sense of the interests inherent in being man. Science is treated as a purpose in itself: the link between systematic knowledge and the fundamental interest structures of the human life is severed.

6.4. Lakatos designed his rationality criterion for research, but he noted that it had also some other applications. Scientific journals should refuse to publish articles that reflect the degeneration of the research program on which they are based; and research foundations are to refuse money for projects evidencing the same defect.[70] Extrapolating from these observations, it seems safe to conclude that, as long as a program does sustain its momentum, it is intended to dominate the scientist's activities also in his capacities of teacher, consultant, and inventor. As a result, the

whole of the scientist's choice-making in his field will be subject to one type
of rationality criterion: to an algorithm which is formal and to be applied
monologically, even if the rule of preference ordering is of two kinds:
objective in the case of program appraisals and subjective in, say, the
scientist's actions as inventor-entrepreneur.

This universality (whether presupposed as a fact or cultivated as a
prescript) has always been the great lure of rationality$_2$, but from the present
point of view it is its main weakness. For scientific knowledge is a product
of a special kind: as Marx observed, even a scientist long dead may be a
member of the present "total labourer"[71] because his labor, while in a
historical sense past labor, is, as far as its employment is concerned, still
today's labor. For a theorem is not passed on to others as an object of a
definite material shape: it is "embodied" only in symbols as the material
carriers of a message. Therefore, scientific knowledge, unlike a tool or
machine, is, so to speak, perfectly elastic: it is capable of unlimited
expansion and of a great variety of employments, some of which might have
never entered the author's mind. Yet it is precisely this knowledge that
changes all the time the material basis and the social structures of human
life. For this reason, it is necessary that the theory of science draw the
practitioner's attention to both the advantages *and* the limitations of the kind
of rationality concept that has its roots in man's action vis-à-vis nature (as
distinct from interaction between men themselves).

6.5. The point can perhaps best be made by choosing an extreme
situation - but on the understanding that extremes are, after all, always
recognized as such only in relation to what is more common or more usual.
Suppose geneticists come to the conclusion that certain directions of
research in their field might lead to disastrous manipulations of the
biological substance of human beings and, for this reason, of their own will
and by genuine consensus decide to place such research activities
permanently "out of bounds."[72] From Lakatos' point of view, this would be
an "external" derailment of the "objective" movement of knowledge in this
branch of science, and therefore (a) an "irrational" act. However, the
geneticists could argue - and legitimately so - that their action is not in
violation, but (b) outside the jurisdiction of, the theory of rationality that
Lakatos propounded. By doing so, they would not be disputing the
historian's right to uphold the logical priority of the "internal" over the
"external." They would merely construe their act *as a part of the historical
process of the science's self-identification*, a process which at this point
required that they limit the area of the "internal" in accordance with what
they themselves felt to be the proper sphere of jurisdiction of the "external."

An appeal to another notion of rationality does not, by itself, make an act
rational. But our concern is not with the act, which is at any rate
hypothetical, but with the concept of practical reason now invoked.

Obviously, the criterion appealed to in (b) is *substantive*: it has to do with the *what* of the knowledge attained or expected to be attained. At issue is a *point* on the curve of ascending knowledge, and the point is regarded as having a property (say, extremity) that renders the slope-criterion invalid. At this point, the scientists concerned act jointly to impose an ethically based boundary within which to conduct their quest for knowledge, and they reserve for themselves the interpretation of the norm by consensus; that is, the monologic behavior associated with rationality$_2$ is replaced by a "dialogue." Thus the formally rational criterion, which is intended to be applied syllogistically, ceases to be the scientist's code of honor (the way it was in iv). The chain of reasoning is reversed: it is the substantive-ethical that becomes rational$_1$.

The moral of the story is, of course, that the danger that changes in the biological substance of human beings may get irretrievably out of hand is, after all, merely a special case of the problem of the science-based technological change which affects the material and social conditions of human life in a perhaps less dramatic, but more widespread and pervasive manner. It also does so in ways that the scientists themselves have even less chance of controlling than (at least the initial) genetic mutations. This is a sobering thought, but should not be taken for a reassuring one.

Beyond Games

7. In Lakatos' argument, scientific knowledge exists only as *intra-disciplinary*. Therefore, the claim to epistemological relevance ("approximating the Truth about the Universe") must also be understood as being made on behalf of a mass of scientific knowledge that is just "out there," divided into branches whose *inter*relations and *inter*actions are represented only by blanks. This is, of course, the obvious position to take as long as the scientist is understood to concentrate on "observable facts" and the functional laws defining the *former's* interrelations. For then the investigator remains naturally and rightfully within the boundaries of his discipline which historically constituted itself as a systematic inquiry into that range of "facts."

However, to the extent that the theorist is prepared to venture into the "metaphysical" sphere of causes and linkages *under*lying the phenomena, he is likely to be more in need of interdisciplinary cooperation too. This is often the case also when he finds that a line of inquiry, conducted under the presuppositions and conventions of one's discipline, or the relevant subdivision of it, has reached the limit inherent in these same presuppositions and conventions. For this is the moment at which these points of departure themselves have to be subjected to a scrutiny from "outside," and this "outside" may have to include a neighboring science. In these and similar instances, interdisciplinary cooperation responds to the *internal* needs of one or more of the participating sciences, rather than to external demand (a motive stressed in 4.4). In what follows, we shall look into one such case which is of special interest because it brings us back, albeit from a different point of view, to the meaning of "rational behavior" and, in due course, leads to a problem that is always present in the wings when the human consequences of techniques are discussed: namely, to the problem of institutional change.

7.1. In the theory of games, the central place is occupied by two-person (or two-homogeneous-group) games which may be, for the present purpose, divided into four types: (aa) strictly competitive games (in which all outcomes are such that what one player gains the other loses) with equilibrium pairs (so that, for each player, there is a pure equilibrium strategy that not only attains the best security level for him, but is also good against the pure equilibrium strategy of the other player that attains his best security level); (ab) strictly competitive games without such an equilibrium pair (so that mixed strategies have to be employed); (ac) nonstrictly competitive games (in which there is at least one outcome such that one player's gain is not equal to the other player's loss) which are noncooperative (no preplay communications, let alone binding agreements); and (ad) cooperative games.[73] We shall be mainly concerned with a limiting case of (ac) which will be denoted ac'. Usually it is called the prisoner's dilemma game, but we shall give it another interpretation.

7.1.1. Suppose there are two (homogeneous) groups of geneticists, each depending for its survival, or at least for its standing in the scientific community, on attaining the best results in their research (and in this sense competing with the other), but also acutely aware of the danger (see 6.5) that certain kinds of investigation might lead to disastrous manipulations of the biological substance of human beings (a concern which, being shared, represents a cooperative aspect of the game). Therefore, each is prepared to discontinue investigations in these fields, provided that the other does so too. For some reason, however, the groups either (f) cannot communicate with each other, or (g) if they actually do come to an agreement, must keep their adherence to it secret (so that, as in (f), neither party can be sure what the other will in fact do). Now, if both abstain from research in the "dangerous" areas, they will both attain the same "gain" in the sense that they will avoid the risk which concerns them and will continue their further research on the basis of equal opportunities. If, however, one group enters the forbidden field, it will obtain an undue advantage over the other. Under these circumstances, the rationality criterion developed on the basis of games (aa) will demand that both groups continue the "risky" research and thus both "lose" (or at least "gain" less than they would if they discontinued it).[74]

7.1.2. Faced with this counterintuitive result, the game theorist may respond in three ways. (i) He will continue to maintain that this is the "rational" outcome of the game; meaning essentially that, while the game has certain cooperative aspects, and if played cooperatively, would allow both parties to "gain," this outcome is irrelevant for the resolution of the noncooperative game itself. (ii) The theorist will say that, although the outcome leaves him uncomfortable, he is not prepared to discuss it in terms of "rationality" or "irrationality":[75] somehow, these concepts have been rendered inapplicable. (The conclusion seems to be that such games should be "banned." But the ban may have to be decided upon by the same kind of game,[76] and if it is played noncooperatively, the injunction will never be imposed.) (iii) The analyst will come to the conclusion that he is confronted with a special case of a more general finding: namely, that the concept of "rational" behavior based on (aa) and justifiably extended to (ab) loses its prescriptive power, if applied to (ac), even though it remains a useful tool of analysis.[77] It is in this last case, and in this case alone, that the theorist ceases to ask the usual question: Is "this" act "rational," given the concept of rationality on hand? Rather, he asks a "metaquestion": Is this concept of rationality valid, given the kind of "situation" now on hand?

The third conclusion (iii) is strengthened - that is, the negative reply to the last question supported - by looking into the actual behavior of people playing (albeit under laboratory conditions) a long *series* of ac'-games. For then the players have been found to exhibit behavior indicating a search for tacit "collusion" which would enable them to play cooperatively and attain a higher degree of social welfare (i.e., the outcome in which both gain). More specifically, (a) the initial phase of each player expecting the other to cooperate is (after some disappointments) followed by (b) a period of the prevalence of noncooperative behavior which is (once the players realize that there is "no percentage" in noncooperation) reversed and replaced by (c) the prevalence of cooperation.[78] The learning process clearly operates both ways; but the general tendency is towards cooperation, this attitude being not so much superior, as more "natural." This seems to be the reason why it was found that in a round-robin computer tournament, where 62 different strategies (for playing a series of ac'-games) were pitted against each other 200 times (and even 1000 times), the winner was the TIT FOR TAT strategy proposed by the game theorist who initiated the earlier tests which revealed the a-b-c pattern outlined above. The rule is simplicity itself: cooperate on the first move; and thereafter, do whatever the other player did on the previous move.[79] In other words: start by showing your willingness to cooperate; reward, and thus encourage, the other side's cooperation whenever it occurs; punish noncooperation, but only proportionately, not excessively.[80]

7.1.3. In sum, what started as a reflection of *one* discipline on itself (in the form of the iii-response to the counterintuitive results of the isolated, once-for-all ac'-game) and gave rise to direct interaction between *two* specialized sciences (the testing of the players' behavior in a series of such games and the interpretation of the resulting behavioral patterns) has the potential of becoming *self*-reflection of a wider *field* (including, say, economics and ethics).

7.2. At this point we shall stop to ask: What do these results tell us about the (imaginary) case of the geneticists?

The tendency to cooperate was observed, and the advantages of the cooperation-based long-term strategy were noted, in a rather long series of ac'-games, and perhaps the first thing that comes to one's mind is that, in the present case, there may be only one game: one of the groups enters the forbidden area, the *djin* is out of the bottle, and there is no occasion for further games. This possibility can again be responded to in several ways, of which two appear to throw most light on the nature of the problem at hand.

7.2.1. If the two parties did agree to cooperate, albeit secretly (see 7.1.1, alternative g), they could have also stipulated a fine for the group which defects (and in order to benefit from the transgression, will at some time have to present research results testifying to the defection). If the fine is included in the payoffs, the players are, in effect, engaged in a new game, and there is always a fine so high that the resulting game leads to the socially preferable outcome (both sides gain), even if the players implement the notion of rationality developed in the sphere of the aa-games.[81] But the fine will modify the payoff matrix only if it (the former) is "enforceable by the rules of the game."[82]

This formulation makes it clear that each player is *sure* that he will have to pay the fine if he defects. But the proviso merely presupposes that there *are* such sure fines: it does not explain how they are *possible*. This question may be beyond the jurisdiction of the theory of games; but the understanding of some of its results still depends on what the answer is. Suppose that, in the present case, the fine is "to be excluded from the community of geneticists" and it is prohibitively high (it converts the gain from defection into a loss). Then we must surely be able to ask: Under what conditions will this fine be (and be known to be) subject to no uncertainty and no game? For, if there is no satisfactory answer, the proposition that the imposition of the fine changes a socially harmful game (both sides lose) into a socially beneficial one (both gain) is left without a definite, clearly understood content.

7.2.2. The principal difference between a single, once-for-all ac'- game and a series of them is, of course, that the latter allows each player to learn from the results of the previous games and to make use of what he has learned. The question then is: What precisely is the learning process about? The laboratory tests which yielded the a-b-c sequence discussed in 7.1.2 indicated also that the frequency of cooperative responses did not depend on the personal (independently established) characteristics of the individuals concerned: the frequency was mainly the product of the players' interaction during the game series, or rather of the dynamic characteristics of the game itself.[83] This suggests rather strongly that the player learned not so much "who" was the person on the other side as "what" was the nature of the game, as revealed by the unfolding and progressing game series.

If so, it seems likely that person A who, in his role of geneticist, faces today person B, appearing in the same capacity, in an ac'-game with "this" payoff matrix can have learned something relevant for this venture from a game of the same type which he, acting as part-time wheat farmer, played last year with persons C....N, acting in the same role, in a situation depicted by a quite different set of payoffs. The conclusion would then have to be that, strictly speaking, there are no isolated ac'-games. All would become parts of a more general learning process about situations involving this kind of game.

This point (7.2.2) calls for empirical studies into the mechanics and dynamics of the wider, more structured, more socially oriented learning: will it confirm the tendency towards cooperation, or will it be otherwise? Item 7.2.1, however, poses a quite different kind of question.

7.3.   The agreement to discontinue certain avenues of research was said to be an expression of a genuine consensus on the part of the geneticists (6.5). More specifically, the assumption has been that (a) they share certain historically developed and substantively formulated norms; that (b) "community of geneticists" is a name for the relations freely entered into by its members on the basis of these norms; and that (c) these relations are transparent to them, so that the group *is* what it *understands* itself to be ("they *know* what they are *doing*"). (See also 4.5.2.) If so, the agreement to stop research in certain areas is a binding consensual interpretation of a shared norm ("thou shalt not do what endangers the human species"), and a violation of the agreement entails self-expulsion from the group. The "fine" is certain - as long as the specified conditions obtain. This means, of course, that the certainty of the fine has been established only for an idealized static situation. But this is also just the introductory part of the argument.

7.3.1.   Turning to the theory of games, we shall for the moment abstract from the transparency requirement (c). The theory subscribes to the freedom of choice (b), but it does not presuppose shared substantive norms (a). In this world, sure fines, too, can only be presupposed, not explained. From the present point of view, the certainty of fines becomes, in effect, a proxy for commitment to ethical norms - except that, first, the imposition of the fine can be (as an assumption) stipulated without any conditions at all and that, second, the imposition is an act functionally separate from the transgression of the agreement on declaring certain research areas "out of bounds." In this case, one has to ask what happens when the geneticists who defected refuse to vote for their own expulsion. In the framework of norms the stress is on the identity of the transgression and the loss of status, but the problem does not disappear. For the principle of self-expulsion can be effective only if the *society as a whole* behaves so as to conform to the view that the defector is no longer a geneticist. In this sense, the geneticists' original agreement is a prototype of institutional change, a reform affecting the identity of the society in its entirety. In this way, the inquiry into the possibility of sure fines leads necessarily to the question of rational behavior with respect to changes in norms and their binding interpretations.

7.3.2. If institutional change is recognized to occur under conditions of uncertainty, the theory of games tends to reply that the most general model of the "constitutional contract" formation is the ac'-game itself. If nothing more were said, of course, no institutional change would ever occur. Therefore, it has to be added that the game must be played cooperatively: the players have to agree that they will choose the socially preferable outcome (both gain), if the costs of enforcing the agreement are less than what they both gain from it. (The enforceability presupposition leads, of course, one way or another, back to the problem of fines.) The willingness to cooperate seems to be associated with the repetition of the game.[84] But "constitutional contracts" are negotiated rather rarely; so it appears that underlying the argument is a tacit reliance on the wider learning process sketched in 7.2.2. The empirical evidence for this kind of behavior is, however, still drawn mostly from the repetition of identical games.

7.3.3. In positive economics, the problem of institutional change is often discussed for the simple reason that the actual state of the economy is rarely, if ever, what the general equilibrium theory demands. One way of explaining the discrepancy is to argue as follows. The theory presupposes that institutions are a *dependent* variable whose "value" is determined jointly by resources, technologies and tastes, given the rationality of utility and profit maximizing. For future reference, it will be noted that this can be the case only if (a) the agents correctly anticipate which institutions will enable them to maximize the gains from all the trades. The argument then asserts that at least some institutions do not in fact respond to changes in the independent variables originally invoked. They remain constant and assume the role of *independent* variables in their own right. Hence the "institutional distortions" of the equilibrium positions. It has been noted, however, that such an approach contradicts the individualistic assumptions underlying the model as a whole; this is especially evident when "welfare losses" are measured relative to the equilibrium positions determined on the basis of the initial, strictly individualistic criteria.[85] And if these are adopted consistently, it must be concluded that (b) the choice of institutions is in no way different from, say, the consumer's choice of the composition of the commodity basket which he can afford, given the price structure and his income constraint.

7.3.4. Against this background, let us now return to the paradigmatic case of the geneticists. The assumption of correct anticipation (7.3.3.a) may be interpreted and justified in various ways, but our interest is now only in its relationship to the transparency requirement (7.3.c) in the static framework of norms. At first sight, the two stipulations may appear to be fairly similar, but in fact there are substantial differences between them. In the first place, uncertainty is not the same thing as lack of transparency. In the simplest case of an all-inclusive auction, in the course of which the general equilibrium positions are established, all information is shared by all those present and there is no uncertainty. But the proceedings are still not transparent to the participants: there are no negotiations among them, they communicate only through the auctioneer, and once the data of the system are given, the determination of the unique solution may be left to a computer.

Secondly, the anticipations in (7.3.3.a) are usually thought to be based on a theory or theories, and if these are correct, so are the expectations. A theory may, however, reveal and *accept* lack of transparency in the whole-constituting relations between the elements. Suppose, for instance, that the bureaucracy in the geneticists' organization manipulated the information flows between the membership and the leaders. An economic theory may consider this behavior a legitimate form of maximizing the value of the bureaucrats' utility functions[86]; and this factor would then have to be taken into account when expectations about the "best" institutional structure are made. In the context of norms, this same manipulation of information is an important cause of the geneticists' inability to really "see through" the whole of which they are constitutive parts: something *in* the community stands *against* it as an unknown power. Therefore, when norms and their binding interpretations are being changed - i.e., when the assumption of transparency (7.3.c) must be replaced by setting forth the conditions leading to this goal - one of the crucial conditions of rational behavior is that information flows are in no way "rigged."

7.3.5. This condition is necessary, but not sufficient. As a way of approach to the latter, it will be convenient to look into the conclusion that institutions are chosen in the same way as, say, scarves (7.3.3.b). Many, perhaps most, of the geneticists who voted for the agreement to abstain from certain directions of research are likely to feel that the reasoning which led them to take this position was by its very nature different from that which results in the choice of a particular consumer goods assortment. Some may speak of values *versus* tastes, others will contrast moral imperatives with the pragmatic ones. However, there is also a distinction which may be phrased as follows: "In the choices reflecting the degree of my preference for, say, shirts and turtle-necks, I am no doubt giving expression to an image of myself; but in this case, I can, and usually do, take 'myself' for granted. Before I could bring myself to abandon a research area - an outside sphere whose theoretical appropriation would change my identity - I had to inquire into what I expect from, and for, myself, into who I am, who I want and deserve to become."

If this volition were unguided by some higher principle and could therefore become arbitrary, we would be back in the sphere of the consumer choice theory. If, however, the interest in *emancipation* is an interest of *reason* - an interest that cannot be separated from the notion of rationality - and if reason itself demands that the reasonable be realized (so that one does *not* have to *adopt* a rationalistic attitude),[87] then we have at least a point of departure for a theory of change of norms and institutions. That is, we have a starting point which surmounts the apparent impossibility of formulating, within a framework where rationality$_1$ was defined *in terms of* norms and their consensual interpretations, a concept of rational behavior for *changes* in norms and the forms of behavior based on them.[88]

7.4.   Until now, the division of labor in science and scholarship and the need for interdisciplinary cooperation have been looked upon from the point of view of the content of the knowledge gained, and to be gained. However, the fact that one knows this or that imposes upon him or her also certain ethical obligations: for instance, it would be morally wrong to propose the employment of a technique of production that is known, or even only suspected, to cause damage to the health of the individuals exposed to it. But there are techniques which endanger, or are on good grounds feared to endanger, the health of whole societies, and if their inventor and proponent does not feel a moral constraint in making them available for actual employment, it is in part because there is nothing in the code of honor of his scientific profession to obligate him to cease and desist. Nor is this surprising or in itself reprehensible: chemists, for instance, may justifiably feel that, *qua* chemists, they are not in a position to assess the gain accruing, or the damage done, to the social whole by a particular technique originating in their field of inquiry.

It has been noted, however, that more cooperation among disciplines would tend to surmount these narrow boundaries of concern (4.4 and 7.1). And it is, indeed, self-evident that the cultivation of interdisciplinarity would extend in each and all the participating sciences the area of jurisdiction of professional ethics. It also stands to reason that more contact between sciences refines the professional's sensitivity to the limits at which the formal rationality of enhancing the rate of increase of knowledge has to submit to the substantive criteria influencing the historical process of the sciences' self-identification (6.5).

Conclusions

8. Even if scientists and scholars assumed and satisfied all the responsibilities listed above, they could still influence the productive use of techniques and their impact on individuals and societies only to a limited degree. In the last analysis, therefore, the crucial, and probably the only lasting way in which they can help is by contributing to the *society's* understanding of *itself*: this is where interdisciplinarity is most needed, where inquiries into the notion of rational behavior are most important, and where it is crucial to distinguish clearly between history which aims at man's emancipation and "history" from which the "point of view" of man must ultimately be excluded (5).

Returning for the last time to history proper, we shall recall that, in the community we started from, universality of knowledge was sought for practical purposes and techniques of production were directly dependent upon, and derived their legitimacy from, their place in the universe constituted, and uniquely shared, by "us" (2.3 and 2.4). A modern society, trying to regain mastery over the tools and machines employed in it, is in effect attempting to reattain the same state of affairs - except that the word "us" refers not to a group united, and also enclosed, by a particular culture (which at the same time excluded all "others"), but to "us" as the bearers of the fundamental interests inherent in *la condition humaine*.

The purpose is to make the ever-increasing technical control over things and "packaged" processes contribute to - rather than permitting it, whether by commission or omission, to override and thwart - the efforts aimed at attaining the practical end of freeing the joint formation of the identity of the individual and his society from as many external constraints as possible, and allowing them (the people integrated in societies and ultimately in mankind) to obtain and enhance their grasp over their destinies.

Notes

1. Dorothy Lee, *Freedom and Choice* (Englewood Cliffs, N.J.: Prentice Hall, 1964), p. 109. In the part of the book referred to, Lee is engaged in partially reinterpreting Malinowski's investigation of the Trobrianders.

2. *Ibid.*, p. 95.

3. *Ibid.*, p. 98.

4. *Ibid.*, pp. 93, 102, 100, 97.

5. "Reality is constituted in a framework that is the form of life of communicating groups and is organized through ordinary language. What is real is what can be experienced according to the interpretation of a

prevailing symbolic system." Jürgen Habermas, *Knowledge and Human Interests*, trans. J.J. Shapiro (Boston: Beacon, 1971), p. 192.

6. Claude Lévi-Strauss, *The Savage Mind* (London: Weidenfeld and Nicholson, 1976), pp. 18-20, 37-38.

7. Habermas, *Knowledge*, pp. 196-7. "Language is self-consciousness existing *for others* .... [Through language] *this* actual self ... fuses directly with others and is *their* self-consciousness." G.W.F. Hegel, *The Phenomenology of Mind*, trans. J.B. Baillie (New York: Harper and Row, 1967), p. 340.

8. Edmund Husserl, *Phenomenology and the Crisis of Philosophy*, trans. Quentin Lauer (New York: Harper and Row, 1965), p. 170.

9. E.E. Evans Prichard, quoted in Cyril S. Belshaw, *Traditional Exchange and Modern Markets* (Englewood Cliffs, N.J.: Prentice Hall, 1965), p. 32.

10. George Dalton, ed., *Primitive, Archaic, and Modern Economies: Essays of Karl Polanyi* (Garden City, N.Y.: Doubleday, 1968), pp. 88-89.

11. Lee, p. 97. Also Belshaw, p. 34.

12. The Trobrianders' case is special in that they did not seem to distinguish clearly between (i) and (ii). For the meaning of "consensus," see J. Habermas' concept of "communicative action," e.g., *Communication and the Evolution of Society*, trans. Thomas McCarthy (Boston: Beacon, 1979), pp. 118-120. Also his *Theory of Communicative Action*, I, trans. T. McCarthy (Boston: Beacon, 1984).

13. A classical example of rationality$_2$ occurs in the constrained maximizing algorithms of modern economics, for which "the question of rationality and irrationality is ... a question of the appropriateness of the means, given the ends, and neither requires or implies any judgment about ends." G.C. Archibald and R.G. Lipsey, *An Introduction to a Mathematical Treatment of Economics* (London: Weidenfeld and Nicholson, 1973), p. 157.

14. Say, "atoms" or even "values" that are (unlike observed prices) theoretical entities.

15. Aristotle, *Metaphysics*, trans. H.G. Apostle (Bloomington: Indiana University Press, 1975), 1003, 1026a.

16. Aristotle, *Ethics*, trans. J.A.K. Thomson (Harmondsworth: Penguin, 1977), 1177b.

17. *Ibid.*, 1177, 1178a.

18. Husserl, p. 159.

19. The working with a given, preexistent set of tools and materials, or more generally, within the confines of a particular state of "this" or "that" civilization, which is not yet subject to a continuous reflection based on concepts (as distinct from signs), a reflection by its very nature capable of transcending the confines of the present. Lévi-Strauss, pp. 18-20.

20. Aristotle, *Ethics*, 1139b, 1140.

21. Aristotle, *Politics*, trans. Ernest Barker (New York: Galaxy, 1962), 1263b.

22. Sir Ernest Barker, *The Political Thought of Plato and Aristotle* (New York: Dover, 1959), p. 289. See also Aristotle's *Ethics*, 1139a.

23. Aristotle, *Ethics*, 1132b, 1133.

24. *Ibid.*, 1133a-1134a.

25. When we meet them, the Sukuma comprise about 1,200,000 people living on the shores of Lake Victoria in what was then the Protectorate of Tanganyika, administered by Great Britain.

26. Peter McLaughlin, *An Economic History of Sukumaland to 1964: Fieldnotes and Analysis* (Fredericton, N.B.: McLaughlin Associates, 1971), mainly pp. 12-27.

27. *Ibid.*, p. 25.

28. In quite a few cases, the target was found to be too high and was scaled down to twenty acres. *Ibid.*, pp. 25-26.

29. *Ibid.*, p. 26.

30. See also Habermas, *Toward a Rational Society: Student Protest, Science and Politics*, trans. J.J. Shapiro (Boston: Beacon, 1971), p. 93.

31. Henri Lefebvre, *Le langage et la société* (Paris: Gallimard, 1966), p. 20.

32. The system of noun-classes is characteristic of Bantu languages in general. (Jack Berry, "Language Systems and Literature," in *The African Experience*, I, ed. J.N. Paden and E.W. Soja (Evanston: Northwestern University Press, 1970)). In what follows, the classification is explained in terms of Swahili, the *lingua franca* of the region.

33. The classes are listed here in an order which is somewhat different from that used in Swahili grammars and the MA-class is omitted because it can hardly be characterized the way the others are. D.V. Perrott, *Teach Yourself Swahili* (London: The English Universities Press, 1969).

34. See also paragraph 4.5 below.

35. See also paragraphs 3.4 and 7.1 as well as 7.4.

36. Karl Marx, *Grundrisse: Foundations of the Critique of Political Economy (Rough Draft)*, trans. Martin Nicolaus (Harmondsworth: Penguin, 1973), pp. 690-700.

37. Karl Marx, *Capital* (Moscow: Progress Publishers, 1971), I, 77-78.

38. Hans Cory, *Sukuma Law and Custom* (Westport, Con.: Negro Universities Press, 1970), p. 103. Cory's manuscript was finished in 1949 and first published in 1953.

39. *Ibid.*, p. 103.

40. *Ibid.*, pp. 103, 134.

41. *Ibid.*, pp. 136-7.

42. J. de V. Graaf, *Theoretical Welfare Economics* (London: Cambridge University Press, 1967), p. 103.

Languages, Techniques, Rationalities   87

43. Martin Heidegger, *The Question Concerning Technology and Other Essays*, trans. W. Lovitt (New York: Harper and Row, 1977), pp. 130-131.

44. See, for instance, Lovitt's Introduction, p. xv, or Wolfgang Stegmüller, *Hauptströmungen der Gegenwartsphilosophie* (Stuttgart: Kröner, 1965), pp. 139, 143.

45. Heidegger, pp. 131, 132.

46. Heidegger denies that Protagoras' statement points in the same direction as Descartes' *ego cogito*. (Appendix 8)

47. Heidegger, pp. 127, 140.

48. Lee, p. 109.

49. Heidegger, p. 10.

50. *Ibid.*, p. 17.

51. *Ibid.*, p. 19.

52. *Ibid.*, p. 38-39. Also pp. 44-45.

53. *Ibid.*, p. 47.

54. An African saying quoted by Dietrich von Rotenhan in "Cotton Farming in Sukumaland," a paper included in *Smallholder Farming and Smallholder Development in Tanzania*, ed. Hans Ruthenberg (München and London: Weltforum and Hurst, 1968), p. 66.

55. Hans-Georg Gadamer, *Hegel's Dialectic*, trans. P.C. Smith (New Haven: Yale University Press, 1971), p. 110.

56. *Ibid.*, p. 107.

57. In the part called "Self-consciousness," the first section is "The True Nature of Self-certainty," followed by that on "Lordship and Bondship."

58. Heidegger, pp. 10-11.

59. *Ibid.*, pp. 47, 48, also 25.

60. Alexandre Kojève, *Introduction to the Reading of Hegel*, trans. J.H. Nichols, Jr. (New York: Basic Books, 1969), pp. 33-35.

61. Heidegger, pp. 126-127.

62. Imre Lakatos, "History of Science and Its Rational Reconstruction," *Boston Studies in the Philosophy of Science* (VIII), pp. 99, 100-102, also 92.

63. *Ibid.*, p. 101-102.

64. *Ibid.*, p. 106.

65. *Ibid.*, p. 105.

66. Wilfred Sellars, "The Language of Theories," in *Readings in the Philosophy of Science*, ed. B.A. Brody (Englewood Cliffs, N.J.: Prentice Hall, 1970), p. 345.

67. Lakatos, p. 92.

68. This is the point of departure of R. Rudner's argument (Brody, pp. 540-546), although the quotation is from R.C. Jeffrey's critique of it ("Valuation and Acceptance of Scientific Hypotheses," Brody, p. 557).

69. Richard Rudner, "The Scientist qua Scientist Makes Value Judgments," Brody, p. 541.

70. Lakatos, p. 105.

71. Karl Marx, *Capital*, III, 104.

72. A decision on these lines was taken several years ago, but the injunction was only temporary.

73. For details, see e.g. R.D. Luce and H. Raiffa, *Games and Decisions* (New York: Wiley, 1967), chapters 4 and 5.

74. Let the two players (groups) be called A and B and the payoffs matrix stipulate the following gains and losses (or more generally, utilities) of the four outcomes, depending on the players' decision either to cooperate (c) or defect (d); the first number in each pair referring to A, the second to B:

	Bc	Bd
Ac	1, 1	-2, 2
Ad	2, -2	-1, -1.

If A as well as B chooses that strategy (c or d) which maximizes his security level (i.e., maximizes the lowest yield in the row for A, and in the column for B), the outcome will be Ad;Bd, for -1 is more than -2 in the case of A and similarly for B. For different games of this kind, the payoffs will be in general different - but the relation between them must in each outcome follow the above pattern.

75. Luce and Raiffa, pp. 96-97.

76. See Dennis C. Mueller, *Public Choice* (London: Cambridge University Press, 1979), pp. 12-13.

77. A. Rapoport and A. Chammah, *Prisoner's Dilemma* (Ann Arbor: University of Michigan Press, 1965), p. 23.

78. *Ibid.*, pp. 65-66, 198-201. The game was played in pairs. Altogether 740 subjects were used (p. 204). See also Luce and Raiffa, p. 101.

79. Robert Axelrod, *The Evolution of Cooperation* (New York: Basic Books, 1984), pp. viii, 13-14, 20, chapter 2 and throughout the book. (The winning strategy was proposed by Professor Anatol Rapoport of the University of Toronto, the senior author of *Prisoner's Dilemma*, where the effects of TIT FOR TAT are summarized on pp. 202, 207, 255.) Again the strategies competed in pairs. The size of the test may be indicated by pointing out that in an earlier round with only 14 strategies 240,000 separate choices were made. Axelrod, p. 31.

80. It is possible, of course, that set against a different assortment of strategies, TIT FOR TAT would not win. But the sample is sufficiently large to suggest that any winning strategy would have to stress the willingness to initiate cooperation and reciprocate it.

81. Suppose we start from the game outlined in footnote 74 and impose a fine of -10 to be paid if either A or B defects, but not if both do so (see

Rapoport and Chammah, p. 26). Then it is easy to see that, following the same minimax rule, the outcome will be Ac; Bc.

82. Luce and Raiffa, p. 114. The fine need not be agreed upon by the two players; it could be inherent in the situation of which they are a part. (Rapoport and Chammah, pp. 25-26.) This means that, in principle, fines could be operative also if the two groups could not communicate with each other (7.1.1.f).

83. Rapoport and Chammah, pp. 199, 223.

84. Mueller, pp. 12-15.

85. H. Demsetz, "Information and Efficiency," *Journal of Law and Economics*, No. 12 (April 1969), p. 1. The problem was first brought to my attention when I read an unpublished paper by my former colleague Geoffrey Newman.

86. Albert Breton, *The Economic Theory of Representative Government* (Chicago: Aldine, 1974), pp. 164-5.

87. Jürgen Habermas, *Theory and Practice*, trans. John Viertel (Boston: Beacon, 1974), pp. 276, 279. Also Habermas, *Knowledge*, pp. 198-201, 205-206. The clause in brackets is directed against Karl Popper.

88. This is to say that interest in emancipation as an interest of reason is a necessary condition for the validity of norms to be based on rational consensus (by contrast with traditional consensus). (For this distinction, see Jürgen Habermas, *Theory of Communicative Action*, I, p. 261.) Of course, this condition is, in itself, not sufficient. See, for instance, the conditions under which norms may be said to "regulate legitimate chances for the satisfaction of needs." Thomas McCarthy, *The Critical Theory of Jürgen Habermas* (Cambridge, Mass.: MIT Press, 1982), p. 313. See also pp. 314-317, and J. Habermas, *Theory of Communicative Action*, I, pp. 88-9.

TECHNOLOGY AND THE PROBLEM OF DEMOCRATIC CONTROL: THE CONTRIBUTION OF JÜRGEN HABERMAS

Marie Fleming

Jürgen Habermas is a social theorist who is determined to work through a wide range of philosophical and theoretical problems related to contemporary society. That he insists on dealing with these problems within the context of a discussion of modernity is worthy of note, for he remains undeterred by what he views as the growing conservatism and defeatism suggested by the use of concepts such as postmodernity and poststructuralism.[1] In the discussion which follows it becomes clear not only that he rejects the perspective of a postmodernity, but also that he has turned his back on many of his predecessors at the Frankfurt School. He is neither convinced by gloomy predictions about the inevitability of the spread of instrumental reason and the domination of technology (Horkheimer and Adorno), nor does he resort to the mysticism inherent in the apocalyptic solution of a New Technology (Marcuse). Refusing to be swayed by old gods and wary of the promise of new gods, Habermas does not seem to know intellectual and political defeatism. On the contrary, he seems able to generate whatever energy is required to push his analysis further. His pursuit of questions dealing with social and political problems is relentless and represents a sustained effort to uncover the relationships which define the society which we, as human beings, have constructed. These relationships take place on a number of levels. In this essay I deal specifically with the political level.

The project of modernity, as initiated by the Enlightenment and interpreted by Habermas, involves human emancipation and the establishment of conditions for the practice of individual autonomy and self-determination. And yet, as we have suspected for some time, the hope for liberation has not been fulfilled and may not even have been justified. As Horkheimer and Adorno wrote in the opening remarks to their *Dialectic of Enlightenment*: "In the most general sense of progressive thought, the

90

Enlightenment has always aimed at liberating men from fear and establishing their sovereignty. Yet the fully enlightened earth radiates disaster triumphant."2   On a descriptive level, it is difficult to dismiss such an analysis. Are we, then, to view Horkheimer and Adorno as essentially correct in their suggestion that humankind has been deluding itself about possibilities for liberation and especially in the belief that such liberation was to come about through technical progress? Must we look upon technology in simply negative terms and nod sagely in resignation at the "failed" project of modernity? Or is it still possible to rescue the project and to reestablish a basis for the fulfillment of the Enlightenment claims? These questions are of considerable importance, for it is most unlikely that technical progress can be halted; and even if it could be, it is improbable that a "restored" pastoral existence could provide for the development of freedom and autonomy. Either way, from within the Enlightenment problematic, we would have to confront the possibility of unfreedom and domination. Even Marcuse viewed the problem of unfreedom as intrinsically connected with science and technology, and consequently he was led to the conception of a New Science and a New Technology. But before we contemplate the implications of these various courses, perhaps we should consider more precisely the nature of the problem.

What Habermas offers is an alternative to those viewpoints which attribute the problem of the loss of freedom to technology itself. As we shall see, he insists on viewing technology as a collective project of the human race, and he attributes what Marcuse perceived to be the dominating aspects of technology to a failure of human beings to place technology under democratic control. He formulated the question in the following form several years ago: "Our problem can then be stated as one of the relation of technology and democracy: how can the problem of technical control be brought within the range of the consensus of acting and transacting citizens?"3 It is not always clear that this basic problem of the democratic control of technology remains a central concern of Habermas' more recent work. His decision to address himself more extensively to theoretical and philosophical problems might leave some of his readers wondering whether he has retreated to the proverbial ivory tower and has lost sight of concrete political problems. We should also keep in mind that Habermas is continually revising and refining his theories, sometimes to the point where it is not always clear whether they have been abandoned or merely reappropriated in a new form.

It seems to me, however, that Habermas' work builds systematically upon those insights which he put forward in connection with concrete political problems. What I should like to do in this essay is to recover the principal themes of Habermas' early writings and thus attempt to set the stage for his move into the world of analytic philosophy and language studies which has characterized so much of his recent work. I shall focus upon Habermas' efforts to define the problem of the relation between technology and democracy within the context of an examination of the theories of Karl Marx and Max Weber. In the first section I discuss some aspects of the relevance of Marx's theories and suggest why Habermas finds it relatively unproblematic to challenge Marxian political economy. In the second and third sections I review his examination of the question of technology in terms of Weber's model of decisionism and show how he uses John Dewey's pragmatic philosophy in order to specify what he views as a central weakness of Weber's analysis. In the final section I attempt to explain how Habermas' critique of Weber merges with his critique of positivism, and how the effort to redefine the question of the relation of technology and democracy leads him to confront Weber with an alternative theory of rationality and rationalization. In conclusion, I suggest that Habermas' examination of the problem of democratic control of technology should be placed within the context of his conception of knowledge-constitutive interests, and I once more take up the question of his relation to the Marxist tradition.

The Relevance of Marx

According to Habermas, the Marxian response to the problem of democratic control of technology is both brilliant and flawed. On the one hand, he acknowledges, Marx demonstrated that the capitalist system of production had become "a power that has taken on its own life in opposition to the interests of productive freedom, of the producers." Under capitalist production, goods which are produced socially are appropriated privately, so that "the technical process of producing use values falls under the alien law of an economic process that produces exchange values." Once it becomes established that the self-regulation of capital accumulation has its origins in the private ownership of the means of production, that is, once the process itself becomes demystified, this alien law loses its power. At this point it becomes possible for humankind to understand "economic compulsion as an alienated result of its own free productive activity and then abolish it." For Marx the problem of democratic control of technology is resolved. The reproduction of the material basis of life can now be "rationally planned" in the form of a technical process which produces use values under the control of a democractic society "in accordance with the will and insight of the associated individuals."4

Habermas claims that Marx made a serious error when he simply "equated" the practice of a functioning democracy with the successful control of technology. He seems to have assumed that there would be no fundamental incompatibility between the demands of technical control and the needs of democracy. In the meantime, says Habermas, we have become aware that we require more than a well-run planning bureaucracy if we are to have any hope of "realizing the associated material and intellectual productive forces in the interest of the enjoyment and freedom of an emancipated society." It was the failure to address this problem, he says, which explains why socialists never anticipated "the authoritarian welfare state" which guarantees citizens a measure of social wealth, but denies them political freedom.[5]

Habermas accepts Marx's political economy as essentially correct for an analysis of liberal capitalism. However, he insists that since the late nineteenth century we have witnessed two trends which demand reconsideration of the applicability of Marx's theory for the analysis of advanced capitalism. One of these is increasing state intervention in the economy. As a consequence of the dysfunctional effects arising out of the private accumulation and utilization of capital, the maintenance of the capitalist system came to depend upon overcoming the instability of the business cycle through a government "corrective" of social-economic policy. This state intervention, necessary for system stability, signifies a fundamental change from the system of liberal capitalism in which the state provides general guarantees of order and leaves the fate of the economy largely to market forces. Thus, since the time of Marx, the capitalist mode of production has lost "its really novel feature," its ability to perpetuate itself "autonomously" through self-regulation. With the economy "repoliticized," the relation between the economy and the political system has changed: politics is no longer "*only*" a superstructural phenomenon in the sense in which Marx had defined base and superstructure. Marx's political economy is inapplicable precisely because the "base" has to be viewed as "in itself a function of governmental activity and political conflicts." It is no longer meaningful to suggest that the "power structure can ... be criticized *immediately* at the level of the relations of production." Marx, says Habermas, "unmasked in theory ... the root ideology of just exchange," and now with government actively involved in the economy, the ideology has also "collapsed in practice."[6]

The second trend isolated by Habermas and said to be characteristic of advanced capitalism is the growing interdependence of research and technology and their transformation into a primary productive force. Planned scientific and technological progress, along with state intervention, represents a powerful tool to be utilized in adjusting imbalances and in mediating conflicts arising out of a production process governed by the imperatives of capitalist investment. In such a situation, state action cannot supplant the law of value, but it can compensate for the tendency of the rate of profit to fall. It may even be possible, despite the presence of economic crisis tendencies, for the system to sustain a steady rate of profit.[7] A related feature of late capitalist development is the pattern that scientific and technological research has assumed. Habermas points to the linking of industrial research with research conducted under government contract, particularly in the military sector. Government-sponsored research thus provides information which can flow back for use in the "private" sectors of the economy. In this way, says Habermas, scientific-technical progress has become an "independent source" of surplus value and has fundamentally altered the conditions for the application of Marx's labor theory of value. It no longer makes sense to calculate capital investment in research and development solely in terms of the labor power of the immediate producers who are coming to play an ever-smaller role in the production of surplus value.[8]

For anyone familiar with the Marxian prediction concerning the collapse of the capitalist economy as a necessary consequence of its internal contradictions, the conclusions which Habermas draws are startling, particularly from one who is so sympathetic to Marx. It is clear, however, that Habermas has found a way in which he can situate himself in the Marxist tradition. First of all, he sees Marx, as he sees himself, as heir to the Enlightenment. He can, moreover, build upon the "revisionism" of the early Frankfurt School which had already established that, even on a descriptive level, Marx's political economy is inadequate for an analysis of contemporary society. Habermas is thus able to elaborate certain key notions in the theories put forward by Horkheimer, Adorno and Marcuse, particularly their notions of the expansion of state power and increasing bureaucratization, along with the steadily diminishing role of citizens in contemporary "democracies."

The Problem as Defined by Weber

Habermas can critically appropriate Marx because he self-consciously remains in the Marxist tradition. With Weber the situation is different. Habermas endeavors to break out of the tradition of Weber and to avoid the fate of Horkheimer and Adorno, who eventually succumbed to the spell of Weber's thesis of the progressive and irreversible (?) rationalization accompanying the disenchantment of the world. Habermas characterizes his major work on *The Theory of Communicative Action* as the "second attempt to appropriate Weber in the spirit of Western Marxism."[9] In the final section of the essay I shall take up this question and show how Habermas traces the spirit of Weber to a tradition of modern scholarship going back to Thomas Hobbes. This perspective is intimately connected with Habermas' conception of knowledge-constitutive interests which gives him an additional arsenal of weapons against Weber.

In an early essay Habermas explains that the concept of "rationality" was introduced by Weber as a descriptive term to refer to the structures of capitalist economic activity, the legal system and bureaucratic administration. This rationality Weber viewed as a *Zweckrationalität*, a purposive or instrumental rationality concerned with the selection of means to fulfill predetermined ends. Rationalization was, for Weber, the extension to ever more areas of social life of the criteria of a purposive-rational action which is always directed to the organization of means or the choice between alternative means. Such a process of rationalization is closely linked with the absorption by social institutions of scientific and technological developments. The logic of purposive-rational action tends towards the establishment, improvement or expansion of subsystems not only at work and in bureaucratic administrations, but also in such everyday areas of life as transportation and communication. As science and technology become institutionalized, former world-views, even the "cultural tradition as a whole," lose their potency for motivating action.[10]

Far from challenging Weber's thesis on progressive rationalization, Habermas confirms it. In another essay he suggests that the modern state, "which arose from the need for central financial administration in connection with the market patterns of an emerging national and territorial economy," was from the beginning dependent on technical expertise. The advice which the state sought from legal experts in setting up its administrative machinery was, in some important respects, not unlike the kind of technical knowledge required to organize the military. This was a period of rationalization in which scientific techniques were applied in the interest of administrative efficiency. Like Weber, Habermas is convinced that in an important sense the "scientization" of political life and administrative organization cannot be held back. He would go further and suggest that it is not even desirable to hold it back. But Habermas is also sympathetic to Weber's view that progressive rationalization leads to the development of a basis for bureaucratic domination.[11] What is at issue is how this tendency toward domination can be brought under control and the form which such control might take. It is at this point that the disagreement between Habermas and Weber emerges.

Weber's *decisionistic model* of political practice demands the complete separation of the functions of the expert and the politician. The relation operates within the context of a strict division of labor, clearly defined responsibilities and institutional norms. The policy decisions of political leaders are informed by technical knowledge, but remain independent of such knowledge, while officials, employing the techniques of rational administration, are charged with the execution of policy decisions. Scientific rules of procedure operate as techniques and thus govern the *means* of political practice, never the political practice itself.[12]

The validity of this model may be questioned on two levels. First of all, as it stands, it may no longer have much heuristic value for an examination of present-day politics. Since Weber's time, and especially in the period following the Second World War, Habermas suggests, Western societies have entered a "new or second" stage of rationalization. Whereas the first stage was characterized by a scientization of politics limited by its subordination to the imperatives of political will, what happens in stage two is that bureaucrats, military personnel and political leaders have been "orienting themselves to strictly scientific recommendations in the exercise of their public functions." Primary examples of the increasing tendency towards a qualitatively different scientization may be found in the scope of research under government contract and the extent of scientific consultation sought by public services. As Habermas explains, we are dealing here not merely with the improvement of traditional instruments for use in formulating and carrying out political decisions. Systems analysis, and especially decision theory, not only introduce new technologies; they also "rationalize choice as such by means of calculated strategies and automatic decision procedures." To the extent that this is done, the experts are able to uncover so-called objective necessities which seem to dominate the choices of political leaders. In this way "the exercise of power domestically and its assertion against external enemies ... have been structurally transformed by the objective exigencies of new technologies and strategies."[13]

Weber's model, which was developed in the first stage of rationalization, may not be adequate to deal with the qualitative changes of the second stage. In fact, Habermas says, it is clear that the Weberian conception of the necessary separation of the functions of the expert and the politician is being eclipsed within a *technocratic model* in which the relation of expert and politician would appear to have reversed itself. According to this model, the politician becomes "the mere agent of a scientific intelligentsia, which in concrete circumstances, elaborates the objective implications and requirements of available techniques and resources as well as of optimal strategies and rules of control." The politician is "left with nothing but a fictitious decision-making power," while the initiative in political decisions has moved to scientific analysis and planning. Habermas acknowledges that the technocratic model has descriptive value for present-day mass democracies, first and foremost, the United States. However, despite its advantages as a heuristic device, this model remains unable to deal with the "politics" of the practical decisions. In this respect, says Habermas, it is not fundamentally different from the decisionistic model developed by Weber and may, in fact, be characterized as an *expanded decisionistic model*.[14] Here we come to Habermas' second, and more important, criticism of Weber.

While the Weberian model of decisionism claims that politicians are equipped with an array of expert knowledge to assist in arriving at policy choices, the model provides no rational basis for justifying the ends of political action. Decisions must be made between "competing value orders and convictions, which escape compelling arguments and remain inaccessible to cogent discussion." Thus, says Habermas, "rationality in the choice of means accompanies avowed irrationality in orientation to values, goals, and needs."15 However, while the decisionistic model would have it that politicians decide - irrationally - between competing value systems, the technocratic model eliminates the discussion of values altogether. The latter model not only presupposes an immanent necessity of technical progress, but also holds that the politicians' *practical* as well as the experts' *technical* problems are equally amenable to technical solutions. Despite the fact that, at a descriptive level, the technocratic model has some advantages over the decisionistic, when it comes to questions of practical politics, values, and social needs, the former abandons the antithesis between politics and expertise and reduces everything to a "logic of reality." Habermas agrees with a critic of the technocratic model who concludes that the "logic of reality" is only "a camouflaging of what is really as political as ever."16

This notion that the technocratic model may be viewed as an *expanded* decisionistic model is misleading. On the one hand, the area for political decision-making is considerably circumscribed. As Habermas himself points out, at a time when politicians have access to technical means which are quantitatively greater and qualitatively more refined than any which had been previously available, they are also confronted with a "logic of reality" which drastically reduces the complex of problems amenable to political intervention. Carried to extremes, this rationalization removes the content from political decisions and reduces them to pure form. Moreover, Weberian decisionism, for all its weakness in dealing with practical interests, nonetheless took cognizance of the distinction between technical and political decisions. The technocratic model, on the other hand, recalls the weakness of the Marxian model in that, in both cases, practical problems are reduced to technical problems.

What then can we say about Weber's model? From Habermas' perspective, Weber clearly was aware that two distinct kinds of problems are involved. He did not, like Marx, reduce the one to the other. In a sense, Weber may even be said to have been sympathetic to the idea of emancipation. After all, he was preoccupied with what many observers perceive to be a central and enduring problem of modern life - bureaucratic domination. And unlike the facile solutions proposed by present-day neoconservatives, his responses, though inadequate, reflect his determination to confront the situation squarely and not to draw away from uncomfortable conclusions. In many ways, Marx, for all his commitment to democracy, did not reach the same level of insight into the operation of modern institutions as that attained by Weber; and this, I believe, cannot simply be written off as a reflection of the period in which Marx lived. It is because Weber reached this level of insight that his thesis on progressive, ever-expanding rationalization demands attention. In the next section I shall examine how Habermas pursues the problem with the help of American pragmatic philosophy.

Towards a Model of Democracy

Neither the decisionistic nor the technocratic model structurally requires democracy. Each may be seen as an attempt to account for the relation between expertise and politics within the context of the scientization of modern life, but in neither case is there any provision for a public discussion of policy issues. It was Weber's concern for the sovereignty of the politician that led him to introduce the notion of the strict separation of the expert and the politician, but this "removal" of the politician from the world also left no room to develop any conception of a meaningful role for citizens. In the end, the only political action accorded to citizens is the election/legitimation of those who will then undertake the task of making decisions. For Weber, explains Habermas, democratic choice assumes the form of acclamation, since the choice refers only to the choosing of the decision-makers and not to the selection of policy guidelines. Democracy is understood in purely procedural terms. The substantive issues dealt with by the politicians who are chosen (acclaimed) by the public, not only must remain beyond *public* discussion; they must also remain beyond *rational* discussion, since it is the prerequisite of power to decide issues without undue pressure from a rationalized administration. This model has been developed by Schumpeter and has become one of the pillars of a great deal of modern political sociology. In the final analysis, democratic decision-making is reduced to "a regulated acclamation procedure for elites alternately appointed to exercise power." In fact, says Habermas, power remains "untouched in its irrational substance ... legitimated but not rationalized."17

The technocratic model goes even further in its demand for the full scientization of politics by reducing political matters to questions of rational administration. Accordingly, it is not even correct to say that citizens "choose" political decision-makers, since within this model there is no longer any question of making decisions, merely the uncovering of the "objective necessity" to which politicians, as well as everyone else, are strictly subjected. Thus, citizens can only select (legitimate) what amounts to administrative personnel and evaluate the professional credentials of competing elite groups. But how, in this case, can we be justified in continuing to speak of any decision-making, let alone democratic decision-making, since there is nothing left to decide, only something to administer.

"A technocratic administration of industrial society," says Habermas, "would deprive any decision-making process of its object."[18]

There are two interrelated factors which may be said to be responsible for this development. First of all, in both the decisionistic and technocratic models there is a failure to perceive the relation between the capitalist mode of production and expanding subsystems of purposive-rational action. Habermas explains this relation by examining the fundamental way in which modern industrial technology differentiates itself from pre-industrial technology. Every "civilization,"[19] he points out, is equipped with a "system of social labour" and a "stock of accumulated technically exploitable knowledge" out of which develop subsystems of purposive-rational action. The institutional framework of traditional societies, legitimated by mythical or religious interpretations of reality, tolerates structural change arising out of potential surpluses in the economic system, so long as such change remains within the bounds of cultural traditions and does not call into question the legitimacy of shared world-views. This constraining action on the development of subsystems of purposive-rational action is the basis for the "superiority" of the traditional institutional framework. Under the capitalist mode of production, however, the relation between the economy and the political system is fundamentally altered. In the modern period, a level of development of the productive forces is reached which makes possible the establishment, in the economic system, of a "self-propelling mechanism that ensures long-term continuous growth (despite crises)." As a "mechanism that guarantees the *permanent* expansion of subsystems of purposive-rational action," the capitalist mode of production "overturns" the established superiority of the institutional framework. Through the emergence of a system of "economic legitimation" the political system, far from being able to constrain the developing subsystems, is now "adapted" to the new requirements of rationality demanded by them. For the first time, says Habermas, domination is legitimated no longer "from the lofty heights of cultural tradition, but instead summoned up from the base of social labour."[20]

It is crucial to see that, with the overturning of the traditional superiority of the institutional framework, the political system is always under the pressure of having to adapt to the rationality requirements of permanently expanding subsystems of purposive-rational action. It is this process of adaptation, he says, that Weber isolated as rationalization. According to Habermas, we can observe the pressure to rationalize coming "from below" in such areas as labor and trade, transportation, information and communication, private law, financial institutions and the state bureaucracy. This pressure from below, however, sets new standards of rationality which give rise to compulsion for rationalization coming "from above." On this level, says Habermas, we can perceive what Weber referred to as "secularization."

On the one hand, world-views based on mythological and religious interpretations of reality lose their power and validity as legitimating forces and are
"reshaped" into personal belief systems. Having thus lost their force,
traditional world-views can no longer fulfill the functions of legitimating
power and motivating action. These functions are now taken over by new
legitimations which develop out of "the critique of the dogmatism of
traditional interpretations of the world and claim a scientific character."21

It is thus in "the mantle of modern science" that the state achieves its
legitimation. However, since the knowledge which the modern sciences
produce is technically exploitable knowledge, the nature of "actual power
relations," which cannot be disclosed through science, must remain
"inaccessible" not only to analysis, but also to public consciousness. While
it is true that social interests still determine the direction and pace of
technical progress, those interests "define the social system so much as a
whole that they coincide with the interest in maintaining the system." The
"quasi-autonomous progress of science and technology then appears as an
independent variable on which the most important single system variable,
namely economic growth, depends." Thus, says Habermas, there emerges "a
perspective in which the development of the social system *seems* to be
determined by the logic of scientific-technical progress." According to the
"immanent law" of such progress, objective exigencies are produced which
seem to be so intimately connected with the functional needs of the social
system that there is no alternative but to obey them. Thus, in modern
societies "the process of democratic decision-making about practical
problems loses its function and 'must' be replaced by plebiscitary
decisions."22

But more important for Habermas than the question of the validity of the
technocratic model is the fact that the technocracy thesis "can also become a
background ideology that penetrates into the consciousness of the depoli-
ticized mass of the population, where it can take on legitimating power."
What is remarkable about this ideology is its ability "to detach society's self-
understanding from the frame of reference of communicative action...and
replace it with a scientific model."23 Technological consciousness is, on the
one hand, "less ideological" than previous ideologies, for it does not
represent merely a delusion that disguises power relations. As a background
ideology which makes a "fetish" of science, however, it appears as "more
irresistible and farther-reaching" than its predecessors. For in orienting itself
to the solution of technical problems, it veils practical problems and thus "it
not only justifies a *particular class's* interest in domination and represses
another class's partial need for emancipation, but affects the human race's
emancipatory interest as such." It is not justifiable, however, to view
technocratic consciousness as only ideology, for it offers no conception of a
projected "good life." It differentiates itself from the ideology of just

exchange in that "it severs the criteria for justifying the organization of social life from any normative regulation of interaction." "Technological consciousness reflects not the sundering of an ethical situation but the repression of 'ethics' as such as a category of life."[24]

Habermas has uncovered a series of political problems which not only appear to defy practical solution, but continually challenge the whole emancipatory thrust of his argument. What is unique to capitalist production is not merely its ability to guarantee permanent expansion of subsystems of purposive-rational action, but also the virtual unassailability of the legitimacy it has acquired through its validation by the modern faith in science. But it is here, where the public interest appears to have been absorbed by objective exigencies of technological progress, that Habermas uncovers what he views as the key to the problem of democratic control of technology - the relation of the sciences to public opinion.

There is an obvious interdependence, says Habermas, between "values that proceed from interest situations and techniques that can be utilized for the satisfaction of value-oriented needs." It was Dewey, he points out, who suggested some time ago that "the introduction of continually augmented and improved techniques does not merely remain bound to undiscussed value orientations but also subjects traditional values to a sort of pragmatic corroboration." In view of the fact that the direction taken by technical progress limits, if it does not shape, value orientations, any model of the relation between expertise and politics would have to deal with the social interests which are bound to the introduction of increasingly improved techniques. While Dewey did not work out the implications of his position, he nonetheless insisted upon "the pragmatic examination and consequently the rational discussion of the relation between available techniques and practical decisions."[25] This *pragmatistic model* transforms the Weberian strict separation of the expert and politician into a "critical interaction" in which all practical decisions are open to a "scientifically informed discussion." The interaction assumes the form of a "reciprocal communication" in which decision-makers consult with scientific experts within the context of a consideration of practical needs and what Dewey refers to as "value beliefs." Rather than allow political decisions to be dealt with - irrationally - in the realm of pure decision, the pragmatistic model makes explicit the problem of making political decisions within the context of value-oriented needs. The discussion of technical progress is necessarily bounded by discussion of practical needs, as these have been historically understood and as they may be reinterpreted in light of possibilities opened up through technological innovation.[26]

Dewey imagined that such critical interaction, relating the question of technical progress to the value orientations of the interested parties, could be managed rather simply with a commonsense utilization of existing decision structures.   Habermas elaborates the pragmatistic model by developing Dewey's notion of the necessary critical interaction and by showing how the communication which takes place between expert and politician must necessarily be increasingly dependent on "mediation by the public as a political institution." As Dewey insists, communication is necessary because of the presence of "value beliefs." Habermas takes this to mean that communication is "based on a historically determined preunderstanding, governed by social norms, of what is practically necessary in a concrete situation." The preunderstanding is a consciousness, open to hermeneutic enlightenment and shared by all members of a community. The enlightenment must take place, therefore, "in the discourse of citizens in a community." "The relation of the *sciences* to *public opinion* is constitutive for the scientization of politics." That Dewey failed to make this relation explicit is not an inherent weakness of the pragmatistic model.[27]

Interaction and Emancipation

As suggested above, it is misleading to refer to the technocratic model as an expanded decisionistic model. Nevertheless, it may be justifiable to agree with Habermas that the technocratic model is a development out of Weberian decisionism. It might be argued, for example, that the irrationality with respect to values required by Weber's model cannot be easily reconciled with the demand for certainty implicit in modern conceptions of science, and that science as ideology requires such irrationality to be progressively removed until all question of values is eliminated from political life. Weber may be viewed, therefore, as laying the groundwork for the emergence of a situation in which technological consciousness comes to dominate modern politics. Weber himself, however, as noted above, is caught within a tradition of social philosophy which Habermas traces back to Hobbes.

From Habermas' perspective, the appearance of *Leviathan* is the culmination of a long intellectual process in which the Aristotelian "classical doctrine of politics" is abandoned. It is Weber's participation in and contribution to this "Hobbesian" tradition which Habermas perceives as the key to understanding the central weakness of his analysis, his inability to deal with values in political life. Before taking up the question of this weakness, I should like to state briefly the principal characteristics of Hobbes' social philosophy, as viewed by Habermas.

The twenty-ninth chapter of *Leviathan* begins, says Habermas, with confidence and self-certainty: "Though nothing can be immortal, which mortals make: yet, if men had the use of reason they pretend to, their Commonwealths might be secured, at least, from perishing by internal diseases....Therefore, when they come to be dissolved, not by external violence, but intestine disorder, the fault is not in men, as they are the *Matter*, but as they are the *Makers*, and orderers of them." This passage, says Habermas, reveals a marked contrast to the political-ethical perspective of the classical doctrine of politics. Whereas Aristotle understood politics to be the "doctrine of the good and just life," with Hobbes we confront a "scientifically grounded social philosophy" which is oriented to the establishment of the conditions for the "correct order" of state and society. These conditions are to have validity independently of any particular historical period. Second, while the old doctrine is built upon the notion of *praxis* as opposed to that of *techne*, within the new version application of the knowledge of the conditions for the correct order becomes a technical problem, concerned with generating rules, relationships and institutions. Third, Aristotle emphasizes *phronesis* or a "prudent understanding of the situation"; but under the new ideal, human behavior comes to be viewed only in the sense in which it is "the material for science." The "categories of ethical social intercourse" can now be disregarded by the "engineers of the correct order" who are to "confine themselves to the construction of conditions under which human beings, just like objects within nature, will necessarily behave in a calculable manner." Politics is finally severed from the "doctrine of the good and just life," and the way is prepared for the emergence of a "scientific" politics to be classified among the social sciences. The complete separation of the social sciences from the normative elements of the classical conception of politics was accomplished through Weber's clarification of the "value-judgment controversy" and the defining of a positivistic "logic of investigation."[28]

Weber's view that there could be no rational approach to decisions on values and convictions, and his consequent judgment that the politician had to have a preserve for decision based on pure will, followed from his positivistic self-understanding. To challenge the validity of this position, however, does not amount to a rejection of his thesis on progressive rationalization. In fact, Habermas affirms the validity of this thesis on almost every page. Moreover, his *Theory of Communicative Action* may even be viewed, in several important respects, as an elaboration and extension of the rationalization thesis. This becomes apparent especially in the notion of the "colonization of the lifeworld" in which the ethical dimensions of everyday interaction are increasingly suppressed and made subject to the system imperatives of bureaucratization and monetarization.[29] What Weber fails to see, according to Habermas, is that the "rationalization" of capitalist society is "imbalanced."[30] In fact, Weber belongs to that tradition, deriving from Hobbes, which Habermas views as having a "distorted understanding of rationality."[31] As we have seen, the rationality which Weber perceives and which he thematizes is that of means-ends relations. Habermas insists, however, that under the capitalist mode of production there has developed a "selective pattern of rationalization"[32] which Weber, through his positivistic approach, has failed to grasp.

There is, Habermas argues, in addition to instrumental or purposive-rational action, a type of action which is by nature fundamentally different from that concerned with means-ends relations. This, he terms interaction or "*communicative action*," an action which is "governed by binding *consensual norms*, which define reciprocal expectations about behavior and which must be understood and recognized by at least two acting subjects."[33] The logic of interaction contexts in which participants in dialogue must orient themselves to the validity claims of truth, truthfulness and rightness is clearly different from the logic of systems of purposive-rational action in which technical rules and strategies are validated empirically.[34] I do not have the space here to go into the controversial questions arising from Habermas' uncovering of "another" rationality which is, at the same time, a necessary and unavoidable feature of our lives as symbolically interacting human beings.[35] While much work remains to be done, it is clear that the theory of communicative action is a challenging endeavor which opens up so many fronts that it will provide for energetic discussion for some time to come. The point that needs to be made here is that Habermas' insistence upon the rational basis of dialogue leads to the notion that we must distinguish between "*two concepts of rationalization*."[36]

Throughout this essay my concern has been to explore questions related to rationalization at the level of subsystems of purposive-rational action. Habermas claims that there is also "*rationalization at the level of the institutional framework*" based upon the logic of the demands of symbolic interaction. Such rationalization, he says, "can only occur in the medium of symbolic interaction itself, that is, through *removing restrictions on communication*." This calls for public discussion which is unrestricted and free from domination, and which ranges over such questions as the "suitability and desirability of action-orienting principles and norms in the light of the sociocultural repercussions of developing subsystems of purposive-rational action." It is crucial that provision be made for such communication at all political and "repoliticized" levels of decision-making. Within this analysis, it becomes clear that when Marx viewed emancipation as a function of the level of development of the forces of production, what he failed to see was that the process of the developing forces of production can be a potential for liberation only so long as this rationalization does not destroy the basis for a development of the "other" rationalization at the institutional level.[37]

In conclusion, I should like to situate the question of democratic control of technology within the context of Habermas' conception of knowledge-constitutive interests. Without going into this thesis of the intimate and necessary relation between knowledge and human interests,[38] I should like to highlight those aspects of the theory which seem to me relevant for the present discussion. The theory rests upon a central fact of human existence: that human life cannot take place outside "a sociocultural life-form dependent on labor and language." It is not difficult to see that the daily reproduction of the material basis of human life through work requires an attitude which objectifies those events and objects capable of being manipulated and controlled. It is also clear that the reproduction of the material basis of life is accomplished through interaction with the other human beings who make up our universe. We can agree, I believe, that this interaction always takes place within the context of a network of communicative relations in which reciprocal expectations are renewed and/or expanded. Thus the *technical interest* in manipulating the environment, shared by all of us in the reproduction of our lives, is inseparable from the *practical interest* involved in the intersubjective communication about how (politically-ethically) such manipulation is to take place. Habermas' claim is that these two "natural" and unavoidable interests give rise to two categories of possible knowledge, the one represented by the empirical-analytic and the other by the historical-hermeneutic sciences.[39]

While there might be some resistance to this notion of the technical and practical interests which govern social relations, it is Habermas' view of the *emancipatory interest* which seems to many to be the most problematic. He argues that, just as the technical and practical interests are linked to work and language, so the emancipatory interest is rooted in power, another form of social organization. In contrast to the practical (political-ethical) action that is involved in intersubjective communication, the action that is associated with the interest in emancipation would appear to take place in the realm of thought and to involve a process of enlightenment, or "liberation from the objectified self-deception of dogmatic power." (That is not to say that there are no consequences for practical action.) As examples of analyses which have self-consciously embodied the emancipatory interest Habermas points to the social critiques of Marx and to the metapsychology of Freud which, he says, are "distinguished precisely by incorporating in their consciousness an interest which directs knowledge, an interest in emancipation going beyond the technical and practical interest of knowledge."[40]

Habermas is particularly concerned to argue that reason must not be viewed as a mere "organ of adaptation" for human beings "just as claws and teeth are for animals." Throughout the course of human history we can witness not only the tendency to fulfill natural drives, but also the tendency "toward release from the constraint of nature." Thus the human interests which have emerged in the course of the natural history of the human species "derive both from nature and from the *cultural break with nature*."[41] There is some justification for taking the position that the emancipatory interest may be immanent in the very utilization of our rational faculties. Habermas even suggests that the normative foundation for a critical (emancipatory) sociology may be "smuggled in surreptitiously" when we "mingle" two senses of the interest in enlightenment: on the one hand, "a relentless discursive validation of claims to validity" and, on the other, the interest in "practical change of established conditions."[42]   The question which Habermas posed concerning the relation of technology and democracy can now be viewed from the perspective of the development of a model which advances the unavoidable technical, practical and emancipatory interests of humankind.

As discussed above, Habermas finds significant parts of Marx's political economy outdated for an understanding of advanced capitalist societies. Nonetheless, he professes to draw inspiration from Marx, and it is not difficult to see that he is heavily indebted to Marxian insights in his conception of knowledge-constitutive interests. For Marx, as for Habermas, the natural history of the human species demonstrates that "*socially organized labor* is the specific way in which humans, in contradistinction to animals, reproduce their lives."[43]   Insofar as Marx incorporates this insight into his work, he is keenly aware of what Habermas refers to as the technical and practical aspects of the coordination necessary to the reproduction of the means for life.   However, while Marx senses the significance of the social nature of this reproduction, it is a great weakness of the Marxian analysis that the technical rationality implicit in the development of the productive forces is offered as the explanation for changes in the relations of production.   The problem for democracy is thus reduced to instrumental or purposive-rational action, and concerned with the organization of means or choices between alternatives.   It would appear that the presence of an interest in emancipation, without an accompanying clearly defined conception of the practical interest, is an insufficient basis for an emancipatory theory and may even subvert the aims of such a theory.   Habermas insists that there are other dimensions of learning that need to be considered.   There are good reasons, he says, for assuming "that learning processes also take place in the dimension of moral insight, practical knowledge, communicative action, and the consensual regulation of action conflicts - learning processes that are deposited in more mature forms of social integration, in new *productive relations*, and that in turn first make possible the introduction of new productive forces."[44]   Without developing Habermas' views, we can suggest that, while "culture" retains its place in the superstructure, the learning processes associated with the rationality implicit in the communicative process would appear to be necessary to the resolution of unresolved system problems which have their origin in the economy.

Marx, says Habermas, instinctively knew the meaning of the relationship between the instrumental action contained in work and the communicative processes of social interaction, and it was in fact this knowledge which informed his notion of critique. Nonetheless, Marx failed to recognize the importance of the insight for historical materialism, and this confusion in his own theoretical self-understanding led him to reduce interaction to work and to present them in their collapsed state as social practice (*Praxis*).[45] Despite the weakness in Marx's theory, Habermas by no means wants to abandon Marxism. In fact, it does not really matter that he finds parts of Marx's theories obsolete: for Habermas it is Marx's spirit and insight into the nature of human relationships which are important. It is for this reason that he sets out specifically to "reconstruct" historical materialism. "*Reconstruction*," he states, "signifies taking a theory apart and putting it back together again in a new form in order to attain more fully the goal it has set for itself."[46] It is in this sense that Habermas has undertaken the "second attempt to appropriate Weber in the spirit of Western Marxism ... inspired by the conception of communicative reason."[47]

Notes

1. See Jürgen Habermas, *The Theory of Communicative Action*, Vol. I, trans. Thomas McCarthy (Boston: Beacon, 1984), author's preface, pp.xxxix-xlii. Cf. Jürgen Habermas, *Der philosophische Diskurs der Moderne* (Frankfurt: Suhrkamp, 1985); Richard J. Bernstein, ed., *Habermas and Modernity* (Cambridge, Mass.: MIT, 1985).
2. Max Horkheimer and Theodor W. Adorno, *Dialectic of Enlightenment* (New York: Herder and Herder, 1972), p. 3.
3. Jürgen Habermas, "Technical Progress and the Social Life-World," in *Toward a Rational Society* (Boston: Beacon, 1971), p. 57.
4. *Ibid.*, pp. 57-58
5. *Ibid.*, p. 58.
6. Jürgen Habermas, "Technology and Science as 'Ideology'," in *Toward a Rational Society*, pp.100-2; also his *Legitimation Crisis* (Boston: Beacon, 1975), pp. 33-40.
7. See the discussion in Habermas, *Legitimation Crisis*, pp. 45-46 and *passim*. Habermas is discussing the appearance of economic crisis tendencies in advanced capitalist societies, but his arguments also support the view that these crisis tendencies may be indefinitely contained.
8. Habermas,"Technology and Science," p. 104.
9. Jürgen Habermas, *Theorie des kommunikativen Handelns* (Frankfurt: Suhrkamp, 1981), II, p. 448.
10. Habermas, "Technology and Science," p. 81.

108   Marie Fleming

11. Jürgen Habermas, "The Scientization of Politics and Public Opinion," in *Toward a Rational Society*, p. 62.

12. *Ibid.*, pp. 62-63.

13. *Ibid.*

14. *Ibid.*, pp. 63-65.

15. *Ibid.*, p. 63.

16. *Ibid.*, p. 65.

17. *Ibid.*, pp. 67-68.

18. *Ibid.*, p. 68.

19. A "civilization" is differentiated from a primitive society insofar as the former is characterized by the presence of state organization of political power, social-economic classes and a central world-view which takes on a power-legitimating function. See Habermas, "Technology and Science," p. 94.

20. *Ibid.*, pp. 95-97.

21. *Ibid.*, pp. 98-99.

22. *Ibid.*, pp. 99, 105.

23. *Ibid.*, p. 105.

24. *Ibid.*, pp. 111-112.

25. Habermas, "The Scientization of Politics," p. 66.

26. *Ibid.*, pp. 66-69.

27. *Ibid.*, pp. 68-69.

28. Jürgen Habermas, "The Classical Doctrine of Politics in Relation to Social Philosophy," in *Theory and Practice* (Boston: Beacon, 1973), pp. 41-44.

29. Habermas, *Theorie des kommunikativen Handelns*, II, esp. ch. VIII. Cf. *Legitimation Crisis, passim.*

30. Habermas, *The Theory of Communicative Action*, I, p. 183.

31. *Ibid.*, p. 66.

32. *Ibid.*, p. 241.

33. Habermas, "Technology and Science," p. 92.

34. Cf. Jürgen Habermas, "What is Universal Pragmatics?," in *Communication and the Evolution of Society* (Boston: Beacon, 1979), pp. 1-68; *The Theory of Communicative Action*, I, pp. 273-337.

35. Cf. Bernstein; for a discussion of questions related to Habermas' formal pragmatics see Marie Fleming, "Habermas, Marx and the Question of Ethics," in Axel Honneth and Albrecht Wellmer, eds., *Die Frankfurter Schule und die Folgen* (Berlin: Walter de Gruyter, 1986), pp. 139-150.

36. Habermas, "Technology and Science," p. 118.

37. *Ibid.*, pp. 118-119.

38. The first systematic statement of this conception was presented in Habermas' inaugural address to the University of Frankfurt in 1965;

published as appendix to his *Knowledge and Human Interests* (London: Heinemann, 1972).

39. Jürgen Habermas, "Some Difficulties in the Attempt to Link Theory and Practice," in *Theory and Practice*, pp. 7-9. Habermas' thesis is that the specific viewpoints from which we apprehend reality arise out of the natural history of the human species. My analysis is based upon a reformulation of this thesis: that the natural history of the human species gives rise to specific viewpoints from which we apprehend reality.

40. Habermas, "Some Difficulties," pp. 9, 15.

41. Habermas, *Knowledge and Human Interests*, Appendix, p. 312.

42. Habermas, "Some Difficulties," p. 15.

43. Jürgen Habermas, "Toward a Reconstruction of Historical Materialism," in *Communication and the Evolution of Society*, p. 131.

44. Jürgen Habermas, "Historical Materialism and the Development of Normative Structures," in *Communication and the Evolution of Society*, pp. 97-98.

45. Habermas, *Knowledge and Human Interests*, pp. 60-63.

46. Habermas, "Historical Materialism," p. 95.

47. Habermas, *Theorie des kommunikativen Handelns*, II, p. 448.

SHADES OF OPTIMISM:
SOVIET VIEWS ON SCIENCE AND MORALITY

László G. Jobbágy

At a time when the future of mankind depends upon our ability to empathize with other men, the ideas, beliefs and hopes of our supposed adversaries in the communist countries constitute an important concern for us. To listen with respect to our critics can benefit us in two ways: we can learn about them, and we can learn about ourselves. Readers who are not acquainted with Soviet literature on the problems of science, technology and morality would probably be astonished by the large number of books, articles and essays devoted to these issues. Because it is impossible in a short essay to review all of this material, I have selected certain typical viewpoints which are representative of the main Soviet approaches.

The most striking characteristic which one encounters in Soviet texts is their overwhelming sense of optimism. Western philosophers frequently consider "optimism" and "pessimism" to be superficial categories, irrelevant from the point of view of theoretical reflection or practical political action. As a doctrine and frame of mind, utopian optimism may neglect or distort crucial facts, while pessimism may perform the opposite function and prevent meaningful action. Soviet thinkers would dispute this approach. They would argue that theorists such as Hans Jonas, whose "ethics of responsibility" is intended to overcome both utopian optimism and pessimistic despair through a combination of "hope, fear, and modesty,"[1] are in fact only discouraging revolutionary action by suggesting its futility in face of impending disasters.[2]

Soviet authors believe that the main weakness of bourgeois social theory lies precisely in its inability to offer an "integral world-view." In other words, the incapacity to provide a "positive program," a "utopia" or a "vision," is said to indicate most clearly the spiritual crisis of bourgeois civilization. Although satisfaction of basic material needs is emphasized by all Soviet philosophers, the need for a *Weltanschauung* that integrates needs, desires, morality and actions - past, present and future - is also considered to be of primary importance in releasing the "spiritual power" that is mankind's "hope for the future."[3]

Soviet philosophers insist that their belief in communism is *not* a question of blind faith, but is based on true scientific and historical knowledge. Thus A. Arsenyev rejects any interpretation of communism as eschatology and points both to the determinants of human action and also to the need for a human determination of goals:

> the historical subject is determined in two opposite ways: from the past to the present (causal determination) and from the future to the present (goal determination). The former is expressed in the dependence of the subject upon the external world (necessity), the latter - in the dependence of the world upon the activity of the goal-positing subject (freedom). The degree of dominance held by the second way over the first could most probably be taken as a criterion, thereby a definition of historical progress (of course, not the sole criterion).[4]

In Arsenyev's view the essence of man is his capacity for "transcendence," a capacity which in turn depends upon ethical projection.

Soviet writers observe that bourgeois ideology has abandoned its youthful optimism and replaced it with "gloomy prophecies about the allegedly inevitable demise of civilization as a result of the uncontrollable development of production, technology and science."[5] In opposition to this bourgeois fatalism, the hopes elaborated by Soviet philosophers rest upon the epistemological premise that the universe is knowable. In his book, *Philosophy of Optimism*, B.G. Kuznetsov claims that the so-called "limits of knowledge" are simply "limits of specific laws that are replaced by other laws."[6] Thus "epistemological optimism," supplemented by a Hegelian interpretation of history, becomes "historical optimism." The Marxist notion of "restructuring social relations on revolutionary lines" further transforms the latter into "social optimism" and finally into "ethical optimism":

> Ethical optimism is a logical continuation of social optimism, generalising the simplest moral norms, the whole body of the working people's ethical experience, and their faith in the working man, in the triumph of justice.[7]

Many critics of Soviet Marxism, including Hans Jonas, believe that communist systems are underdeveloped versions of industrial societies and are therefore equally prone to the excesses of growth, consumption and waste. Soviet analysts reply that the current predominance of economic tasks means only that under objective historical influences "particular aspects of Marxism [were] promoted to the foreground."[8] Nevertheless,

> The substance of the matter is by no means located in the reduction of moral consciousness to the consciousness of the "economic individual." (This ... is one of the most widespread interpretations of Marxism in contemporary bourgeois literature.) The substance of the matter, in fact, lies in the elevation of moral consciousness itself by means of science to the vantage point of the *ethico-social* and *ethico-historical* view over society.[9]

In the Soviet interpretation, the principal obstacle to mankind's ethical development is capitalism, which prevents the world from entering a new era free from the old irrationalities, injustices and irresponsibilities. The new world which they anticipate would not be a paradise, free from contradictions, but they are confident that with a new system of social relations mankind will be prepared to meet new contradictions and challenges. With this general orientation of Soviet thought in mind, let us now consider the differences of emphasis which distinguish the contours of Soviet writing. For this purpose, I propose to group various opinions and concepts under three headings, which I shall call "Propaganda Optimism," "Historical Optimism" and "Cautious Optimism."

Propaganda Optimism

Soviet writings devoted to the simple propaganda of optimism are frequently published anonymously and are characterized by a gross oversimplification of problems, supported by quotations from party leaders and from Marx, Engels and Lenin. Their principal theme is that science and technology are wonderful under socialism, while under capitalism they are a "rapacious" malady of society and lead to disaster. A typical publication of this genre is the book *Capitalism, Socialism and Scientific and Technical Revolution*, published in the series entitled "The Library of Political Knowledge." The authors claim that scientific and technical progress aggravates capitalism's "general crisis," whereas socialism "gives full scope to revolutionary changes in science and technology in the interest of all working people."[10]
One of the most frequent claims of "propaganda optimism" is that under socialism science becomes a "direct productive force." What this appears to mean is that socialist societies are able to utilize science fully, whereas in capitalism scientific development is frustrated by the contradictory economic laws of the market. Capitalism displays "impotence" in its effort to integrate the different branches of science, the main obstacle to full-scale automation being suppression of inventions by monopolies.[11] One of the authors

writing these propaganda works claims that "Socialism alone provides the necessary horizons for the development of science and technology,"[12] the result of which will be an automated world wherein "Man is replaced by scientific knowledge embodied in machines (apparatuses, instruments, etc.) which effect 'conscious' or 'rational' acts."[13] Propaganda optimism speaks of "subjugating nature's forces"[14] for the purposes of production and expresses simplistic confidence in the miracle-working character of modern science. As Ye.K. Fyodorov remarks, "Never throughout history, has science failed to solve a problem confronting mankind."[15] Socialist society is said to generate rapid economic growth, "which spares the working people constant upheavals, knows no crises or unemployment, and ensures the planned and balanced development of the productive forces."[16] Such claims exclude the possibility of any moral doubts concerning the role of science and technology in a planned, socialist society. Thus, Abid Sadykov's statement could serve as the *ars poetica* of propaganda optimism: "The very conception of 'science' is synonymous with progress. Scientific development therefore cannot have unfavourable consequences."[17]

Historical Optimism

The type of Soviet publication which I have designated under the heading of "propaganda optimism" is clearly targeted upon a relatively unsophisticated readership. The optimistic outlook of the largest portion of Soviet academic writing is more solidly grounded in the central themes of what is called "historical materialism." This concept originates in Hegelian philosophy. Following Marx's critique of Hegel, however, the development of "objective spirit" is here replaced by development of the actual man, as the real, historical subject. Viewed from this perspective, the meaning of science, technology and morality is intimately tied to historically evolving social relations. The optimism of this theory is based on trends and tendencies of consciousness and social relations, which are revealed by critical inquiries into the laws of social development and then projected into the future.

Soviet philosophers claim that the separation of human consciousness, into the two distinct spheres of science and morality, began with the appearance of class-divided societies and has continued ever since. As a result, both science and morality are considered to be historically determined manifestations of given class relations. Moreover, it is argued that the final split of knowledge into knowledge of things (science) and knowledge of man (morality) occurred parallel with development of the capitalist system of production relations in sixteenth- and seventeenth-century Europe. This final division however, does not imply for Soviet theorists - as it would for positivist thinkers - that "science reflects reality whereas morality does not."[18]

In the view of Soviet theorists, the fragmentation of human reality and consciousness has brought serious adverse consequences for man. On the one hand, "Mankind is being enlisted in the service of science and is becoming the obedient executor and even the slave of its despotic design."[19] On the other hand, capitalist morality, because of its class content, endorses and perpetuates this subordination of man to the products of his labor. Nevertheless, Soviet authors believe that social relations can be positively altered and the unity of consciousness restored on a higher level. The new and integrated world which they anticipate is supposed to eliminate the "distinction between the two modes of investigating man and nature in terms of the existent and the imperative."[20] Thus, the assumed advantage of Marxist philosophy over its bourgeois counterparts is its determination to reject the "idolization of any given institutionalized form of human activity"[21] and to contemplate transcendence of bourgeois division between the "is" and the "ought."

Since the primary obstacle to overcoming the fragmented and alienated existence of man is thought to be the capitalist mode of production and private property relations, abolition of these conditions is considered to be the minimum requirement for change. Consequently, radically transformed social relations provide the foundation for the "all-round development of the individual," which is the *sine qua non* of historical optimism. The meaning of the term is synonymous with Marx's view of the "emancipation of man" and implies the "free development of all the capacities of the integrated individual."[22]   The first step towards this ideal is the "emancipation of labour and its conversion into a means of broadening and enriching the entire life process of the workers."[23]   The nature of consumption is also altered, and both asceticism and consumerism are rejected as "one-sided modes of existence."[24]   The realization of the individuals' creative powers and abilities further includes:

> an increasingly high level of education; the need for comradely relations and a wide range of human contacts; the need to realize one's individuality and to develop an integrated personality able and willing to respond to others; the need for physical activity and close contact with nature, and finally the need for beauty in every form.[25]

Hence, the "all-round, harmonious development of the individual" becomes the goal of communist civilization, "the first civilization in history" to extend these values "not only to humanity as a whole but also to each individual."[26]

In contrast with these prevailing themes of historical optimism, Soviet writers on science and morality discern two different schools of bourgeois philosophy which are said to dominate Western consciousness. The first school is thought to overemphasize the role of science in its craving to save capitalism through "technomania"; the second and more recent school of bourgeois thought, whose adherents are overwhelmed by a sense of capitalism's decline, extends its apocalyptic vision to encompass the entire world and mistakenly blames science for all of capitalism's woes. As a reflection of the general consciousness, the spiritual life of the bourgeois citizen is said to be hopelessly torn between "outward well-being," achieved through the self-indulgence of hedonistic consumption, and the reality of atomized and alienated existence, a consequence of the bankrupt capitalist mode of production.[27] Soviet authors insist that Western philosophy, consciously or unconsciously, obscures the real causes of modern problems and so prevents the masses from coming to grips with reality. Sergei Popov is even less generous in his account of pessimistic bourgeois thinkers:

> All these gloomy pictures of the future, the allegedly inevitable global disasters and catastrophes are meant to intimidate the people, to blunt their minds and paralyze their will.[28]

Soviet exponents of historical optimism are in general agreement that Western ideology is fragmented and exhausted, incapable of viewing the world in its wholeness. Capitalist pessimism is justified insofar as it is reflective of capitalist reality. In opposition to this Western pessimism, however, Soviet writers contend that Marxist-Leninist philosophy offers a viable alternative. The optimism of the Marxist-Leninist world-view is founded on the morality and creativity of the working people; and on this foundation Soviet philosophers propose a radical transformation of social relations and anticipate that social planning will effect a reunification of human consciousness and human *praxis*.

Cautious Optimism

By use of the term "historical optimism" I have classified that group of Soviet writers who most forcefully argue that the march of history is in the direction of human emancipation through a planned reconciliation of the objective needs of scientific cognition with the human needs of society. There are, however, differentiations within the trend of historical optimism; some of the writers in this category are more *cautious* than others about how "social laws" or "historical necessity" should be interpreted. Thus "cautious optimism" can be distinguished from less discriminating optimism through its tendency to be relatively more critical of the presumed benefits of science.

In his book, *The World of Man in the World of Nature*, for example, I. Laptev takes scientists to task for intellectual arrogance and criticizes their "unbound faith in technology" and their unquestioning "conviction that technology will rework nature in the best possible way."[29] The Lithuanian philosopher, Jacovas Minkevicius, in an essay analyzing the relation between nature and culture, states that "the present-day level of society's development has clearly shown the incorrectness of the absolutization of [scientific] progress."[30] Ivan Frolov has questioned "the idea of unlimited research,"[31] and E. Solovyov has similarly been skeptical of science's messianic ambitions.[32] Solovyov is one Soviet philosopher who acknowledges the problems inherent in the institutional autonomy of science and who warns that "ethically oriented control is needed not for the sake of science, but for controlling the social organization of science and its relation with technology and [the] economy."[33] A. Arsenyev shares these concerns: he concedes that science serves human emancipation by allowing men to master the "world of things"; but he also notes that science subordinates men to material goals, resulting in "the dehumanization of human relations." From this point of view, science itself "turns out to be immoral."[34] In order to counter this tendency, Arsenyev demands a reorganization of the Soviet educational system with the purpose of placing more emphasis upon education in ethics.[35]

Like historical optimism, cautious optimism sees the purpose of social progress in the "emancipation of man." However, it is emphasized here that the "all-round and harmonious development of the individual" must also include "moral progress."[36] This moral progress is incompatible with the value relativism of "conformist and pragmatist maxims ('the end justifies the means')."[37] As Otar Dzhioev writes, it is moral progress which gives meaning to history:

> The problem of the meaning of history is the problem of realizing values which are ultimately universal values. In order that history have a meaning, it is not enough that it be only a law-like process, it should also lead to moral progress.[38]

This emphasis on human values has far-reaching political implications. If the making of history presupposes fully developed individuals, with a shared commitment to universal values, the implication must be that it is no longer enough to replace the "creativity of the masses" with the creativity of an "expert" bureaucracy. Thus Arsenyev concludes that the individual's ethics is only distantly dependent on "historical forms of culture and social relations" and is more directly related to ethical ideals encountered through personal contacts. It is through personal relations that universal values are determined; and the universality of personal relations requires, in turn, a socialist process of liberalization.[39]

Still another difference between the "cautious" and the less discriminating optimists is the willingness of the former occasionally to praise bourgeois theorists for their assessment of global problems. Thus Laptev, in a commentary upon the reports issued by the Club of Rome, makes the following comment:

> Analyzing them, one cannot but feel profound respect for the humanist standpoints of their authors and welcome the noble quest of scientists concerned for the future destinies of mankind.40

These shades of difference in emphasis are not fundamental, but neither are they without significance. In the writings of "cautious optimists" ethics has been accorded greater social significance, while science has correspondingly been treated with greater circumspection. For writers of this approach, the true and proper ground for optimism is not simply faith in history or in man, but also a conviction that man will be able to identify his own limits and to act accordingly. Determination of the human limits to science and technology presupposes social and political relations which will permit man to achieve self-control in order that he might more adequately control the products of his thought and his labor. Human progress requires transcendence of capitalism and alienation.

Conclusions

This brief survey of the "shades of optimism" in Soviet writing suggests the need to address at least two important questions. First, do science and morality play a different role in Soviet society than they do in the West? And second, is Soviet philosophy really capable of addressing the problems of modernity?

Many Western observers believe that the Soviet Union is far less reservedly committed to the cause of science than any other country in the world. The strength of this commitment provokes fears - particularly after the disaster at Chernobyl - that Soviet behavior may become increasingly irresponsible and dangerous. There is certainly no disputing the fact that Soviet ideology places great hope in the potential of science, a hope most directly expressed in propaganda references to the "Scientific and Technical Revolution," which is said to characterize the current period of history. But it is also clear from the ideas which I have examined that Soviet writers have diverse opinions and are not one-dimensionally committed to "technomania." It is true that even the more "cautious" philosophers are not so opposed to science and technology as certain of their Western counterparts. Yet it is equally true that these writers expose and openly question the alleged excesses of science and of scientists. Even the more conventional historical optimists declare that scientific goals must be subjected to the "objectives of the owners of the means of production,"41 which in the Soviet Union is supposed to imply subordination to the "interests of the working people."

The real problem is not some Soviet "cult of science." Rather it is the gap between ideals and reality and the resulting inability of the Soviet system to realize the promises of its own ideology. The central fact is that the "working people" have precisely no control over social processes. Indeed, upon reading the works of the "cautious optimists" one is pressed to inquire whether even the Communist Party, with its powerful apparatus of planning and control, has succeeded in supervising scientific research and the resulting application of technology. From this perspective, it does appear legitimate to question the extent to which ethical and political constraints upon science have the prospect of becoming as effective in the Soviet Union as might theoretically be possible in the more pluralist societies of the West.

This consideration leads me to the second question, which concerns the ability of Soviet philosophy to grasp and respond to the problems of modernity. To my mind it is clear that Marxism, as a theoretical system, does possess some clear advantages over contemporary Western thought. First, it approaches the world in a holistic fashion, striving for the integration of different scientific disciplines. Second, its historical method brings together past, present and future. And finally, it appeals for technical rationality and social justice simultaneously, thus seeking to unite the "true" with the "good." Marxism aspires to be a universal and comprehensive economic and social theory. For this reason, however, it is all the more remarkable that Marxism contains one decisive weakness in the sense that it neither has, nor even realizes the need for, a political theory. Marx did not write a political theory of socialist society, and Soviet philosophers have never noticed that it was even missing. Thus politics is conventionally reduced in Soviet writing to economics. And economics, in the Soviet Union as elsewhere, has less to do with ethics than with relations of power.

Politicians - even Soviet politicians, who feel compelled to present themselves as theorists - know very well that guns are more important than theory. That is why the Soviet Union excels in production of nuclear weapons and not in consumer goods, to say nothing of philosophy. "Economizing" our understanding of the world does nothing to promote human understanding in either personal or international relations. And it is equally clear that war between two "socialist" countries (China and Vietnam), as well as Soviet aggression against other "socialist" countries, cannot be explained either by property relations or by economics.

It is this lack of political theory which helps to account for the short-sightedness of some Soviet propagandists who hold capitalism exclusively accountable for the present state of the world. Unless Soviet theorists realize that capitalism signifies not only the enslavement of man by "things," but also a step towards emancipating man through political liberation, they will always have a distorted picture of the true meaning of capitalism. Moreover, without an adequate political theory they will never understand why the abolition of private property relations did not, of itself, bring about a socialist society in the Soviet Union. Nor will they understand that paternalistic redistribution of goods is not emancipation, but only a lower form of social intercourse. The political liberation of individuals is the fundamental phase in the "all-round development of man"; and all other aspects of social emancipation, including the control of science and the exercise of morality, are subject to this condition.

It is the reality of political life in the West, however constrained it may be, that has caused private capitalist monopolies to become habituated to a regime of state regulation and to forget the glorious past when they could freely subordinate the public interest to the private. Soviet critics are perfectly correct when they point out that restraints on monopoly power in the metropolitan countries of capitalism do nothing to discourage its exercise elsewhere in the world. It is also beyond doubt that the abolition of private property relations had (and still has) the potential for creating a more favorable environment for the emancipation of man in the "socialist" countries. The fact remains, however, that replacing private monopolies with the universal monopoly of an uncontrolled state bureaucracy has nothing to do with the "all-round development of the workers." The current state of Soviet society affords an instructive example of where this kind of "emancipation" leads.

The Soviet theory of social emancipation, with its traditional disregard for social diversity and politics, is inevitably marked by the historical context in which the country underwent forced industrialization in the 1930s. Isolated from the West, Soviet politicians had no choice but to subscribe to the Stalinist ideology of a besieged fortress, committed to "socialism in one country" and the authoritarian practices which it entailed. However, Soviet Marxist philosophers cannot allow themselves to be deceived by such shallow propaganda. They must realize that capitalism is the last "socio-economic formation" that could begin as a national project. Precisely because of capitalism's success, there is no longer even "hunting and gathering" in one country. It is this consideration which encourages me to believe that there is a real potential for partnership in finding mutually acceptable solutions to global problems confronting capitalism and socialism alike.

The global structure of human civilization, which emerged spontaneously long before capitalism, is the structure of power. No country within this structure can unilaterally alter it. Attempts at isolation can only be temporary. To be "ethical" or "peaceful," for a single state, ultimately means being eliminated by a stronger state. Today "peace" inevitably means preparation for the next war. Neither aggressor nor defender can be meaningfully separated in this structure: in fact, they are bound up with each other. Clearly, this situation cannot continue indefinitely, and the "sword of Damocles" has to be lifted from over the head of mankind. If one accepts the view of those Soviet philosophers who anticipate the "moral progress" of mankind, then one may also countenance the elimination of this horror through the consent and political cooperation of all nations. The major factor which could interfere with this potential for a political commitment to universal human values is the tendency of Soviet officialdom to disregard and deny the significance of politics in the life of the individual. Few Soviet philosophers would presume to make this argument explicitly. Nevertheless, their emphasis upon the "all-round" development of socialist citizens is at least an implicit critique of the Soviet bureaucracy and its tendency to subordinate citizenship to "science," and "moral progress" to the objectives of power. One may disagree with particular conclusions of Soviet philosophers, but such disagreement need not prevent one from sharing their optimism and their faith in humanity, or from respecting their devotion to humanist causes and their growing awareness of the global effects of science.

As I indicated at the beginning of this essay, there are numerous Western analysts who would consider the optimism of Soviet writings to be both unfounded and ultimately dangerous. Many would claim that such hopes as I have discussed here, including my own, are based upon longings which are impossible to realize, as history allegedly demonstrates. In this regard, however, I am reminded of the Soviet scientist G.F. Khilmi, who once commented that life emerges as the "dialectical negation of both the Second Law of Thermodynamics and the Law of Organizational Degradation."[42] This condition implies that man is forever set against the impossible. To face the impossible, therefore, does not seem to be a new task for mankind, nor should it be viewed as reason for pessimism. On the contrary, it is our permanent historical condition. Besides, we know that the impossible is what challenges life and imparts meaning to its struggles. Thus, to attempt the impossible is a duty, worthy of human beings. Those who still lack practice in this vitally important activity are encouraged to read Lewis Carroll's *Through the Looking-Glass*:

"I can't believe that!" said Alice.
"Can't you?" the Queen said in a pitying tone.
"Try again: draw a long breath, and shut your eyes."
Alice laughed. "There's no use trying," she said:
"one can't believe impossible things."
"I daresay you haven't had much practice," said the Queen.
"When I was your age, I always did it for half-an-hour a day.
Why, sometimes I've believed as many as six impossible
things before breakfast."[43]

Notes

1. Hans Jonas, *The Imperative of Responsibility* (Chicago: The University of Chicago Press, 1984), p. 201.

2. T.I. Oizerman, "Historical Materialism and the Ideology of 'Technical Pessimism'," in *Philosophy and the Ecological Problems of Civilization*, ed. A.D. Ursul, trans. H. Cambell Creighton (Moscow: Progress, 1983), p. 360.

3. Ivan Frolov, *Man-Science-Humanism: A New Synthesis* (Moscow: Progress, 1986), p. 336.

4. A. Arsenyev, "The Relationship Between Science and Morality (Philosophical Aspects)," in *Science and Morality* (Moscow: Progress, 1975), p. 183.

5. S.I. Popov, "Optimistic and Pessimistic Interpretations of the Social Process," in *Civilization, Science, Philosophy*, ed. T. Perfilyeva (Moscow: USSR Academy of Sciences, 1983), pp. 239-240.

6. B.G. Kuznetsov, *Philosophy of Optimism* (Moscow: Progress, 1977), pp. 15-16.

7. S.I. Popov, *Socialism and Optimism* (Moscow: Progress, 1977), p. 283.

8. Frolov, p. 241.

9. E. Solovyov, "Knowledge, Faith and Morality," in *Science and Morality*, p. 129.

10. *Capitalism, Socialism and Scientific and Technical Revolution* (Moscow: Progress, 1983), p. 45.

11. *Ibid.*, p. 125

12. M.G. Chepikov, *The Integration of Science* (Moscow: Progress, 1978), p. 245.

13. *Ibid.*, p. 224.

14. *Capitalism, Socialism*, p. 21.

15. Ye. K. Fyodorov, "From a Description of Nature to the Planning of Nature," in *Society and the Environment* (Moscow: Progress, 1983), p. 83.

16. E. Plimak and A. Volodin, *The Way Society Develops* (Moscow: Progress, 1981), p. 120.

17. Abid Sadykov, "Science and Society," *Social Sciences*, 1 (1973), 161.

18. A. Alexandrov, "A Scientific Approach to Morality," in *Science and Morality*, p. 35. See also Drobnitsky in *ibid.*, pp. 206-207.

19. E. Ilyenkov, "Humanism and Science," in *Science and Morality*, p. 270.

20. O. Drobnitsky, "Scientific Truth and Moral Good," in *ibid.*, p. 200.

21. Ilyenkov, p. 272.

122   László G. Jobbágy

22. Valentin Tolstykh, "Communist Civilization as a New Mode of Human Life," in *Civilization and the Historical Process*, ed. Y.K. Pletnikov, trans. Cynthia Carlile (Moscow: Progress, 1983), p. 376.

23. *Ibid.*, p. 382.

24. *Ibid.*, p. 384.

25. *Ibid.*, p. 385.

26. Lyudmila Buyeva, "Man as an End in Himself Within Social Development," in *ibid.*, p. 159.

27. Y. Sogomonov and P. Landesman, *Nihilism Today* (Moscow: Progress, 1977), p. 131.

28. Popov, *Socialism and Optimism*, p. 201

29. I. Laptev, *The World of Man in the World of Nature* (Moscow: Progress, 1979), pp. 207-208.

30. Jacovas Minkevicius, "Interaction between 'Cultura' and 'Natura'," in *Civilization, Science, Philosophy*, p. 78.

31. Frolov, p. 153.

32. Solovyov, p. 94.

33. E. Solovyov, "Nauka, etika i gumanizm," *Voprosy filosofii*, 8 (1973), 105.

34. Arsenyev, p. 176.

35. *Ibid.*, p. 180.

36. Grigori Kvasov, "Sociology and Moral Progress," *Social Sciences*, 3 (1978), 130.

37. *Ibid.*, p. 131.

38. Otar Dzhioev, *Priroda istoricheskoi neobkhodimosti* (Tbilisi: Mecniereba, 1967), p. 132.

39. Arsenyev, p. 187.

40. Laptev, p. 168.

41. L.I. Abalkin, *The Economic System of Socialism* (Moscow: Progress, 1980), p. 42.

42. G.F. Khilmi, "Organizovannost' biosfery i kosmicheskaia tendentzia k khaosu," in *Resursy biosfery na territorii SSSR*, ed. I.P. Gerasimov (Moscow: Nauka, 1971), p. 43.

43. Lewis Carroll, *Through the Looking-Glass* (London: Oxford University Press, 1982), p. 177.

PART II

PROSPECTS FOR DEMOCRACY

LIBERAL DEMOCRACY AND THE PROBLEM

OF TECHNOLOGY

Jerry Weinberger

For the most part, it seems, liberal democratic theory has had little to say about the "problem of technology." This is not to say that liberals have not been concerned with the moral and political problems generated by advancing technology. Indeed, in American universities whole new academic specialties have arisen to treat the ethical dilemmas generated by technological advances and by the increasingly technical orientation of business, industry, and medicine. Today's philosophy Ph.D.s can look forward to gainful employment as advisors to corporate boardrooms and as practising "bioethicists." But to these new specialties there is no problem of technology that cannot be confronted with the language and concepts familiar to the liberal view of the world: technology presents a problem because it poses new questions of individual rights, such as the right to privacy, the right to life, the right to free choice over one's reproductive functions, and so forth. For liberals technology is a danger, to be sure - one threatening humanity itself if one considers the nuclear peril and the degradation of the environment. But it is a danger posed somehow from without; that is, it is conceived as the unintended consequences or "externalities" of the well-meant and legitimate pursuit of happiness and security, or as a friendly but rambunctious genie released from the atom or from nature in general. It seems that technology in no way forces liberals to rethink their views of liberty, freedom, politics and society, let alone to wonder if these views are themselves somehow technological. For instance, neither of the two most influential recent accounts of liberal justice, Rawls' *A Theory of Justice* and Nozick's *Anarchy, State, and Utopia*, has anything to say about technology.

But to see technology as "just another problem," as by no means fundamental, is to miss its obvious character as a horizon within which every other problem comes to light. For the possibilities of technology constitute not just any modern world view; they refract our experience of any possible world, whether it be past, present, or in the future.   It is impossible to conceive of modernity without reflecting on technology.   Moreover, although as moderns we live in the possibilities of boundless choice and conquest, we cannot choose our modernity.   Thus we cannot live outside the power of technology, which means that however familiar or subdued it may be, it is also menacing and strange because it is never wholly within our grasp.   Our age of so much freedom is stalked by forebodings of oppression by forces beyond our control.   To see technology as just something we need to tame is to miss the ubiquity of technology; it is to ignore its character as a destiny, to hide the fact that "the essence of technology is by no means anything technological."[1]   But if we miss the essence of technology we cannot hope to understand just how it is a problem and a danger.   Liberal thought seems superficial in the face of technology, and having quoted from Heidegger we suspect that alternatives to liberal thought offer a more promising grasp.   However, for these alternatives the problem or question of technology involves liberal democracy itself.   Therefore, if technology is a problem, then so too is liberalism.   It is not just that liberal democracy is wedded to the promise of economic growth and that such growth is impossible without the ever expanding and potentially harmful power of technology.[2]   Rather, the relationship between liberalism and technology is said to be deeper than this obvious dependence, which is, after all, acknowledged proudly by liberals themselves.   For the nonliberal analysts of technology, the very principles of liberal democracy embody technology, are blind to its essence,   and thus merely serve its danger.

To speak very briefly, the argument goes as follows.   With the rise of modern science, the world was conceived as a tripartite whole, whose parts are: the demonstrably knowable ground that renders every object manipulable; the manipulable objects; and the human subject who discovers the ground and who, in manipulating the objects, endows them with "values." Since the values do not belong to them essentially, every natural object stands neutrally between the necessity of its natural ground and the freedom of subjective human art, between "fact" and "value."   But because of the difference between fact and value, it becomes possible for the being of subjectivity to be understood in terms of the manipulable objects it discovers: freedom and manipulability are akin when compared to the necessity of natural ground.   Modern science was technological from the outset, because for it "to be" is, for every practical purpose, "to be manipulable." And liberal democracy is scientific because its conception of the person is grounded on, or reflects, the scientific conception of subjectivity as a worldless, isolated and independent ego, defined concretely in terms of those objects over which it has mastery, beginning with, but not necessarily ending with, itself. The essence of technology animates the very heartbeat of liberalism - its individualism.

Now the problematic consequences of technology and liberalism are interpreted differently according to whether the critique disclosing them inclines to the right or the left of the political spectrum. For the right, liberal individualism isolates the human person from every location that gives life depth and meaning. If to be is to be manipulable, and if the medium for exchanging the products of such manipulation is money, then for liberals there is literally nothing that money cannot buy. Technological liberal democracy thus transforms human experience into an endless business transaction, with every human possibility or value being interchangeable and thus ultimately the same. The phenomena of art, politics, and the gods are flattened in being understood as the objects of scientific knowledge, in the light of which they become merely useful; real creativity, reverence, loyalty and rootedness, and astonishment and estrangement are obliterated from human life, which becomes the stage merely for the mass man or the last man.

Like the right, the left worries that technological liberal democracy abstracts the individual from the social whole of which it is a part and within which its life gets meaning. But for the left, the danger of technology is not the disappearance of rank, order and mystery from the community of life. Rather, the left argues that the techno-scientific project at once hides the possibilities of human practice, understood not as political art but rather as free communication between equals, with forms of domination, and legitimizes those forms with its power to satisfy the "individual's" infinite variety of material needs.[3] The infinity of these needs, once thought by Marx to provide wholeness to individual human life,[4] have become in the technological age the chains that bind real human freedom.

For both left and right technology does not have to oppress or distort the possibilities of human experience. Rather, when we grasp it as a destiny we can let it fulfill our human being. Thus the left claims that when social forms catch up with and adapt to the full promise of technological bounty, human life can be constituted by "discourse" rather than by force and exploitation. And Heidegger, to cite an instance on the right, argues that while technology deepens the forgetting of Being that began with Socratic philosophy, as technology ripens it will in fact turn men toward their own relationship to Being and so to Being itself. In either case, however, technology cannot overcome itself while in its liberal garb, which as ideology or as oblivion of Being is unaware of its merely historical role in the course of human life. To see technology for what it is, and thus to participate in its jumping over its darkening shadow, is not possible within the bounds of liberal thought. Technology will call forth either critique of ideology or *Gelassenheit*, but not talk about individual rights and dangers to representative government.

So for liberal democrats, and I count myself as one, there appears to be the following dilemma: There is something about modern technology that makes it different from the many practical problems facing us today, perhaps even different from the great problems identified by the tradition of political philosphy, which, as it embraced modern science, stands accused as the real source of the problem of technology.   But if it is a special problem, then it seems that we must reject the principles of liberal democracy, or at least find them insufficient for grappling with the most important phenomenon, and danger, of modernity.   However, liberals face such a dilemma only if the problem of technology is what the nonliberal critics of technology say it is. To refute these critics would require showing that the rationalism of modern liberalism is different from scientism, that, while they are linked, liberalism is not simply identical with the project of modern science and is thus not within its power as a destiny.   This is indeed a tall order, but it is not impossible to discover some directions for thinking about it from the first liberals, who, because they fashioned the liberal tradition, neither took its principles for granted nor were charmed by the terms of its presentation.5

    There certainly seems to be no clearer connection between liberalism and the scientific project than can be found in Hobbes, the founder of representative government.   It is true that we cannot see Hobbes' intention if we do not grant that the principles of his political science are independent of his account of natural science - that they derive ultimately from the teaching of the human heart, which can in its own way be available to reason.6   But Hobbes argued that this teaching is neither self-evident nor always heard. On the contrary, until his political science it had been misunderstood or ignored.   And for Hobbes the new science of nature, or at least a set of opinions reflecting it, was the best means for transcending the traditional perspectives - especially the perspectives of religion and everyday citizenship - that obfuscated the truths of the heart.7   As Hobbes describes individuals in the state of nature, they need not be philosophers or natural scientists to recognize the rights and laws of nature.   In fact, Hobbes' state of nature does not describe what men know in actual life, where they have always been formed by some false or misguided moral view.   Only when we know from science that, contrary to religion, philosophic tradition, and common political opinion, there is no *summum bonum* , will some come to see man's natural condition for what it really is.   That is, only the scientific construction of the state of nature can disclose the reality beneath the natural propensity of men to live in worlds fashioned by partial and dangerous opinions. Therefore, it should not be surprising that Hobbes does not expect all individuals spontaneously to be or act rationally: his political science is not directed to all individuals, but rather to "he that is to govern a whole nation."8   For Hobbes the light of science will shine indirectly, by way of illuminating the art that can fashion individuals so that they will behave as if they were enlightened by science. By means of this art that transcends the perspective of the citizen, those who do not transcend this perspective can be made into a new kind of citizen, one better than human experience has ever known. For Hobbes, scientific politics is not a deliberative activity in which the new citizen will be involved, but the ground of an art that forms him. While modern science is the gateway to Hobbes' teaching about natural man, rather than its substance, his political teaching as a whole is indeed a form of scientific instrumentalism.

The latter point is clear when we realize that the Hobbesian citizen is construed by Hobbes to be artificial. One could in fact argue that Hobbes describes the origin of government from an act of consent in a prepolitical "state of nature" in order to guarantee precisely that citizens and the sovereign who represents them will be artificial. His argument is roughly as follows: Having gained access to and listened to our hearts, we realize that prior to any government or positive law, or in a condition of nature, individuals are equal because each is able to destroy every other; no one has a natural right to absolute power over another. Each individual is capable of choosing his own ends and has an equal hope to attain them. But when one individual's ends are the same as another's they become enemies and mistrustful of each other. And since the most reasonable way for each to secure himself is to anticipate and prevent threats from an enemy, reason tempts individuals "by force, or wiles, to master the persons of all men [they] can, so long, till [they] see no other power great enough to endanger [them]: And this is no more than [their] own conservation requireth, and is generally allowed." Moreover, because some individuals simply love the pleasure of conquest, men who are by nature satisfied with more moderate security are compelled to this mastery of others. And finally, because each individual is equally able to choose his own ends, men come to be convinced that there are few as wise as themselves. Therefore, men come to be offended by "signs of contempt, or undervaluing," and hence attempt to extort "greater value" from others. Thus from competition, mistrust, and glory, each individual in the state of nature is at war with all other individuals. Despite these several causes of conflict, each individual has the natural right to do whatever is necessary to preserve himself. Under such conditions even the moderate and reasonable cannot but act as do the lovers of power and glory, for which reason the state of nature is a condition in which life is "solitary, poor, nasty, brutish, and short" for all.[9]

Reflection on the state of nature discloses the dictates of reason, which clearheaded men are motivated to follow by the fear of violent death and by the hope for "commodious living." According to Hobbes, once these two passions are freed from false opinions they can be trusted to sober even the most dangerous and irrational persons. Moved by fear and hope, individuals create government when all consent to transfer to one man, or to an assembly of men, what they have discovered to be their right to do whatever is necessary for their self-preservation. By consent, then, every individual authorizes a sovereign to do for himself what he has a right to do in the state of nature but which, when exercised by prepolitical individuals, frustrates the very end of that right, self-preservation. When only one single power maintains this right in actual use, every individual can be secure in the knowledge that others will keep the contracts that bind and facilitate every human relationship. They can be secure because the existence of a right in use to do whatever is necessary, with no other such right in use to dilute and frustrate it, is a sufficient sanction to guarantee that individuals will obey the law of nature that enjoins men to keep their contracts and covenants. By virtue of authorization, the sovereign's actions, which are by right whatever is necessary to guarantee obedience to the laws of nature, become the actions of the subjects.[10]

The object of Hobbes' political science is to reinterpret our actual political experience on the model presented in the account of the state of nature. Ultimately, what citizenship can become depends upon how actual citizenship is interpreted, for actual citizenship - at least before the advent of Hobbes' political science - is not characterized by the rational consent of individuals in the state of nature. If it were, there would be no need for Hobbes to have written his book in the first place. Now there is no doubt that Hobbes conceives the citizen represented by the sovereign to be a formalized abstraction of something like the natural individual. But even in the account of the state of nature, depicting a time before consent to government, the individual is presented in a double way: on the one hand the individual is defined abstractly, by formal rights that determine a range of phenomena over which he has actual or potential dominion, and on the other hand the individual is described concretely, as being moved by particular opinions about substantive practical ends, opinions that can be construed as superior to others and that can be understood to involve shared moral experience. Thus men come to conflicts not just from competition and mistrust springing from scarcity, but also from "glory." In describing individuals in the state of nature, Hobbes assumes the abstract posture of the political scientist, but the abstraction involved in describing the individual in terms of formal rights is quite evident *as* an abstraction. Hobbes does not assume the abstraction in describing the individual; rather, he aims to justify it by a concrete argument about politics and justice.

Hobbes' intention was to put an end to the terrible consequences of political life - especially insofar as it was agitated by religious enthusiasm and traditional morality - by transforming our interpretation of just what government is. This transformation required replacing the traditional concepts of political rule, especially the concept of the regime, with the concepts of representation and sovereign power. Put very briefly, a regime was understood to consist in the rule over the political whole by a part, for the sake of the ruling part's conception of the human good. By contrast, sovereign power stands not for the ruling good of some part, or for the common good determined by some part, but for the unmediated common good of all. In providing for such a common good, government secures commodious living without determining the ends of commodious living, controversy about which Hobbes believed was at the root of most political evil. And such a common good is understood to be *represented* by sovereign power because the sovereign acts for each and all in doing what they have a prepolitical right to do but cannot do for themselves, which is to do whatever is necessary to secure the conditions for self-preservation and commodious living. But there is a more important sense in which the sovereign "represents" the individual and common good: in acting for the good of each individual, the sovereign *represents* particular opinions about the good that cannot themselves determine the common good, but that also cannot be wholly separated from any act of sovereign political power. This point calls for explanation and elaboration.

Even though government's task is not to determine for individuals their particular ends of life, it is still inevitable that any public deed of a sovereign will tend to some particular end rather than another, will answer to some opinion about the goodness or badness of such ends, and will thus benefit some individuals more than others. In fact, disputes about the justice or injustice of such benefits (or harms) are what Hobbes aimed to extirpate from political life. The task of his political science was to separate the public character of sovereign deeds from their measurability by such ends, opinions, and benefits. Therefore, his account of representative government turns on the distinction between the artificial opinions of the abstract, formal individual and the natural opinions of the concrete, actual individual: it distinguishes between the natural individual who is liberated by government and the same individual in the artificial role of represented citizen. By focussing on the origins of government from the need all natural individuals have to escape the prepolitical war of all against all, Hobbes argues that sovereign power can satisfy this need that all share equally only when its sovereignty is absolute, that is, when in doing whatever it judges necessary to guarantee covenants and contracts between citizens its deeds cannot be judged to be just or unjust. Sovereign power cannot exist, and so prevent the horrors of the state of nature, where its word is not the last. In acting to secure peace and preservation for the natural individual, whatever the sovereign does or opines in a particular instance is an individual's own, even if it conflicts with that individual's concrete, actual, opinion about particular ends. But this is to say that the sovereign stands for natural individuals, who always have particular opinions they hold to be as true as they are dear, only by speaking and acting for them as artificial citizens, that is, by representing the opinions of the natural individual. Lest this seem an arbitrary interpretation, we note Hobbes' explicit claim that in generating political power from the consent of individuals in a state of nature, one individual, or an assembly of individuals, is transformed from a natural individual into an "artificial man."11

If the sovereign is artificial, then so too are those who empower him to the extent that the sovereign's concrete deeds and opinions are their own. In the transformation that creates sovereign power, the sovereign's natural opinions become artificial, which means that they are taken to be necessary for the common need for self-preservation, rather than persuasive because of their particular content regarding more specific ends. And natural individuals become citizens, much smaller artificial men, whose opinions are just those of the sovereign.12   With such transformations, sovereigns and citizens make up the world of public life, and natural individuals are then freed, within the realm of private liberty cleared by sovereigns and citizens, to pursue the arts producing commodious living. By way of Hobbes' political science, the particular opinions about ends that must inevitably determine any concrete exercise of political power are emptied of their moral power to form and direct individuals, to define the particular ends of commodious living in the vast natural expanse of private, individual liberty protected by artificial public life. Only when such opinions are taken to be effectively arbitrary - to be artificial - can they represent every natural individual's need for government by representing his natural opinions about particular ends in terms of the common end of self-preservation. For Hobbes, such artificial *representation* is the only way that what a natural individual needs most can be *represented* in the senses of "standing for" or "acting for." To think that representation requires consultation and accountability is a typical mistake springing from our natural opinions. For Hobbes there is no genuine contradiction between representation and re-presentation, and to see a problem here is to ignore his liberal intention to remove opinions about the particular ends of the public good from the act of generating political energy.13

Now for Hobbes government must *always* be representative, because it is impossible for any art, even one so powerful as that revealed by Hobbes' political science, literally to make natural individuals into artificial citizens. The sovereign must govern opinion and doctrine, but he cannot, indeed ought not, alter the fact that men will always have their natural opinions about particular ends, opinions formed in the space of their natural liberty.14 These opinions by their nature tend to cover up the teaching of the human heart, the harsh truths of the state of nature and self-preservation, which can only be uncovered by political science. Consequently, for Hobbes the will behind public law - that is, the sovereign - must always be up-front and evident, in fact awesome, which is not necessarily the same thing as having the last word in all matters of justice. For in order for natural individuals to let sovereign power represent them, they must always be reminded of the harsh prepolitical necessity requiring the soverign's deeds. The sovereign's will stands in for the science that only a few can know. Thus the sovereign's will, not his argument, must stifle the political self-assertion to which individuals convinced of their superior wisdom and ends will be tempted. To be sufficiently fearsome for this task, sovereign power must be monarchical and undivided. As artificial citizens, individuals must be motivated continually - by fear - to love their natural opinions about ends less than they respect the artificial, represented counterparts of these opinions.

Assuming as Hobbes does that an individual cannot do an injustice to himself, his doctrine of representation and artificial citizenship solves the problem of justice: to know what is just, one must merely know the sovereign's will, whether it appears in law or in prerogative act; for the sovereign's will, whatever it is, is always the individual's own - but only by way of artificial citizenship. If sovereign opinions are representative, establishing the conditions for justice only when they are artificial and arbitrary, then no questions about their justice can arise. And according to Hobbes it is precisely appeals from the law to some extra-legal justice that cause political life to resemble the condition of war. For Hobbes, the perspective of science discloses natural right, and the science of politics reveals the artful device - representative government - that harmonizes natural right, material justice, and positive law. One might say that like all liberals, Hobbes thinks that since justice, not virtue or the good, is the sole political good, then justice misconstrued is the cause of all political evil. And for Hobbes, justice is secured not when individuals deliberate about the form and ends of society, nor when they accept their rootedness in blood and soil, but when they become the objects of an artificial will disclosed by science. Hobbes' instrumentalism was not assumed, nor did it simply determine his understanding of the natural human individual. Rather, it was quite consciously intended to solve the problem of justice, which Hobbes thought to be coeval with natural political life.

Therefore, liberals can argue that Hobbes' instrumentalism is not simply ideological. This is important if only because it shows that Hobbes did not take the scientific project, or its conception of the individual, for granted. But it is still instrumentalism, and it cannot be denied that Hobbes' conception of liberty is purely negative; to the extent that it has any specific content it consists in the endless pursuit of the means to commodious living. It does seem, then, that Hobbes' conception of liberty is "technological" in the contemporary sense: the free individual is free precisely for acquisition, which depends upon the Baconian project for manipulating nature, and in order to be free the individual must be manipulated as well, albeit by the science of representative government. Hobbes' instrumentalism does seem open to the charges leveled by the right and left critics of technology: on the right hand it seems to announce the stultifying baseness of the last man, and on the left hand it is wedded to the scientific project that conquers nature not by the efforts of "humanity," but by the increasingly specialized expertise of a few, including the new techno-ethicists who could well boss men in the name of science when other technocratic elites will not. Although he did not presume it, Hobbes engendered the exaggerated faith in science that would substitute productive art for all other forms of practice, including the deliberation that determines the end of art itself. For Hobbesian liberalism, "art for art's sake" does not announce the noble, the beautiful or the sublime, but the utilitarian solution to the problem of justice.

We wonder, then, if there is an account of liberal democracy that is less wedded to the acquisitive promise and instrumental project of modern science. There is - to be found, I will argue, in an unlikely place: in the argument for representative government presented by Locke in the *Second Treatise of Government*, perhaps the most explicit argument for the acquisitive conquest of nature in the entire liberal tradition. My contention doubtless will seem implausible, for anyone will rightly object that Locke makes an explicit argument for the modern conception of art or *techne*. Thus, as is often noted, in the *Second Treatise* Locke rejects the traditional notion that art complements or imitates nature and claims that artful human labor is responsible for almost all that nature can be made to provide. Against the tradition Locke argues that there is no limit to artful acquisition once the invention of money makes it possible for one man's gain not to be another's loss. In fact, Locke's is not just the first but also, perhaps, the most comprehensive defense of limitless acquisition. Although it proceeds from formal equality of rights to private property, Lockean acquisition is justified on more materially egalitarian grounds because the natural prohibition against waste requires that private acquisition always improve the lot of others, including the poorest individuals. And Locke's account of acquisition does not reduce men to purely economic animals. For unlimited acquisition is also described as the incentive for men's protecting their political liberty. The right to unequal private property is the means to acquisition, for which reason men will want to secure the right. But in securing the right to unequal property men secure more than just their individual property. They secure along with that property not just their "lives, liberties and estates," but also the more general "*peace, safety*, and *public good* of the people."[15]

But even if Locke's doctrine of property is consciously political and less ideological than has been assumed in recent interpretation - even if its dependence on the Baconian project for the conquest of nature was, like Hobbes', intended to overcome the oppression of enthusiastic politics - it is not helpful for liberals if in fact it overlooks the oppressive possibilities of modern *techne*. It would seem that Locke could not even see these possibilities, much less overlook them, because like a typical modern he in effect assumes that *techne* has no natural, moral, or practical limits. Thus, without a more complex argument that seems indeed to be lacking, it is hard to see how he could have conceived of a conflict between acquisition and liberty, between technical means and their end. If for Locke there is no circumstance in which such conflict is possible, then his conception of liberty is really just technological and ideological: it takes the free person to be a subject who conquers objects, and it merely presumes that such conquest can only increase the liberty of one and all.

Now this plausible argument is just what I intend to deny. For Locke thought not only that liberty and acquisition might be opposed but also that artful acquisition is the ultimate source of political conflict. Moreover, he conceived of unlimited acquisition - and its problems - in the light of a natural measure, in the light of natural acquisition. To see these points clearly, we have to examine Locke's accounts of the state of nature, property, and the concrete stages in the development of government from the first consent to monarchy to the development of a well-formed commonwealth. When we do, we find that Locke's account of liberal government is suggestive for thinking about the problem of technology as we have come to know it from the nonliberal critics.

According to Locke, individuals leave the state of nature because in that state the natural law enjoining men to preserve their property (the most rudimentary of which is the individual's own body) and that of all mankind does not have sufficient sanction. When individuals sanction the law of nature by themselves, the resulting inconveniences compel them to create a single public sanction who can judge and execute the law of nature so as to guarantee its end. But such was not always the case in the state of nature. For prior to the invention of money there was no reason to fear for one's property at all, because, as Locke says, God or nature has given "all things richly." The point is not just that at this time the boundaries of property were perfectly clear because they were determined by the bounds of the individual human body. Rather, prior to the invention of money the natural law simply needed no sanction. At this time, as Locke says,

the measure of property nature has well set, by the extent of men's *labour* and the *conveniency of life*: No man's labour could subdue, or appropriate all: nor could his enjoyment consume more than a small part; so that it was impossible for any man, this way, to entrench upon the right of another, or acquire to himself, a property to the prejudice of his neighbor, who would still have room for as good, and as large a possession (after the other had taken out his) as before it was appropriated. This *measure* did confine every man's *possession* to a very moderate proportion, and such as he might appropriate to himself, without injury to any body, in the first ages of the world, when men were more in danger to be lost, by wandering from their company, in the vast wilderness of the earth, than to be straitened for want of room to plant in.16

In describing the state of nature, Locke actually distinguishes between a natural and a conventional economy, with both being prior to government but only the latter being the condition out of which government arises.   In the former, individuals are related to nature much as are any other animals, for whom acquisition is limited to the body's most rudimentary needs. By provision of the law of nature, individuals have a right to whatever they appropriate, but only provided that there is enough left over for others and provided that it does not spoil before being used. Thus where anyone's appropriating of anything would be another's loss, everyone would have a right to property but no appropriation would be just or unjust, including the forceful taking from others. But in the natural economy, where there is virtual plenty and certainty about the bounds of property, not only would such extreme circumstances not arise, but there would be no occasions for disputes about just and unjust appropriations. Scarcity of land and conflict about property are the products of the conventional economy.

Now as Locke describes it, the natural economy is in fact evanescent. The only circumstance in which it would not give way to a conventional economy based on money, where property extends beyond the limits of the body, would be where there is no medium that could serve for money. But of course any durable good can serve for money.   With the invention of money, men consent to unequal property that can be unlimited in extent because money does not spoil and facilitates the conserving exchange of those things that do. If the property to which one has a right is determined by an individual's labor (as Locke maintains), and if money "has its value only from the consent of men, whereof labor yet makes in great part *the measure*," then in consenting to the use of money individuals recognize a right to unequal property.   And because money facilitates conserving exchange, exchange that circumvents spoilage, it liberates productive labor to increase the store of material goods far beyond the gifts of untended nature. When exchange is possible, an individual can both appropriate and produce beyond the limit of what could be used by that individual before it spoils. Thus in consenting to money individuals consent not only to unequal property, but to such property in unlimited extent. And the ultimate result of money and exchange is that all individuals, from the richest to the poorest, are better off than they would have been in the natural economy.17   As property in land becomes scarce, property as such - the means of a "standard of living" - grows beyond anything to be measured by the dimensions of the land as such. According to Locke's account of property, labor "*puts the greatest value upon the land*, without which it would scarcely be worth anything: 'tis to that we owe the greatest part of its useful products."18

Prior to the application of developed human labor, nature's unlimited value is merely latent, with its actual or real value being limited to the "rudimentary conveniency" of life that characterizes the natural economy.[19]

Having identified the distinction Locke draws between the natural and conventional economies, the following questions arise: If the natural economy is evanescent, why does Locke bother to describe it? And again, if in the natural economy property is not a problem, because of its rudimentary extent, should it not remain unproblematic in the conventional economy for just the opposite reason, that is, because of its unlimited extent? That is, should not the extraordinary power of labor in the conventional economy, unleashed by the invention of money, recreate the "rich" (i.e., perfectly sufficient) natural provision of the peaceful natural economy? The answer to the second question is obviously no. For to think otherwise would make the consent to government in the state of nature unintelligible. Locke tells us that in consenting to government to protect the prior consent to the right to unequal property, individuals fulfill God's intention in giving the world "to the use of the industrious and rational (and *labour* was to be *his* [the industrious and rational laborer's] *title* to it); not to the fancy or covetousness of the quarrelsome and contentious."[20] It seems that in the conventional economy individuals are compelled to government by the irrationality of the quarrelsome and contentious. But how did the quarrelsome and contentious come to be? Locke makes no mention of the Biblical account of the Fall. Rather, his account of how property is private, despite having been given to "Adam and his posterity in common," subverts the Biblical distinction between Adam's leisure in the garden of Eden and his (and mankind's) need to toil after the Fall. For by Locke's account, the most rudimentary appropriation - simple gathering or picking up - is labor no more or less than any other. And of course Adam had to appropriate even in the prelapsarian garden.[21] In fact, Locke's account of the difference between the natural and conventional economies replaces the Biblical account of the Fall. Therefore, it explains just how the quarrelsome and contentious come to be. In accounting for the rise of the conventional economy from the natural one, Locke gives an account of the character of art and artful acquisition. Only from the latter can we see the reasons why government is necessary at all.

Earlier we surmised that government could have arisen only from the conventional economy. But Locke does nothing to make this clear and in fact suggests the contrary. According to Locke's description of the origins of government, men first consented to government within the family. The first government took the form of a benevolent, paternal monarchy because, given the simplicity and poverty of the time, there were little covetousness and ambition and consequently few controversies. At this time individuals were more in need of "defense against foreign invasions and injuries, than of multiplicity of laws," so that their concern "cannot but be supposed to be, how to secure themselves against foreign force."22 As is the case for the Indians in America, which is still "a pattern of the first ages in *Asia* and *Europe*," paternal kings were little more than "*generals of their armies*," because "want of people and money gave men no temptation to enlarge their possessions of land, or contest for wider extent of ground."23 By this argument, the first consent to government preceded the invention of money. But it seems implausible that government should arise at all in the natural economy, and of course government does not arise from such an early age, as Locke shows rather subtly in describing the actual beginnings of political society.

During the period of the natural economy, it was impossible for an individual to entrench upon the right of another by any acquisition by means of labor. Therefore, in such a "first age of the world" individuals would have consented to government not because of doubts about the bounds and title of property, but only out of fear of those who would appropriate without laboring, an unlikely possibility given the sparseness of human population and the very meager needs that moved men to labor in the first place. Before money there was no incentive to acquire beyond the limits of the natural economy, which would have been met by the simplest gathering, and during the natural economy human population was very sparse. The world was plentiful because needs were simple, and robbery or theft would certainly have been more difficult, and more dangerous, than gathering by means of one's own labor. Under such circumstances, Locke tells us, men would not have enlarged their possessions of land even if land were both rich and free for the taking.24 How, then, could large families have feared the encroachments of other such families? Moreover, Locke knows perfectly well that the Indians in America - the contemporary pattern of the first age - have money, although he makes it difficult for us to know that he does. Toward the end of the *Second Treatise*, in describing the limits of conquest in a just war, Locke distinguishes between land and nature's goods produced by labor, on the one hand, and money, on the other hand, arguing that money has no value by nature's standard any more than the "wampompeke of the *Americans*" has to a European or silver money would have to an American.25 If the contemporary Americans are the pattern for the "first ages of Europe and Asia," when the first consent to government occurred, then these first ages knew the institution of money. The truth seems to be that only the invention of money causes the circumstances that require men to consent to government, and we wonder first how this is so and second why Locke is reluctant to admit that the origin of government is in the family *after* the invention of money and not before. Why should the conventional economy before government be an embarrassment to the family? To answer these questions, we must consider Locke's distinction between natural and artificial, or imaginary, value.

The invention of money is the difference between the natural economy, where there is no incentive for consenting to government, and the artificial economy, where there is. Now Locke remarks that money gets its value from fancy or agreement rather than from "real use, and the necessary support of life."26 And in the later chapter on the limits of conquest, he argues that "...money: and such riches and treasures taken away, these are none of nature's goods, they have but a phantastical imaginary value: nature has put no such upon them." That is, the value of things prized as plunder is purely imaginary in contrast to "nature's goods," which are land and nature's goods improved by labor in a conventional economy.27 But we are not to think that unlike money and plunder improved natural goods are simply natural. For by the measure of the natural economy they are not.

Rather, the time of the natural economy was "before the desire of having more than man needed had altered the intrinsic value of things, which depends only upon their usefulness to the life of man."28 In the natural economy what was useful to the life of man was limited to "very moderate proportion" by the character of labor and the "conveniency of life," i.e., the rudimentary tools necessary for gathering.29 By liberating the desire to have more than man needed in the natural economy, the nonnatural value placed upon money in turn liberated the arts that produce the difference between the natural economy's acorns, water, and leaves or skins, on the one hand, and the conventional economy's bread, wine, and cloth, on the other hand. Locke comments that in describing the difference as he does he refers to merely "ordinary provision." But the very homeliness of the examples emphasizes the important point: from the point of view of the natural economy, bread, wine, and cloth are *luxuries*. Such luxuries could only be imagined in the natural economy, if only because they presuppose a development and division of labor and art so elaborate that it would be even for Locke "almost impossible, at least too long, to reckon up."30 If Locke could make such a reckoning the value of the "luxuries" in question would be no less imaginary as measured by natural "real use and necessary support of life."

In other words, it is not just the medium of exchange, or money, that depends upon the alteration of "the intrinsic value of things." Rather, the entire fabric of production beyond the natural economy depends upon such an alteration. As measured by the natural economy, "nature's goods" produced by labor in a conventional economy begin in "intrinsic value" but end in "phantastical and imaginary value," far beyond what satisfies purely natural needs. For Locke, nature differs from convention as conventions - such as European silver money and American wampompeke - differ from each other: never completely. From the standpoint of the natural economy, in the conventional economy the "industrious and rational," to whose labor God gave the world, are moved by a desire for imaginary value beyond the intrinsic value of things. Human progress beyond the limits of the natural economy is moved not by the press of harsh necessity, but by the love of luxury. Money and the artful natural products facilitated by money are not wholly different: one might just as easily say that men can love money because they can prefer wine to water as to say that because they come to love money they can produce wine.

Having clarified the distinction between the natural and conventional economies, we can see why Locke is reluctant to advertise the origin of government from the family in the conventional economy. As we know, Locke has claimed that the first government was a moderate and kindly monarchy because it was but the political extension of benevolent paternal authority. But any careful reader of the first chapter should doubt this claim, since it requires that an actual father have possessed and have been willing to use the right to inflict capital punishment on his offspring. If the conditions in such a family were as amicable as Locke describes them, why would it require laws to be enforced "with penalties of death"?31 Just what kind of father and family is this?

To fit the pieces of the puzzle together, we have finally to consider Locke's description of the rise of complicated government - what he calls well-regulated commonwealth - from the original paternal monarchy. Locke argues that the paternal monarchy occurred during a "golden age" before "vain ambition, and *amor sceleratus habendi,* evil concupiscence, had corrupted men's minds into a mistake of true power and honor," when peoples, from these vices, questioned the prerogative of princes and princes, from "ambition and luxury," came to have different interests from peoples. If we ask about the cause of this change, the answer is obvious: the invention of money. For only with the invention of money does human striving move toward its natural horizon, which is located, for men, beyond "the intrinsic value of things" and in "phantastical and imaginary value." But then, as we have already seen, the origin of government in the family could not have preceded the invention of money. No wonder Locke has been reluctant to admit this fact, which must mean that the prepolitical but postconventional family cannot have been the golden institution he describes, but rather one in which evil concupiscence and vain ambition called forth the need for laws to be enforced with "penalties of death."

The important point for us is not *that* the origins of government were harsh, although this does have broad implications for Locke's argument about sovereign power, but *why* they were. The vices which Locke says required the development of more complicated government, and which in fact call for government as such, are not said to be limited to a few, to the "quarrelsome and contentious" as opposed to the "rational and industrious," whose right to private and unequal property government is instituted to protect. Rather, Locke describes the vices as characterisics of rulers and subjects in general. The reason is that these vices are grounded precisely in the artfulness of the rational and industrious. Having reflected on the natural human economy, Locke knows that human art is put to work to produce commodities whose measure begins with natural need but always proceeds beyond the "intrinsic value of things" to "phantastical and imaginary" value. The artfulness of the industrious and rational, grounded as it is on the desire for goods beyond the most limited needs of the body, is the very source of luxury and vain ambition.

This is not to say that Locke thinks there is no difference between the rational and industrious and the quarrelsome and contentious. Such an exaggeration would be untrue to Locke's intention and argument. But it does mean that Locke knows that human art is possible only because men are open to the good that is beyond the merely needful as such. And this is the same as to say that human art takes place only because men are open to the possibility of glory. Strictly speaking, there is no human need to be met by art that is not at the same time in fact luxurious and the product of human imagination. Therefore, Locke knows that by their very nature the rational and industrious are likely to be moved by opinions about "power and honor" that are controversial if not always "mistaken." And if so, they will be moved not only by the desire to acquire, but also by political self-assertion. Moreover, the artfulness of the industrious and rational provides the pretexts for such self-assertion: artful labor produces the greater part of all that is of value, and its product is always a man's own and not common. But just because artful labor is differentiated in a complex division, what each individual contributes to every item of value is "almost impossible to reckon up."32 And in the absence of demonstrable signs, one can expect the rational and industrious, moved as they are by opinions of power and honor, to mind other men's business in the process of minding their own.

There was never a "golden age" for man, nor is the family by nature a tranquil locale, because the natural economy is evanescent. But this is to say that the very artfulness that creates government and so calms and softens not just the real human age, but also the family itself, is the ultimate source of the quarrels and contentions that call for government in the first place. Locke hides his agreement with Hobbes about the harsh origins of government by consent because, having better understood the nature of human art, he does not think that the artifice of representation can operate as immediately in human affairs as did Hobbes. For Hobbes, a loud artificial will disclosed by science will make that science effective in practical life. For Locke, the scientific truth of the state of nature must operate at once more subtly and more indirectly, lest it exacerbate the danger of the artfulness it empowers. Thus Locke rejects absolute monarchy, or absolute government of any kind, for that matter, because he cannot trust the rationality or industriousness of any individual or body, arguing rather that unrestrained political power tends to corrupt its possessor.33

It is true that a majority must "conclude" the whole of a representative assembly and that the actual majority ultimately has absolute, sovereign power to direct the whole of political society. But for Locke such sovereign power must be removed from government by means of subsovereign representative institutions, not brought to bear on government itself, except in the most extreme cases of oppression by government itself.[34] It is also true that Locke describes the people, by which he means the actual majority, as very slow to anger and to act, which seems to contradict our argument about the contentious nature of the "rational and industrious." Perhaps the "rational and industrious" do not make up the majority, in which case the people's sobriety highlights the problem of rationality and industriousness. But if the majority is assumed to be rational and industrious, so that they ought to be described as contentious, we note that Locke's argument assumes a people who have governed themselves by means of constitutional and representative institutions. That is, it assumes a people who have been formed into a particular people and thus deterred from indulging in the vices of princes and peoples as such, vices that in the beginning led to the origin of government.[35] Unlike Hobbes, Locke cannot trust any sovereign, whether prince or people, *especially* when they join in the project of artful acquisition. An artificial will is no proof against tyranny, and artful acquisitiveness is no proof against sedition.

For Locke, human beings need government *because* life is characterized by artful production rather than by natural acquisition. Therefore, while it is possible for men to govern themselves according to political science wedded to art and acquisition, such a science cannot be expected to be perfect and can operate in political affairs only from a standpoint farther removed from actual practice than Hobbes had thought - at best it can work through constitutionally managed majority rule. There is, therefore, no complete replacement of deliberative practice by *techne* or art, or by an artificial will: the right of revolution is recognized in the most extreme situations, sovereignty is delegated and divided between institutions in everyday practice, and participation is expanded within them. The citizens' natural opinions are thus brought to bear in determining the common good, but only at a point removed, by the devices of constitutionalism, from the source of absolute sovereign power.[36] Likewise, individual freedom cannot be understood to be simply technological, as if the artful conquest of nature were its certain guarantee. Locke does not take men to be political, and so always in danger of losing their freedom, because their art has not yet conquered scarcity. Rather, they can experience both scarcity and art only because they are by nature political, because they are by nature drawn to glory and the good as well as pushed by the merely necessary. This is why Locke describes the natural economy as at once natural and evanescent.

Locke's liberalism is not ideological, and it is not simply technological as the nonliberal critics understand technology: Locke has much to tell us not only about the consequences of our inventiveness, but also about the problematic character of inventiveness itself. But Locke's liberalism also provides a clue to the uniquely modern problem of technology. For despite being able to take the natural measure of art and acquisition, Locke also rejects the traditional argument that they can be subordinated to nonproductive ends such as knowledge, philosophy, or moral virtue. Locke without doubt announces the modern destiny, which is for mankind to be inseparably bound to the artful, and endless, mastery of nature. But Locke shows that this destiny need not blind us to its character or to its special danger. We might then say that Locke is important precisely because he illuminates a distinctly modern problem without the luxury of premodern assumptions. Or at least we might say that he can respond with responsible urgency to our modern predicament, having brought to the acquisitive project a natural measure that does not depend for its power upon a partial and controversial account of perfecting natural ends. From Locke we learn that liberals can both understand the essence of technology - its ubiquity and the impossiblity of ever outstripping it - and manage its ultimate danger, which has little to do with the material or moral consequences of technological things.

If we follow up on Locke's teaching about art and politics, we see that every useful activity springs from some natural need, but that human beings differ from the animals because our useful actions are experienced as toward some good, which, as good, is not merely useful or necessary. Human needs are never experienced as *mere* needs, however needful in fact they are. Human life is certainly at first and always the experience of being in need. But no need can be a human need apart from some counterpart, which, by comparison, is or at least appears to be self-sufficient or useless, or an end in itself. This simple truth has important implications for the nature of human art, which includes not just the works of the hands, but also the interpretive arts of the poet, the rhetorician, and the spokesman for the gods. For although there is no useful action that is not related to some useless (luxurious) counterpart, no art can fully know its ultimate subordination to such counterparts - to its purposes - lest it prefer them to its own activity. Socrates, we recall, refused to practise his manual art not for the sake of making useful speeches, but so as to question and doubt the claims of every such speech.

If only a natural slave is content to be merely useful rather than good, it follows that productive activity can, indeed must, be able to take its needful work as essential or self-sufficient, being needed more than being in need. Every productive art can serve human need only by being potentially oblivious of its own mere usefulness, of the fact of its being defined within a context of useful activities and items. Thus every art harbors relative to other arts what amounts to a political claim - that it alone is the (useless) end of the particular order of any whole of (useful) arts. No such claim is ever demonstrable, however, and so every order of human arts is constituted by force as well as persuasion. But with its merely partial grasp of its own relation to the good, each art is susceptible to the "vain ambition" and "mistake of true power and honor" that ignores the neediness of every attempt to persuade and compel. Such ignorance is essential for art, but it also causes the most violent forms of coercion. The ignorant competence of art is the source of unreasoning tyranny. When Locke tells us that there is no limit to human acquisition, he is not simply telling us, as he does indeed, that there is no such thing as a natural end that defines human dignity. Rather, he tells us that unlimited needs call forth controversial arts only because men are by nature dignified. Without assuming with Locke (and with Aristotle, I would add) that the good is an inseparable and immanent cause of both making and doing, rather than somehow separate in space and time, it is impossible to explain why need should ever be answered by art, or why the natural economy should ever give way to the conventional one.37 Neither materialism nor simple teleology can account for the actual phenomena of social and political life.

Extrapolating from Locke's teaching, we learn the simple truth that if ends are the causes of means, then *techne* is at once inseparable from political life and the source of the greatest political danger. So long as politics and *techne* are coeval - and by nature they always are - political life will be ordered by a combination of force and persuasion. But *techne* always tempts men to exercise political will as if it were artful but not coercive, as if it were the spontaneous and self-evident end of the order of productive arts. And of course such political will is the harshest form of coercion because it is not open to and so limited by its own need to persuade. The real danger of modern technology, which in knowing no limits makes every conceivable promise, is the extent to which it promises that political life can be overcome. The more technology promises freedom from scarcity, the more we are tempted to think that the need to manage and moderate coercive rule can be overcome, thus blinding us to the many guises of tyranny and oppression.

From this perspective, the danger of technology is more a problem for the left than for the liberal, and the left is more likely than liberalism to be blind to it. For whether one's Marx be materialistic or humanistic - that is, whether one's Marx sees an infinity of bodily needs or the activity of self-conscious *praxis* as the sufficient telos of human life - it is possible that, unlike Locke, he mistook altogether the character of human art and human need. Without seeing these phenomena clearly, it is all the easier to succumb to the siren song of art, louder now in the form of modern technology that promises the reduction of political practice to one or another of the productive arts. In our time the arts seem ever more competent. Moreover, they do not really have to persuade or compel the material upon which they work.[38] Thus they are ever more powerfully the source of political conflict and the model for oppressive politics. For all of the left's hostility to art and preference for "*praxis*," it was Marx, not Locke, who vainly saw the productive colossus of technological capitalism as the precondition for the disappearance of politics.

There really is no right wing alternative embodying the serious argument from the theoretical right. We need not dwell, then, on the extent to which the fascist regimes' love of their cooked-up traditions depended on their mastery of revolutionary and modernizing technology. However, the serious concern for the flattening and tyrannical effects of technology does occur in the strain of nonliberal but democratic thought that respects what is most sober and powerful in Nietzsche and Heidegger.[39] But again, technology may be more of a problem for the nonliberal democrat than for the liberal. For in preferring the realm of "autonomous politics" to the liberal's politically hedged sphere of private liberties, the nonliberal democrat may simply expect too much from politics. From the Lockean point of view politics is to be feared, and so managed rather than embraced, precisely because it is inevitably technological and thus always characterized not just by persuasion, but also by force. Perhaps the most subtle technological hope is not that politics will disappear, but that it can be perfected by the softest of all the arts, the speechmaking art. From the Lockean point of view the freedom of human ends can never be separated from the hard urgency of material needs, precisely because the former animate the latter. And the consequent danger is always that one or another necessary art - including the art of persuasion - will present itself as entirely free and self-sufficient, as if it has no need to compel as well as persuade the other arts.

It is possible, then, that Locke's liberalism is uniquely helpful for grasping the deepest problem of technology. Its combination of individualism and constitutionalism recognizes that technology, so apparently different from nature, is at once natural to man and the power that makes political life both inevitable and dangerous. Indeed, men conquer nonhuman nature only to confound their own. But such is the human condition. This is not to say, however, that liberalism or liberal thought is a useful tool simply ready to hand, or that technology does not present a danger through liberalism itself. Indeed, to defend liberalism we have had to remember a liberal source, and a reluctant one at that, now long forgotten by most liberals. Locke prescribed constitutionalism as the political hedge to the acquisitive individualism that would replace religious politics. But as technology has become ever more modern, that is ever more technically adept, the tension between individualism and constitutionalism has become much more fragile.

On the one hand, individualism conceives the individual as an abstract person, defined by formal rights that prevent him from being formed by or forming others according to some conception of virtue or the good life. When engaged in private acquisition, justified by formal rights, men can be encouraged to mind their own business and seem to need rather little persuasion to do so. On the other hand, constitutionalism recognizes the need to regulate and moderate tendencies to political opinion and ambition, which Locke knew to be both a cause and an effect of artful acquisitiveness. Liberal politics depends on the careful balance of these contradictory and interwoven elements, a balance that culminates in the liberal moderation of majority rule. Modern technology threatens to disturb this balance by tipping it toward the abstract person. For as technology promises new freedoms from hitherto natural necessities, with each new freedom the object of an individual right, we are tempted to think that we can likewise be free from need to moderate and manage majority rule. Thus rights come to be understood not as the hedges of an individual capable of political liberty, but as guarantees against the need to be constrained by any controversial coercion, however liberal or moderate it may be. A growing array of rights appears as a warrant against the need to be constrained or formed to the virtues of self-government, as if it were not always necessary to manage conflict about the public good and the need for coercive rule. For liberals, the danger of technology is that it tempts them to believe that an element of their creed, the abstract individual, is not just a politically necessary perspective for viewing the real, human person, but a concrete reality by itself. Judged by such a standard, the political elements and characteristics of liberal democracy will appear anachronistic at best and oppressive at worst.

As for its nonliberal alternatives, the danger of technology for liberals is that as it appears more and more plausible that material scarcity can be overcome, it appears more and more likely that political conflict will disappear. The more liberals take this view to heart, the more it is tempting to believe that all public controversy is to be resolved by one or another field of technical expertise, whether it be the lawyer's, the economist's, the judge's, or the bioethicist's, rather than by well-formed and moderate majority rule. If, as reflecting on Locke teaches, human beings are technological only so far as they are political, then the growing power and legitimacy of experts who do not claim to rule can only be a new form of despotism. In our modern technological age, it is urgent that liberals recover the lessons taught by the debate between Hobbes and Locke, the very first liberals.

It is not to be denied that liberalism depends dangerously on the modern technological project. But this need not mean that liberals must be blind to the problem of technology, for we have discovered a liberal source for understanding the complex interrelationship of political and technological life. Liberals need not succumb to technological faith. Indeed, they may be better able than others to avoid it. But neither must they forgo technology's most important gifts, which need not merely succor the last man. The modern technological project makes way for new possibilities of greatness and excellence as well as for equality, comfort and long life. Surely the conquest of space is as grand in its way as was the Roman conquest of half the ancient world, and the threat of nuclear holocaust must broaden the responsibilities and enliven the possibilities of statesmanship and diplomacy beyond anything heretofore experienced. What nobler deed than saving mankind, and what more thrilling danger than managing nuclear deterrence, which approximates antiquity in making the statesman and the soldier share the same risks? And in approaching nature through technology, are we not more turned to wonder at the being of nature, man, and the divine than at any time since the flourishing of philosophy in Athens? For liberals technology is a danger. But liberals ought to consider that perhaps only they can see the danger clearly, and thus see how it can be a danger that saves.

Notes

1. Martin Heidegger, "The Question Concerning Technology," in *The Question Concerning Technology and Other Essays*, trans. William Lovitt (New York: Harper & Row, 1977).

2. As Leon Kass has observed, the only right recognized in the body of the U. S. Constitution is the right to the patent. See *Toward a More Natural Science* (New York: The Free Press, 1985), p. 135.

3. See Jürgen Habermas, "Technology and Science as 'Ideology'" in *Toward a Rational Society*, trans. Jeremy J. Shapiro (Boston: Beacon Press, 1971).

4. See *Early Writings*, trans. R. Livingstone and G. Benton (New York: Random House, 1975), pp. 348, 356, 358.

5. For an extended discussion, see my *Science, Faith, and Politics: Francis Bacon and the Utopian Roots of the Modern Age*, (Ithaca: Cornell University Press, 1985).

6. Hobbes, *Leviathan*, ed. C.B. Macpherson (Baltimore: Penguin, 1971), pp. 82-83.

7. See J. Weinberger, "Hobbes's Doctrine of Method," *The American Political Science Review*, LXIX, No. 4, December, 1975, 1336-1353.

8. Or to the few who are educated by the university curriculum, as opposed to the many who are educated within the largely autonomous family. *Leviathan*, pp. 83, 264, 408, 728. See Nathan Tarcov, *Locke's*

Education for Liberty (Chicago: The University of Chicago Press, 1984), pp. 42-51.

9. *Leviathan*, pp. 183-188.

10. *Ibid.*, pp. 217-239.

11. *Ibid.*, pp. 81-83.

12. For the important exception to this in the case of religious conscience, see Clifford Orwin, "On the Sovereign Authorization," *Political Theory*, 3, No. 1, (February, 1975), 26-44.

13. Cf. Hannah Pitkin, *The Concept of Representation* (Berkeley: The University of California Press, 1967), pp. 14-37.

14. See note 8 above.

15. *Second Treatise of Government*, sects. 27, 31, 34-41,123, 131. In this and in all subsequent quotations from Locke the italics are his. See Harvey C. Mansfield, "On the Political Character of Property in Locke," in *Powers, Possessions and Freedom*, ed. Alkis Kontos (Toronto: University of Toronto Press, 1979), pp. 35-38.

16. Sect. 36.

17. Sects. 40-41, 46-50.

18. Sect. 43.

19. Sect. 36.

20. Sect. 34.

21. Cf. sects. 25-35, *Gen.* 2-3.

22. Sect. 107.

23. Sect. 108.

24. Sect. 48.

25. Sect. 184, cf. sect. 49.

26. Sect. 46.

27. Sect. 184.

28. Sect. 37.

29. Sect. 36.

30. Sect. 43.

31. Sects. 3, 107.

32. Sects. 43-44.

33. Sects. 90-94, 143, 156, 159.

34. At the origin of government, all individuals consent to submit to the power of the majority, which has "the whole power of the community" and the "right to conclude the rest." The first positive law of a commonwealth is the "establishing of the legislative power," which means the establishment of this power in the form of perfect democracy, oligarchy, hereditary or elective monarchy, or some form mixed or compounded of them. The legislative power "in the hands where the community once placed it," i.e., in the particular form, is then "sacred and unalterable," except under the extreme conditions that justify revolution. And in the course of the *Second*

Treatise, Locke describes a well-regulated commonwealth as one where the legislative power is placed in the form of an occasional representative assembly, with the executive function of political power separated from the legislative. Sects. 95-99, 132-134, 143-144, 153, 156, 159.

35. Sects. 211-230.

36. Cf. sects. 98, 135-140.

37. The press of increasing population would not be a sufficient explanation for the development of money, luxury and art, and political society. For with the very limited needs described in the natural economy, even unimproved nature is a bountiful store. But if, before the demise of the natural economy, scarcity were to result from natural population increase, Locke implies that it would not produce government more complex than the simple, benevolent, and paternal monarchy he describes. Indeed, in the only mention of natural population increase Locke describes it in the same breath with money: thus the first ages were a time when "the inhabitants were too few for the country, and want of people and money gave men no temptation to enlarge their possessions of land, or contest for wider extent of ground...." Sect. 108. And at any rate, the natural economy is evanescent, so that the invention of money must have preceded increase in population. But even if overpopulation could precede money, only wars of necessity would ensue between clans, and govenment would not have to be complicated precisely because without money there would be no "vain ambition," not to mention potential conflicts between the rational and industrious and the quarrelsome and contentious. It is difficult for us to imagine what a war of necessity would be like, for since the invention of money there has not been one in the entire course of human history. Again, the cause of political conflict is man's natural dignity, which can never be outstripped or overcome, and without which *movement* to some historical telos - if indeed such a telos exists - would be impossible. The various appearances of dignity, in the individual, rights, social class, and the gods, are not reflections of our grappling with need; they are the conditions for the very experience of need.

38. To be sure we speak of the technological conquest of nature. But technologically speaking, nature cannot be conquered, for she puts up no resistance, let alone demands an accounting for her surrender or demise. Art is nonmoral precisely because what it works on is but "stuff."

39. For one important source of this strain, see Hannah Arendt, *The Human Condition* (New York: Doubleday & Company, 1959).

40. The two most recent liberal intepretations of liberal justice, those of Rawls and Nozick, reject constitutionalism altogether. See my treatment of them in "Liberalism, Constitutionalism, and the Rediscovery of the State of Nature," in *Towards a Revival of Constitutionalism*, ed. James Muller, University of Nebraska Press, forthcoming.

ROUSSEAU VERSUS INSTANT GOVERNMENT: DEMOCRATIC PARTICIPATION IN THE AGE OF TELEPOLITICS

Joseph Masciulli

I

Bernard Lonergan has correctly observed the premise of modernity: "the challenge of history is for man progressively to restrict the realm of chance or fate or destiny and progressively to enlarge the realm of conscious grasp and deliberate choice."[1] The dominant theme of modernity has been to control chance through technology. Technical mastery has broadened our choice in consumer goods, relieved many of the necessity of burdensome toil, enlarged the amount of free time, and empowered humans to combat disease, hunger and even death. Indeed, technological mastery could be said to be above all an attempt to conquer our mortality. Rousseau, one of the strongest opponents of modernity, was at the same time paradoxically one of its partisans, though he advocated the control of human destiny by political not technological methods.

Rousseau was one of the first critics of the emerging modern state, with its dedication to an unlimited increase in economic prosperity and technological power over nature. He thought its archetypical members, whom he labeled "the bourgeois," were committed to the goal of staying alive as long and as comfortably as possible through "involvement in commerce and the arts, avid interest in profits, softness and love of comforts, that replace personal services by money."[2]

The English liberal tradition celebrated property and liberty, commerce and representative government. But in Rousseau's view, Hobbes and Locke championed *bourgeois subjects* of a representative government, not *autonomous citizens* participating in formulating the rules by which they conducted their lives. Engaged in profitable commercial transactions in a society increasingly characterized by division of labor and technological development, bourgeois subjects would merely pay their taxes and thus hire representatives and soldiers to act on their behalf in the public sphere. While feverishly active in the acquisition of commercial wealth and in the industrial transformation of nature, they would be mere spectators in the public realm, for the most part apathetic as long as the political referee functioned competently in protecting their lives, property, and individual independence to seek happiness as they themselves saw fit.[3]

This spectator consciousness - the apolitical individualism of men and women whose primary goal is comfortable self-preservation, the acquisition of power from wealth, and domination of nature through technology - is nourished, Rousseau contended, by the social fragmentation that results from the excessive industrial division of labor that accompanies urbanization and unbridled, runaway capital-intensive growth. This rootlessness in the context of bigness encourages centralized power and the dark art of manipulating strangers through the cunning use of money and force.[4]

Locke and Smith saw the market as integrating the socio-economic division of labor (with some additional basic education oriented towards technical competence and a watered-down religious, non-militant secular consciousness). For Locke it was the division of labor, unified through monetary exchange, that alone is creative, transforming "the almost worthless materials" provided by nature into commodities which give even the worst off a better material life than the best off in simpler economies based on hunting and gathering or subsistence agriculture.[5] Smith defended "the propensity to truck, barter, and exchange one thing for another" as an attribute of human nature and the only fruitful basis of economic growth, since an "appeal to self-love" is more effective than reliance on people's benevolence. Yet he granted that as the world market extended the division of labor, and as everyone became enmeshed in living to some measure by exchange, the majority of workers would come to be confined to very few operations, frequently one or two, in which a decrease in understanding, inventiveness, and initiative would occur. In these conditions workers would be "as stupid and ignorant as it is possible for a human creature to become," incapable of "conceiving any generous, noble, or tender sentiment, and consequently of forming any just judgment concerning many even of the ordinary duties of private life."[6]

Though the division of labor can result in increased technical efficiency and economic productivity on the one hand, its costs in terms of increasing human passivity and brutalization on the other hand are very high indeed. Following Montesquieu's analysis (though not his prescriptions), Rousseau defended the political and social virtues which he saw being negated by commercial-technological development. Although Montesquieu saw that the "corruption of the purest morals" would result from the triumph of the spirit of commerce, he nonetheless sided with the partisans of the expansion of material wealth, luxury, and the "perfection of the arts" and sciences, rejecting as a thing of the past republican participatory politics grounded on austere virtue.[7]

Warning his contemporaries that the modern liberal commitment to economic and technological power was resulting in a tyranny over nature and a "tyranny of the rich" over the poor,[8] Rousseau advocated suppressing technological growth, opting out of technological systems, and returning to natural simplicity and austerity as much as possible. In order to preclude the brutalization of human specialists in an extensive division of labor, and to preserve or re-create conditions for citizen-generalists, who would be active participants rather than passive spectators, Rousseau defended a socioeconomic order characterized by the predominance of an agrarian, low-technology sector, with the commercial, high-technology sector being tempered and curbed by conscious political decisions. Though he did not advocate a primitive or undifferentiated economy of small producers tied to subsistence agriculture, he did wish to harness a differentiated economy to the satisfaction of human potential and the needs of everyone - as interpreted politically, not as determined by market forces.[9] Rather than production in response to monetary and market rewards, he encouraged a renewal of dedicated craftsmanship, motivated by the desire for skill and pride. In place of conspicuous consumption and luxury, from which only minorities could benefit, he preferred responsible consumption which would be consistent with a planned economic environment and would aim to preserve prosperous, healthy, and free living and working conditions for the vast majority.[10]

From the perspective of democratic community, rootedness in the land and craftsmanship, he espoused policies that would result in widespread and relatively equal ownership of land and small capital. A discretionary kind of technological negation, he contended, would include selective banishment of some technologies; a rejection of the development of military technology and regular armies that would replace citizen militias (because of the economic disequilibria and potential for tyranny inherent in them); and the proscription of labor-saving machines and inventions (for some type of productive occupation is the indispensable basis of responsible citizenship in democratic community).[11] Rousseau's sense of environmental responsibility pointed to appropriate technology. He was not hostile to all technical progress as such, but favored the kind of renewable, small-scale technologies that encourage natural productivity and reintegrate our activities with biospheric processes.[12] (In this sense there is a similarity between Rousseau and today's advocates of solar energy systems, wind generators, organic farming, etc.)

II

Through the encouragement of discretion in the development of technology and commerce, Rousseau hoped to nourish human activity and generalist occupations, to minimize material inequality and rural-urban imbalances, and to protect the rootedness of human beings in the land. These, he believed, were the conditions necessary to support the life of the family and of small communities, which in turn would facilitate a participatory and democratic political process. Citizens would be able to acquire and express their political virtue (their commitment to the general will of the community, or the common good, and their willingness to sacrifice for it when necessary).[13] A political community, made up of virtuous citizens, would share a transparent common life - full communication in citizen assemblies - in which the voice of the general will of the people would be experienced as the voice of God. As a result of their patriotic commitment, citizens would be desirous of contributing personal services to the public realm and would seek public recognition for their contributions to the security, prosperity, and harmony of their community. In the best possible case, citizens would desire to be recognized not for their conspicuous consumption and market power - as implied by the spectator consciousness - but rather for their practice of austerity, of doing more with less and preventing the multiplication of needs beyond natural simplicity.[14]

Rousseau's participatory democratic model is meant to assure that citizens attain a relatively high degree of intimacy through face-to-face communication in public assemblies and other gatherings. A sense of intimacy and trust results from the familiarity of people seeing one another often, with the consequence that citizens come to know one another and at the same time come to share a sense of compassion. According to Rousseau human beings, though essentially malleable through time, are originally defined in a state of nature by their self-love and compassion. Rousseau explains humanity's change from independent animals, loosely herded together, to a potentially noble existence in virtuous political community, by the human faculty of perfectibility. In the long run, however, this faculty has made human beings tyrants of nature and of themselves, involved in dependent relations of conventional wealth, honor, and power. This perfectibility has manifested itself above all in their other-directed pride, developing as an extension of self-directed biological self-love (*amour propre* out of *amour de soi-même*).[15] The primitive compassion of human beings was always subordinate to their individual desire for self-preservation (*amour de soi-même*), but as their pride and vanity (*amour propre*) and their historically acquired needs have expanded beyond any limits, their compassion has grown more limited.[16] Our *amour propre* propels us to seek recognition from others; our natural compassion is a kind of "natural virtue" which keeps us from harming other humans and, indeed, all sentient beings (unless our self-preservation is directly threatened). Through our pity or sentiment of humanity we identify with those who suffer, realizing that "all are born naked and poor; all are subject to the miseries of life, to sorrows, ills, needs and pains of every kind. Finally, all are condemned to death....This is what no mortal is exempt from."[17] From compassion comes an inner strength that extends us beyond ourselves, for in pitying the suffering of another we realize that we ourselves are not suffering presently. On the other hand, the "hard" person wants "to dominate everywhere" because his desire for vain recognition has submerged his sense of pity, and he can never possibly get sufficient recognition for his unlimited desires.[18] In the modern world, as humans have become more technological, they have correspondingly become harder and more given to the vain demands of the spectator consciousness, often wishing to appear what they are not for the sake of distinguishing themselves.[19]

Though Rousseau claims that compassion can be extended and generalized to the whole human species and beyond, and implies that political virtue can promote even the general will of "the great city of the world," in fact, he concludes, both compassion and political virtue are most efficacious when they are symbiotically joined to one another within a relatively small political community, in which the limited faculties of average citizens suffice to establish bonds of intimacy among them. Citizens who are at once virtuous and compassionate care for one another; their bond is that of concrete patriotic love, which includes shared suffering.[20]

Given these personal affective bonds and their intimate knowledge of one another, citizens are able to come together in the public assemblies as independent peers, ready to listen to each other's interpretation of what is the general will or common good of the community. True, because of inequality in political talents and the limitations of time and energy, a division of political labor between full-time political specialists and part-time citizen generalists is necessary. Some type of elective "aristocratic" government is needed, whereby those recognized as wiser and more competent would administer particular policies and make discretionary decisions under the pressure of time and circumstances. Though Rousseau maintained that political understanding is always limited and fallible - being mere probabilistic knowledge, grounded upon "combinations, applications, and exceptions, according to time, place, and circumstance" - and always subject to "ever-new prejudices" and blind spots in every epoch, he nonetheless accepted the essential gap between those who possess specialized political knowledge and citizen generalists who do not.[21] His solution for assuring political responsibility and direct democratic participation was periodic citizen assemblies, during which sovereign citizens alone would exist, the politicians becoming simply citizens once again.

Though Rousseau stressed that there would always be tension between these two groups, with the citizen-politicians seeking to guide ordinary citizens towards accepting laws, policies, and particular decisions they (the politicians) preferred, nonetheless love, compassion, and intimate knowledge of each other's characters would preserve the community's unity.22 Each would respect the conscientious decision of the others as to what promoted the common good, a decision emanating from each citizen's inner commitment to community life. Lastly, Rousseau insisted that his idealistic alternative to the modern materialistic state, committed to technological domination, required rare moral leadership by a "legislator" totally uninterested in political power for himself. The "legislator" must be committed to a religious horizon, affirming that "everything is good as it leaves the hands of the Author of things; everything degenerates in the hands of man." He must affirm God's providential and just governance of the universe as a whole, as well as of human beings in particular, for political conscience requires a religious horizon.23

Rousseau intended his model of participatory democracy to be applicable primarily to small states which met the economic, technological, and social conditions he outlined. Nevertheless he granted that with some institutional creativity this model might be applied to medium-sized states or federations of small polities, allowing for personal intimacy among citizens. He envisaged national deputies as mediators (not representatives) of a people's legislative will, who would have to seek the ratification of local, direct citizen assemblies for their national decisions. Through various modes of election, politicians would be required to govern with considerable discretion while remaining responsible to citizen assemblies.24 These institutions, however, could only function without giving rise to tyranny if citizens had been politically educated in compassion and virtue, though the institutions themselves could become in due time media of public education. While he did not limit the potential for effective citizenship exclusively to small face-to-face communities, Rousseau was clearly not sanguine about the possible success of experiments in direct democracy which went beyond small-scale and appropriate technology.

III

In our time we experience modes of mass politics that are informed by significantly different types of elite manipulation. This is true in liberal-democratic, communist and authoritarian systems. All uphold a spectator, consumerist consciousness and promise ever-greater technological domination of nature for the sake of greater individual wealth, health, leisure, and hedonism. Absolute technological power is greater than at any time in the history of the human species. Increasing inventiveness, and especially the widespread application of computer and electronic technology to everyday life, have created unprecedented possibilities for democratizing and further humanizing our planet. At the same time, they have also increased the danger of totalitarian manipulation by technocratic and political elites, who would seek to construct a world beyond freedom, dignity, and affective participatory communities, abrogating the demand for accountability and responsibility on the part of politicians to the general will of the people.

This threat to political life has provoked many thinkers and activists to emphasize the potential of modern technology to contribute to greater democratic participation. Benjamin Barber, for example, recognizes the dangers of enhanced manipulation but goes on to argue for a pro-technological attitude that accepts fully the orientation of dominating nature on the grounds that "the ultimate permissible size of a polity is now as elastic as technology itself." Indeed, Barber claims that "today the boundaries of the technological community push against global limits."[25] To realize the democratic potential of technology, Barber sees the need for a variety of reforms. These include neighborhood assemblies, tied to national referenda and initiative processes; electronic town meetings, whereby television would integrate neighborhood assemblies on a regional basis and coordinate them with delegates on a national level; multichoice voting and polling; and a videotext information service, organized as a public utility and directed by a civic communications cooperative.[26] This new media-political elite would then have the task of implementing guidelines for regional and national town meetings, for tie-ins to neighborhood assemblies, for institutional networking, and for other interactive forms of public discussion. At the same time, the civic communications cooperative would be "establishing or providing guidelines for video coverage of civic events, hearings, trials, and other public activities of civic interest" and would protect viewers from the possible abuses of computer data, surveillance services, polling, and voting procedures.[27] With reforms such as these, Barber believes that over time common talk, an empathetic imagination, and common action can be extended certainly over a national scale, and possibly an international or global one.

The alleged democratic potential of telepolitics, and its presumed capacity to generate greater universal compassion, are worthy of careful, critical reflection. Along with greater access to information, made possible for the average citizen by the exploitation of "user-friendly" computers, the telephone, and the increase in television channels through cable and satellite technologies, all of which allow for "horizontal," non-hierarchical modes of access,[28] the kind of institutional innovations related to interactive television suggested by Barber and others would certainly increase public participation to some degree. At the very least, more citizens could experience the sense of participation now felt by members of the media covering political press conferences.[29] Using telephone/television interactive hookups, tele-democracy and televoting could function by providing advance information-al programing on selected issues, interactive phone-in debate on the issues, a press-distributed ballot, and, lastly, a follow-up televised program discussing the results with the audience.[30] In conjunction with national initiative and referenda processes, telepolitics could well dissipate some of the current political apathy and cynicism in liberal democracies.

Despite these great expectations from the enhancement of existing tele-politics, however, we must also realize that there are considerable limita-tions: intimacy, in the sense of the face-to-face communication which Rousseau advocated for small-scale polities, can never be characteristic of town meetings on a large scale. Some analysts have muddled this central point by failing to distinguish clearly between the kind of rooted intimacy and transparency that Rousseau had in mind, and the mere familiarity and informality that people might experience through telepolitics.[31] It is true that telepolitics does eliminate the mystique which politicians could previ-ously cultivate by virtue of their distance from the voters. Thus the camera reveals their nervous twitches, perspiration, errors of fact and expression; it documents their moments of instability and tears that cannot be forgotten; and investigative reporting exposes traits of greed, lust and paranoia by increasingly "politicizing the personal." At the same time, however, tele-politics also subordinates policy issues and debates over questions of sub-stance to the style of political actors. Are they witty, lively and humorous, friendly and alert, profound in their off-the-cuff remarks, etc.?[32] This kind of mediated communication replaces face-to-face intimacy with the kind of familiarity that can breed contempt, cynicism, or the idol-worship associated with Hollywood actors and rock stars; it does not generate either the trust that arises from immediate knowledge of character or the distrust that arises from more direct experience of a politician's duplicity.[33]

Telepolitics exposes viewers to the global afflictions of a suffering humanity. It compels us to reflect upon mass starvation, illiteracy, infant mortality, the demonic use of violence, warfare and terrorism; it also alerts us to the perils of attempts by the superpowers to generate new and more sophisticated weaponry, both for offensive and for defensive purposes. While there may be individual viewers who will not remain "spectactors" when confronted by issues of such magnitude, even those who have some minimal sense of global responsibility and compassion will find it increas-ingly difficult to assimilate such volumes of information and to respond effectively to such a multitude of problems. The majority of viewers will hope and pray that someone will do something; alternatively they will react to the drain on their psychological resources by becoming more cynical and turning in upon themselves.[34] An expanded awareness of the global suf-fering of the poor, the innocent, and the victimized, will not in itself guarantee a compassionate response from telecitizens who cannot immediately relate to global issues of the common good. In short, a technological reconstruction of a Rousseauian transparent assembly appears to be highly implausible.

IV

If the democratic potential of electronic participation seems questionable at best, the dangers of tyranny inherent in telepolitics are clear and undeniable. One variant of telepolitics, for example, would involve a direct-input module through which viewers could gain access to central computers, register their votes, order services, or call up information. One such system, already in operation, scans subscribers' homes every six seconds, in some cases recording the comings and goings of family members, while at the same time storing data concerning polling, shopping, banking and viewing.[35] The manipulative potential of such technology is too obvious to require elaboration. The average citizen becomes more susceptible to technological tyranny, the more dependent he or she becomes upon experts to provide essential information (and opinions) regarding a world that is becoming increasingly bewildering in its complexity.[36] What is gained in terms of the information necessary for citizenship is simultaneously lost through the numbing effects of information overload and psychological stress.

Rousseau would have understood this problem very well. In his view political knowledge was always imperfect, much too imperfect to satisfy the ambitions of technocracy. In addition, Rousseau was also alert to the fact that political specialists will remain subject to the temptation of substituting their particular wills for the general wills of their political communities. The passions of political leaders, their ambition for public recognition and the pleasure of commanding others, their prodigality, greed, sexual desire, vindictiveness, jealousy, and overall weakness are forever in conflict with their intention to act for the common good of all.[37]

Barber seeks to accommodate these realities by way of various institutional checks and balances, including his proposal for a civic communications cooperative. Some of its members would be elected by neighborhood assemblies or their regional associations and sent as mere delegates; others would be selected by several different governmental and nongovernmental constituencies; a congressional watchdog committee would oversee operations to assure that the cooperative did not stray from its mandate; and existing private media corporations would continue in existence.[38] The fact remains, however, that this elite would have to be made up, for the most part, of media experts of all types. The iron law of oligarchy should caution

us against the real possibility of a Walden II type of manipulative technocracy, whose real expertise would be in psychological engineering.

The dangers of plebiscitary tyranny are too palpable for us to ignore or
minimize. The prospect exists of this technocratic elite further manipulating
mass telepolitical audiences, so that public opinion could be daily revised,
and elected officials could be replaced with the same ease as performers are
now taken off the air in the case of amateur talent shows which employ a
degree of interactive television. Such instantaneous, dynamic politics would
abolish all distinctions between experienced politicians, dedicated citizens,
and merely frivolous spectators playing politics until the activity became
relatively boring in relation to the competing entertainment, sports, and education programs. It would be a reinstatement of mobocracy, though the
public square could now extend over the entire planet. Instantaneous telepolitics, for the amusement of anonymous viewers, would necessarily discourage inner commitment and political responsibility. The political ratings
game, arbitrated by computers, would reward short-term thinking and policies, which in the context of enhanced technology could mean longer-term
harm to the environment and to future generations for centuries to come.
This political process would be a travesty of Rousseau's model of
knowledgeable politicians and dedicated citizens interacting periodically
(with enough time elapsing to allow for reflection and learning from
experience) as peers to discern the general will of their community - a
community bonded together by shared compassion, patriotism, and an
intimate sense of transparency.

At present, media and corporate elites have preserved a high degree of
privacy and are relatively impervious to the monitoring processes of investigative journalism, which destroys the careers of public personalities, political and religious, on a regular basis. Media experts and their support staffs
are expert at giving scripted and managed performances while appearing to
be spontaneous.[39] Such masterful techniques, even though they fall short of
the dreams of Skinnerian technocracy, could not be easily countered by
watchdog committees whose very hearings would have to conform to the
guidelines established by those being monitored. If private and public
mediacrats began to monitor each other systematically, there would be some
hope for effective checks and balances. But there is no greater likelihood of
this occurring than there is of the various branches of the armed forces
monitoring and revealing each other's abuses through public disclosures
going well beyond their current internal struggles and bureaucratic in-
fighting. On the contrary, expansion of telepolitics poses the threat of a
media-political complex, arising alongside of the military-corporate complex
and creating even greater dangers to public accountability. The likely
symbiosis of all of these elites would result in the nightmare of an
authoritarian or totalitarian process, sheltered from political responsibility

and deceptively justifying policies opposed to the public good by recourse to the broadly shared but ill-defined goals of national security.[40]

We need not, in fact, even go so far as to impute a tyrannical intention to a media-political complex, for as a group they would have the corporate interest to push ahead with further technological innovation and implementation. That, after all, would be their *raison d'être*. Using the latest generation of supercomputers as they become available, the media-political elites, organized as "cyborgs" or human-machine teams in close symbiosis, might well usher in the tyranny of technological organisms, whose junior partners they would themselves become. Then an iron cage of political existence, shutting out the values of personal dignity on the part of the innocent and technologically illiterate, of the poor, weak and inefficient, would have triumphed absolutely.[41]

We are aware from our own experience that telepolitics is a new and powerful integrating force; yet we also know, from Rousseau, that only politicians can and should exercise the intergrating power of last resort in any society. That is why they require and possess that discretionary authority necessary to deal with public emergencies that threaten the stability or survival of polities. The large-scale emergencies that have occurred and are likely to occur in the future in highly interdependent technological societies (e.g. nuclear accidents, power blackouts, terrorist blackmail on television, the unforeseen consequences of unbridled experiments in biological engineering or their failures) confront political and technocratic elites with the temptation to increase and consolidate their power. Whether their particular motivations be ideological or personal - whether they be motivated by a fanatical or demonic vision, or merely by corruption stemming from debilitating passions for power, sex, revenge or greed - the end result would once again be some version of authoritarian or totalitarian politics justifying itself by false appeals to the public good.

V

There is no doubt that techology may enable us to explore the planets, cure diseases, and emanicipate millions from the deprivations of illiteracy and brutalizing labor. It is also undeniable that technological societies have evolved much too far since Rousseau's day for radical negation of technology to be a viable option, except for small creative minorities willing to form rooted communities in the interstices - between the bars, as it were - of the iron cages that constitute our contemporary political existence. Clearly, modern socictics cannot banish technology. On the other hand, we can at least seek to temper the excesses of technological enthusiasm. Although Rousseau's democratic aspirations often motivate his present-day followers to speculate about the democratic potential of technology, there are abundant reasons for us to treat such speculation with healthy skepticism. We need to sober up, going beyond a spectator consciousness and an attitude that abides technological domination, and reaffirm our potential for an autonomous political consciousness beyond technocracy and human-machine symbiosis. What we need, first of all, is the resolve to explore diverse possibilities of "fasting" from telepolitcs and liberating ourselves from enclosed techno-logical environments.[42] We must experiment with a variety of means by which we might return to the realities of interpersonal political dialogue in our neighborhoods, in the large organizations of which we are members, and outside the parameters and biases of telepolitical images (even though these images cannot be escaped entirely).   Second, we should seize every opportunity to experience or re-experience solidarity with nature - not only in our leisure, but also in our work - whenever we can devise to be craftsmen of hand or brain instead of appendages to animate or inaminate machines, to bureaucracies and factories respectively, with their shared biases towards standardization, precision, and quantitative efficiency. Part-time liberation through such prudent technological negation, combined with attempts to become "specialists in generalism," to see the patterns of truth and bias across the rigid divisions of intellectual labor,[43] would, I think, be salutary pathways to traverse. By searching in these directions we may rediscover our ability to question radically and comprehensively the problem of tech-nology and to partake in attempts by citizen groups to assess technological innovation and implementation.[44]

In his political theory, Rousseau has left us a valuable perspective that inspires us to be autonomous, to be self-directing, and to own ourselves as free and compassionate beings capable of inner political commitment and of sacrifice for the common good. His noble vision is one of a return to nature in forms of solidarity with and receptivity towards its "imperishable beauty," which we can consciously and contemplatively grasp in the midst of the variety of natural species and the harmony of our lakes, rivers, mountains, oceans, and life-giving seasons. The ecological responsibility to which he appeals encourages us to become stewards and protectors of all existing life forms, including the rich, human gene pool, which we now have the capacity to destroy through misuse of our increased technological powers.[45]

Indeed, Rousseau's portrayal of the imperishable beauty of transparent participatory democracy should inspire us, I would hope, to labor hard and uncompromisingly to protect the democratic ideal from being destroyed by the complacent notion that advanced technology has already actualized democracy in principle. Despite our technological might, we must see how weak and fallible we remain politically, both in terms of our inability to attain participatory democracy in the mainstream of our political life and also in terms of the urgent threats to even the minimal degrees of democracy we have managed to preserve. Perhaps by accepting the limits of our

162   Joseph Masciulli

contemporary political wisdom, by rejecting the illusions of our blind
technological pride, and by waking up from the irrational dream of
conquering death, we might proceed to act more moderately as fallible
human beings, fully aware that we are, as Rousseau contended, but a part of
an orderly whole entrusted to us by the Author of our being.

Notes

1. Bernard Lonergan, *Insight* (New York: The Philosophical Library,
1957), p. 228.
2. Jean-Jacques Rousseau, *On the Social Contract*, book III, chapter 15,
in *Oeuvres complètes*, ed. Bernard Gagnebin and Marcel Raymond (Paris:
Gallimard, Bibliothèque de la Pléiade, 1964), vol. III, p. 429 (hereafter *O.C.*,
III).
3. Cf. Thomas Hobbes, *Leviathan*, chs. 10, 13, and 14; John Locke,
Second Treatise of Government, sects. 212 ff.
4. Rousseau, *Discourse on Political Economy*, in *O.C.*, III, pp. 252-54,
258-59; *Emile*, trans. and ed. Allan Bloom (New York: Basic Books, 1979),
p. 321.
5. John Locke, *Second Treatise of Government*, sects. 41, 43.
6. Adam Smith, *The Wealth of Nations*, book I, chapters 2, 3; book V,
chapter 1, pt. 3, articles 2 and 3. Smith also calls for a renewal of militias,
alongside of a well-disciplined standing army, but according to a market
model.
7. Montesquieu, *The Spirit of Laws*, book XX, chapters 1, 2; book XXI,
chapters 20, 6, and 14; bk. XXIII, ch. 29.
8. Cf. Rousseau, *Discourse on Inequality*, in *O.C.*, III, p. 142; *Discourse
on Political Economy*, in *O.C.*, III, pp. 258, 271-72.
9. Cf. *On the Social Contract*, bk. I, ch. 9; bk. II, ch. 11; *Discourse on
Political Economy*, in *O.C.*, III, pp. 262-278.
10. *Discourse on Political Economy*, in *O.C.*, III, pp. 262, 266-67;
Discourse on Inequality, in *O.C.*, III, pp. 205-207; *On the Social Contract*,
Bk. I, Ch. 9.
11. *Discourse on Inequality*, in *O.C.*, III, p. 112; *Discourse on the Arts
and Sciences*, in *O.C.*, III, pp. 28, 525 ("Fragment"); *Discourse on Political
Economy*, in *O.C.*, III, pp. 268-69.
12. Cf. Hazel Henderson, *Creating Alternative Futures* (New York:
Berkley Publishing Corporation, 1978), pp. 323, 325; *Emile*, pp. 195-203.
13. Cf. Carole Pateman, *Participation and Democratic Theory*
(Cambridge, England: Cambridge University Press, 1970), pp. 22-27.

14. Cf. *Discourse on Political Economy*, in *O.C.*, III, pp. 246, 258-59, 261, 273-74; *On the Social Contract*, bk. III, ch. 15; bk. II, ch. 3; bk IV, ch. 1; and Jean Starobinski, *Jean-Jacques Rousseau: la transparence et l'obstacle*, 2nd ed. (Paris: Gallimard, 1971), pp. 13-35.

15. *Discourse on Inequality*, in *O.C.*, III, pp. 142, 219; 156, 168.

16. *Ibid.,* pp. 156, 168, 170-71.

17. *Emile*, p. 222.

18. *Ibid.,* p. 229.

19. *Discourse on the Arts and Sciences*, in *O.C.*, III, p. 19.

20. Cf. *Discourse on Political Economy*, in *O.C.*, III, pp. 247, 254-55; *Emile*, p. 253.

21. *On the Social Contract*, bk. III, ch. 5; bk. II, ch. 7; "Letter to Mirabeau," in *Jean-Jacques Rousseau: Authoritarian Libertarian?*, ed. Guy H. Dodge (Lexington, Mass.: D.C. Heath and Company, 1971), p. 35.

22. *On the Social Contract*, bk. III, ch. 18; bk. IV, ch. 1.

23. *On the Social Contract*, bk. II, ch. 7; bk. IV, ch. 8; *Emile*, p. 37.

24. Cf. *On the Social Contract*, bk. III, chs. 5, 13, and 15.

25. Benjamin R. Barber, *Strong Democracy* (Berkeley and Los Angeles: University of California Press, 1984), pp. 246-47; cf. Henderson, *Creating Alternative Futures*, pp. 374-75; Alvin Toffler, *The Third Wave* (New York: Bantam Books, 1981), pp. 427 ff.; Joshua Meyrowitz, *No Sense of Place* (New York: Oxford University Press, 1985), p. 323.

26. Barber, pp. 266-299.

27. *Ibid.* pp. 277.

28. Meyrowitz, p. 325.

29. Barber, p. 274.

30. *Ibid.,* p. 275.

31. Meyrowitz, pp. 282, 320-21; Barber, p. 274, grants that "the electronic town meeting sacrifices intimacy, diminishes the sense of face-to-face confrontation; and increases the dangers of elite manipulation."

32. Meyrowitz, pp. 275-283, 304, 315.

33. *Ibid.*, pp. 281, 290; cf. *On the Social Contract*, bk. IV, ch. 1.

34. Meyrowitz, p. 318.

35. Barber, p. 277.

36. Cf. Meyrowitz, pp. 326-27.

37. *On the Social Contract*, bk. III, ch. 10.

38. Barber, pp. 277-78.

39. Meyrowitz, p. 324; cf. B.F. Skinner, *Walden Two* (New York: Macmillan, 1976), pp. 218 ff.

40. Cf. *On the Social Contract*, bk. III, ch. 18; bk. IV, ch. 6.

41. Cf. Max Weber, *The Protestant Ethic and the Spirit of Capitalism*, trans. Talcott Parsons (New York: Charles Scribner's Sons, 1958), pp. 181-83; Arthur Gibson, "Visions of the Future," in *Humanism and*

Christianity, ed. Claude Geffré (New York: Herder and Herder, 1973), pp. 122-23.

42. Cf. Langdon Winner, *Autonomous Technology* (Cambridge, Mass.: Cambridge University Press, 1977), pp. 331 ff.

43. Meyrowitz, pp. 327-28.

44. Henderson, pp. 366-67.

45. Cf. Hans Jonas, "Technology, Ethics, and Biogenetic Art," *Communio*, XII, No. 1 (Spring, 1985), 94-96.

ANARCHISM AND TECHNOLOGY

Frank Harrison

Whenever we discuss anarchism we must first remind ourselves that we are not considering a finished system of social and political thought. Within the spectrum of writers who are properly called anarchists there are various approaches. Consequently, if we are to discuss anarchist views on any particular issue, such as technology, it will be helpful if we have a sense of what they hold in common. What ties together the various thinkers to whom I shall refer in this essay, linking them in a single school of thought?

We can begin by recognizing that anarchists, when they are not thought of as bomb-throwing nihilists in black cloaks, are most often viewed as having one thing in common: an uncompromising opposition to the political state in any and every form, which is combined with the proposal of alternate structures of social organization. This is a correct perception. It has been the anarchists' consistent rejection of the state, not only as an end but also as a means of achieving their goals, which has ever been the wedge between them and the Marxists. It was Bakunin's rejection of the state, even the transitional state of a dictatorship of the proletariat, that was the principal ground of his conflict with Marx. The state in whatever form was presented by Bakunin as an independent source of hierarchy and repression, not simply the executive committee of the owners of the means of production.[1]

However, the *archons* that are attacked by the *an-archists* have never been understood as solely political in form. What characterizes the anarchist has been a sensitivity to all forms of domination, and an opposition to all sources of control (power) over individuals in society. Be the anarchist a Proudhonian "mutualist," a Bakuninist "federalist," an "anarchist communist" like Kropotkin, or an "anarcho-syndicalist" like Pelloutier, they have all sought to identify and replace *the multiplicity of causes preventing the development of autonomous individuals who control their own social lives.* Alexander Berkman showed this breadth of concern when he stated:

Authority controls our lives from the cradle to the grave - authority parental, priestly and divine, political, economic, social, and moral....And as you are invaded and violated, so you subconsciously revenge yourself by invading and violating others over whom *you* have authority and can exercise compulsion, physical or moral. In this way all life has become a crazy quilt of authority, of domination and submission, of command and obedience, of coercion, and subjection, of rulers and ruled, of violence and force in a thousand and one forms.[2]

Anarchist analysis of authority is, therefore, much broader than might at first be thought. Moreover, as a result of this, anarchists have usually defined themselves as either socialists or communists when they consider property - stateless socialists, of course. Where anarchists have accepted private property it has always been in a form which was grounded in equality of ownership as the basis of free association, as was the case with both Proudhon and his follower, Benjamin Tucker. Indeed, it might well be argued that any thinker not concerned with economic repression is not an anarchist at all, so glaring is any absence of a critique of property. Thinkers like Robert Nozick, an advocate of a minimal state rather than an anarchist as is sometimes supposed, are no more than neoconservative ideologists of old-fashioned liberalism - as I have shown elsewhere.[3] So-called "anarcho-capitalism" attacks the welfare state and the socialist state, but in the name of the liberal right to unequal property and, in consequence, exploitation and domination. It is a strange anarchism indeed, with nothing in common with the humanism, egalitarianism, and demand for a free community that has characterized anarchist thought for the past two centuries.

That being the general character of the anarchist, what is the anarchist's view of technology?

Technology must be regarded by the anarchist with some suspicion. As the extension of human control over the environment by means of implements or tools, technology has always had the capacity to control the human beings who are part of the environment, to make of them "means" rather than "ends," to destroy autonomy. For the anarchist the state itself is an example of technology, its bureaucratic organization being a tool that has always performed a dehumanizing role. Therefore, Rudolf Rocker argued that the statist mentality, characterized in Rousseau's insistence that we subordinate ourselves to the "common will," was a technological mentality. Considering the centralized state issued in by the French Revolution, Rocker accuses its rulers of viewing the machine of state as more important than the individuals within and under it:

the weal and woe of millions was entrusted to the higher wisdom of a central body whose members felt themselves to be the "mechanics of the machine" - to use Rousseau's term - and quite forgot it was living men whom they used as guinea pigs in their experiments to prove the political wisdom of the "citizen of Geneva."[4]

The technological imagination exists where efficiency of control becomes an end in itself. It is expressed in and through the state, for which reason it might be said that a central concern of anarchism has always been technology, its application, and the mentality which goes with it.

The machines with which our modern imaginations are concerned when we use the term "technology" are, however, conceived somewhat more particularly than the state structure. Technology usually refers to the mechanical hardware, produced by human invention and skill, that allows us to manipulate and to change the physical universe. It is seen as the application of scientific knowledge and engineering skill to the goal of dominating nature for purposes defined by human beings. We live today in what is often termed a "technological society," where capacity for control has been established in an unprecedented manner, and where change is so rapid that each new generation is faced with a world radically different from that of its parents. When asked if they approve of this increased capacity of control of our new Prometheans, anarchists must reply that, "It depends upon the consequences for human beings." Technology is never, in itself, desirable. For example, the computer promises a broadening of communications and an expansion of our understandings. In cybernetic combination with sophisticated machines, we see the possible abolition of toil in a robotics revolution. Yet we also see these technologies being used as means of police control by the state, with the growth of data relating to any citizen who is perceived as a threat. Much has been written by anarchists concerning this aspect of our modern world.[5] Moreover, the promise of a leisured society, reaping the benefits of labor-free productivity, is hardly seen in the expansion of unemployment, insecurity and misery that the ongoing cybernetics revolution has initiated. In Rocker's words, we have been "sacrificed without compunction to technique, degraded into a machine, changed into a nonentity, a 'productive force' deprived of all human traits, in order that the productive process might function with the least possible friction and without internal obstruction."[6] He wrote that some fifty years ago. In its present form and under its current controllers, whether they call themselves communists, capitalists, or social democrats, technology can still be seen to degrade us. Anarchists are still concerned with it.

Science and its offspring, technology (the practical application of our understanding of the physical universe), have facilitated not only the manipulation of nature to human ends (if only the ends of a minority), but also the manipulation of human beings themselves. Science has enabled the control of persons through improved methods of coercion and persuasion; and what the riot stick cannot get, the propagation of information through the media can attain through discrete selection of the parameters of truth. This has been carefully documented by Noam Chomsky, who summarized the situation in the United States as follows:

> The mass media of the United States are part of the national power structure and they therefore reflect its biases and mobilize popular opinion to serve its interests. This is not accomplished by any conspiratorial plotting or explicit censorship - it is built into the structure of the system, and flows naturally and easily from the assorted ownership, sponsor, governmental and other interest group pressures that set limits within which media personnel can operate, and from the nature of the sources on which the media depend for their steady flow of news.[7]

Those who control the techniques of production also control the techniques of persuasion. For anarchists, of course, this is also true in states where property is under the direct control of political bureaucrats, such as the Soviet Union. If anarchists are to be accused of being subversive, they must be seen as subversive of both capitalist and socialist (Marxist-Leninist) states alike.

When we turn from the owners and controllers of technology, and consider science and technology in themselves, as they operate and have been operated, it has been argued that they contribute to a framework of thought that is at once both limiting and oppressive. Such a framework of thought results in the uncomplaining and uncritical acceptance of increasingly unsatisfactory human arrangements. We rape the environment, oppress our populations, and allow the majority of the human race to fester in starvation and poverty. The gods of science and technology are seen to require this sacrifice as the price of progress. The horrible identification of the "is" and the "ought" is our new culture of fatalism. And the philosophers of optimism, like Bell and Brzezinski, look to the technotronic and technocratic resolution of society's evils without pain or turmoil in the non-zero sum game of building a post-technological society. We witness the presumption that science treads a pristine path of neutral progress when, equally and perhaps more feasibly, it can be either the prostitute of established interest, or a blind Frankenstein monster blundering along in pursuit of each new interest mindless of the consequences.

There is no need here to make a distinction between science and technology, the latter being properly regarded as an adjunct of the former. Pure science and applied science, with the managerial organization of the latter, have in fact been drawn together conceptually within a single operational framework. "After 1850, the application of science to technology became a more and more important factor in the advance of industry, and during the present century most of the outstanding technical discoveries have stemmed in the main from scientific researches."[8] Since the 1920's we have had mission-oriented research laboratories, providing permanent links between science and corporations, and between science and government (particularly the military). This unity of science and production, of the pure and applied, of research and technical applications, has become so close a bond that it becomes impossible to consider one without the other; and a "scientific approach" is presumed desirable in all fields of human enquiry in order to gain exactness of understanding and capability in the implementation of goals. Scientific discoveries are transformed into the technical hardware for their practical exploitation in every field. Scientists can say with pride that,

> The exponential growth of the enterprise of science marks the modern era. With it has grown the public following for the sciences - the popular infatuation with discovery and with what is understood as the scientific method of explanation....Radar. Nuclear fission. Antibiotics....Television. Opinion-polling. The green revolution. And here comes genetic engineering. The checklist is piled high on the shelves around us. We now wallow in the practical payout.[9]

A brave new world indeed.

Even in the social sciences the prevailing sympathy persists, with the modern descendants of Auguste Comte seeking exactness of understanding behind the veil of "behaviorism." We have the likes of B.F. Skinner telling us that although we are beyond freedom and dignity, everything will be alright in the realm of behavioral modification. If pigeons can be trained to play ping-pong through systems of reward and punishment, positive and negative reinforcement, then why not use the same methods to train human beings to behave nicely towards each other? Or is there some reason why we might not want our psychologists as new philosopher-kings? Is it perhaps true that social engineers have no more ability to discern the outlines of a just society than have mechanical engineers?

We will return to these questions shortly. At this time, however, let us note that the scientific ethos of the modern period, now so all-encompassing, has involved a distinctive reorientation in the way we regard ourselves and our relationship to our environment or nature. It has dislocated the psyche from any sense of participating in any existential project larger than the satisfaction of immediate biological and material needs. The hierarchical ownership and/or control of resources, and the development of consumer societies, can be seen as intrinsic to this process. *Homo economicus* in both capitalist and socialist (Marxist-Leninist) contexts, exists in psychological isolation from other members of society. Possessed of no sense of purpose beyond immediate needs, incapable of seeing ourselves as participants in a global project of mutual interdependence with our own and other species, we fail to take the necessary actions to ensure even our survival. Such is the central concern of Murray Bookchin, who is perhaps the best known North-American anarchist. Ecology for Bookchin is a question not of discovering less destructive ways of exploiting nature, but of developing an entirely new relationship with nature. That relationship must involve a new view of society, of human relations, of the relationship of humanity to nature. To achieve an ecological society involves a cultural revolution, escaping a mentality of technological domination of which both bourgeois and Marxist ideologists are guilty - if we are to believe Bookchin, who writes, "Marx's own imagination is completely tainted by Promethean, often crassly bourgeois, design images."[10] Bookchin wants to identify ecology with a new social outlook:

> We must try to create a new culture, not merely another movement that attempts to remove the symptoms of our crises without affecting their sources. We must try to extirpate the hierarchical orientation of our psyches, not merely remove the institutions that embody social domination.[11]

An ecological mentality is for him indissolubly linked with anarchist goals; and that mentality must involve a total reconsideration of science, to establish a "new science that accords with libertarian reason,"[12] which is founded in an "ecological ethics." His anarchism is, therefore, a rebellion against the historically developed character of science.

The current prestige of science goes hand in hand with the whole secular emphasis of modern life, the abandonment of transcendental concerns and the concentration upon earthly and empirical matters. The scientific viewpoint comes to be linked with the notion of hedonism, amorality, and the absence of either individual or social restraint. The Christian and conservative Eric Voegelin explained this in terms of the victory of "gnosticism." In the beliefs of that early and largely forgotten Christian sect, he saw as central a dissatisfaction with the world, combined with a belief in the possibility of changing it by human action - action based on knowledge. "Knowledge - gnosis - of the method of altering being is the central concern of the gnostic."[13] This was for Voegelin the equivalent of the murder of god, the victory of Prometheus amongst a humanity assured of the ability to save itself through its own efforts. In his own theological terminology, "Prometheus, Cain, Eve, and the serpent become symbols of man's deliverance from the power of the tyrannical god of this world."[14]

Now anarchists tend to be on the side of those who say that, if god exists in the patriarchal and domineering form that he is usually given to us, then they are with the Prometheans and serpents. However, what is significant is a shared recognition that science cannot replace ethics. Technology has developed the chain saw, which can be used to cut down trees or, somewhat less efficiently than other weapons, to cut off the limbs of other human beings. Science and technology tell us nothing concerning how their products can best be used. An additional judgment must be made, a further assessment concerning the application of the knowledge, the direction and use of technology. Without that judgment science and technology are left to flounder according to the whims of their controllers. Florence Nightingale's application of medicine, Hitler's genocide towards Semitic and Slavic races, Harry Truman's decision to murder the civilian populations of Hiroshima and Nagasaki, the use of medicine to improve health, and giving Indians in South America blankets carrying anthrax; without some kind of extra direction, direction which science does not provide, all of these actions stand isolated from approbation or disapprobation. At the extreme, science and technology have produced the most splendid devices for the destruction of humanity, with sufficient nuclear weapons in the hands of state elites to destroy the human race hundreds of times over. It is a grander version of the salesman who sells a Saturday-night special to a mindless mugger, now providing barbarians with nuclear clubs.

During the nineteenth century anarchism's major proponents had regarded science, the ability to understand the "laws of nature," as crucial to both revolution and the development of social alternatives. Bakunin, Reclus, Kropotkin, Malatesta, and numerous lesser-known thinkers express this embracing of the Promethean vision. This confidence in the revolutionary capacity of the sciences, both physical and social, was expressed by Kropotkin as follows:

> Anarchism is a world-concept based upon a mechanical explanation of all phenomena, embracing the whole of nature - that is, including in it the life of human societies and their economic, political, and moral problems. Its method of investigation is that of the exact natural science, and, if it pretends to be scientific, every conclusion it comes to must be verified by the method by which every scientific conclusion must be verified.[15]

To the extent that this was attained humanity could progress along the path of liberation.

Liberation would have three principal forms. First of all, science, as knowledge of nature's laws, would involve a *liberation from myth*, secular and religious, which inhibited our ability to choose rational courses of action. Reason here was understood to be the capacity of the human mind to appreciate cause and effect, and to implement this knowledge in the satisfaction of life's needs. Usually this was taken in the utilitarian manner of improving one's physical and mental happiness. The second form of liberation was more closely linked to the developing capacity to control and to exploit the resources of nature, and can be summed up by the phrase *liberation from want*. In the third sense, liberation was to be provided from oppression by others by the pursuit of the destruction of social relations which involved the power of a minority over a majority in both economic and political spheres. This can be summed up as a *liberation from hierarchical human organization*. Science and technology might contribute to the triple liberation; indeed, it must. However, even in the nineteenth century Bakunin was sensitive to intrinsic problems.

Bakunin asked: To whom are scientists responsible? Do scientists provide a potential for making themselves a new elite of designers and implementors of new programs of social and industrial reorganization? Does scientific method itself generate a special kind of psychological orientation which has social consequences? Who should determine the goals and projects of science and technology? In answering these questions Bakunin was drawn towards, rather than guided by, anarchist conclusions.

Looking at the scientific community, Bakunin was convinced that they were the bought servants of the bourgeoisie. "The modern universities of Europe," he wrote, "which form a sort of scientific republic, render in the present day the same services to the bourgeoisie which at one time the Catholic church rendered to the nobility."[16]   Science, therefore, is not automatically neutral in its activity and consequences. It serves a master, and that master is the owners of the means of production in capitalist society.

One must take control of science and put it in the service of the masses. However, if one merely took possession of that which already existed, then one would take a biased piece of merchandise. That was the error of the Marxists for Bakunin. Marx had not rid his scientific *Weltanschauung* of its statist links, and it remained a means of domination. "Mr. Marx and his friends ... would concentrate the reins of government into strong hands, for an ignorant people needs strong guidance."[17]   They "demonstrate that the alleged popular state will be nothing more than the very despotic rule of the popular masses by a new and numerically small aristocracy of real or imagined scholars."[18]   Like the witch doctors and the priests of earlier societies, scientific socialists would present their special control of the environment as a basis for forming themselves into a new ruling caste. Consequently, Bakunin talked not just about the destruction of economic privilege (the historical product of a specific science and technology), but also about the destruction of property in the form of knowledge. Destruction of intellectual privilege was seen to be as important to human relations as destruction of property. On the matter of technical progress under capitalism, he argued that it had been "stupendous." However, "the more it grows, the more does it become the cause of intellectual and consequently of material slavery, the cause of poverty and mental backwardness of the people; for it constantly deepens the gulf separating the intellectual level of the privileged classes from that of the great masses of the people."[19] According to Bakunin, Marx had either deliberately or accidentally failed to take this into account with his own political programs.

To break the barrier between a sophisticated elite, which could control the intricate mechanisms that were intrinsic to modern society, and the people, Bakunin resorted to what might be termed educational democratization. This is reminiscent of Babeuf's earlier demand that all must be equal in any human society that is to be regarded as just, including equality of knowledge. Bakunin asserted that the workers *must*

> acquire knowledge and take possession of science - this mighty weapon without which, it is true, they can make revolutions, but lacking which they will never be able to erect upon the ruins of bourgeois privileges the equality of rights, justice, and liberty which constitute the true basis of all their political and social aspirations.[20]

To be wise is thereby turned into a revolutionary responsibility, as is the obligation to propagate knowledge. Its revolutionary fulfillment may involve the lowering of the peaks of human intellectual achievement and "fewer illustrious scientists." Instead "there will be millions who, now debased and crushed by the conditions of their lives, will then bestride the world like free and proud men; there will be no demi-gods, but neither will there be slaves."[21]

This conforms with the moral necessity that people organize their own lives collectively through voluntary associations and confederations of such. It also allows Bakunin to avoid the anti-industrial agrarian anarchism such as that advocated by anarchists like William Morris. Appalled by the ugliness of the industrial environment, an ugliness both aesthetic and ethical, Morris had looked to a dismantling of industry and a depopulation of the towns as necessary for a happy life. Such Luddite aspirations are not without their attractions, especially in the modern era of production of so many "non-goods" - particularly weapons. Bakunin however, like most anarchists, did not look for a society of sophisticated peasants after the manner of Morris. He embraced industrial gains. Control, however, was not to be hierarchical with specialists and managers in superior positions using their "mental labour." Social inequality, generated by one's specialist status in the production process, must be organizationally removed. Status must be destroyed by insisting on equality of income and equality of condition for everyone. The following was Bakunin's formula: "Everyone will work and everyone will be educated."[22] Manual labor, collectively performed, obligatory for all, was seen to be the educational and organizational device for the achievement of solidarity between equals. Such was Bakunin's prescription to ensure that distinctive skills did not carry differential status and rewards. Equality was not just a literal material equality (although he also insisted upon that), but also entailed the ability to perceive all human beings as equal participants in self-governing communities organized nonhierarchically, "from the bottom up."

For Bakunin, as for all anarchists, liberty, equality, and fraternity are not three distinct goals, but are bound together as a single ethical imperative. Structural factors in society must be adjusted to enable their realization. Combined with this is, therefore, a denial of the organizational myths which have encompassed the development of production methods in East and West. The idea that the manager, the technician, the technocrat, is somehow worthy of separate status and reward is regarded as neither functionally necessary nor socially acceptable. The view that workers are to be organized from above, directed like some form of unintelligent subspecies, is attacked as an elitist ideological sham. Anarchist organizational theory and practice constantly stress the cooperative features which exist in all human organization, pointing to the fact that efficiency is served as well as justice when hierarchical methods of production are dispensed with. Typical of this orientation was Kropotkin's description of his own efforts in the famous *Encyclopedia Britannica* article of 1905, where he stated that he had tried

> to indicate how, during a revolutionary period, a large city - if its inhabitants have accepted the idea - could organize itself on the lines of free communism; the city guaranteeing to every inhabitant dwelling, food and clothing to an extent corresponding to the comfort now available to the middle classes only, in exchange for a half-day's, or five hours work; and how all those things which would be considered as luxuries might be obtained by every one if he joins for the other half of the day all sorts of free associations pursuing all possible aims - educational, literary, artistic, sports and so on.[23]

The same concerns, perhaps without quite so much optimism, still involve the anarchist imagination.

Anarchist recommendations concerning how one might move away from the technological centralization characterized today by the gigantomania of American transnational corporations, will sometimes point to the desirability of reduced consumption by the removal of false needs - elegant poverty being the price of autonomy for such as Paul Goodman, in the tradition of William Morris. George Woodcock on the other hand, recommends the following pragmatic changes:

We shall have to reverse the direction of technology, to use it for the simplification rather than the complication of production, for the reduction in size of manufacturing units and power grids, for the recycling of materials and the use of renewable forms of energy, like sunshine and the tides....All this retrenchment will be easier if we have abandoned the habit of seeing such things, in imitation of the Americans, on a megalomaniac national scale.[24]

Woodcock thinks that technology has taken the form of an uncontrollable colossus. His orientation is similar to that of Lewis Mumford (not an anarchist), who used the term "megamachine" to describe the overbearing development of automation and cybernetics to the extent that we have become subordinate to the onrush of technological development. Mumford advocated a withdrawal from the "myth of the machine," which he saw as a fatalistic acceptance of a dehumanized, mechanized sense of ourselves. "We now have sufficient historic perspective," he thought, "to realize that this seemingly self-automated mechanism has ... a man concealed in the works; and we know that the system is not derived from nature as we find it on earth or in the sky, but has features that at every point bear the stamp of the human mind, partly rational, partly cretinous, partly demonic."[25] Cultural revolution and withdrawal of cooperation with the interlinked systems of technological-political domination became his hope. Anarchists do not disagree.

This brings us back to the question of the ethical direction to be given to science and technology, and by whom this direction is to be given. As we saw earlier, there is no implicit direction. Worse perhaps, the scientist might be considered to develop psychological traits which lead to the denial of humanity to those who experience the consequences of "progress." For science deals with "abstract" human beings, not real human beings:

Since by its very nature science has to ignore both the existence and the fate of the individual - of the Peters and the Jameses - it must never be permitted, nor must anyone be permitted in its name, to govern Peter and James. For science in that case would be capable of treating them much the same as it treats rabbits. Or perhaps it would continue to ignore them. But its licenced representatives....would finally end up by fleecing those individuals in the name of science, just as they have hitherto been fleeced by priests, politicians of all shades, and lawyers....[26]

In this statement Bakunin indicates the dehumanizing and authoritarian consequence of a scientific rationality, the Baconian mentality that removes the observer, the scientist, from any identification with the object of study. Nature comes to be regarded as alien raw material, a resource for manipulation and exploitation. Where human beings become part of the object of examination they too are denied their humanity. So the social scientists after Marx, and the managerial scientists after Taylor, treat people "like rabbits." Control of the environment, and control of the individuals within it, is regarded as normal in both state-socialist and capitalist societies. Technical change, to the extent that it is pursued on grounds of simple efficiency, measured by output and profit, regards human beings as production units. If those units become redundant, they are to be thrown away along with the old machines. They cease to be a consideration. Logic demands that they be released from their occupations and from the concern of the planners and implementors of the industrial organization. Technology, going in no particular direction by itself, and implicitly dehumanizing, must be given other parameters than those that it has had thus far. The directions in which anarchists would point technology are necessarily revolutionary. Technology is at present a tool in the hands of the owners and/or controllers of the means of production, be they capitalists or communists, and is intimately linked with existing hierarchies. To change the direction of technology necessarily involves taking it out of the hands of these hierarchies - as was seen most clearly in the writings of Bakunin referred to above.

The revolutionary project, however, is by no means necessarily apocalyptic in form, seeking to provoke class war by propaganda of the word and deed. Few anarchists these days scan the horizon for the red flags of a revolutionary proletariat erecting barricades. Nor are they terrorists, the propaganda of the deed seeming largely futile and productive of negative consequences. Sometimes the anarchist will even take the modest position of George Woodcock:

> The anarchists ... will never create their own world; the free society of which they have dreamed is as pleasant and as remote a myth as the idyllic libertarian society William Morris portrayed in *News from Nowhere*. The material and social complexity of the modern world obviously precludes such simplistic solutions. But this does not mean that the libertarian ideas that have emerged in the libertarian tradition are - outside the context of an anarchist utopia - irrelevant in the real world. Taken individually ... they often have a striking relevance to current positions. At the same time ... the liberalization of society is, in fact, an evolutionary and not an apocalyptic process, and can only be attained by concentrating on piecemeal changes.[27]

For Woodcock, the principal role for anarchists is to criticize the nature of hierarchy and suggest where democratization and decentralization of decision-making can be made within the current framework. It is a framework of thought, a libertarian orientation, which allows specific situations to be analyzed in a manner that avoids false compromises and simplistic choices. In this way Woodcock thought that anarchist positions could remain central to contemporary debates and avoid marginalization. At times this view has even placed Woodcock in the strange position, for an anarchist, of advocating Canadian nationalism. However, we must remember that this is not support of the Canadian state, but a stance in favor of a developing federalism in a country far more politically decentralized than the USA. It also means an advocacy of alternatives to the control of industry north of the forty-ninth parallel by transnational corporations. In his own way Woodcock is reiterating the position of Malatesta who, whilst hating the Italian state, said that he loved Italy.

In a similar vein the American Len Krimerman has drawn a contrast between "classical anarchism" and a "reconstructed anarchism." He regards the former as having a "stubborn streak of self-destructiveness," its emphasis on ideological purity making it a "peripheral voice." A reconstructed anarchism would de-emphasize the goal of a stateless society, work with nonanarchist organizations, and look to "cumulatively evolving transitional stages." In this way he hoped to direct anarchists' attention more towards the workplace and the everyday considerations of working Americans.[28]

Not all anarchists agree with the modest proposals suggested by such writers as Woodcock and Krimerman. In response to Krimerman, Howard Erlich argued that worker cooperatives are either revolutionary projects or alternatives within capitalism; and he could not extend his support to the latter. His stoical conclusion was that anarchists "are required, as revolutionaries, to live our lives as persons marginal to the society and culture we seek to change."[29] Many anarchists have done just that. We must remember, however, that in spite of its bad press and terroristic image, anarchism has usually presented itself as an integral element in all human cultures, not the promoter of strange new utopias, but the cultivator of that which is already there. Kropotkin, for example, did not promote mutual aid as an alternative to our nature, but tried to show that it was intrinsic to every improvement of the human condition. Spontaneous, mutually beneficial and voluntary interaction between individuals is a large and normal element in all of our lives, combined with an instinctive hatred of those who demand involuntary obedience. In the words of Alexander Berkman, "every human being who is not devoid of feeling and common sense is inclined to anarchism."[30] Bookchin presented this common position more recently as follows:

A basic sense of decency, sympathy, and mutual aid lies at the core of human behaviour. Even in this lousy bourgeois society we do not find it unusual that adults will rescue children from danger although the act will imperil their lives; we do not find it strange that miners, for example, will risk death to save their fellow-workers in cave-ins....What tends to shock us are those occasions when aid is refused - when the cries of a girl who has been stabbed and is being murdered are ignored in a middle-class neighborhood.[31]

What we might call a natural solidarity (which does not discard the need for organization) lies at the root of all anarchist argument and expectations. It is this solidarity which permits anarchists to promote unashamedly the idea of an end to hierarchical organization based on power, and the substitution of the free organization of society.

There are few blueprints in anarchist writings, and those tend to be indicative rather than final. Anarchism leaves final forms to the decision of the participants themselves. Certain liberatory directions do seem obvious, however - the principal one being the use of technology within a framework of organizational decentralization and expansion of authentic self-management.

The pursuit of decentralization can take place at the everyday level, looking for incremental or transitional goals such as those put forth by Woodcock and Krimerman. All anarchists do this, living their ideology through the promotion of solidarity in associations with which they are connected. Anarchists are active participants in trade unions, day-care centres, local community meetings, the peace movement, cooperatives, etc., promoting the advance of community and workers' control in the immediate situation. This grasping after immediate opportunity is probably what led some Spanish anarchists to participate in the revolutionary government during the Civil War, much to the dismay of other anarchists.

There is no doubt that anarchists must tread carefully in the attempt to keep theory and practice complementary. But there are good reasons why anarchists should spend energy supporting trade-union initiatives such as the ones suggested by the National Union of Provincial Government Employees in Canada. These include the demand that electronic monitoring of work be prohibited, as an invasion of privacy and a cause of unnecessary stress; that there should be mandatory consultation between employers and unions concerning the introduction of technology; that employees be given at least one year's notice of warning concerning the introduction of new technology. With changes such as these, more general goals might be attained, such as the forging of "new alliances to avoid the risk of social isolation. We must end the fragmentation of the labour movement. Mergers, coalitions and a more cooperative style of work are necessary to resolve jurisdictional disputes and face the future effectively."[32] The aim of NUPGE in the 1980s is explicitly stated to be "control over technological change." No anarchist could object to this. Working towards such immediate goals is not a sellout, but part and parcel of their contribution towards the creation of an acceptable alternative to the use of technology for control.

Nevertheless, beyond these immediate concerns is the anarchist perspective, which involves inevitably a distrust of the trade-union operation as being satisfied with established processes and limited goals. The direction that is the constant conditioning variable in the intellectual framework of the anarchist, which keeps him/her demanding ever "more," is the confidence that any gains in self-management and self-determination are but indicators of a vaster potential. In this sense the anarchist has a perpetual ability to be dissatisfied, and is always looking for the next opportunity to dismantle another element of hierarchy.

That task of formulating an alternate approach to what has been loosely called the postindustrial society has been Bookchin's principal concern during the past twenty years. His analyses and speculations have developed within the framework of the idea of *ecology*, and the practical necessity of redefining the total relationship between humanity and Nature. Bookchin explains how the present problems of technological development, from pollution to starvation to the prospect of nuclear war, are problems of "social ecology" - problems of the way in which human beings relate to each other and to all of the other interconnected ecosystems that make up our total environment. In his 1965 essay, "Towards a Liberatory Technology," he outlined the possibility of an affluent but less wasteful society using technology to establish egalitarian relationships in which urban and rural occupations are integrated to provide an existence which is materially, morally and aesthetically beneficial to all. This is an invitation to speculate originally, to move away from the "technological rationality" towards an ecological reason which will use (rather than be used by) technology. We are given the possibility of decentralized communities with established and alternative technologies, communities which might be self-governing entities of freely associated individuals.

Seriously doubting the future of humanity if we do not reorient our view of human society and its relationship to nature, Bookchin communicates a sense of urgency. We must consider "whether a future society will be organized around technology or whether technology is now sufficiently malleable so that it can be organized around society."[33] He points the way towards the latter possibility through the development of a "libertarian rationality," as he calls the necessary reorientation of our attitudes and values:

We have only to sculpt reason into an ethically charged sensibility that is personally and socially emancipatory....Reason, whose defeat at the hands of Horkheimer and Adorno evoked so much pessimism among their colleagues, can be lifted from its fallen position by a libertarian ethics rooted in a radical social ecology.[34]

The direction in which Bookchin points us is away from the intellectual narrowness and elitism of the academic journal and ideological system. It is an invitation and stimulus to alternative styles of thought, speculations that are unpolluted by hierarchical associations, involving a participation in aesthetic indiscipline in preference to the dry inhibitions of the critical styles with which we are more familiar.

> The greatness of the Dadaist tradition, from its ancient roots in gnostic Ophites to its modern expression in Surrealism - a celebration of the right to indiscipline, imagination, play, fancy, innovation, iconoclasm, pleasure, and a creativity of the unconscious is that it criticizes the "hidden" realm of hierarchy more unrelentingly and brashly than the most sophisticated theoretical games in hermeneutics, structuralism, and semiology so much in vogue on the campuses of contemporary western society.[35]

Narrow systems of thought, defined by thinkers trapped in the specialized logic and concepts of a narrow corner of their disciplines, are not likely to break free from the inhibitions of the present or cultivate a broad and popular consideration of alternatives. Conceptual straitjackets must be torn off and less rigid frameworks of thought encouraged and accepted.

We are not given an ideological system by Bookchin, nor a definitive program for change. The direction is clear, however, and has been summarized by John Clark as follows:

> a new technological practice aimed at ecological regeneration and founded in a respect for nature must be accompanied by a new political practice aimed at social and cultural regeneration. Such a practice will seek to transform all social institutions by replacing mechanistic, power-based structures by organic social forms. It will oppose centralization with decentralization, hierarchical control with self-management, manipulation with mutuality, atomistic individualism with community, and domination with cooperation.[36]

All of this is merely indicative of the direction in which common sense should take us. It is an appropriate intellectual response to the problems that are given to us by the hierarchical uses of technology. To the degree that we move in that direction, life will become more satisfying for more people; and that must be reward enough as we look forward to the next situation, the next opportunity to demolish an aspect of hierarchy and abuse of technology.

On the other hand, the state and its officers appear more and more alien and irrelevant in the context of that most obvious product of modern technology, the thermonuclear bomb. The "nuclear state," the state which possesses thermonuclear weapons, would appear to contradict the logic of its own legitimacy. States are supposedly there to protect their citizens; but, as Joel Kovel argues, the nuclear state places its population in a position of perpetual threat of death:

> its own citizenry must increasingly be regarded as adversaries. Essentially this is because the promotion of any nuclear policy means that the state must be willing to destroy its own society to get what it wants....If the truth were generally appreciated, it would destroy the state's legitimacy and so bring down its power from within through the very exercise of the means of securing it from without.[37]

Contemporary power and modern technology are at the point of wiping us all out. If that is not a stimulus to thinking about alternatives, nothing is. And of those alternatives, the anarchist theoretical perceptions and practical proposals at least manage consistently to place technology in a proper subordinate relationship to individual human beings.

Notes

1. For a discussion of the theoretical conflict between Bakunin and Marx see Chapter Three, "Anarchism and Revolutionary Socialism," of my book, *The Modern State: an Anarchist Analysis* (Montreal: Black Rose Books, 1983), pp. 75-121. For a more general discussion of the theoretical differences between Marxism and anarchism, see my "Marxists and Anarchists," in *A Critique of Marxist and Non-Marxist Thought*, ed. Ajit Jain and Alexander Matejko (New York, Praeger Publishers, 1986), pp. 158-177.
2. Alexander Berkman, *A.B.C. of Anarchism* (London: Freedom Press, 1964), p. 8.
3. See my article, "Rights and the Right Wing: Nozick Reconsidered," in *Our Generation*, 16, No. 2 (March, 1984), 27-34.
4. Rudolf Rocker, *Nationalism and Culture* (Los Angeles: Rocker Publication Committee, 1937), p. 171.
5. See for example D. Roussopoulos and M. Hewitt (eds.), *1984* (Montreal: Black Rose Books, 1984). This is a collection of essays by North-American anarchists on various conceptual themes found in George Orwell's *1984*, examining how contemporary western states and societies possess the same repressive features as those shown in Orwell's dystopian novel.
6. Rocker, p. 524.

7. Edward S. Herman, *The Real Terror Network*, (Montreal: Black Rose Books, 1985), p. 139.

8. Stephen F. Mason, *A History of the Sciences*, (New York: Collier Books, 1962), p. 503.

9. Horace Freeland Judson. "Century of the Sciences," in *Science*, 5, No. 9 (November 1984), 41-42.

10. Murray Bookchin, *The Ecology of Freedom* (Palo Alto: Cheshire Books, 1982), p. 226.

11. *Ibid.*, p. 340.

12. *Ibid.*, p. 308.

13. Eric Voegelin, *Science, Politics and Gnosticism*, (Chicago: Gateway, 1968), p. 87.

14. *Ibid.*, pp. 36-37.

15. Peter Kropotkin, *Revolutionary Pamphlets* (New York: Dover Publications, 1970), p. 150. From "Modern Science and Anarchism" (1913).

16. G.P. Maximoff (ed.), *The Political Philosophy of Bakunin*, (London: The Free Press, Collier MacMillan, 1964), p. 82.   From Bakunin's "Federalism, Socialism, and Anti-Theologism."

17. M.A. Bakunin, *Statism and Anarchy*, ed. J.F. Harrison, (New York: Revisionist Press, 1976), pp. 263-264.

18. *Ibid.*, p. 260.

19. Maximoff, p. 82. From Bakunin's "The Knouto-Germanic Empire and the Social Revolution."

20. *Ibid.*, p. 83. From Bakunin's "The Lullers."

21. *Ibid.*, p. 412. From Bakunin's "Integral Education."

22. *Ibid.*, p. 411.

23. Kropotkin, p. 298. From Kropotkin's "Anarchism"(1905).

24. George Woodcock, *The Rejection of Politics* (Toronto: New Press, 1972), p. 81. From "Up the Anti-Nation."

25. Lewis Mumford, *The Pentagon of Power* (New York: Harcourt Brace Jovanovich, 1970), p. 434.

26. Maximoff, p. 78. From Bakunin's "The Knouto-Germanic Empire and the Social Revolution."

27. George Woodcock, p. 43. From "Anarchism Revisited."

28. Leonard Krimerman, "Anarchism Reconsidered: Past Fallacies and Unorthodox Remedies," in *Social Anarchism*, 1, No. 2 (October 1980), 1-16.

29. Howard J. Erlich, "Commentary: Anarchism Reconsidered." *Ibid.*, p. 26.

30. Alexander Berkman, p. 20.

31. Murray Bookchin, *Post-Scarcity Anarchism* (Montreal: Black Rose Books, 1977), p. 138. From "Toward a Liberatory Technology."

32. NUPGE, Document #19 of the 15th Constitutional Convention: "Workers' Rights in the Silicon Age." (Ottawa, no date).

33. Bookchin, *Post-Scarcity Anarchism*, p. 106.

34. Bookchin, *The Ecology of Freedom*, p. 353.

35. *Ibid.*, p. 350.

36. John Clark, *The Anarchist Moment* (Montreal: Black Rose Books, 1984), p. 198.

37. Joel Kovel, *Against the State of Nuclear Terror* (Boston: South End Press, 1983), p. 33.

HEGEL AND MARX:
PERSPECTIVES ON POLITICS AND
TECHNOLOGY

Richard B. Day

The struggle of the Solidarity trade union has brought into focus important areas of theoretical weakness in classical Marxism. At a time when many socialists are arguing the need to replace Stalinist planning with some form of market, the Solidarity program has tended to be interpreted in terms of two central themes. First, there is the demand that Stalinist bureaucrats respect their own constitution and the *rule of law*. And second, there is the related awareness that re-creation of civil rights appears to presuppose a new autonomy for *civil society*.[1] The rule of law is normally understood to mean the absence of discretionary economic power in the hands of the political authorities. Yet to constrain the state in this way seems to imply, as traditional liberals would argue, that civil society has rights which are *antecedent* to the state and that economic actors should be essentially self-governing within a framework of established statutory rules. In the liberal interpretation the laws of the state should have the same objectivity as the laws of nature or the economic laws of the capitalist market.[2] In that way individuals can plan their own economic activity, knowledgeable of the consequences and without fear of arbitrary intervention.

Marx believed that such a separation of the economic from the political was the essence of political alienation. Socialism was to be the transcendence of this contradiction, bringing the anarchic economic activities of individuals in civil society under the conscious communal control of the associated producers. Numerous critics, including many critical Marxists, have now come to the conclusion that Marx dealt with the society-state relationship in a tragically inadequate manner. On the one hand he believed the commune-state would provide the transitional form of political *emancipation*; on the other hand he charged the *dictatorship of the proletariat* with responsibility for overcoming economic scarcity through planning. The problem is that Marx provided no indication of how socialist planning might be accomplished democratically. The historical consequence has been a "scientific" plan alien to the producers. In Stalinist societies the plan is said to be "rational," yet in reality it functions as a mystery to those whose human creativity Marx thought would be emancipated through social planning.

It is this dilemma which prompts Agnes Heller to write of the need for "a relative (never complete) separation of state from society." Insofar as the particular interests of civil society retain an independent existence, Heller believes that the socialist state must be characterized by constitutional law, democratic civil liberties, pluralism, the system of contract and the principle of representation.3 "Whoever wants to avoid tyranny has to reconsider what kind of relations have to exist between state and society, the public and private spheres....If we cannot imagine a society expressing one homogeneous will, we have to assume the system of contracts which ensures that the will (and interest) of all has to be taken into consideration. Consequently, we have to presuppose democracy."4

Other Marxists believe that the alternative to Heller's approach is to locate the hope for human emancipation in the scientific and technical revolution. Instead of reverting to the rule of law and a market, this view would rely upon the new production technologies to overcome the socially divisive consequences of scarcity. From the standpoint of classical Marxism, however, this argument raises equally serious problems. To Marxists it should be obvious that the new means of production and communication have both an alienating and an emancipating potential. If capitalism, as Marx argued, appropriates the inorganic *body* of the workers and transforms it into the alien power of capital, there is surely an equal danger that "scientific Stalinism," equipped with computer technology, will perpetuate itself by appropriating society's inorganic *mind.* As private ownership of embodied labor established capital's tyranny over living *labor,* so in this case bureaucratic control of embodied thought would imply unprecedented possibilities for manipulating the living *consciousness.* The result would be to eliminate any prospect of replacing "scientific" control from above with democratic control from below.

That modern Marxists should confront such a dilemma is a direct consequence of Marx's own rejection of the state and his resulting failure to recognize the need for a theory of socialist politics. Although Marx's critique of the market economy was expressed most coherently in *Capital,* his understanding of the relation between civil society and the state grew out of his youthful repudiation of Hegelian philosophy. Hegel's *Philosophy of Right* subsumed the unconscious activity of market individuals under the higher authority of rationally determined laws. Unlike the liberal tradition, which interprets statutory law by analogy with the "objective" laws of the market, Hegel's laws were to embody the will of associated citizens. Hegelian theory provides a vision of a society dialectically articulated, wherein citizens consciously determine the conditions of their freedom. In this paper I shall argue that Hegel's approach to the question of *right* affords more constructive insight into the dilemma of modern Marxism than either the liberal or technological alternative.

Whereas Hegelian philosophy treated the state as ontologically necessary, in *The German Ideology* Marx and Engels traced its origin to historically transitory conditions arising from the division of labor and economic needs. The first human needs were satisfied within the family. Wife and children became the "slaves" of the husband, and this first form of property corresponded perfectly to "the definition of the modern economists, who call it the power of disposing of the labour power of others."5 Through the development of industry and commerce, men acquired the ability to appropriate nature more fully in satisfaction of their needs, creating in the process their own second nature. Human labor transformed the world, but appropriation of the *collective* second nature in the form of *private* property resulted in an alien power no less threatening than primordial nature had been to the first men. The products of human labor came to control their creators; social labor became forced labor in exchange for access to privately owned means of production; and the antagonistic economic relations of civil society created the need for the capitalist state.

The claim of the modern state was to re-create at a higher level the original prepolitical community. To this contention Marx and Engels responded that the state was but an "illusory communal life"; its enforcement of the illusory "communal interest" merely expressed the particular interest of the ruling class.6 Marx was certainly aware that even in communist society certain "social functions" would remain and be similar "to the present functions of the state."7 But as class divisions receded, Marx expected these functions to assume a technical-administrative rather than a political character and to be fulfilled in accordance with a "settled plan."8 Industrialization was to advance to the point where human labor would be all but displaced by machines, allowing every "social individual" the disposable time in which to develop human potential to the full.9 Economic life would be transformed into a "technological application of science"; and men would control the new technologies to the extent that disposable time equipped them with universal skills. The fully developed human being would be one "in whose head exists the accumulated knowledge of society."10 A truly human community would transcend the division of labor, in particular the division between mental and physical labor, allowing social individuals to regulate their relation with nature "rationally" and to pursue development of their own creativity as an end in itself. The Realm of Necessity (economic production) would coexist dialectically with the Realm of Freedom (disposable time), the result of which would be free and endless human becoming.

Marx's economic treatment of the dialectic of freedom and necessity was a response to Hegel's political interpretation of the same dialectic in the *Philosophy of Right*. Hegel had followed the approach of Aristotle's *Politics*, where justice was said to be the "bond of men in states" and "the principle of order in political society."[11] Hegel agreed with Aristotle that the principle of the state was ethical (rather than economic) life, or community with others experienced as its own end. In contrast with Marx, Hegel believed the state did not arise *from* the family and civil society, but was logically *prior* to both in the sense that neither could exist apart from a political order. The family was not the first division of labor, rather it was the moment of ethical life "in its natural or immediate phase"; civil society, the real domain of the division of labor, was a necessary moment of economic association brought about by pursuit of particular needs; and the state was the concrete realm of freedom, welding its particular components together into the mediated totality of conscious ethical life.[12]

Whereas Marx and Engels viewed the legal framework of civil society as a "cult" of concepts, necessitated by class antagonisms, Hegel regarded the system of right as "the realm of freedom made actual." Marx found man's second nature in the objective world created by human labor; Hegel described the laws as the living consciousness of freedom, "the world of mind brought out of itself like a second nature."[13] For Marx the problem with Hegel's system was its foundation in civil society and private property: unable to contemplate transcending the division of labor, or the compulsive pursuit of individual needs in the market, Hegel had produced merely the consciousness of freedom, "the dialetic of pure thought," or false consciousness on a universal scale.[14] Thus Hegel's highest achievement was merely a philosophy of freedom, whereas Marx sought the material substance of freedom through a scientific economic plan. For the law-making role of the Hegelian state Marx substituted the plan-making activities of a voluntary, ultimately nonpolitical association of producers, freed from the determination of economic necessity.

A fundamental distinction between these two approaches lies in their different understanding of reason. Hegel saw reason in *practical* terms, as the process whereby citizens consciously determine the conditions of their mutual recognition and affirmation; Marx understood reason in the *technical* sense, leading to the instrumental knowledge required to manipulate a world of things in pursuit of human objectives. Hegel emphasized the need to define the objectives themselves through political discourse; Marx thought that until society had technically resolved the economic problem of scarcity, it remained capable only of "philosophizing" over ends. When Hegel declared that the principle of the modern state required "that the whole of an individual's activity shall be mediated through his will,"[15] or through self-determined rights and duties, Marx replied that in capitalist society *market laws* operate "independently of the will, foresight and action of the producers."[16] Hegel saw the world governed by reason; Marx pointed out that the rationality of the market prevails only *post festum*, through repeated economic crises·necessitated by unplanned disproportionalities between the different branches of industry. Hegel saw finite spirits as vehicles of the World Spirit, or the rational necessity which prevailed throughout nature and history; Marx countered with the demand that men become "the authors and actors of their own drama," which in turn depended upon *ex ante* integration of their labor through conscious planning.[17]

Hegel was certainly aware of both the egoism of civil society and the reality of class differences, but he believed that individuals were "the unconscious tools and organs of the world mind at work within them."[18] Thus within the self-seeking of civil society Hegel found implicit reason at work: "That is to say, by a dialectical advance, subjective self-seeking turns into the mediation of the particular through the universal, with the result that each man in earning, producing and enjoying on his own account is *eo ipso* producing and earning for the enjoyment of everyone else."[19] Familiar with the work of Smith, Ricardo and others, Hegel believed the new science of political economy had proven itself a credit to thought by discovering rational laws for a seeming mass of accidents in the market.[20] But while poliltical economy remained a positivist science, focused upon abstract individuals and the implicit reason of Smith's "hidden hand," Hegel argued that the role of the state was to mediate this abstract subjectivity up to the level of conscious totality. In civil society unity was present "not as freedom but as necessity."[21] The purpose of the laws was to subsume the particular economic activities of the market under the rationally determined and freely accepted obligations of an integrated community of ethical life.

The political community was the concrete universal, within which the particular and universal consciousness were united through "self-determining action on laws and principles which are thoughts and so universal."[22] In its *universality* the state transcended the particular wills of civil society; its *concreteness* lay in the fact that as a mediated totality it affirmed and upheld these particulars by raising them to awareness of mutual rights and duties as the necessary foundation of private contracts. The laws were rational insofar as they continuously emerged from the exercise of practical reason on the part of citizens themselves. "Hence in this identity of the universal will with the particular will, right and duty coalesce, and by being in the ethical order a man has rights insofar as he has duties, and duties insofar as he has rights." Hegel thought individuals had an abstract right to property, as the embodiment of their reason and their labor, but property rights presupposed a higher right "to be subjectively destined to freedom."

The right to freedom was fulfilled when citizens belonged to an ethical order.[23]   The "supreme duty" of an individual, therefore, was "to be a member of a state."[24]

The typical critique of Marx from an Hegelian perspective begins with the observation that Marx replaced political mediation of class differences with an economic theory of class struggle.   Moreover, as R.N. Berki comments, Marx assumed that the end of civil society would result in an *immediate* and stateless "community of universal harmony."[25]   Charles Taylor similarly observes that Marx had a "wildly unrealistic notion of the transition as a leap into untrammelled freedom" - a freedom devoid of internal structure and therefore utterly empty.[26]   The Hungarian Marxist philosopher, Mihaly Vajda, shares identical concerns in *The State and Socialism.*   Society, he argues, must be based upon "the confrontation between its interwoven particular groups ... and not on the abolition of particularities."[27]   Democracy involves a process of "enlarging the opportunity for each particular group ... to articulate their needs and to assert their interests."[28]   Humanized forms of social interaction are required in order to accommodate "unavoidable clashes of interest."   In the absence of a mature civil society, with civil rights for all groups, one group is bound to prevail: the political bureaucracy will pursue its own group interest "as if it were the interest of the whole of society."[29]

This new Marxist awareness of the need for political mediation is related to the persistence of the division of labor, a condition which Hegel believed to be ontologically necessary.   For Hegel all being is syllogism, and the individual is mediated into the universal through the particular associations of which he is a member. Although he shared the political economists' belief in the general beneficence of the market,   Hegel was also aware of its contingent nature: for reasons beyond his own understanding, uncontrolled market forces brought in their wake the danger of economic crises.   The particular interest, he wrote, "invokes freedom of trade and commerce against control from above; but the more blindly it sinks into self-seeking aims, the more it requires such control to bring it back to the universal. Control is also necessary to diminish the danger of upheavals arising from ... the working of a necessity of which [individuals] themselves know nothing."[30]   Unless subsumed under explicit reason, the market had the potential to create a "pauperized rabble," and once society is established "poverty immediately takes the form of a wrong done to one class by another."[31]   Price controls over the major branches of industry were one means with which to avert class polarization;   another was to lay the burden of maintaining the poor on the wealthier classes and on public resources. "The important question of how poverty is to be abolished is one of the most disturbing problems which agitate modern society."[32]

Comments such as the above help to explain the origins of Marx's theoretical project and also the uniqueness of its solution. When Hegel said that men are subjectively destined to freedom, Marx reinterpreted the remark to mean that through embodying their human subjectivity in technology, men would overcome the necessity of the division of labor. Whether or not modern Marxists share this original vision, the fact is that the nominally "socialist" societies are far from overcoming economic scarcity or its social implications. For this reason it seems appropriate, despite the fundamental differences between Marx and Hegel, to suggest that modern Marxists might learn from Hegel's theory when addressing the problems of socialist civil society and democratic planning. To acknowledge the necessity of a socialist civil society requires nothing more than to recognize that within "actually existing socialism" particular needs persist. Unless these needs are politically mediated, they will necessarily result either in social disintegration or in a scientific tyranny of bureaucratic technique.

Influenced by liberal theories of the rule of law, many of the dissident intellectuals in Soviet-type societies have reacted to this prospect by reasserting the importance of rights, law and legality. Andrei Sakharov, for instance, has appealed to Soviet leaders to commit their legal system to "the pursuit of justice as an abstract concept"[33] in the hope that a "flexible, pluralist, tolerant society" might result from legal reforms.[34]   Roy Medvedev, another prominent Soviet dissident, has called for restoration of a long list of liberal freedoms, including "freedom of conscience, freedom of movement, free elections by secret ballot and absolute equality before the law ... with a separation of powers between the legislative, executive and judicial branches."[35] But the experience of the Solidarity trade union has demonstrated that in order for socialist workers to realize self-determination, it is not enough to appeal for the abstract rights of individuals. Thus while Solidarity's program repeated the traditional demands for liberal rights, it combined these with the further demand for universal democratization and for codification of the new relations between state and civil society in the form of a *social contract*.

The fact that Solidarity spoke of a social contract has encouraged many observers to interpret the movement's significance in terms of a reassertion of liberal values. The notion of two parties negotiating a contract certainly appears to imply their separation and thus to emphasize the potential for a self-governing civil society. As Hegel argued in the *Philosophy of Right*, however, the very act of entering into a contract is simultaneously a movement beyond abstract particularity. "Existence as determinate being is in essence being for another....This relation of will to will is the true and proper ground in which freedom is existent. The sphere of contract is made up of this mediation ... [and of] participation in a common will."[36] Solidarity's social contract was to determine the disposition of labor and the

products of labor on a social scale. Like any other contract, it logically
presupposed a social system of rights and duties; that is, a political
community of which the contracting parties are both members.

Solidarity did not aim for a *separation* of state and society, but for their
dialectical *reintegration*: its goal was not to perpetuate the externalization of
political authority but to achieve the very opposite, or "socialization of ...
government and state administration." The first section of the union's
program declared that "we are not just a force of *rejection*. Our aim is to
rebuild a just Poland." The universal legal forms of a just society were to
receive concrete content through recognizing the legitimacy of particulars
and the duty of citizens to participate in determining the conditions of their
freedom: "Respect for the *person* must be the basis of action: the state must
serve the people instead of dominating them....The state must really *belong*
to the whole nation."[37]   Whereas Stalinism had separated the ruling
bureaucracy from the people, the goal of Polish workers was to restore "a
just relationship between the citizens and the state" - a relationship which
presupposed an "indissoluble unity" between civil society and the political
authorities.[38] The dialectical expression of this unity was to be the "self-
governed republic," a political universal made concrete through "independent, self-governing institutions in every field."[39]

Solidarity proposed to rebuild a socialist community from the factory
floor, beginning with election of workers' councils. Enterprise directors
were to be appointed with the participation of the councils and would be
subject to recall by the councils. On this necessary foundation of particularity, the entire economy was to be reconstituted so as to combine
"planning, autonomy and the market."[40] Individual enterprises were to
dispose of their own output on the market, with the plan controlling their
activity from above and bringing them back to the universal through
supervision of prices, taxes and interest rates. At the same time, the democratic functioning of control from above was understood to require that the
plan itself be "subject to the control of society."[41] When civil society was
fully reconstituted, this responsibility for social control would be shared at
various levels by the Sejm (the legislature), local governments and the
workers' councils. In the interim, the mediated unity of civil society and the
state was to be embodied in a Social Council of National Economy, bringing
together workers' delegates, government and the Church. In other words,
the state was to retain its necessary presence in the system of needs at the
same time as civil society established its own rightful presence in the
political state. The organizational principle of such a dialectically rein-
tegrated community would have become, in Hegelian terms, mediation of
particular interests through the universal of a democratic plan. Notwithstanding the theoretical differences which divided Marx and Hegel,
Polish workers demonstrated in practice the possibility of pursuing Marx's

ambition through the kind of organizational structures discussed in Hegel's *Philosophy of Right.*

Solidarity went beyond Sakharov's and Medvedev's appeal for civil rights in the knowledge that citizens can only claim the rights they give to themselves. This was what Marx meant when he wrote that "In democracy the constitution, the law, the state, so far as it is political constitution, is itself only a determination of the people, and a determinate content of the people....all forms of state have democracy for their truth, and for that reason are false to the extent that they are not democracy."[42] Stalinist states are "false" in exactly this sense: they are an abstract totality in which the particular interest of the ruling bureaucracy presumes one-sidedly to be present in all other particulars. Hegel wrote that "fanaticism is just the refusal to give scope to particular differences."[43] Stalinism is fanatically committed to "despotism," which in Hegel's view meant "any state of affairs where law has disappeared and where the particular will ... takes the place of law."[44] The fatal flaw in Marx's *Critique of Hegel's 'Philosophy of Right'* was Marx's acceptance of the notion that "in true democracy the political state disappears," that when all members of society are in the state, separation of the two falls away and is replaced by immediate unity.[45] As a practical response to this weakness of Marxist theory, Solidarity's self-governed republic was neither an abstract parliamentary regime of liberal forms nor the stateless unity which Marx associated with scientific planning. Instead, it was a mediated unity of individual, particular and universal, incorporating the socialist division of labor and pointing towards subordination of technical reason to practically determined social ends.

Whereas Marx expected the *political state* to fall away, as the institutionalized "other" of civil society, Hegel referred to the state *as such* in much broader terms: it extended beyond the practice of politics to include, as T.M. Knox remarks, "the totality of human life ... as ... the life of moral beings united in a community."[46] The universal was continuously sundered through internal differentiation into necessary particulars, but as a living entity it "perpetually re-creates itself in its dissolution."[47] Civil society was the "external state, the state based on need," but its internal structures had the purpose of educating citizens into the life of the universal. The state affirmed the legitimacy of civil society's *corporations* by recognizing their right to care for their members' shared interests; within the corporation the individual found his "rank" and "dignity," recognition that he is a "somebody" and not merely the abstract individual of the liberal market.[48]

The corporations were relatively autonomous within their own sphere of particular right, but like Solidarity's trade unions and workers' councils, the legitimacy of their right presupposed participation in a higher universal. The state must be present in civil society, and civil society must be present in state. The state's presence in particular corporations would be signified through selection of their officers by a combination of election and appointment; conversely, the corporations would establish themselves in the political state through corporate appointment of deputies to the legislature (or the estates). The principle of directly representing the particulars of civil society in the legislature reflected Hegel's conviction that freedom would be vacuous and the people would be powerless unless organized: "it is of the utmost importance that the masses should be organized, because only so do they become mighty and powerful. Otherwise they are nothing but a heap, an aggregate of atomic units. Only when particular associations are organized members of the state are they possessed of legitimate power."[49] The role of deputies was to ensure that "the state enters into the subjective consciousness of the people and ... the people begins to participate in the state."[50] Through their representatives in the legislature the people would participate in determining the laws, and the strength of the state would therefore reside in "the unity of its own universal end ... with the particular interests of individuals."[51] Individual and corporate interests could be neither suppressed nor ignored if the state was to remain a *concrete* universal: "instead they should be put in correspondence with the universal, and thereby both they and the universal are upheld."[52]

Just as corporations were to mediate particular interests in the direction of the universal, so Hegel thought the civil service might rise above the economic "battlefield" of particular classes and groups and bring their particular consciousness back to conscious awareness of the universal.[53] The civil service was to be Hegel's "universal class," but lest its members be tempted to behave otherwise, he believed the authority vested in the corporations would constitute "a barrier against the intrusion of subjective caprice into the power entrusted to a civil servant."[54] Legitimate corporations completed "from below" the system of state control from above. Hegel believed the "personal arbitrariness" of officials would be "broken against such authorized bodies. Action in accordance with everyone's rights, and the habit of such action, is the counterpoise to officialdom which independent and self-subsistent bodies create."[55] A dialectically articulated community would prevent the civil service from assuming "the isolated position of an aristocracy and using its education and skill as means to arbitrary tyranny."[56]

Insofar as Marx's vision of communism involved universalization of education and skills, it was understandable that Marx did not share Hegel's awareness of the need for a popularly controlled public administration. In the absence of a civil society, Marx could see no need for a civil service. For Marx, Hegel's bureaucracy was merely another particular embodiment of the "corporation mind," another negation of true universality waiting to be negated. "The same mind that creates the corporations in society creates the bureaucracy in the state." As the "spiritualism of the corporations," the bureaucracy took the "spiritual being of society" into its own possession as "private property" and turned out to be "a particular, closed society within the state." Marx was not surprised, therefore, to find every bureaucrat treating the state as his own "private end," to be used in pursuit of wealth and a private career.57 In Marx's system the contradiction between bureaucracy and civil society would be transcended when society repossessed its own alienated "spiritual" and objective being.

The problem with Marx's solution, as Leon Trotsky realized in the early days of the Bolshevik revolution, is that so long as scarcity and the division of labor exist, neither a socialist nor any other society can organize its collective affairs without a bureaucracy. A specialized knowledge of public administration is essential in organizing the struggle against scarcity. And while Trotsky hoped that bureaucracy might be kept "within limits," he also understood that "Bureaucratism is an epoch in mankind's development, during which he overcomes the darkness of the middle ages ... and creates certain habits and modes of management....We must adopt these good aspects of bureaucracy....Precision - this is the greatest lever of economic development."58 As in the case of Hegel and Solidarity, Trotsky's main concern was to control the public authority by preserving the "relative independence" of particulars. In order to protect the legitimate interests of their members, Trotsky argued that the trade unions "must remain trade unions just as long as the state remains a state."59 At the same time, however, socialist trade unions had the further responsibility of mediating particular interests into the universal of a democratic plan. For this purpose Trotsky proposed a "coalescence" of union and planning bodies, or a sharing of personnel at all levels. In this way administrative authority might be reconciled with autonomy: workers would implement production decisions at the same time as they participated in determining the social plan.60

Like Hegel, Trotsky also saw that a dialectically articulated community implied the need for reconciliation through politics. Once the old Bolshevik party had been destroyed by Stalin, he argued that it must be replaced by "several parties."61 Heterogeneous in its internal composition by virtue of the division of labor, the working class would realize its human potential for freedom through "an inner struggle of tendencies, groups and parties."62 Through the mediation of political practice, the "humiliating control" of the Stalinist bureaucracy would be replaced by self-imposed "cultural discipline,"63 growing out of "education, habit and social opinion."64 New socialist values could not be scientifically determined by planners alone, but would have to arise from "a free conflict of ideas" and "spiritual creativeness."65

By subsuming bureaucratic technique under the collective exercise of practical reason, both Trotsky and Solidarity acknowledged that a socialist plan is ultimately an expression of ethical as well as technical values, or a determination of human relations as well as the community's relation to the world of things. Marx initiated the exclusion of this ethical dimension from socialism, but a far more direct origin of Stalinism can be found in Lenin's writings on philosophy, particularly in *Materialism and Empirio-Criticism*. Lenin replaced Hegel's concern for *human* laws, as the self-determination of human necessity, with a narrower focus upon *objective* laws, said to act "*independently* of our will and mind." Freedom for Lenin meant technical domination of nature: when men master natural laws, when these laws are accurately reflected in the human consciousness, then we possess "objective, absolute and eternal truth."[66] In *Dialectical and Historical Materialism* Stalin followed Lenin in declaring that "mind is secondary [and] derivative, since it is a reflection of matter."[67] "Marxist philosophical materialism holds that the world and its laws are fully knowable, ... and that there are no things in the world which are unknowable."[68] In *Economic Problems of Socialism in the U.S.S.R.* Stalin added that while economic laws are objective and therefore cannot be abolished, "men can discover laws, get to know and master them, learn to apply them with full understanding, ... and thus subjugate them, secure mastery over them."[69]

Lenin's "copy" theory of truth represented a radical degeneration of Hegel's dialectic. For Hegel, nature was the embodiment of mind: it possessed no truth other than that imparted to it by consciousness. The truth of consciousness was freedom, or the conceptual necessity whereby embodied consciousness returned to itself through self-determination in a "world which mind has made for itself."[70] The truth of the particular, whether natural or social, lay in the mediated consciousness of the totality. In order to realize their freedom in nature and history, men had first to establish the social conditions for freedom in their relations one with the other. Lenin translated Hegel's ontological dialectic into the technical dialectic of political organization through "democractic centralism." In *What is to be Done?* Lenin claimed that workers are constrained by the particularity of their consciousness: they interpret the class struggle as a particular conflict in their own factory. *Professional revolutionaries*, in contrast, are political technicians who study the panorama of history as a totality and situate the particular conflict according to the universal laws of class struggle. Translated into Stalinist terms, what this meant is that the truth of the particular party organization - its destiny - lay in obedience to "totalitarian" decisions made by *professional rulers*. Rendering the same proposition in terms of economic planning, it meant that party leaders and bureaucrats "know" and "subjugate" the laws of political economy, while the latter continue to operate "independently" of the will and mind of the workers.

In place of Hegel's practical reason, whereby particular groups of citizens are mediated by laws of their own making into the concrete universal of the state, Stalin expressed his view of social organization in terms of the laws of simple mechanics. Society was to be understood by analogy with a nineteenth-century factory. A central steam engine, the party-state leadership, would provide the driving force for all operations, and every moving part of the social "factory" would be connected to the center by a "transmission belt." Stalin's list of transmission belts included all of the potential Hegelian "corporations" of a socialist civil society - the trade unions, the soviets, the cooperative societies, the Young Communist League, and every level of the party apparatus. The ascending movement of Hegel's dialectic was replaced by unilateral control from above; ethical life was reduced to the smooth operation of a machine; the purpose of the machine was its own technical efficiency.

Familiarity with this ideological background is essential for a realistic appraisal of recent Marxist arguments that the scientific and technical revolution will make men free. One writer who has attempted to apply Marx's theory of technological emancipation to the modern context is Rudolf Bahro. In *The Alternative in Eastern Europe* Bahro contends that the philosophical potential for overcoming the division of labor has now become a practical possibility. Traditional class divisions have now been replaced by a new type of social structure, one deriving from education and the resulting hierarchy of knowledge.[71] If hierarchical control persists in "actually existing socialism," Bahro attributes its survival to centralized control over information and a corresponding differentiation in the "structure of consciousness."[72] The party-state apparatus maintains its hold over society by virtue of its claim to "absolute, divine knowledge."[73] Hence the initial step toward socialist self-determination must be a "cultural revolution" aimed at transforming "the entire subjective form of life of the masses."[74]

According to Bahro, modern means of production are solving the economic problem and replacing it with the new problem of "surplus consciousness," or "an energetic mental capacity that is no longer absorbed by the *immediate* necessities and dangers of human existence and can thus orient itself to more distant problems."[75] The disjunction between the possibility of freedom and the reality of domination is explained by what Hegel would have called pursuit of the "false infinite," or the difficulty experienced by human consciousness in shaking itself free from the historical obsession with accumulation of things. By subscribing to the same cult of material growth, the same fundamental "madness of our epoch" as capitalist societies, the so-called socialist countries negate their potential for freedom by shutting themselves up within self-imposed necessity.[76] Thus the masses are diverted from *emancipation* into *compensation*, or consumerism, like their counterparts in the reified world of capitalism.

In order to free people's minds from the fetishized world of things, Bahro claims that the cultural revolution must reduce material aspirations to "a natural normal level."[77] Universal educational opportunities must allow the masses to experience "psychologically productive activity"; intellectuals must join in physical labor and participate in the condition of the majority; and by thus overcoming the division between mental and physical labor, society will finally realize the possibility of dissolving itself into "an association of communes."[78] In place of existing particulars, with the accompanying hierarchy of knowledge and power, the new communal organization will express its freedom through a "general will," made possible through electronic communication: "Now that the problem of a general assembly of the people is solved ... by modern computers and means of mass communication, it would be possible at least in principle for all individuals to participate regularly in ... establishing future perspectives for society."[79]

The fundamental weakness of Bahro's projected alternative to Stalinism is his disdain for the system of needs and therefore for real politics. Believing that the thoughts of "little people" stand in the way of humanity's universal redemption, Bahro provides no space in his theory for particular needs and concerns of socialist citizens. Humanity as a whole must storm the barricades of bureaucracy; mere democratic demands "do not reach deep enough and do not touch the heart of the matter."[80] In Bahro's view it is nothing but a distraction to attempt to emulate "bourgeois democracy," with its one-sided fixation upon legal guarantees and rights.[81] Democracy is indeed an attribute of communism, but Bahro is convinced that it is certainly not "in the last instance a question of constitutional law."[82] What is really at stake is "a revolution against the *state* itself."[83] Bahro's most fervent hope in *The Alternative* is to put an end to "socialization in a totally alienated form"; his greatest failure is his commitment to the principle of all or nothing. A political theory without a theory of politics is an abstraction which can only reproduce the void now filled by the Stalinist bureaucracy.

The consequence of detaching the theory of scientific and technical revolution from a theory of socialist politics is most clearly revealed in the writings of V.G. Afansyev, the leading Soviet exponent of "scientific Stalinism." Like B.F. Skinner in the West, who believes human society is beyond freedom and dignity, Afansyev hopes to reduce human beings to things through manipulation of their social environment. In his most influential book, *The Scientific Management of Society*, he provides a revealing self-portrait of the modern Soviet bureaucracy. In his view the mission of the bureaucracy is to create "*a society controlled scientifically*," wherein "control of society emerges as *control of people*."[84] Expressing a technician's contempt for the unpredictable, he claims that freedom in such a society means "freedom from the influence of spontaneous factors"[85] and requires establishment of social "harmony" by making "subjective activities consistent with the objective laws and conditions."[86] True to his Stalinist heritage, he assigns responsibility for defining objective laws and conditions to the bureaucrat: "the subjective factor does not coincide with the activities of all ... but is the expression of those who fulfil control functions."[87] The subject of control is not the working class, but "a complex system of government and non-government organizations ... headed by the Communist Party."[88] The party's purpose is to protect the minds of the people from "alien bourgeois ideology."[89]

Having described the Prussian bureaucracy of his own day as the "spiritualism of the corporations," Marx would not have been surprised to find Afanasyev declaring that even "social and spiritual relations" must fall within the province of the bureaucracy. In Afanasyev's words: "Nothing corrodes a person's consciousness and behaviour so much as the absence of efficient control, order and organization. Lack of organization leaves him confused, damps his enthusiasm, causes him to neglect his duties and ignore his fellow-workers, society and leaders, and destroys his sense of responsibility."[90] Hegel would have replied that it is Afanasyev who is confused: "A slave can have no duties; only a free man has them."[91] A slave has only his "absolute right to free himself" and thereby to realize his destiny as a thinking being.[92]

Afanasyev's work goes beyond traditional Marxism-Leninism in two principal directions. In the first place, scientific Stalinism has finally abandoned, even in theory, Marx's hope to overcome the divison of labor and replace it with an immediate community of freely associated producers. Afanasyev declares that "a group of workers is unthinkable without each being assigned a definite place and function in the group. Division of labour and establishment of certain proportions between various spheres of production are necessary in any society."[93] Associated with this conviction is the typically Stalinist corollary: "Administrative relations are not something transitory: they have always existed and will always exist as long as human society endures."[94] A second distinctive contribution to Soviet doctrine is the need which Afanasyev sees to bring the administrative superstructure of society into conformity with the new base being created by the scientific and technical revolution. Abandoning the philosophic language of "right" in favor of the scientific language of cybernetics, he argues that a new "social technology"[95] must incorporate computer and information-processing technology in order to permit all social decisions to be reached "through mathematical decision theory."[96] The informational-cybernetic model of society replaces Stalin's "transmission belts" with electronic communications and the technical rationality of instantaneous feedback. The purpose of organizing society as an "integral system," however, remains unchanged, namely, to convey more efficiently "the content of socialist ideology to the consciousness of each person."[97] "In the

Soviet Union it is the Communist Party that is responsible for the political information system, and all the components of this system - the press, radio, television, films and verbal channels of political information operate under its direct guidance."98

The aspirations of Stalin's heirs dramatically underline the need for modern Marxists to reconsider the political implications of the scientific and technical revolution. Bahro was perfectly correct to draw attention to the positive implications of science, particularly to the referendum potential of electronic instruments for processing information and communicating knowledge. They do indeed create an explosive universalization of communication, which in turn might enable human beings to find one another with an ease not previously imagined. The fact remains, however, that ease of communication does not necessarily imply an emancipated "general will." Information processing is like manufacturing in the sense that it too is subject to economies of scale. For this reason it tends to generate both user stratification and centralization of data. Here we are confronted with an unprecedented capacity for manipulated consensus, for "protecting" people's minds, for "modelling" their subjectivity and for denying their right to be free.

In his *Critique of the Gotha Program* Marx declared that "right" can never be higher than the economic structure of society and the cultural level conditioned by that structure.99 The problem is that when Marx finally returned to the Hegelian problematic of "right," he had nothing more in mind than the right of an individual to his share in social consumption. By collapsing Hegel's *Philosophy of Right* into a simple economic claim, Marx believed that "right" could be quantitatively measured in terms of each individual's contribution of labor to the satisfaction of society's needs. Similarly, when Marx referred to culture what he meant was the culture of technical reason. Marx believed that living labor would be displaced by machinery, as objectified knowledge, which in turn presupposed knowledgeable workers. Communist society would elevate the level of "right" through raising economic productivity. In that way it would eliminate the divisive consequences of scarcity and therewith all concern over "right." Communism would be characterized by economic abundance, enabling each individual to draw upon the social product in accordance with his needs.100 There would be no need for Hegel's dialectic of recognition, for as scarcity receded, each would spontaneously recognize the "right" of all. There would be no need for politics, for there would be no particular claims to "right" which could not immediately be satisfied.

At a time in history when the human "right" to consume confronts the necessity of nature to survive, Marx's technological theory of emancipation invites skepticism from many directions. But the most serious challenge has now been posed from within the Marxist tradition. Afanasyev and his cothinkers in the Soviet Union have seen that the scientific and technical revolution does not make individuals into immediate universals. "It is well known," claims Afanasyev, "that a division of labour is taking place within the sphere of regulation and that [this] process is no less intensive than in the sphere of production....Just as specialized workers appeared within production at an earlier time, so persons specializing in particular regulating activities have begun to appear in the sphere of regulation."[101] Rejecting Hegel's view that men are vehicles of the World Spirit, Marx believed that emancipated workers would carry their own universality within themselves. The scientific Stalinists have found that Marx was wrong: the principle of science is not freedom but *control*. They have also realized that by suppressing any possibility of a democratic political culture, they preserve the possibility of maintaining a tyranny. That is why the scientific and technical revolution, instead of eliminating concern for the political, has the contradictory effect of making it all-important. Marx himself hoped to transcend politics. But it is Marx's own commitment to human dignity which must impress upon modern Marxists the inhuman implications of that ambition.

Notes

1. Andrew Arato, "Civil Society Against the State: Poland 1980-81," *Telos*, 47 (1981), p. 23.
2. Friedrich A. Hayek, *The Constitution of Liberty* (Chicago: University of Chicago Press, 1960), p. 142.
3. Agnes Heller, "Past, Present and Future of Democracy," *Social Research*, 45, No. 4 (1978), p. 867.
4. *Ibid.*, pp. 882-3.
5. Karl Marx and Frederick Engels, *The German Ideology* (New York: International Publishers, 1963), pp. 21-2.
6. *Ibid.*, p. 23.
7. Marx and Engels, *Basic Writing on Politics and Philosophy*, ed. Lewis S. Feuer (Garden City, N.Y.: Doubleday, 1959), p. 127.
8. Marx, *Capital* (Moscow: Foreign Languages Publishing House, 1957-62), I, 80.
9. Marx, *Grundrisse: Foundations of the Critique of Political Economy* (New York: Vintage, 1973), p. 708.
10. *Ibid.*, p. 712.
11. *The Politics of Aristotle*, trans. Benjamin Jowett (New York: Modern Library, 1943), p. 55.

12. *Hegel's Philosophy of Right*, trans. T.M. Knox (London: Oxford University Press, 1967), p. 110.

13. *Ibid.*, p. 20.

14. Robert C. Tucker, ed., *The Marx-Engels Reader*, 2d. ed. (New York: Norton, 1978), p. 112.

15. Hegel, p. 292.

16. Marx, *Capital*, I, 75.

17. Marx, *The Poverty of Philosophy* (New York: International Publishers, n.d.), p. 98.

18. Hegel, p. 217.

19. *Ibid.*, pp. 129-30.

20. *Ibid.*, p. 268.

21. *Ibid.*, p. 124.

22. *Ibid.*, p. 156.

23. *Ibid.*, p. 109.

24. *Ibid.*, p. 156.

25. R.N. Berki, "Perspectives in the Marxian Critique of Hegel's Political Philosophy, " in *Hegel's Political Philosophy*, ed. Z.A. Pelczynski (London: Cambridge University Press, 1971), p. 207.

26. Charles Taylor, *Hegel and Modern Society* (London: Cambridge University Press, 1979), p. 146.

27. Mihaly Vajda, *The State and Socialism* (London: Allison & Busby, 1981), p. 10.

28. *Ibid.*, p. 13.

29. *Ibid.*, p. 8.

30. Hegel, pp. 147-8.

31. *Ibid.*, pp. 277-8.

32. *Ibid.*, p. 278.

33. Andrei Sakharov, *Alarm and Hope* (New York: Vintage, 1978), p. 38.

34. *Ibid.*, p. 17.

35. Roy A. Medvedev, *On Socialist Democracy* (New York: Alfred A. Knopf, 1975), xxvi.

36. Hegel, p. 57.

37. Stan Persky and Henry Flam, eds., *The Solidarity Sourcebook* (Vancouver: New Star, 1982), p. 206.

38. *Ibid.*, p. 225.

39. *Ibid.*, p. 213.

40. *Ibid.*, p. 208.

41. *Ibid.*, p. 211.

42. Marx, *Critique of Hegel's 'Philosophy of Right,'* ed. Joseph O'Malley (London: Cambridge University Press, 1970), p. 31.

43. Hegel, p. 284.

44. *Ibid.*, p. 180.

45. Marx, *Critique of Hegel's 'Philosophy of Right,'* p. 31; cf. p. 121.

46. Hegel, p. 364.

47. *Ibid.*, p. 283.

48. *Ibid.*, p. 153.

49. *Ibid.*, pp. 290-1.

50. *Ibid.*, p. 292.

51. *Ibid.*, p. 161.

52. *Ibid.*, p. 162.

53. *Ibid.*, p. 189.

54. *Ibid.*, p. 192.

55. *Ibid.*, pp. 290-1.

56. *Ibid.*, p. 193.

57. Marx, *Critique of Hegel's 'Philosophy of Right,'* pp. 45- 7.

58. Leon Trotsky, *Sochineniya* (Moscow: Gosudarstvennoe Izdatel'stvo, 1925-7), XV, 420.

59. *Trotsky Archives*, No. T-3542.

60. Trotsky, *Rol' i zadachi professional'nykh soyuzov* (Moscow: Gosudarstvennoe Izdatel'stvo, 1920), pp. 25-6 *et passim*.

61. Trotsky, *The Revolution Betrayed* (New York: Pioneer, 1945), p. 267.

62. *Ibid.*

63. *Ibid.*, p. 262.

64. *Ibid.*, p. 46.

65. *Ibid.*, p. 180.

66. V.I. Lenin, *Materialism and Empirio-Criticism* (New York: International Publishers, 1927), p. 192.

67. Joseph Stalin, *Dialectical and Historical Materialism* (New York: International Publishers, 1940), p. 16.

68. *Ibid.*, p. 17.

69. Stalin, *Economic Problems of Socialism in the U.S.S.R.* (New York: International Publishers, 1952), p. 11.

70. Hegel, p. 285.

71. Rudolf Bahro, *The Alternative in Eastern Europe* (London: NLB, 1978), p. 165.

72. *Ibid.*, p. 151.

73. *Ibid.*, p. 246.

74. *Ibid.*, p. 257.

75. *Ibid.*

76. *Ibid.*, p. 263.

77. *Ibid.*, p. 427.

78. *Ibid.*, p. 435.

79. *Ibid.*, pp. 300-301.

80. *Ibid.*, p. 309.

81. *Ibid.*, p. 151.
82. *Ibid.*, p. 380.
83. *Ibid.*, p. 33.
84. V.G. Afanasyev, *The Scientific Management of Society* (Moscow: Progress, 1971), p. 84.
85. *Ibid.*, p. 36.
86. *Ibid.*, p. 89.
87. *Ibid.*, p. 91.
88. *Ibid.*, p. 116.
89. *Ibid.*, p. 130.
90. *Ibid.*, p. 176-7.
91. Hegel, p. 261.
92. *Ibid.*, p. 242.
93. Afanasyev, p. 32.
94. *Ibid.*, p. 120.
95. Afanasyev, *Social Information and the Regulation of Social Development* (Moscow: Progress, 1978), p. 84.
96. *Ibid.*, p. 156.
97. *Ibid.*, p. 344.
98. *Ibid.*, pp. 314-15.
99. Marx and Engels, *Basic Writings*, p. 119.
100. *Ibid.*
101. Afanasyev, *Social Information*, p. 182.

POLITICAL TECHNOLOGY, DEMOCRACY
AND EDUCATION:
JOHN DEWEY'S LEGACY

Frank J. Kurtz

For John Dewey education is "the supreme human interest in which ...
other problems, cosmological, moral, logical, come to a head."[1] As the
supreme human interest, education must also be the public or political interest; in Dewey's philosophy of education we should discover the charged
core of his political theory. For this reason political theorists should focus
on the relation of his pedagogy and politics.

Yet political theorists have widely ignored Dewey. Much of the better
literature has seized upon the epistemology of his political thought. The
domination of the methodological interest has meant that theorists have not
probed for the heart of Dewey's conception of politics; they have virtually
ignored his psychological critique of corporate capitalism, and the role of
technology and education in his democratic idealism.

I argue that for Dewey, technology - material and political - is the necessary condition of genuine democracy. The democratic potential of this force
cannot be liberated because of the social psychology of capitalism. Formal
education can release technology, for it alone can transform character and
establish a new social psychology consistent with democracy. Dewey's
view of technology as an engine of democratic social change cannot be fully
appreciated unless it is seen in relation to his social psychology and educational theory. In this light, Dewey leads us to a surprising conclusion: only
the school and the teacher enjoy the political power sufficient to liberate the
enormous democratic potential of technology. Plato taught that the state
must educate its citizens, and Marx claimed that the proletariat must educate
- in the pregnant historical sense - the state. Dewey learned from both: he
fully accepted economic determinism, technology as a revolutionary social
force, and the interpretation of politics as *paideia*. This synthesis enabled
him to define the locus of political power in an unconventional fashion.
Through this redefinition Dewey's political thought shares in the spirit of the

204

modern theoretical preoccupation with power. For this reason Dewey ultimately deserves the attention of political theorists.

I

Behind the great changes following the industrial revolution, according to Dewey, lie two forces, "one dynamic, the other relatively static." Science and technology constitute the former, and capitalist property relations constitute the latter. The methods, conclusions, and technological fruits of science represent a historically protracted, cooperative endeavor. Science and technology are the significant forces of modernity: they have revolutionized the conditions of social life and have become the great, active forces of production. These forces have generated unprecedented productivity, which has brought us into an "age of potential plenty." The entire physical basis of economic life now depends upon the issue of science.[2] Capitalism, that "complex of political and legal arrangements centering about a particular mode of economic relations," has not been responsible for the creation of modern forces of production; it has counted only in the distribution of this new productivity. The Baconian hope for the relief of the common estate by command over nature has been largely frustrated; the blessings of the scientific and industrial revolutions have been appropriated by that class which privately owns the means of production and exchange. Since their birth the modern forces of production have been the servants and prisoners of capitalist property relations.[3]

The modern command of technique is so complete that the most serious problems of men are now social and no longer associated with the domination of nature. The exploitation and control of technology by an industrial oligarchy enables organized economic interests to exercise a coercive influence overshadowing that of the state: for Dewey capitalism "operates as a standing agency of coercion of the many." The control of technology by "interest in private profit" constitutes "the serious and fundamental defect of our civilization."[4]

In *The Public and Its Problems* Dewey argued that the public is lost and unsure of itself. The public cannot identify or distinguish itself because of the indirect and extensive social consequences of technological change. "There are too many publics and too much of public concern for our existing resources to cope with." For Dewey "the problem of a democratically organized public is primarily and essentially an intellectual problem, in a degree to which the political affairs of prior ages offer no parallel."[5]

This diagnosis is no less compelling today. The complicated social implications of, and physical interrelations between, a high-technology economy, its energy requirements, and its ecological effects, typify the veracity of Dewey's assessment. He accurately foresaw that future social problems would require a highly dependable and refined intellectual tool for their statement, if not solution. If Dewey erred in thinking that experimental logic could become the basis of this new tool or "political technology"[6] - and most scholars agree that he erred - the overwhelming need for improved ways to institutionalize political knowledge and criticize political methods testifies to his sagacity. Thoroughly convinced that the future problem of American liberal democracy was intellectual, Dewey decided that only the "courage of the fool" could endorse democracy without a new political technology.[7] In this sense Dewey was not unconditionally democratic in his thinking. It is misleading to see him as a populist ideologue, or as the philosopher of the common man, as he is often depicted. Neither common sense nor the common man can be the firm foundation of a socially and technologically complex society.

Individualism Old and New offers Dewey's most finished portrayal of the psycho-social effects of the modern capitalist society. The "lost individual" is the tragic personification of the unprecedented nihilism which Dewey found in this society. "The significant thing is that the loyalties which once held individuals, which gave them support, direction, and unity of outlook on life, have well-nigh disappeared. In consequence, individuals are confused and bewildered. It would be difficult to find in history an epoch as lacking in solid and assured objects of belief and approved ends of action as is the present."[8] This nihilism is not an abysmal psychological vertigo, an active repudiation of meaning, or a beatification of evil. Rather, it is flat, passive, and a dismal gray: it is the nihilism of the empty, hollow life. This loss of meaning arrests, suspends, and victimizes mind. And this loss is universal; the lost individual is not a class phenomenon. The captains of finance and industry are no more the "captains of their own souls - their beliefs and aims" than the many. As the interpretive and directive moral power resident in action, mind is lost to all. In social terms this vexation makes all easy prey to the sensational, the outlandish, or to whatever seems momentarily charged and forceful. Overshadowed by meaninglessness, we either scurry about for these factitious supports or languish in distress, uncertainty and nervousness. According to Dewey, these traits signify "widespread pathological phenomena."[9]

Dewey initially associates this pathology with two major sociological conditions of modern capitalist society - corporateness and impersonality. Associations, corporations, and organizations now so thoroughly pervade and dominate society that they define social life itself. "The influence business corporations exercise in determining present industrial and economic activities is both a cause and a symbol of the tendency to combination in all phases of life." The development of corporate capitalism has entirely transformed the character of social life; in contrast with the days when personal effort had social weight and effect, social life has now become corporate. In

1929 Dewey wrote that economic corporateness had advanced sufficiently to overturn the historical, intellectual and social conditions of agriculture, art, education, labor, leisure, politics and even criminality.[10]

As industrialism broadened, the social nexus became ever more impersonal. The dissolution of direct, intimate social ties and their replacement by distant, indirect connections, is so radical that it constitutes a social revolution. This new social order has yet been unable to reinvest men with a shared, living sense of purpose. The attendant impersonal forces and indirect social consequences of corporate capitalism, which stem from "the new means of technological production," are so vast and complex that the social meaning of economic activity is unknown. Since economic activity touches all aspects of modern life, this means that we do not recognize what we are about; by virtue of the form of modern economic life, we literally are not self-conscious about our life's work.[11]

Without the attachments normally established by the community, we nonetheless gravitate towards consensus through "artificial and mechanical means." Consequently, both adventitious uniformity and "emotional instability and intellectual confusion" characterize corporate capitalist society.[12] This is the obverse of nihilism. Corporate capitalist society ultimately rests upon the balance of two principal forces - the drive toward a mediocre and perjured sense of community and the dissipating symptoms of nihilism.

The phenomenon of the lost individual has its roots in the failure to address successfully the increasingly corporate, impersonal and oppressive character of the social forces unleashed after the industrial revolution. The lost individual is the artifact of a society still faithful to an atavistic form of economic individualism. The renewal of community and the redemption of the lost individual thus depends, first of all, upon the sacrificial death of private economic profit as the animating principle of capitalism:

> For the chief obstacle to the creation of a type of individual whose pattern of thought and desire is enduringly marked by consensus with others, and in whom sociability is one with cooperation in all regular human associations, is the persistence of that feature of the earlier individualism which defines industry and commerce by ideas of private pecuniary profit.[13]

What is the alternative to this regime? For Dewey, mind appears when feelings reach that "organized interaction with other living creatures which is language, communication."[14] This implies that we become "a conscious center of experience" only in association with our fellows; it implies also that goods are "consciously realized" only under "public, social" conditions.[15] Hence, the moral value of a regime can be appraised by appealing to two ideal generic social traits: the degree to which social interests are held in common, and the extent of free and cooperative interchange among different groups. Theoretically, democracy best satisfies these criteria.

Democracy means much more to Dewey than a form of government based on universal consent. It is that way of life which concretely realizes the necessity of the full release of the potentials of human nature.

> From the standpoint of the individual, it consists in having a responsible share according to capacity in forming and directing the activities of the groups to which one belongs and in participating according to need in the values which the groups sustains. From the standpoint of the groups, it demands liberation of the potentialities of members of a group in harmony with the interests and goods which are in common. Since every individual is a member of many groups, this specification cannot be fulfilled except when different groups interact flexibly and fully in connection with other groups.[16]

Dewey realized that the promise of democracy was an unanswered question; he knew also that history too often witnessed rising waves of social liberation swell into whirlpools of novel forms of authoritarianism. Hence he sought a method which would protect his vision from this fate. Of the "ultimately but three forces that control society - habit, coercive and violent force, and action directed by intelligence," the first two have historically failed to balance the claims of social change and individual freedom on one side, and social stability and collective authority on the other.[17] Although history itself suggests that the third force, action directed by intelligence, deserves to direct the societal destiny, the opportunity to replace habit and force has yet to occur. Dewey argues that establishment of a genuinely democratic social order is not possible apart from the use of "a new conception and logic of freed intelligence as a social force."[18]

"Intelligence" is:

> a shorthand designation for great and ever-growing methods of observation, experiment and reflective reasoning which have in a very short time revolutionized the physical and, to a considerable degree, the physiological conditions of life, but which have not as yet been worked out for application to what is itself distinctively and basically human....It is ... the method of observation, theory as hypothesis, and experimental test.[19]

For Dewey, thought itself has a natural history. The progress of experimental science confirms as fact the hypothesis that knowing is a function of doing. As the most authentic form of knowing, experimental inquiry represents the pattern of all genuine knowing; in all its phases, conditions, and organs, knowing should be understood according to this form. In the classic interpretation pure thought was the sole authentic avenue to higher knowing; experience set definite limits to true knowledge for it furnished only opinion. Thought turned away from experience and the realm of changing empirical things to the world of changeless, eternal forms. As it excludes practical activity as a component of inquiry, Dewey rejects the classic interpretation as atavistic. In experimental knowing, experience in the form of observation and verification is indispensable to knowledge. "The method of physical inquiry is to introduce some change in order to see what other change ensues; the correlation between these changes, when measured by a series of operations, constitutes the definite and desired object of knowledge."[20]

Precisely because science acts upon and marks the interrelations of changes in natural objects, it yields the potential for producing and averting other events; it liberates man from the world as he finds it. As modern science denudes natural objects of their intrinsic teleology, it releases them for new ends through action. In the past, men thought experience could not sustain their cherished ideals and meanings; uncertainty drove them toward a transcendental realm of good. The experimental method of knowing emasculates this dread of change and disparagement of the phenomenal world because it exposes it as a profound error. It reveals that "knowing is itself a mode of practical action and is the way of interaction by which other natural interactions become subject to direction"; it teaches us that the goods we cherish can be secured "only through regulation of processes of change, a regulation dependent upon knowledge of their relations."[21] Due to the rise of the experimental method, "the quest for certainty by means of exact possession in mind of immutable reality is exchanged for search for security by means of active control of the changing course of events." Thus the experimental method offers the possibility of a new philosophy of experience.[22]

The political significance of this trial cannot be underestimated. In practical terms this means that the principles supporting social institutions and public policy would be considered tools for philosophic inquiry, not political absolutes. The value of these principles would be established pragmatically by observing the specific consequences of the social practices they inform. Following this logic, social institutions and public policies would be framed and treated as the working hypotheses of experimental political philosophy. "Such a change involves a great change in the seat of authority and the methods of decision in society."[23] Political change would be an integral element of the normal method of political discourse; it would not be an external attack upon a regime which is philosophically certain of itself or set in its institutional patterns. The advocacy of experimental logic as the basis of political discourse is synonymous with the continual and systematic query, reevaluation, and reconstruction of the most basic social beliefs and practices; it is synonymous with a "continuously planning society." Philosophically, this political methodology - this "political technology"[24] -

constitutes but a special case of Dewey's contention that all moral judgments are experimental; politically, this means nothing less than a regime which institutionalizes the means of its own subversion, for even the extent of political sovereignty is experimentally determined.25

The imposing practical problem with this approach centers on the value of pragmatic value itself. In principle social utility can be measured. While the moral judgment of this utility is developed experimentally, moral alternatives remain matters of conscience, vying for recognition in the field of conflicting social interests. Yet this makes the political and social application of experimental logic all the more necessary. Dewey argues that precisely because society is charged with serious conflicts, a social force more flexible than habit, and less destructive than violence, is needed to demonstrate how conflict can be resolved in the name of the greatest number. Experimental logic does not legitimate ultimate political purpose; it rationalizes social procedure. But this rationalization is a profound social contribution.

This rationalization of politics is not its emasculation. Intelligence is a social force in the literal sense. In two articles, written in 1916, Dewey argued that force is the indispensable condition of all our accomplished ends, and power is the effective "ability or capacity to execute, to realize ends."26 Thus Dewey not only reduced the morality of power to the question of its economical use, but also implicitly aligned himself with the political theorists of the seventeenth and eighteenth centuries who, he claims, reduced all political questions to the question of the exercise of power.27 Intelligence is the highest form of political power for Dewey because it is the most effective force for the solution of social problems. Far from being all the weaker for its political technology, society will be strong and stable: "the best guarantee of collective efficiency and power is liberation and use of the diversity of individual capacities in initiative, planning, foresight, vigor and endurance."28 Dewey's advocacy of political technology entails a radical democratization of political power. For this reason he freely admitted that predominant class interests would oppose this method and that, as his Marxist critics argue, this method cannot be utilized in a class-divided society.

While experimental logic does not legitimate political purpose, the redistribution of power implicit in the new political technology affects political purpose: "The general adoption of the scientific attitude in human affairs would mean nothing less than a revolutionary change in morals, religion, politics and industry."29 The social use of experimental logic would encourage each continually to rediscover and re-create his world: it would free each from social and political dogma. The experimental method is the method of democracy, for it fosters moral and intellectual growth. The social and political application of this method has a revolutionary impact because it endeavors to change the way we imagine the world.

II

Considering the onerous significance of economic reform for a democratic future, Dewey is curiously silent about the political and social difficulties of the reformation of property relations. He emphasizes the social control rather than the social ownership of the economy in his democratic idealism, but the political implications of current property relations cannot be ignored. As concentrated economic power effectively acts as political power, capitalism looms like a mountain blocking the passage to a democratic future. Yet Dewey virtually ignored the question of the political consequence of property relations: he neither developed nor adopted any theory of political economy. Given the importance of the question of property to his democratic idealism, this indifference requires explanation.

Dewey's philosophic career was extraordinarily long and encyclopedic. In some seventy years he wrote on aesthetics, education, ethics, law, logic, metaphysics, philosophy, politics, psychology, religion, science and more. This wide range of interests makes the objects of his indifference as intellectually intriguing as his philosophic vision is challenging. This is especially true of his social and political thought. Though Dewey led an active public and political life, travelled widely, and witnessed a period of singular social, economic, and political change in the United States, he left no systematic treatment or critique of political economy.

More than once he claimed not to be an economist. As early as 1894, he nonetheless argued that "the same fundamental problems and attitudes have underlain philosophic and economic thought from the onset, simply assuming different statements and outward garbs"; there is a "reflection of philosophic conceptions over into the region of political economy, influencing and even controlling the economic writer without any consciousness on his part of the ideas of which he was the mouthpiece."[30] Since Dewey thought himself a philosopher, we should reasonably expect a philosophic critique of political economy from him. In *Individualism Old and New* he recognized that the relation of the economy to politics - the issue Karl Marx "raised" - "forms the only basis of present political questions."[31] Dewey suggested, on both philosophical and political grounds, that political economy deserved serious attention. He raised and then ostensibly dropped the issue of its significance. C.B. Macpherson explains this indifference to political economy by reference to Dewey's disinterest "in any analysis of capitalism. He was entirely taken up with the prospects of a democratic liberalism."[32]

Yet an analysis of capitalism need not necessarily be political-economic. Dewey was interested in, and offered a critical analysis of, capitalism. His analysis was not political-economic but psychological; it was based upon his theories of mind and community. Dewey circumvented political economy because he interpreted economics psychologically rather than politically: he applied an economy of the healthy psyche to economics. However, Dewey's critique was truncated. He failed to appreciate the central psychological importance of property relations for our moral habits. Dewey misread the social conditions required for the full liberation of the profit motive and, as a result, failed to provide a complete indictment of capitalism which a critical theory of political economy could have produced.

The human potential of science and technology has been denied us by capitalist property relations. Yet Dewey holds that "for the most part, economic individualism interpreted as energy and enterprise devoted to private profit, has been an adjunct, often a parasitical one, to the movement of technical and scientific forces."[33] This statement sets the problem of Dewey's indifference to political economy. If Dewey identified the separation of labor from capital as the necessary social condition of a thoroughly liberated profit motive, he clearly failed to explicate the institutional foundation of the moral history of technology. If he identified private property as such with economic individualism, his indifference to political economy can be treated sympathetically because he provided a prodigious critique of the philosophy of individualism. The question is, then, how Dewey related or confused the interest in private profit with capitalist property relations.

Dewey found the genesis of community in the transformation of force by symbols. Community originates when the forces which exist and pass between human beings become charged with meaning. This transformation is never fully consummated; in each generation the young must be initiated into the community. Yet education is no guarantee against the domination of the merely "physical and organic" aspects of human association:

> The old Adam, the unregenerate element in human nature, persists. It shows itself wherever the method obtains of attaining results by use of force instead of by the method of communication and enlightenment. It manifests itself more subtly, pervasively and effectually when knowledge and the instrumentalities of skill which are the products of communal life are employed in the service of wants and impulses which have not themselves been modified by reference to a shared interest.[34]

Science and technology are collective arts: they represent a cooperative endeavor and are the "products of communal life." Their history has been morally truncated because they have been diverted away from general humane purposes by the interest in private economic profit. Thus science and technology are "employed in the service of wants and impulses which have not themselves been modified by reference to a shared interest." As "harmony of social interests is found in the widespread sharing of activities significant in themselves, that is to say, at the point of consumption,"35 the interest in private profit vitiates the shared meaning of the consequences of social activity; it annihilates the communal because consumption is directed to serve distinctly private, rather than social, ends. Wherever it reigns, the interest in private profit establishes the kingdom of the old Adam. Since meaning is the characteristically human need, the social institution of the interest in private profit denies man his essence.

Since we become conscious centers of experience through association, Dewey defines "assured and integrated individuality" as the "product of definite social relationships and publicly acknowledged functions."36 Under capitalism this individuality is denied to the class of workers: the separation of labor from capital and the division of labor mean that the worker has only the most cursory idea of the social justification and consequence of his labor. The worker is unable to appreciate the full meaning - the social relationships - of his own labor. The separation of labor from capital destroys the unity of body and mind which Dewey considered "the ultimate source of all constant nurture of the spirit." With no architectural share in the designs they execute, workers are reduced to mere means. Inevitably the meaning of labor for the laborer does not transcend the struggle of wages and profits. These conditions make freedom and growth impossible if, as Dewey teaches, "everywhere and at all times the development of mind and its cultural products have been cognate with the channels in which mind is exercised and applied."37

This is no less true of the industrial oligarchy. The meaning of their activity is not referred to society because "the deflection of social consequences to private gain" is their reward. For Dewey, "a unified mind, even of the business type, can come into being only when conscious intent and consummation are in harmony with consequences actually effected."38 Dewey argues that the desires and purposes of those who control the economy are not integrated with the objective social consequences of their activity because these consequences are inherently irrelevant to the drive for private power and advantage. This class finds no complete satisfaction or inner contentment through their work.39

Through his theories of community and mind Dewey evolved a psychological analysis of capitalism. Since both theories direct attention towards the essentially human need for meaning, Dewey was primarily interested in the effects of economics on mind and character and criticized the economy for its pedagogic effects. In terms of his own thought, a psychological critique of economics was the most profound form of economic analysis, for Dewey believed that "education - in the broad sense of formation of fundamental attitudes of imagination, desire and thinking - is strictly correlative with culture in its inclusive social sense."40 A psychological critique of economic life is, therefore, the best method for assessing the widest social meaning of the economy. Dewey dissolved the question of property relations into a question of social psychology: thus psychology supplanted political economy as the critical method of economics. Dewey was indifferent to political economy because he found the essence of capitalism in the philosophical anthropology of classic economic liberalism. For this reason he defined capitalism as "a systematic manifestation of desires and purposes built up in an age of ever threatening want and now carried over into a time of ever increasing potential plenty," and attacked the underlying psychology of capitalism. In short, Dewey took capitalist property relations as the objective form of the interest in private profit; when he spoke of the effects of the separation of labor from capital, he meant those of "pecuniary individualism."[41]

The problem with Dewey's approach to capitalism is that it is too psychological. Dewey interpreted the birth of individualism historically, but ignored the issue of how classic economic individualism reflects a specific set of property relations. It is capitalist property relations, not the psychology of economic individualism (the profit motive in itself), that fully liberates production for private profit. For this reason Dewey's psychological critique of economics requires as its necessary complement a critical political economy.

Macpherson accounts for this lacuna by placing Dewey with twentieth-century political theorists who stand in the tradition of J.S. Mill. Since Mill there has been a decreasing economic penetration of political theory in this tradition. Dewey, like other theorists of the first half of the twentieth century, "increasingly lost sight of class and exploitation." Macpherson argues that these theorists tended to ignore class as a political question, for they thought that "class issues had given way, or were giving way, to pluralistic differences." Dewey was uninterested in "any analysis of capitalism" and "entirely taken up with the prospects of a democratic liberalism," because he had not seen how the party system moderated and smoothed over "a conflict of class interests so as to save the existing property institutions and the market system from effective attack." Dewey took the reduction of "the democratic responsiveness of governments to electorates" by the party system to mean that "pluralistic social groups" and an "overriding citizen rationality" had supplanted class interest as a basis for politics.[42]

While Macpherson is correct to argue that Dewey lost sight of class in his analysis of capitalism, Dewey did not misunderstand the historical role of the party system in western democracies, nor was his pluralism the logical consequence of any such misunderstanding. As early as 1888 Dewey taught that a nondemocratic economy compromised political democracy. More than fifty years later he exclaimed that "the idea of a pre-established harmony between the existing so-called capitalist regime and democracy is as absurd a piece of metaphysical speculation as human history has ever evolved."43 Dewey consistently urged that the class concentration of economic power effectively denies political and social freedom to most citizens and that our political institutions tend to minister to a dominant propertied class. Despite its clear advantage, Dewey also agreed that "American party politics seem at times to be a device for preventing issues which may excite popular feeling and involve bitter controversies from being put up to the American people." And he found "the idea that the conflict of parties will, by means of public discussion, bring out necessary public truths ... a kind of political watered-down version of the Hegelian dialectic."44

As for Dewey's pluralism, it appears explicitly for the first time in *Democracy and Education*, where he criticizes Plato for not recognizing that "each individual constitutes his own class." As an individual's "infinite diversity of active tendencies and combinations of tendencies" are inexpugnable, the static individual or society is mere romance.45 As individuality is originally a potential for a distinctive manner, perspective and preference continually and simultaneously mature and change:

> We should forget "society" and think of law, industry, religion, medicine, politics, art, education, philosophy - and think of them in the plural. For points of contact are not the same for any two persons and hence the questions which the interests and occupations pose are never the same.46

Dewey likened the state to a "conductor of an orchestra" on the empirical grounds that various "groupings for promoting the diversity of goods that men share have become the real social units."47 He never crossed the Rubicon of a strict class analysis of society because he believed that the mode of social analysis itself must be flexible and pluralistic: his objection to class analysis was logical, not ideological. Dewey intended not to denigrate the seriousness of class conflicts, but to insist upon the use of class analysis as a hypothesis of social inquiry and a pragmatic tool of public policy.

Other critics, such as George Novack and C. Wright Mills, who also are indebted to Marx, have identified Dewey's indifference to a critical political economy as a relic of his class origins. Novack finds the sociological essence, historical function and class significance of Dewey's thought in one unadorned fact: "the outlook of the educated petty bourgeoisie." Since this class had a "formless outlook," Dewey could never settle the class issue in his own mind.48 Mills attributes that "intellectualist slant," by which Dewey interpreted the method of social change, to this bourgeois origin.49 For both of these thinkers Dewey missed the irreconcilability of class interests because of the class bias of his own experience. Though the tenor of Novack's indictment is vulgar and demeaning, it cannot easily be dismissed.

Dewey himself sanctioned and used a historical sociology of mind as a method of psychological and political analysis. Yet Dewey never reduced mind to its history; its environment is not the explanation of mind. Individuality is inexpugnable and original; creative genius is a fact, however uncomfortable for historicist interpretation. Heroes of the intellect assuredly wear the colors of their times; this is how we recognize them. But uncommon thoughts are their valor and greatness, and this is why we recognize them. The characteristic subjects of thought may be settled by history, but the character and speech of a great man is not simply historical.

It is incorrect to assign Dewey's indifference to political economy to his logical objections to Marx's class analysis of society and history. Political economy would not have bound Dewey to an antiquated, rigid logic of class analysis. Political economy could well have been part of Dewey's favored political technology; as C.E. Ayers suggested, Dewey's thought lends itself to an "instrumental economics."[50] Chapter four of *Freedom and Culture* is Dewey's most trenchant critique of Marx. Dewey praises Marx there for going "back of property relations to the working of the forces of production as no one before him had done." Marx's criticism of the contemporary "subordination of productive forces to legal and political conditions" was "penetrating and possessed of enduring value."[51] In *The Public and Its Problems* Dewey seems to have taken a page from the "Preface" to *A Contribution to the Critique of Political Economy*:

> The consequences of conjoint behavior differ in kind and in range with changes in "material culture," especially those involved in exchange of raw materials, finished products and above all in technology, in tools, weapons and utensils. These in turn are immediately affected by inventions in means of transit, transportation and intercommunication. A people that lives by tending flocks of sheep and cattle adapts itself to very different conditions than those of a people which ranges freely, mounted on horses. One form of nomadism is usually peaceful; the other warlike. Roughly speaking, tools and implements determine occupations, and occupations determine the consequences of associated activity. In determining consequences, they institute publics with different interests, which exact different types of political behavior to care for them.[52]

Resigned to economic determinism as a fact, Dewey never even coquetted with Marx's conclusion that "the anatomy of civil society is to be sought in political economy." Dewey's highly idealistic definition of technology accounts for this theoretical coyness.

A tool embodies "a sequential bond of nature"; it expresses and endows meaning, for it exhibits relation. Thus language is the condition of the genesis of tools. A tool is considerably more than a physical object: it is a mode of language, "for it says something, to those who understand it, about operations of use and their consequence."53   Language is a natural result of human association.   When organic signals, gestures and cries are "used within a context of mutual assistance and direction" they acquire meaning: the signal becomes significant of the shared activity.54   The essence of language is found through the establishment of cooperation in an activity in which the activity of each partner is modified and regulated by the other. "To fail to understand is to fail to come into agreement in action; to misunderstand is to set up action at cross purposes."   The community of action which Dewey understands as communication bridges existence and essence; through communication, "events in their first estate" - "brute efficiencies and inarticulate consummates" - are elevated to the plane of meaning.55

Language clearly enraptures Dewey; but, like all lovers, he suffered for his enchantment.   Tools may say something to us, but they also do something to us, depending upon their social organization.   Dewey's idealistic interpretation of technology as another mode of language and, therefore, of community, turned his attention away from the actual social organization of technology.   Tools act as "brute efficiencies" insofar as the final outcome of their use is not communally shared.   Since the interest in private profit, which capitalist property relations thoroughly liberate, refers consumption to private ends, it destroys the idealistic status of technology and reduces tools to their "first estate."   For the industrial oligarchy, tools are the instruments of private power and advantage; for workers, tools are mere conditions of livelihood.   There is no common understanding of purpose; indeed, the social organization of technology sets action at cross purposes.   Dewey was so taken with his idealistic interpretation of tools that, while he saw that the differential social organization of technology affects its moral status, he gave it no serious, systematic recognition.   Dewey tended to see past his insight: he envisioned technology as a form of communication.   But, dominated by a liberated interest in private profit, technology acts as a foundation for a tower of Babel.

Dewey was indifferent to political economy because he interpreted technology too abstractly and idealistically; since technology implied peace, political economy was superfluous.   Dewey's thoughts on socialism, and especially on its salutary psychological effects, are quite literally the sociological extrapolation of his idealistic interpretation of technology.   For this reason he left no conscientious schema of a socialized economy; in these matters he was more the dreamer than the architect or stone mason.   In short, Macpherson is right to conclude, though he does so for the wrong reasons, that in Dewey's political thought we encounter a "retreat from economic penetration to idealism."56

In agreement with Dewey, Macpherson argues that the productive potential of technology is so great that we can dispatch the concept of man as an infinite appropriator, and embrace a more democratic notion of the human essence which emphasizes growth and developmental powers.[57] They agree as well that technology itself cannot drive this change. Unless the idea of man as a consumer of utilities within the bourgeois social structure is overcome, technology is likely to frustrate the emergence of the more democratic vision of human nature[58] Macpherson sees more clearly than Dewey how, under capitalism, a rise or a decline in technological productivity would strengthen the image of possessive individualism.[59] The crucial question for both of these thinkers is not whether we can live more fully human lives, but what must be done in order for us to do so. They concur that abandonment of the classic liberal definition of man is primary.[60] Macpherson argues that this requires a "conjuncture ... of partial breakdowns of the political order and partial break-throughs of public consciousness." Clarification of the Western philosophic anthropology by political scientists is an important first step in this direction.[61]

In reply, Dewey would probably have argued that Macpherson's logic of social change is illogical because of the primacy of habit in conduct. Ultimately Dewey's social psychology compelled him to argue that only formal education - specifically the teacher and the primary school - can overcome the old individualism and release the enormous potential of technology for democracy. Through the school marm, the Baconian hope for the relief of the common estate of man can be satisfied. Dewey did not run to the advocacy of education as the singular means of change: he was dragged to it by social psychology. The apparent naiveté of this theory of change is not an expression of Dewey's liberalism; rather, the problems and paradoxes of this theory measure the sophistication of Dewey the psychologist.

III

Dewey understood his own democratic idealism as both the completion of, and a unique break with, the history of modern democracy. He thought modern political democracies were moving toward the "idea" of democracy. And the realization of a "spiritually democratic society"[62] would be historically unprecedented: under its auspices the "idea" would finally fulfill itself. Yet this movement has been restricted to the political realm, and undemocratic habits still prevail in the economy. The psychology of capitalism is, for Dewey, the principal obstacle in the way of a truly democratic culture and the realization of the Baconian vision through the potential of technology.

Dewey argues that men are not primarily rational animals: "Man is a creature of habit, not of reason nor yet of instinct." Human nature is originally ambiguous. Original plasticity both enables and compels us to learn from experience and to develop habits. Native "impulses" acquire social meaning only through a social medium: under the tutelage of society original impulses are "educated" into habits.63

Habits are not simply modes of technical proficiency. They are inclinations and affections which provide the impetus and demand for activity. Habits encompass both our "working capacities" and our "effective desires"; as such, they govern the origin, direction, and intensity of thought.64

> The essence of habit is an acquired predisposition to ways or modes of response, not to particular acts except as, under special conditions, these express a way of behaving. Habit means special sensitiveness of accessibility to certain classes of stimuli, standing predilections or aversions, rather than bare recurrence of specific acts. It means will.65

The primacy of habit in conduct means that the psychology of thinking itself is politically problematic as thought depends on habits which are legacies of the social environment. Native biological capacities do play their role in the formation of mind. However, if mind means the objects of our attention and the way we understand them, then it is clearly tradition which gives our world meaning. As Dewey says, "in conduct the acquired is the primitive."66 What is true of mind is true of morality: the principal determinant of morality is custom. Thus the social psychology of habit is at the very heart of political continuity and change.

For this reason the formation of the appropriate habits of its young is as vital to the survival of society as it is indispensable to the existence of the youthful individual himself. In order that a society may persist through time, it is obliged to engage and interest its youth in its distinctive methods and ends. Towards this purpose, the creation of a "like-mindedness" in the immature must be insured by the mature members. Like-mindedness is established by "means of the action of the environment in calling out certain responses."67 This process educates because it transforms original impulse: through it, the young accept as their own the ideas and emotions that drive and characterize society. This transformation makes their interested participation in social ends possible and is the fundamental basis of social cooperation and control. Education fulfills its foremost social function when, from an initiate, it fashions a fellow.

Since mind depends on habit, and habit on custom, changes in objective conditions can break the continuum of history. This answer is a paradoxical problem rather than a solution. As Dewey says:

> The direction of native activity depends upon acquired habits, and yet acquired habits can be modified only by redirection of impulse. Existing institutions impose their stamp, their superscription, upon impulse and instinct. They embody the modifications the latter have undergone.

> How then can we get leverage for changing institutions? How shall impulse exercise that re-adjusting office which has been claimed for it? Shall we not have to depend in the future as in the past upon upheaval and accident to dislocate customs so as to release impulses to serve as points of departure for new habits?[68]

The political implications of this paradox cannot be underestimated. It means nothing less than that men accept as universal their own historical and political circumstances and, therefore, find the apotheosis of morality in their own history.

The dynamics of the social psychology of habit mean that a social order is an educative force; it fashions thought and character in ways which support rather than subvert it for the same reasons that a new order would liberate the mind from its old patterns. A new complex of habits cannot simply emerge: it must be fashioned out of objective conditions. But these necessary conditions will not arise, for the present order produces a form of mind and morality which is, at the very least, indifferent to change. Hence the social environment is nor merely pedagogical insofar as it educates original impulses into habits. It also has profound ideological effects since it inculcates the acceptance of a particular organization of power, poverty and wealth.

The social education of original impulse creates specific habits that agree with established custom, and these habits effectively act as self-assertive moral standards. Thus the effective moral authority of any established order rests principally upon the fact of its existence, and the continued existence of this fact is assured by the obdurateness of habit. As Dewey says, "When habits are so ingrained as to be second nature, they seem to have all of the inevitability that belongs to the movement of the fixed stars."[69] What is past becomes what is best: history becomes morality. The inexpugnable predominance of habit in conduct assures that a reasoned argument for political change is, by definition, unreasonable.

A shared vision of a new order presupposes the existence of that very same order. Since our ideas depend upon our habits, and habits are embodiments of objective conditions in a personal form, Dewey concludes that our ideals must be preceded by "some accomplished objective situation."[70] As habits and acts precede thoughts, memory of the experienced good is a necessary condition of the imagination of that good. Dewey's social psychology poses a major political dilemma, for it means that a generation's vision of a new order is always retrospective: it is possible only after that order has been constructed. Political idealism is essentially political anamnesis.

Unless new habits or dispositions have, by some mystery, already formed, political change in the traditional sense is futile; it fails to transform the psychological basis of the older order. A "modification of emotion and intellectual disposition" is the "only way" to resolve social conflict or to reform politics.[71] Since education forms and transforms disposition, the philosophy of education suggests, and pedagogical practice actually is, the mode of social transformation.

Dewey redefined the terms of the problems of change. His reduction of the political aspects of social change to questions of educational practice implies that orderly and effective social and political change is an educational, not a political, problem; the achievement of change falls squarely within the province of the philosophy and practice of education and beyond the realm of political science as it is commonly considered. Dewey radically circumscribed the political realm because his theory of social change implies that change is a problem which lies beyond the reach of strictly political activity. Though most of his students have failed to see it, he offers an interpretation of social progress and reform as a theory of education; his philosophy of education is his theory of social and political change.

Dewey thoroughly psychologizes social conflict; a social problem is a psychological problem. The method of social control is also thoroughly psychological; if politics seeks to resolve, control or maintain social conflicts, there can be no practical difference between politics and education as the latter forms and transforms disposition. Thus Dewey implicitly generalized the circumscription of politics in his theory of social and political change; he defined all social problems as problems for the philosophy and practice of education. Dewey not only collapsed the problems and methods of the reformer and revolutionary into those of the pedagogue; he also collapsed all political categories into pedagogical categories. Education is the method of solving all social and political problems: it constitutes the public control of social acts and is the art of politics. For this reason political philosophy is congruent with the philosophy of education.

This means that the most profound divisions between human beings are not those of opposing economic or political interests, of sex, of race, or of culture: the most important political difference is the difference of age. If the origin and limits of our morals are found in the habituation to custom, then any contest claiming to be a struggle for justice necessarily must be a war against the ways of the elders. Any genuine social transformation depends upon overturning the pedagogic power of the elders and replacing it with a new education. As Immanuel Kant taught, man is "merely what education makes of him."[72] The Good is either what our elders command or what our children obstinately desire. For this reason the struggle between the old and the young is the most profound form of class conflict.

This conflict is the essential form of the struggle for political power because children are the only animals that can be politicized as habits and character are fixed early in life. The identity of our morality and our education means that education, whatever its form, is the most secure protection of the rulers against the ruled. Since the elders must always educate the youth, the conflict between generations is at the very heart of the struggle for political power. This analysis does not distill power from politics; it only recasts the locus of power. Dewey accepted Marx's parturient, but aborted, aphorism: "Whomever one seeks to persuade, one acknowledges as master of the situation."[73] Inspired by Plato, he found the neology in it: since children are, in the most profound way, naively unpersuaded about everything, their education is the social vortex of the struggle for power. Pedagogical processes explain society: it is not unfair to suggest that Dewey attempted to give the educative process the same importance as Marx gave to the productive process in the determination of the social whole.

Those with true political power are those who can cast the habits of the young - parents, relatives, and elementary school teachers. Politics is that activity which makes children of the same mind as adults. It is an element of our prosaic, everyday life, and proceeds quietly, beneath the surface of things reputedly political such as elections. Like those things, politics is rather disorderly; it is a motley sort of democracy because the education of children is a shared responsibility. But politics by no means is uncontrolled; it is not a chaos because adults generally respect the division of rights and powers over the young. Like those things putatively political, politics depends upon extraordinary personalities for decisive turns in its direction. Parents, teachers, day-school workers and the like are real statesmen. Hardly a parliament of owls, they forge the habits of children; though unassuming and nearly invisible, they are our governors.

Among these governors, one stands above all others because of its decisive political power. In technically and socially complex societies the young find it impossible to appreciate fully the adult world simply through informal and indirect contacts. In these societies, according to Dewey, the broad social function of education can be achieved only through formal education: only that special institution, the school, successfully preserves the social continuity of life.[74] Formal education is the indispensable condition of social continuity and change. The school and the teacher have decisive political power because they alone can complete our education. For this reason the political fate of the social order balances upon the role of the school and the teacher.

As the facts of social psychology forced Dewey to conclude that the general theory of education must be the theory of social and political change, his philosophy of education should be interpreted as a sort of political surrogate for change by economic reform; education should beget those psycho-social effects which the democratization of the economy would have generated, were it not the indomitable inertia of habit. In this sense Dewey's philosophy of education is an economic revolution writ small in the society of the classroom. It is through this revolution that the democratic potential of technology - material and political - will at last be freed. Against Marx, but not against revolution, Dewey encourages us to seek justice and the means of political change in the moral sensibilities of children. Following Plato, he encourages us to envision political theory and the political science of revolution as a form of social psychology: the theory of learning.

Notes

1. *John Dewey: The Later Works, 1925-1953*, ed. Jo Ann Boydston, (Carbondale-Edwardsville, Illinois: Southern Illinois University Press, 1984), V, 156.

2. Dewey, *Liberalism and Social Action* (New York: G.P. Putnam's Sons, Capricorn Books, 1963), pp. 58, 73, 81; Dewey, *Freedom and Culture* (New York: Capricorn Books, 1963), pp. 9, 168. Dewey defines technology as "all the intelligent techniques by which the energies of nature and man are directed and used in satisfaction of human needs; it cannot be limited to a few outer and comparatively mechanical forms." See *John Dewey: The Later Works, 1925-1953*, V, 270.

3. Dewey, *Liberalism and Social Action*, pp. 73-75, 81; *John Dewey: The Later Works*, II: 302, 344-45.

4. Dewey, *Liberalism and Social Action*, p. 63; also see pp. 64, 75, 82; *John Dewey: The Later Works*, V, 55-56.

5. *Ibid.*, II, 307-14.

6. *The Philosophy of John Dewey*, ed. Paul Arthur Schilpp (La Salle, Illinois: Open Court, 1951), p. 592; see also   Robert L. Heilbroner, *An Inquiry into the Human Prospect* (New York: W.W. Norton & Co., 1975) and Yehezkel Dror, *Public Policymaking Reexamined* (San Francisco: Chandler Publishing Co., 1968).

7. *John Dewey: The Middle Works, 1899-1924*, ed. Jo Ann Boydston (Carbondale-Edwardsville, Illinois: Southern Illinois University, 1976), I, 128.

8. *John Dewey: The Later Works*, V, 66.

9. *Ibid.*, pp. 66-69.

10. *Ibid.*, pp. 58-61.

11. *Ibid.*, II, 295-97, 300-302, 366-68; Dewey, *Liberalism and Social Action*, p. 82.

12, *John Dewey: The Later Works*, V, 64-65, 81-83.

13. *Ibid.*, p. 84.

14. *John Dewey: The Later Works*, I, 198-99.

15. Dewey, *Reconstruction in Philosophy* (Boston: Beacon Press, 1957), 206-7.

16. *John Dewey: The Later Works*, II, 327-28.

17. Dewey, "The Teacher and His World," in *Philosophy of Education (Problems of Men)* (Totowa, New Jersey: Littlefield, Adams & Co., 1975), p. 79.

18. Dewey, *Liberalism and Social Action*, p. 55.

19. Dewey, *Reconstruction in Philosophy*, pp. viii-ix, 95-96.

20. *John Dewey: The Later Works*, IV, 68.

21. *Ibid.*, pp. 82, 85-86, 116-17, 175-77.

22. *Ibid.*, pp. 86, 163.

23. John Dewey, *Reconstruction in Philosophy*, p. 160; see also pp. 96-97, 145, 148, 156-60.

24. *Intelligence in the Modern World: John Dewey's Philosophy*, ed. Joseph Ratner (New York: The Modern Library, 1939), p. 431.

25. *John Dewey: The Later Works*, V, 119-123.

26. John Dewey, "Force and Coercion," in *Characters and Events: Popular Essays in Social and Political Philosophy*, ed. Joseph Ratner, (New York: Henry Holt & Co., 1929), II, p. 784; see also p. 638.

27. *Ibid.*, II, pp. 783, 787, 789; see also p. 637.

28. John Dewey, *Reconstruction in Philosophy*, p. 209; see also pp. 207-208.

29. *John Dewey: The Later Works*, V, 115.

30. *John Dewey: The Early Works*, IV, 215.

31. *John Dewey: The Later Works*, V, 90-91.

32. C.B. Macpherson, *The Life and Times of Liberal Democracy* (Oxford: Oxford University Press, 1977), pp. 74-75.

33. *John Dewey: The Later Works*, V, 85; *Liberalism and Social Action*, p. 75; *Freedom and Culture*, p. 144.

34. *John Dewey: The Later Works*, II, 331-33.

35. Dewey, *Human Nature and Conduct: An Introduction to Social Psychology* (New York: The Modern Library, 1957), p. 251; see also pp. 249-50.

36. *John Dewey: The Later Works*, V, 67; see also pp. 66-73.

37. *Ibid.*, pp. 106-7.

38. *Ibid.*, p. 69.

39. *Ibid.*, pp. 67-68.

40. *Ibid.*, p. 103.

41. *Ibid.*, p. 85.

42. C.B. Macpherson, *The Life and Times of Liberal Democracy*, pp. 49-50, 65-66, 69-76; C.B. Macpherson, "The Economic Penetration of Political Theory: Some Hypotheses," *Journal of the History of Ideas*, 39 (January-

March, 1978), 112, 115; C.B. Macpherson, *Democratic Theory: Essays in Retrieval* (Oxford: Clarendon Press, 1973), pp. 201-203.

43. Dewey, *Freedom and Culture*, p. 72; also see pp. 65-66, 76, 93.

44. Dewey, *Liberalism and Social Action*, p. 71; see also pp. 36, 54, 64, 70, 85; *John Dewey: The Later Works*, II, 310.

45. Dewey, *Democracy and Education: An Introduction to the Philosophy of Education* (New York: The Macmillan Company, 1961), p. 90.

46. *John Dewey: The Later Works*, V, 120; see also pp. 121- 123.

47. Dewey, *Reconstruction in Philosophy*, pp. 203-4; see also pp. 202, 205.

48. George Novack, *Pragmatism versus Marxism: An Appraisal of John Dewey's Philosophy* (New York: Pathfinder Press, 1975), p. 41; see also pp. 7,13, 35-40, 80, 240, 276, 284-85, 291.

49. C. Wright Mills, *Sociology and Pragmatism: The Higher Learning in America*, ed. Irving Louis Horowitz (New York: Galaxy Books, 1966), p. 354; see also pp. 331, 352-55, 392-94, 405, 410-13, 432-33.

50. C.E. Ayers, "Instrumental Economics," *The New Republic,* 121 (October 17, 1949), 19, *passim.*

51. Dewey, *Freedom and Culture*, p. 78.

52. *John Dewey: The Later Works*, II, 263.

53. Dewey, *Logic: The Theory of Inquiry* (New York: Henry Holt & Co., 1955), p. 46.

54. *John Dewey: The Later Works*, I, pp. 138-39.

55. *Ibid.*, pp. 132-33, 141.

56. C.B. Macpherson, "The Economic Penetration of Political Theory: Some Hypotheses," p. 116; also *Democratic Theory*, pp. 201-3.

57. C.B. Macpherson, *Democratic Theory*, pp. 20-21, 24-25.

58. *Ibid.*, pp. 24-25.

59. *Ibid.*, pp. 37-38; C.B. Macpherson, *The Rise and Fall of Economic Justice and Other Papers* (Oxford: Oxford University Press, 1985), pp. 30-31.

60. C.B. Macpherson, *Democratic Theory*, pp. 25, 140.

61. *Ibid.*, p. 140; also pp. 21-23, 25, 76; C.B. Macpherson, *The Rise and Fall of Economic Justice*, p. 51.

62. *John Dewey on Education: Selected Writings*, ed. Reginald D. Archambault (New York: The Modern Library, 1964), pp. 292-94.

63. Dewey, *Human Nature and Conduct*, p. 118; see also pp. 85-91, 188, 206.

64. *Ibid.*, p. 26; also pp. 25, 30-33, 36-44, 49, 64-66; Dewey, *Democracy and Education*, pp. 48-49.

65. Dewey, *Human Nature and Conduct*, pp. 39-41; also pp. 32, 36; Dewey, *Democracy and Education*, pp. 46-49; Dewey, *Logic*, pp. 31-33.

66. Dewey, *Human Nature and Conduct*, p. 85.

67. Dewey, *Democracy and Education*, p. 11.

68. Dewey, *Human Nature and Conduct*, p. 119; also pp. 23-24, 29-30, 55, 86-88, 108-11, 115, 118, 120-22, 138-40, 154-57, 272, 287-91, 297-98, 300.

69. Dewey, *Freedom and Culture*, p. 47; also pp. 18-23.

70. Dewey, *Human Nature and Conduct*, p. 24; also pp. 23, 30, 32, 50-51, 217.

71. Dewey, *Democracy and Education*, pp. 331-32; also pp. 323-29.

72. Immanual Kant, *Education*, (Ann Arbor: University of Michigan Press, 1960), p. 6.

73. Karl Marx and Frederick Engels, "The Eighteenth Brumaire of Louis Bonaparte," *Selected Works*, (Moscow: Progress Publishers, 1960), I, 452.

74. Dewey, *Democracy and Education*, pp. 7-9, 19-22, 36-38.

DAHL, DEMOCRACY, AND TECHNOLOGY

H.D. Forbes

> The first task of thought in our era is to think what that technology is: to think it in its determining power over our politics and sexuality, our music and education.
>
> George Grant

If the rapid growth of industrial or technological society is the great fact of the present century, then every contemporary writer, and especially every writer about politics, must somehow respond to that fact. Robert Dahl, one of the most prominent American political scientists of the past generation, is not someone whose name springs to mind, however, in connection with the theme of this anthology. Dahl is known for his writings on democracy, pluralism, and the behavioral approach in political science, not for his writings on technology. Nonetheless his most recent book, *Controlling Nuclear Weapons,* squarely confronts the complex problem of technology and modern democracy. What he says in that book, though apparently at odds with positions he has argued in earlier writings, represents no radical departure from his earlier principles. What he proposes, in effect, is a technological solution to the problems of technology.

This paper will first briefly describe Dahl's analysis of the problem technology poses for democracy. Then it will explain Dahl's objection to a kind of "participatory democracy" sometimes considered a remedy for the ills of contemporary society. The third section will summarize the various suggestions for democratic reform Dahl has made over the past twenty years, and the fourth will outline his most recent proposals for increasing popular participation in politics and popular influence over government. The last two sections will sketch a possible alternative to Dahl's approach and in the light of that alternative offer some suggestions about the relation of Dahl's thought to technology.

227

I

Nuclear weapons are the outstanding example of a new political problem created by technological progress. A few scientists, partly from natural curiosity, it seems, partly from patriotic motives, have conferred on mankind the ability to destroy itself. All of us who live in large cities in Europe or North America know, whether we are inclined to reflect on the fact or not, that plans have been carefully made for our instantaneous destruction and that the machines to accomplish the task are kept in the highest state of readiness. How many rockets would fail to rise, should the command to launch be given; how many Soviet rockets would fall on Soviet cities, and American rockets on American ones; how many warheads would simply be duds; how extensive the disruption of biological and atmospheric processes would be in the wake of a general nuclear exchange, we cannot, of course, know. But we do know that the fireworks would be spectacular, and that we live on the brink of disaster - thanks to technological progress.

Among the problems associated with nuclear weapons is the one Dahl discusses in his latest book. "No decisions can be more fateful for Americans, and for the world, than decisions about nuclear weapons. Yet these decisions have largely escaped the control of the democratic process."[1] Nuclear policy is in the hands of a tiny group of experts - physicists, engineers, statisticians, economists, politicians, and bureaucrats - who decide what new weaponry will be developed, how it will be deployed, and when and against whom it will be used. The American public - the people who theoretically rule the United States - know almost nothing about the relevant issues; they do not and cannot exercise any detailed supervision over policy-making; the most they can do is give the process an occasional nudge in the direction of a faster or a slower (usually a faster) arms race by electing one presidential or senatorial candidate rather than another.

Popular control is of course so drastically limited for good reasons. Grand strategy dictates almost complete secrecy among the decision-makers. Profound ignorance closes the mouths of most of the public. How much control should ordinary Americans have over nuclear weaponry? Are ordinary people competent to make the sorts of decisions that have to be made? Isn't it better to let the experts handle the explosives?

Dahl, it should be noted immediately, is no wild-eyed democrat. He recognizes that nuclear policy-making requires knowledge "far outside the realm of ordinary experience ... that ordinary citizens not only do not possess but cannot reasonably be expected to possess."[2] Technical knowledge about bombs and rockets is obviously relevant and obviously lacking among ordinary citizens. Equally important is *political* knowledge of relevant adversaries. "What *is* Soviet policy? What are the intentions of Soviet leaders? What risks will they take and in what circumstances?"[3] The ordinary citizen may feel more confident answering questions like these than questions about neutrons and electrons, but there is no reason to believe that his answers will be any better in one case than in the other. Foreign policy has always required expertise that ordinary citizens do not and cannot reasonably be expected to possess.

It is easy for most of us to recognize these limitations of the common man, for most of us are in the relevant respects common men, and we recognize them in ourselves. What is the significance of these limitations? Should the ordinary citizen be excluded from participation in making the decisions that might end his life? Should he be compelled to participate in these decisions even if he would prefer not to be involved? In fact, as Dahl notes, "an overwhelming proportion of the citizen body has until quite recently totally abdicated its rights to participate in any way in making nuclear decisions even of the most general sort."[4]

Now what is true of nuclear weapons is true to a lesser extent of many other fields of contemporary policy-making: effective debate is confined to a narrow circle of specialists; the ordinary citizen is bewildered; he takes little or no part in the discussion; and his cogitations have virtually no effect on the outcome. Consider some of the issues governments face today: recombinant DNA research, nuclear reactor safety, clean air, ozone depletion, government debt, and the cost of medical care. "What problems like these have in common is that they have enormously important consequences for a vast number of people, they seem to require government decisions of some kind, and in order to make wise decisions, decision-makers need specialized knowledge that most citizens do not possess."[5] The control of nuclear weapons is thus an extreme but not misleading example of a much deeper problem in contemporary democracy. The democratic process as we know it today - the institutions of liberal, representative democracy - seem incapable of achieving democratic control of the "crucially important and inordinately complex" issues of modern technological society. As a result "small groups of decision-makers exercise a degree of influence over decisions that, from a democratic perspective, is excessive and illicit."[6]

What to do about this situation is at the heart, I suspect, of all Dahl's reflections about politics, from his earliest writings about the British Labour Party to his most recent books on democratic reform. To understand his most recent proposals properly, one must begin by considering what he has said in the past about size and democracy and about practical strategies for democratic reform.

II

What Dahl recommends, it will be clear presently, is a kind of "participatory democracy," but he does not favor the radical decentralization commonly associated with that phrase. His proposals are best understood against the background of his objections to such decentralization.

Few generalizations will fit all the partisans of participatory democracy. During the past generation many intellectuals have advocated it, and many different ideas are now associated with the phrase. But one simple idea is common to all: true democrats should not be content with the very imperfect kind of democracy represented by countries like Canada and the United States. In such countries - *representative* democracies - there is a division of labor between representatives and the people they represent. The result is government by politicians and bureaucrats and, it is feared, for politicians and bureaucrats. At any rate, politicians and bureaucrats participate directly in the making of decisions, while ordinary citizens, busy with other tasks in the division of labor, do not. Ordinary citizens obviously have some influence over the politicians through their power to vote them in or out of office at election time, but the power of the average citizen - the ability of average A to get average B to do what average B would not otherwise do - is obviously much less than the power of the average president or prime minister.

This is the situation that the partisans of participatory democracy generally find unsatisfactory. They tend to think that all those whose lives are affected by a decision should participate in making the decision. A genuine democracy, they assume, would be one in which all citizens participated equally in making decisions and in which no one citizen or group of citizens - no "power elite" - dominated all the others. This underlying ideal of democracy - equal influence for all - is extremely influential among contemporary social scientists.

How might the ideal be realized? The standard examples of direct, non-representative democracy are the popular assemblies of ancient Athens, the town meetings of New England, and the *Landesgemeinden* of some Swiss cantons. Let us leave aside the problem of how these models should be described: would the New England town meeting, for example, be better depicted in the style of Norman Rockwell or that of Judy Chicago? The more pressing problem is how to adapt these models to countries the size of the United States. What kind of deliberation could take place in a popular assembly of one or two hundred million people?

The partisans of participatory democracy do not pretend to have any simple solution to this problem. To the extent that they talk about it, they reveal much about their thought. Some lean towards anarchism and the belief that coercive government is simply a big mistake that an enlightened humanity will one day relegate to a museum. Others clearly favor the Soviet model of democracy. Many seem to be basically men of faith.

Institution-building, they suggest, belongs to *praxis*; academics who try to draw up blueprints for the new society are wasting their time. The citizens themselves must be left free to decide how they want to live; for the present, the watchword must be "nothing ventured, nothing gained." Most, however, cannot resist dropping some hints about what the new society will be like, and most of these suggest that power will be much more decentralized.7

Dahl stands out in this company because he clearly denies that the problems of representative democracy can be overcome by radical decentralization. Yet he also clearly accepts the now standard conception of democracy as equality of influence. There is no need to cite all the evidence for these generalizations, as I think their truth will be accepted by those familiar with Dahl's work. It will suffice to summarize a few passages from some of Dahl's better-known publications.

In his textbook of American politics, Dahl concludes his discussion of democracy by noting that the definition of democracy has long been a source of controversy. He proposes to reduce the confusion by clearly distinguishing two common uses of the term, to denote an ideal political system, which may not actually exist anywhere, and to denote a number of actual systems that do exist in our world of experience. He reserves "democracy" for the ideal and introduces "polyarchy" to denote the actual systems that approximate the ideal. He asks us to imagine a continuum from ideal democracy at one end to its negation, autocracy, at the other:

Autocracy (-)  (+) Democracy

The extremes of this dimension are perfect inequality (all power in the hands of one man, the autocrat) and perfect equality (every citizen exercising the same power over decisions as every other citizen). Actual systems are distributed along this dimension. The Soviet Union is found to the left of the United States, but neither system is at an extreme of the dimension: in the Soviet Union Gorbachev does not have *all* the power, and in the United States Reagan has a larger share than does, say, the average citizen of New Haven.8

The contrast between democracy as an ideal of equality of influence and democracy as a set of institutions called "polyarchy" that approximate the ideal, goes back to *Politics, Economics and Welfare*, which Dahl published with Charles E. Lindblom in 1953. There the condition of political equality was defined as follows: "Control over governmental decisions is shared so that the preferences of no one citizen are weighted more heavily than the preferences of any other one citizen."9 Democracy in this sense is clearly distinguished from general equality of control: it does not require that all organizations be democratically governed. Families, armies, and businesses, for example, may be organized hierarchically, provided that government is democratic and citizens thus have the "last word" on where in society the condition of equality is to be enforced or forgone. "So long as the condition of political equality is approximated [in government], citizens can always decide in what situations and in what organizations they wish to tolerate hierarchy in order to achieve goals that cannot be satisfied by organization on an equalitarian basis."[10]   Nonetheless, political equality suffers in the presence of hierarchy of any kind, for "the plain fact is, of course, that a leader at the top of a modern hierarchy - corporations, trade unions, government   agencies, political parties - tends inevitably to exert more control over government policy than does any one of his subordinates. The hierarchical leader is more than simply a spokesman for all or a majority of the people in his organization counted as equals; that is, his own preferences count for significantly more than those of any one of his subordinates."[11]

Leadership of any sort is a problem for democratic theory, as Dahl has observed more recently. "To portray a democratic order without leaders is a conspicuous distortion of all historical experience; but to put them into the picture is even more troublesome. Whether by definition, by implication, or simply as a fact, leaders, as individuals, exercise more direct influence on many decisions than ordinary individual citizens. Thus the superior influence of leaders violates strict criteria for political equality."[12]

In short, an ideal democracy would be one in which all citizens had the same power, one in which all were able to participate equally in making the decisions that affected their lives. Dahl differs from most partisans of participatory democracy, not because he has a different conception of the democratic ideal, but because he is less sanguine about what is practically possible.

Equal participation through decentralization must be rejected as impractical because it would fragment political power when it needs to be consolidated. The basic units of a simple participatory democracy would have to be so small that they could not deal with the main problems of contemporary life. Dahl draws attention to the necessary relation between the size of an association and the amount of time each member can have for expressing his own opinions in the group's legislative deliberations. "To take an absurd example: if an association were to make one decision a day, allow ten hours a day for discussion, and permitted each member just ten minutes - rather extreme assumptions, you will agree - then the association could have no more than sixty members."[13] To drive the point home: six hundred members would imply that each would have one minute to state his views. Six thousand members would leave each member six seconds. Sixty thousand, six tenths of a second. Evidently any association that wanted to equalize power by equalizing participation would have to be very small - more like a family than a state.

Even the classic models of direct democracy could not have ensured literally equal participation by all, and the modern world (or modern *technology*) clearly demands large political units. Any contemporary state that broke itself into tiny shards in pursuit of the participatory ideal, Dahl points out, would obviously be much worse off than before with respect to a vast range of problems. His examples include pollution, nuclear testing, public health, medical care, the control of economic enterprises, monetary and fiscal policies, racial discrimination, poverty, crime, access to raw materials, capital, consumers' goods, markets, and, finally, the baffling problem, even for those willing to go back to the stone age, of interstate rivalry.

> In a world of microstates, let there arise only one large and aggressive state and the microrepublics are doomed. Either they must suffer subjugation or they must unite in mutual defense. Neither outcome will allow all important decisions to be made in primary assemblies. The force of these objections is so strong that one wonders how the advocates of primary [i.e., decentralized participatory] democracy can fail to feel it. I do not myself know any answer except that the capacity of a human mind, however brilliant, to be dazzled by beautiful but insubstantial schemes has no more limits in politics than in real estate or the stock market.14

In short, many partisans of participatory democracy simply fail to understand how very small the political units would have to be before every citizen could participate equally in legislation, and how necessary large political units are in our high-tech, interdependent world. Their rhetoric is the abracadabra of the vaudeville stage, not the sober analysis of scientific political science. "The magician who puts polyarchy into a hat and pulls out primary democracy may confound the very innocent and the true believer; everyone else sees that what looks like a town meeting of a hundred million people is pure razzle-dazzle."15

III

Rejecting popular panaceas is often confused with supporting the status quo; the tendency to do so accounts for Dahl's reputation, in some circles, as a conservative. During the past twenty years, however, Dahl has put forward bold proposals for sweeping reforms of American politics.

Dahl's judgment of contemporary democracy is a mixture, as we have just seen, of pluses and minuses. By comparison with the alternatives cast up by history rather than the imagination, it must be appraised, he recognizes, "as a superior instrument for achieving a decent government among a very large body of citizens." Yet it is still "light years distant" from achieving the ideal of equality of influence by every citizen that is the finest product of the democratic impulse.16

What is to be done to bring ideal and reality closer together? *After the Revolution?*, which Dahl published in 1970, recommends two major reforms that would effect revolutionary changes in power and privilege and that could hardly be adopted without a tremendous upheaval, two more modest reforms that would change only the institutions of government and the distribution of the population on the land, and finally a transformation of international politics, the framework of contemporary democracy, to do away with the threat of nuclear war.

Dahl's most widely discussed proposal has to do with taming "the corporate Leviathan." Dahl rejects the common idea that corporations are purely private associations rightly ruled by those who presently own them. They are, in fact, great public bureaucracies providing public services, and as such they flagrantly violate, in their present form, the simplest principles of democratic legitimacy.[17]   But the solution does not lie simply in nationalization as traditionally conceived. "The Post Office, after all, is hardly a model of democratic government."[18] It lies rather in an innovative combination of workers' self-management (based upon workers' councils, as in Yugoslavia), interest-group management (involving participation in management by representatives of affected interests such as consumers, downwind neighbors, etc.), external market controls (to set limits to prices and quantities of production), and hierarchical governmental controls (to bind the whole thing together). Dahl confesses that the optimal combination of controls will not be easy to find and that they may, in effect, shift with the wind. "Yet it seems obvious that if we place much value on democracy at the work place, the present arrangement is ludicrously far from optimal."[19]

Dahl suggests that this transformation in the control of wealth be matched by a vast transformation in the distribution of income. Inequality of rewards is of course compatible with democratic government: it is not clear what free citizens would be free to do if not to give each other unequal rewards. But the people must be cautious lest their most highly paid servants become their masters. All the authorities are agreed that democracy is threatened by extreme inequalities. Dahl offers a number of concrete proposals to strengthen democracy by reducing inequality. Racial discrimination must be eliminated. The "contemptible" injustice that links the fortunes of children to the fortunes of their parents must be rectified. The welfare mess - "the enormous network of bureaucratic regulations and restraints that have bedeviled the life of the welfare recipient in the United States" - must be replaced by a guaranteed annual income large enough to eliminate extreme inequality. The costs of political campaigns must be reduced, or financed differently, so that the man of average means can reasonably aspire to high office. Democracy, in short, requires higher taxes and a stricter control over the use of wealth.[20]

These economic reforms would revolutionize the American class structure. Perhaps not overnight, but in a generation or two, today's wealthy families would find themselves with neither the wealth nor the leading role in society that they presently enjoy. Political democracy would be enhanced and secured by a revolution in power and income that would amount to an expropriation of the expropriators.

By themselves, however, even these large changes would not be enough. They represent no "once-for-all leap into permanent utopia,"[21] but an arduous climb to a new plateau from which new and higher ideals can be perceived.

One of Dahl's most novel and intriguing proposals is to reintroduce the ancient democratic device of choosing public officials at random from the general population (selection by lot). In *After the Revolution?* Dahl recommends that councils be created to advise all major elected officials (mayors of large cities, state governors, members of Congress, and the President) and that their members be chosen by lot.

Let us imagine that the membership of each advisory council were to consist of several hundred constituents picked by the same procedures used to ensure randomness in modern sample surveys; that the citizens selected would be required to serve, as is supposed to be the case now with jury duty, though honored in the breach; that suitable provisions would insure against hardships arising from the obligation to serve - for example, the citizen selected would not only have all relevant expenses taken care of but if he (or she) were poor or unemployed he (or she) might receive a stipend, while an employed person would continue to receive his (or her) regular pay; that one would serve for a year and be ineligible for a second term; that a council might meet at intervals for a total of several weeks in the course of a year; that it would have its own presiding officer (and a professional parliamentarian); that it would invite the elected official to meet with it, to answer questions, hear the debate and discussion.[22]

Dahl advises against choosing the officials themselves by lot rather than election. The "very thin and fragmented" political knowledge of the average citizen counts against any such idea. Most of those chosen by lot would be bewildered by their new responsibilities and would be even more dependent on expert advice from permanent officials than elected politicians are today. "One hundred more or less average citizens snatched out of their daily lives by random selection would find the work of the United States Senate, for example, formidably complex."[23]

The uncontrolled growth of modern cities creates problems for politics that have long concerned Dahl. In *After the Revolution?* he urged that steps be taken to reverse the trend to bigness, so that individuals could live in and help to govern cities of human proportions. He suggested that giant cities like New York be considered states and that each of their neighborhoods have its own city government. He recognized, however, that the most important reform would have to be the development of a system that would, so to speak, put megalopolis on a diet: "We would have to plan consciously to prevent cities from growing too large and how best to do so. We would have to establish a vast program of creating new cities and in this way thin out megalopolis."24

Perhaps Dahl's most significant suggestions for reform have to do with the international order. He urges that we abandon conventional ideals of national independence and accept the necessity of world government. To approach politics today with the ideal in the back of one's mind of many autonomous, completely independent democratic states, is to neglect the obvious and very threatening problem of nuclear war. "It is an invitation to suicide."25 No more satisfactory, he concedes, is the background idea of a world state consisting of nothing but elections and a representative body on the one side and a cabinet and bureaucracies on the other. "Let your mind play for a moment with the thought of the World Minister of Education regulating your schools."26 Plainly any practical world government must employ the federal principle of decentralization with "extensive mutual guarantees limiting the scope of the majority principle."27 Dahl uses the metaphor of "Chinese boxes" to explain what he has in mind: "the people" entitled to "rule" at one stage would be a subset of "the people" entitled to "rule" at a more inclusive stage, and the rights and obligations of "the people" at various stages would be embodied in a system of mutual guarantees. The smallest boxes in such a system could be very small and very democratic, though with nothing very much to decide democratically about. The largest box would contain all the others - some 3 or 4 billion citizens - and at best its procedures could not be very "participatory." It would probably exercise its authority by delegation from "national" governments, at least initially, and would come into being only if democratic purists were willing to relax some of their principles of legitimacy.

> To insist that no system of world government can be rightful unless it operates with the full panoply of polyarchal institutions - elections, representatives, competing parties, and the rest - means that there cannot possibly be a rightful world order in time to rescue man from the gradual or sudden destruction that seems so inevitable a destiny if relations among nation-states cannot be brought more effectively under the control of law. Most nation-states do not now practice polyarchy within their own boundaries. How can they possibly be expected to permit free

elections for representatives to a world parliament when they do not permit free elections for representatives to a national parliament?[28]

In short, we are inexorably impelled to larger and more inclusive units of government in which the fundamental principles of democracy become increasingly problematic.

IV

Why not abandon democracy altogether? If modern life requires vast, transnational bureaucracies to control the intricate and potentially explosive interdependencies of our global village, why even attempt to subject these bureaucracies to the control of ordinary citizens? If the issues faced by governments today are so complex that only a few experts can really understand what should be done, why confer any authority at all on the uninformed opinions of the mass electorate? As Dahl recognizes in his most recent book, "a perennial alternative to democracy is government by meritocratic rulers or guardians."[29]

Controlling Nuclear Weapons is such an interesting and important book because Dahl squarely confronts there the problem of "democracy versus guardianship." The second chapter presents "the case for guardianship." The central issue posed by all theories of guardianship, from Plato to Lenin and B. F. Skinner, is, as Dahl states it, "whether the good or interests of ordinary folk are best protected by themselves, acting through the democratic process, or by a meritorious elite possessing unusual knowledge and virtue."[30]

Dahl argues that two kinds of knowledge and one key disposition qualify rulers to rule. True rulers must have an adequate understanding of the proper ends or objectives that government should strive to reach, and they should also know the best, most efficient means to achieve those ends. The right ends will not be pursued, however, unless rulers are also "virtuous": they must possess a strong disposition actually to seek the desirable ends. Would-be rulers who qualify by all three tests Dahl calls *politically competent.*

The three tests of competence he outlines are as relevant to democracy as to any aristocratic system of guardianship. Why are children denied the vote, Dahl asks, if not because they lack the necessary qualifications to use it wisely? Even democracies evidently accept "the premise that people who are definitely unqualified should not be permitted to participate fully in governing."[31]

The issue between democracy and guardianship, then, turns on the political competence of the average citizen. The *moral* competence of the average citizen - his knowledge of the right ends of government and virtuous disposition to seek those ends - has long been debated, and Dahl concedes that the critics of democracy have some strong arguments. He and they point to the average citizen's shortsightedness, lack of self-knowledge, and egoism. The wise of all ages and all cultures, for example, almost with one voice have condemned materialism - "searching for happiness through the endless gratification of desire, particularly through the acquisition and consumption of things." Yet the average citizens of the world seem to devote themselves above all to this end, heedless of the damage they are doing to the natural environment and the interests of future generations.32

The *technical* competence of the average citizen - his knowledge of the best means to attain given ends - is even more questionable. As noted earlier, nuclear weapons illustrate a general problem. Government makes greater and greater demands upon specialized knowledge as knowledge itself becomes more and more fragmented. The contemporary democratic citizen is typically a tiny cog in a vast machine whose intricacies he only dimly apprehends. He has his slogans, to be sure, and perhaps his party (or ethnic) identification to guide him, but what else lies behind his typical act of political participation, his vote for a party politician, whose very demanding task it will be, if elected, to coordinate all the other specialists? How is the ignorant voter to judge the comparative expertise of experts who disagree among themselves?

Democratic politics often presents a depressing spectacle. Is there not a clear and attractive alternative to it, the proponents of guardianship ask? Rather than having the incompetent citizenry elect leaders whose real skill is flattery, would it not be better to have officials selected by co-optation from among those who had shown special aptitude for ruling in the course of a long and rigorous education for the task? (The new constitution might resemble the papacy and college of cardinals that rule the Soviet Union.) The moral and technical shortcomings of humanity can be overcome, the argument goes, only by a minority and only as a result of special education that can be provided for only a minority.

> Even if most people were potentially capable of acquiring the qualifications desirable for ruling, they would lack the time to do so. A society, after all, needs many different kinds of activities. Ruling is only one activity. We also need plumbers, carpenters, machinists, doctors, teachers, physicists, mathematicians, painters, dancers, and in a modern society thousands upon thousands of other specialists far more various than anything Plato could have imagined. Acquiring the skills necessary for these tasks and then performing them makes it impossible for very many people to spend the time needed to gain the moral and instrumental [technical] competence for ruling. As I have already indicated, the art and science of ruling is difficult; in a world as complex as ours,

extraordinarily difficult: it is probably easier to become an excellent mathematician than to become an excellent ruler. To suppose that many people have the capacity to acquire and use well a great number of specialized skills is merely romantic. True polymaths are a rarity. Would you entrust yourself to a physician who was also attempting seriously to be a ballet dancer, an opera singer, an architect, an accountant, and a stockbroker?[33]

The case for guardianship is thus an extension of the case for specialization: better to be ruled by a well-educated elite than to be at the mercy of the whims of a mass of ignorant citizens stirred up by demagogues.

Dahl states the case for guardianship clearly and succinctly, because he recognizes that it needs to be taken seriously. To test it he turns (in chapter 3 of the book) to the practical problem of controlling nuclear weapons. He begins from the fact that the control of the nuclear forces is now in the hands of a tiny minority ("our *de facto* guardians"[34]) and asks whether they have the qualifications for the role they play. After reviewing some of the extremely difficult moral questions involved in nuclear policy, he concludes that they do not. "Their specialization is, after all, of a very different kind and may, if anything, blunt rather than sharpen their moral sensibilities."[35] He next considers the possibility that some "real guardians in Plato's sense," who united moral understanding with the instrumental knowledge and virtue required for true guardianship, might replace "our *de facto* guardians" (better, our *technocrats*). Dahl clearly rejects any such shift from technocracy to guardianship, saying that it is impossible. His main objection is clearly and forcefully stated:

> Plato's royal science simply does not exist, and therefore its practitioners cannot exist. Thus, *pace* Plato, there is no single art or science that can satisfactorily demonstrate a claim to unite in itself the moral and instrumental understanding required for intelligent policy making in today's world. Perhaps a few philosophers, social scientists, or even natural scientists might make such an extravagant claim for their own specialty. But the weakness of any such claims could easily be shown to the satisfaction of most of us by a simple test: let them explain what their policies would be in a dozen different areas of policy, let them be subjected to examination by experts in each area, and let us be the judges of their performance.[36]

An important supplementary consideration has to do with "virtue," the disposition among rulers to seek the common good. Is it reasonable to suppose, Dahl asks, that a class of guardians versed in modern natural science, free of popular controls short of revolution, and trained to have contempt for public *opinion* as not true *knowledge*, would long persist in selfless devotion to the common good as opposed to their own?   The encouraging example of ancient and early modern republics is less relevant in this connection than the discouraging example of recent technological tyrannies.37

Prudence and practical wisdom, then, dictate that we not look for salvation to the ancient vision of guardianship. Rulers and philosophers are different sorts of people, Dahl suggests, and it is just as well that they go their separate ways.   "Rulers are unlikely to have much interest in [a passionate search for truth], and few would find the results comforting. Nor can philosophers in Plato's sense have much desire to rule, for it will impede their search for truth, as they well know."38

Where then are we to turn? Dahl turns towards more democracy - the kind made possible by home computers and cable television. A brief summary cannot do justice to the ingenuity of his practical proposals in chapter 5 of *Controlling Nuclear Weapons*, but it can convey something of the spirit of the original.

Dahl begins this last and most practical chapter of the book by noting his objections to four popular panaceas: more participation in politics by all citizens (more participation by incompetent citizens will only increase the weight of incompetence in decision making); more conventional education for all citizens (at best the result would be a larger supply of specialists demanding coordination, and we would be no closer to solving our political problem); better public officials (a good thing in itself, of course, but not a step towards real democracy); and, finally, the fuller development of modern policy science (counterproductive, since modern policy science turns Plato on his head: it perfects the instruments of rule without considering the ends for which these instruments should be used).

Having rejected these alternatives, Dahl outlines a "quasi-utopian solution" that involves increasing the competence as well as the numbers of ordinary citizens who participate in decision-making. His main proposal is to provide, through interactive telecommunications systems, more information about the political agenda, appropriate in level and form for all citizens and accurately reflecting the best knowledge available.

> Imagine that with [a system of cables and computers] a citizen indicates that he has a high school education and would like to see and hear a discussion, lasting about an hour, during which the various alternatives [in some area of policy] are fairly represented. After watching and listening to the discussion, he asks for a print-out of certain facts, observations, or arguments offered during the discussion. When he discovers that some of these are presented in a way too difficult for him to grasp, he asks for them in a more easily understood graphical form. Even the

graphics, he discovers, are a bit too difficult, and he requests and receives a simpler and more understandable version.39

The opportunity to obtain information in a suitable form is essential, as Dahl emphasizes. For the functionally illiterate - some 20% of the population, he suggests - the best form might be "an animated cartoon or the equivalent of 'Sesame Street'."40 To ensure that the information appearing on the home computers is not biased and manipulative, its preparation could be entrusted to advisory commissions of scholars similar in operation to the National Academy of Sciences.

By itself, of course, this scheme for computerized adult education would only increase the influence of the scholars over public opinion and not bring us any closer to true democracy. How can we ensure that the concerns of the ordinary citizen, which we cannot assume would be the same as those of the scholars, get sufficient attention? Dahl suggests, first of all, that the scholars be required to provide information (appropriate in level and form even for the functionally illiterate) not just about the issues they themselves consider important, but also about those a random sample of 1600 citizens considers important, and finally those "that other people who are like [the potential users of the service] in some important ways feel are important." Thus there would be different agendas of issues and different packages of information for different genders, races, levels of education, jobs, and incomes.41

To ensure that decision-makers, and not just scholars, are aware of the aspirations and opinions of ordinary citizens, Dahl makes a second important suggestion similar to the one noted earlier for advisory councils selected by lot. He proposes that *minipopuli* of about a thousand citizens be selected at random from the general population. Several could exist at any one time, and each would serve for a year as a kind of parliament to consider a single important issue. Their members, who could serve on such a group no more than once in a lifetime, would remain in their own communities, with their own friends and acquaintances, and they would "meet" by means of the telecommunications network. Each minipopulus could seek the advice of an advisory committee of scholars and would be served by an administrative staff monitored by the advisory committee. It could hold hearings, commission research, and engage in debate and discussion. By the end of its year it would be expected to "indicate the preference ordering of its members among the most relevant alternatives in the policy area assigned to it."42 Its "decision" would not be binding on any legislative or administrative body, but the elected decision-makers (Senators, Congressmen, etc.) would have to reckon with its existence and recommendations, for it would "reflect public opinion at a higher level of competence." Each minipopulus could reasonably insist that it had dealt authoritatively with those value judgments and assessments of risk on which "specialists can make no special claim to expertise."[43] Decisions about nuclear weapons, for example, or about recombinant DNA research, are jampacked with such assumptions about values, risks, and so on. "Who could justifiably claim to possess a more reasonable judgment on these matters than a minipopulus that had grappled with the issue for a year?"[44]

V

Some scholars pondering this last rhetorical question may be tempted to answer that they themselves can justifiably claim a more reasonable judgment. They may hesitate to press their claim from fear of being challenged to face the test of a dozen experts on a dozen policies mentioned earlier, but they may reflect that the minipopulus, too, even after a year's prepping by the experts, with the assistance of cartoonists and puppeteers, would probably fail this test.

Scholars pursuing such reflections may come upon another, rather different "quasi-utopian solution" to the problems of technocratic politics. It may occur to them to maintain the institutions of representative democracy but to have the people elect and the elected leaders select "quasi-guardians" - individuals who resemble guardians more closely than do the politicians, bureaucrats, and experts who now rule us.

The foundations for this "solution" have already been laid. In *After the Revolution?* Dahl drew attention to the way that representative institutions join the aristocratic principle of competence to the democratic principle of political equality.

> A single solution to both these problems [of moral and technical competence] might be to allow the citizens to elect the superior minority for a fixed term of office. This solution looks so much like a prescription for representative democracy that doubtless it will frighten both the aristocrat and the democrat - the one because it concedes the need for popular sovereignty and the other because it recognizes the desirability of competent rulers.[45]

But Dahl does not explore the possibility suggested by this remark. What would it involve and what could it promise?

The aim would be to educate and employ a class of public servants who could justifiably claim a greater measure of broad political competence, more or less as Dahl defines it, than can the ordinary citizen or the highly trained but also profoundly deformed technologist. The necessary changes might well begin with a reform of political science designed to clarify its authority over all the other sciences. Complementary changes would be necessary in the broader curriculum of our schools and universities, and particularly in the teaching of law and journalism. The hiring practices of our civil services might be changed to favor general competence over technical expertise. The nomination procedures of our political parties might be reformed to give more weight to peer review and less to popularity with convention delegates or party members. Both the people and the politicians would have to be educated to distinguish genuine authority from technological wizardry combined with a knack for public relations. They would have to be persuaded that it is proper to defer to guardians and shameful to assert an equality that has no rational basis. The ordinary citizen would have to approach his duties as a voter in the same spirit as he now approaches jury duty: it would be his task to declare his opinion about the merits of the candidates, not to bargain for special consideration of his private interests.

"Realists" will, of course, object that such "elitist" suggestions are hopelessly utopian. They were tried in the past, they will say, and they failed. Democracy had many overt enemies a century ago, and they were constantly telling the ordinary citizen that he had a duty to defer to his political betters. What reason is there to expect that similar sermons today will have any significant effect on the behavior of ordinary citizens and their ordinary leaders? How did we get to our present level of democratization if not by overcoming far more impressive bastions of elitism than any that exist in the late twentieth century?

"Philosophers" may wonder whether there is really any objective better or worse in the realm with which we are here concerned. No one pays any attention to the sermons today, they may suspect, because everyone knows that values are subjective and cannot be proved. Dahl is surely on solid ground when, alluding to the apparent consensus among philosophers today, he points to the limited authority of moral philosophy. "The few who [believe that absolute, objectively valid, and verifiable moral judgments are possible] have so far not succeeded in demonstrating satisfactorily the absolute and objective status of the moral judgments they assert."[46] Everything seems to be permitted in the realm of values; no one should try to impose his own values on others. The claims to rule of would-be guardians are just so much special pleading. Why should their preferences override the preferences of the vast majority and their political leaders, who also demand the fullest possible measure of power and prestige for themselves? If values are tastes and tastes cannot be disputed, need anyone feel guilty if his tastes happen to be democratic?

The difficulties of elitism are obvious, but so are the practical objections to Dahl's proposals. They would work as planned only if the general public were much more interested in politics than they are now. Dahl's constitutional and educational innovations would quickly atrophy unless large numbers of ordinary citizens watched the educational channels and then, on voting day, punished any representatives foolish enough to have ignored the advice coming to them from their advisory councils and the minipopuli. Without an aroused electorate the educators would have no audiences and the politicians would run rings around the random sample of ordinary citizens charged with advising them. Only fundamental social and economic reforms like those Dahl suggests would be likely to produce the necessary interest. But the prospect of such exciting reforms is likely to stir up intense interest among the rich as well as among ordinary folk. The result might be closer to Chile than utopia. The elitist alternative, by contrast, does not presuppose any social or constitutional revolution. It would be almost completely in harmony with the deepest traditions and natural exclusiveness of our educational and political institutions. No more would be required than a firm determination to moderate or undo some of the democratizing reforms of the last century in academic and political life.

This "solution" would be only "quasi-utopian" since it would not aspire to or achieve the union of philosophy and rulership in a single person or group. It would aim no higher than a serious effort to work our existing liberal-democratic institutions in a spirit closer to the aristocratic spirit in which they were conceived. The practical and theoretical problems of technology would remain. The ordinary citizens would remain the final authorities, and all political arguments would ultimately be addressed to their ears. Politics would still be, as it has perhaps always been, a matter of making the best of a bad situation.

VI

Dahl's recent proposals reflect higher hopes for modern democracy and a quite different conception of its fundamental shortcomings. Dahl wishes to go forward, not backward. His proposals are designed to limit the power of political elites and to increase the authority of public opinion by instituting a form of participatory democracy. More broadly, Dahl's democratic theory is populist in spirit, not aristocratic. The "behavioral" kind of political science he has promoted tends to ignore the philosophical tradition, of which it is the uncritical legatee, and to become a collection of narrow specialties within empirical science. Not only does Plato's royal science not exist, according to Dahl, but no efforts must be made to bring it into being.[47]

Radical as some of his practical suggestions may be, Dahl accepts the overall pattern of contemporary political and academic life with surprisingly few reservations. Democracy must become more democratic, he says, and science more scientific. Dahl is obviously aware that some grave practical problems can be associated with contemporary science or technology, but he looks to that science and technology for palliatives. At one level this point is easily illustrated: home computers and cable television are products of the same kind of knowledge and inventiveness that earlier yielded radar, missiles, and nuclear bombs. At a deeper level, the sharp distinction between facts and values characteristic of modern natural science, and its exclusive concern with efficient causation, have shaped Dahl's behavioral political science and underlie his proposed civic education, which would employ experts to explain the facts (including the facts about the causes of human behavior?) but leave the citizens free to choose their own values as they chose practical policies. The basic problem, as Dahl sees it, is to harness technology more tightly to the popular will, so that it will serve the people and not just the technocrats. Technology itself is not a theme for investigation or questioning in Dahl's work.

Technology is more easily illustrated than defined, but it is plainly more than particular techniques. In politics it is not simply the rule of engineers and statisticians. That such specialists should have a large say in the development of public policy for large, complex, technological societies like the United States is hardly surprising. But neither is it surprising that politicians, intellectuals, and ordinary citizens should try to limit the authority of technical specialists by stressing the narrowness of their expertise. Technology may tend to produce technocracy, but it also invites and accommodates democratic protest. Dahl is one of many who would confine experts to the investigation of facts and the provision of means while ordinary citizens determined values and chose the ends of government. The captain should sail the ship, he implies, but leave the choice of destination to the passengers. It appears a sensible division of labor: passengers cannot sail ships, but they know where they want to go, and captains know the sea but not the needs of their passengers. How else are we to reap the benefits of technology while avoiding its pitfalls? Dahl's linking of technocratic expertise with democratic politics may illustrate a basic feature of technology as a way of life.

Notes

1. Robert A. Dahl, *Controlling Nuclear Weapons: Democracy Versus Guardianship* (Syracuse: Syracuse University Press, 1985), p.3. See also Robert A. Dahl and Ralph S. Brown, *Domestic Control of Atomic Energy* (n.p.: Social Science Research Council, 1951), especially pp. 105-9, and Robert A. Dahl, "Atomic Energy and the Democratic Process," *The Annals of the American Academy of Political and Social Science*, 290 (1953), 1-6.

2. *Ibid.*, p.15.

3. *Ibid.*

4. *Ibid.*

5. *Ibid.*, p. 3.

6. *Ibid.*, p. 16.

7. Recent books that make some attempt to sketch the institutions of participating democracy include Benjamin Barber, *Strong Democracy: Participatory Politics for a New Age* (Berkeley: University of California Press, 1984); John Burnheim, *Is Democracy Possible? The Alternative to Electoral Politics* (Berkeley: University of California Press, 1985); and Philip Green, *Retrieving Democracy: In Search of Civic Equality* (Totowa, N.J.: Rowman & Allanheld, 1985). Burnheim puts the greatest emphasis on radical decentralization; Green best exemplifies the common tendency to assume that solutions will eventually be found for problems that now seem intractable. C. B. Macpherson, *The Life and Times of Liberal Democracy* (Oxford: Oxford University Press, 1977) illustrates the tendency to find merit in the Soviet model. For earlier discussions, see Daniel C. Kramer, *Participatory Democracy: Ideals of the Political Left* (Cambridge: Schenkman, 1972) and C. George Benello and Dimitrios Roussopoulos, eds., *The Case for Participatory Democracy* (New York: Grossman, 1971).

8. Robert A. Dahl, *Democracy in the United States*, 4th ed. (Boston: Houghton Mifflin, 1981), pp. 426ff.

9. Robert A. Dahl and Charles E. Lindblom, *Politics, Economics, and Welfare* (New York: Harper & Brothers, 1953), p. 41. Italicized in the original.

10. *Ibid.*, p. 42.

11. *Ibid.*, p. 256.

12. Robert A. Dahl, *A Preface to Economic Democracy* (Berkeley: University of California Press, 1982), p. 152.

13. Robert A. Dahl, *After the Revolution?* (New Haven: Yale University Press, 1970), p. 68. See also Robert A. Dahl and Edward R. Tufte, *Size and Democracy* (Stanford: Stanford University Press, 1973) and Robert A. Dahl, *Dilemmas of Pluralist Democracy* (New Haven: Yale University Press, 1982).

14. *After the Revolution?*, pp. 86-87; cf. p. 81.

15. *Ibid.*, p. 146.

16. *Ibid.*, pp. 140, 141. "For those who believe that the essential value of democracy is in the opportunities it offers individual citizens to participate in and exercise control over public life, the attempt to apply democratic processes on a scale as large as the nation-state is bound to produce a sorry substitute for the real thing." *Dilemmas of Pluralist Democracy*, p. 13.

17. *After the Revolution?*, pp. 115, 116.

18. *Ibid.*, p. 126.

19. *Ibid.*, p. 140.

20. *Ibid.*, pp. 106, 112, 114. Cf. *A Preface to Economic Democracy*, especially pp. 139 and 160.

21. *After the Revolution?*, p. 104.

22. *Ibid.*, p. 149-50. Ellipsis in the original.

23. *Ibid.*, p. 150.

24. *Ibid.*, pp. 164-65.

25. *Ibid.*, p. 93.

26. *Ibid.*, p. 90.

27. *Ibid.*, p. 89.

28. *Ibid.*, p. 97.

29. *Controlling Nuclear Weapons*, p. 19.

30. *Ibid.*, p. 24.   Cf. Robert A. Dahl, "Procedural Democracy," in *Philosophy, Politics and Society*, Fifth Series, ed. Peter Laslett and James Fishkin (Oxford: Basil Blackwell, 1979), pp. 97-133, and *Democracy in the United States*, pp. 414-16.

31. *Controlling Nuclear Weapons*, p. 25.

32. *Ibid.*, p. 27.

33. *Ibid.*, pp. 29-30.

34. *Ibid.*, p. 34.

35. *Ibid.*, p. 42.

36. *Ibid.*, p. 44.

37. *Ibid.*, pp. 30-31, 49.

38. *Ibid.*, p. 50.

39. *Ibid.*, p. 80.

40. *Ibid.*, p. 79.

41. *Ibid.*, pp. 70, 78.

42. *Ibid.*, p. 88.

43. *Ibid.*

44. *Ibid.*, p. 89.

45. *After the Revolution?*, p. 37; cf. *Controlling Nuclear Weapons*, pp. 6-7.

46. *Controlling Nuclear Weapons*, p. 62.

47. The following books and articles by Dahl are particularly relevant: "The Science of Politics: New and Old," *World Politics*, 7 (1955), 479-89; *A Preface to Democratic Theory* (Chicago: University of Chicago Press, 1956); "Political Theory: Truth and Consequences," *World Politics*, 11 (1958), 89-102; "The Behavioral Approach in Political Science: Epitaph for a Monument to a Successful Protest," *American Political Science Review*, 55 (1961), 763-72; "The Evaluation of Political Systems," in *Contemporary Political Science: Toward Empirical Theory*, ed. Ithiel de Sola Pool (New York: McGraw Hill, 1967), and *Modern Political Analysis*, 4th ed. (Englewood Cliffs, N.J.: Prentice-Hall, 1984). Three sentences can do only rough justice to the above contributions. Compared to the related writings of many of his contemporaries, Dahl's are distinguished by balance, circumspection, and moderation. Nonetheless, it is clearly a very "modern" political science Dahl teaches.

PART III

PONDERING OUR DESTINY

POLITICS AND PROGRESS IN HEIDEGGER'S
PHILOSOPHY OF HISTORY

W.R. Newell

The question of the significance of Martin Heidegger's thought for political philosophy has always been a vexed one. This is due in part to a problem of terminology. Heidegger does not claim to possess a "political philosophy" as such because, as a historical thinker, he does not accept the concept of a permanent human nature within the larger order of nature. He believes that authentic freedom and fulfillment will be achieved, if at all, only through some future deliverance. But this is no less true of Hegel, Nietzsche and Marx, who for similar reasons do not embrace the traditional meaning of political philosophy in the sense in which it is understood by Aristotle or Hobbes: the study of human nature in relation to nature. And yet we do not ordinarily hesitate to speak of their significance for political philosophy broadly considered, that is to say, their views of the modern state, alienation and the prospects for greater freedom and community. Heidegger's writings are also concerned with these themes.

The most serious obstacle to assessing the significance of Heidegger's thought for political philosophy is his involvement with the National Socialist regime in Germany during 1933. Feelings run high over this episode, and even the best intentioned efforts at balance and impartiality frequently shade into polemics or apologetics.[1] I have nothing to say about Heidegger's activities in 1933 as a biographical matter. They continue to receive close attention from historians of the period. But I want to suggest that the intense controversy over the character of Heidegger's actions and self-understanding in 1933 has frequently caused the question of his larger significance for the course of contemporary political and social thought to be misposed. Often, those who are most eager to pillory Heidegger and those most eager to fence off his philosophy from any taint of Nazism are oddly agreed in treating 1933 as being virtually exhaustive of the significance of Heidegger's thought for political philosophy altogether. Given this premise, one is forced to choose between a Heidegger who made over his philosophy heart and soul to Nazi doctrine and who afterward, retreating into contemplative passivity, had nothing of significance to say about the social and moral crises of our century, and a Heidegger who, before and after a brief personal lapse into the muck of politics, is equally seen as being at a lofty remove from such worldly matters.

Quite apart from Heidegger's lively interest in contemporary politics, literature and art which we know of from his biographers, and even apart from his manifest interest in and influence on contemporary existentialism, critical theory and Marxism, this way of posing the question of Heidegger's significance for political philosophy is a misleading characterization of his philosophy as a whole. Just as Heidegger would never grant that his philosophy could be seen as reflecting mere "politics" in the sense of some class interest, party platform or ideology, he would likewise never grant that philosophy can remain at a contemplative remove from the social, moral and cultural upheavals of our age. Accordingly, I want to suggest that Heidegger's interest in National Socialism - an interest which, as I will indicate, had little to do with the actual content of Nazi doctrine - was symptomatic of a concern with the destiny of Europe and mankind which is consistent throughout his works. Moreover, Heidegger's subsequent reflection on 1933 and on the whole German experience with National Socialism deeply influenced his later diagnosis of the technological essence of modernity and, in particular, his lengthy engagement with the works of Nietzsche.[2]

What I am arguing, then, is that we should not assume that Heidegger's Party membership and rectorship (succeeded within a few years by official disfavor and ostracism) are sufficient for understanding the political bearing of Heidegger's philosophy and then attempt to see whether or not his works of that period or other periods show traces of that one overt public commitment. Instead, I believe that Heidegger's significance for political philosophy is most fruitfully explored if we see him as a successor to such comprehensive philosophical and social thinkers of the nineteenth century as Hegel, Marx and Nietzsche. If I am correct, Heidegger's brief enthusiasm for the "German Revolution," as well as his subsequent disillusionment with and reflection on that period, are best seen as emerging from his inheritance of German Idealism's long-standing concern with authentic human freedom and community. This in no way mitigates the error of his judgment in 1933, but it allows us to see it as one instance of a life-long, developing critique of modernity with roots in an older and more enduring intellectual context than that of the 1930s. Like Hegel, Marx and Nietzsche, Heidegger resists splitting off metaphysical, epistemological and aesthetic issues from the broader prospects for human freedom and ennoblement through collective historical release. Like them, he believes the alienation of the present era may yield the as yet barely glimpsed deliverance of mankind on a global scale in the future. But unlike them, Heidegger does not believe that the understanding of history as a cumulative progress toward greater human mastery of natural and social conditions is tenable or liveable in light of the cataclysms of the twentieth century. Moreover, he believes that this conception of progressive mastery has in some measure contributed to those cataclysms. In time, he came to see National Socialism as one mode of the global imperative of technological mastery.

In this essay, I will try to show the fruitfulness of approaching Heidegger's political thought through its relationship to German Idealism by focussing on this issue of progress in history. Specifically, I mean the idea, inherited from Hegel and Marx, of history as a "mediated" dialectic, progressing through changing empirical circumstances toward a   universal outcome in which all previous antagonisms are overcome. Heidegger's critique of this "world-historical" conception of progress helped significantly to demolish the notion of an all-encompassing "science" of history,[3] and tracing the critique allows us to see both Heidegger's profound debt to the tradition of German Idealism and the profound exception which his philosophy takes to it. It is in Heidegger's rejection of this idea of progress as a legitimizing doctrine for what he took to be the spiritual wasteland being spread inexorably over the globe by the forces of technology, that one can see most clearly his contribution to contemporary radical thought.

In pursuing my theme, I will comment selectively on four representative works.[4] *Being and Time* provides Heidegger's initial critique of the idea of progress. *An Introduction to Metaphysics* develops this critique along with a phenomenologically more rounded evocation of the destinies of "peoples," fraught with the dark background of 1935 and the actual unfolding of the German "revolution." The postwar *Letter on Humanism* and *The Question Concerning Technology* are noteworthy for their de-emphasis of the sometimes belligerent "resolve" of the earlier works in favor of a more tolerant stance of "letting-be." And yet this withdrawal from any overt commitment to action on the level of a "people" is accompanied by a deepening of Heidegger's analysis of the sources of contemporary alienation as originally expressed in *Being and Time*, culminating in what may be called an "unmediated" conception of historical progress. As we see, while rejecting the understanding of history as a teleological development, Heidegger believes that the very absence of any such immanent development of freedom in history to date yields the prospect of a grand reversal that will bring future generations "near to Being."

Fundamental Ontology and the World-Historical Idea of Progress

The language of *Being and Time* is notoriously recondite. Yet we must begin with it if we are to see how Heidegger's view of historical progress remains rooted in his earliest philosophy even as it expands and develops its categories. Central to the "fundamental ontology" of *Being and Time* is Heidegger's characterization of man as the "being" (*seiend*) for whom "Being [*Sein*] is an issue."[5] In other words, man is the being who wonders about the source of all beings. "Care" (*Sorge*) burdens man with an insight into the finitude of all beings (pre-eminently his own), an "anxiety" (*Angst*) which is thrust upon him by the mutability and impermanence of Being itself.[6] For, as the generative origin of all beings, the source from which they emerge and into which they pass away, Being "is" nothing or nihilation.

Man's resoluteness (*Entschlossenheit*) in facing the finitude which surges through all things establishes his "freedom-towards-death" or "finite freedom."[7] Because he can face the necessity of his world passing away, he can grasp the possibility of this world being generated anew. As a participant in the "destiny" which shapes each "people" from its historical origins, man can rechoose that destiny for his own "time" and "generation."[8] Resolve will free him from the "inauthentic" state of affairs prevailing in "everyday" life - the delusion that the world will always exist just as it is now.[9] A people under the sway of everyday life have forgotten their active participation in the genesis of the world, and their continuing responsibility for its destiny. Instead, the world has been reified as an objective realm standing over against them as subjects.[10] They can conform to this world passively or exert their control over it. Both responses, though superficially different, presuppose the cleavage of the world into subject and object, and therewith the "alienation" of man from Being.[11]

The spurious permanence of the world is fortified by the "they-self," the public authority which orders our lives as fearful conformists or efficient managers of the surrounding environment. Resolving upon its finitude enables a people to shatter this "dictatorship" reared out of their own alienated "potentiality-for-Being."[12] They give themselves to Being by "coming back" to their particular historical destiny, which enables them to strike out into the future rooted in a past so "primordial" as to bear little if any resemblance to the inauthentic present. As the people projects its future - a future whose goals cannot be "known explicitly" in advance, since the present cannot be relied upon to provide any guidance for it - only then in fact will its past reveal itself retrospectively in its essence (*Wesen*). The authentic ways of the people's "heritage" will re-emerge, having been "tranquilized" and "dimmed down" by an official history of the past designed by the they-self to repress any heterodox alternatives.[13]

One commentator has seen in this evocation of the people's recovery of its destiny through freedom-towards-death "the language of 1933" already anticipated in 1927.[14] Others have been struck by the way in which these terms combine a kind of revolutionary dynamism with an extreme abstract formalism. For Löwith, the "revolutionary radicalism" of fundamental ontology in political terms stems from the active yet utterly contentless unity of Being and existence striven for by the people's resolve upon its destiny.[15] Adorno writes of the "unmediated" character of fundamental ontology - Heidegger's refusal to let it be defined in any way by the observable socio-economic conditions of everyday life.[16] David C. Hoy and Werner Marx note the inability of fundamental ontology, in comparison with Hegel's dialectic, to supply empirical and ethical standards for achieving specific, limited reform.[17]

In order to understand the "unmediated" character of Heidegger's conception of historical change, we must look more closely at "everyday" life, the way in which he believes we experience life "first of all and most of the time."[18] Within the everyday world, the stable aspect of beings as they emerge - the "present-at-hand" - is elevated into their sole and absolute reality. In other words, Being, the generative organ of all things present-at-hand, is reified as a higher present or being which causes the visible beings according to the principles of logic, mathematics and the empirical sciences.[19] The search for Being in the "reflected" image of "the looks of the world" is, Heidegger asserts, the flaw in all traditional metaphysics from Plato to Hegel.[20] Although Hegel understood that Being was historical (rather than, as for Plato, eternal), he nevertheless conceived of it as an Absolute Subject which progressively overcomes its contradictions, completing itself at the end of history as a world ruled by reason.[21]

There is a crucial difference between Hegel and Heidegger on the relationship between the historical process and the present-at-hand, first broached in *Being and Time* and developed in subsequent works. For both, the present-at-hand (what Hegel calls the real or actual) is negated by Being (the generative process of history). But for Hegel, the nothingness to which Being reduces its instantiations is a "determinate nothingness."[22] That is, Being is developed and enriched by the very beings it supersedes. What is overcome leaves a residue which is taken up into the next stage of overcoming. This principle may fairly be called the core of Hegel's dialectic. Applied to the events of history, it explains his argument, for example, that the Master/Slave relationship, after its pagan morality has been superseded by Christianity, continues to mediate the new morality as the "unhappy consciousness" of the believer who cannot bridge the distance between his spiritual master, God, and his bondage to the world of the flesh.[23] To take another example: When Protestantism supersedes Catholicism, the salvation previously banished to heaven is brought down to earth as the faith within the individual believer. But the previous, literal otherwordliness is preserved in a mediated form, inasmuch as the internalized salvation of the Protestant is still unable to transform the external world (a development which must await the French revolution). The principle of "determinate nothingness" thus enables Hegel to interpret history as a cumulative progress through an ever richer resolution of contradictions. When the outward transformation of the world has run its course in tandem with the inner reconciliation of man with himself and with his fellow human beings, Spirit will be absolutely manifest. Although Marx rejected what he regarded as Hegel's idealism for mediating the world's actual conflicts out of existence into an imaginary, wholly inner reconciliation, he preserved the dialectical method in his examination of how the starkly opposed "positive" antagonisms of the modern world had emerged from the cumulative conflict between labor and capital.24

The contrast with Heidegger in this regard could hardly be more striking or instructive. For Heidegger, we may say, the negation of the present-at-hand by Being develops neither one nor the other. The "notness" (*Nichtigkeit*) underlying beings cannot be conceived of in a determinate way, that is, as the absence of a being.25 The negation is, so to speak, absolute rather than determinate, leaving no "mediated" residue. Hence Being is not, as it is for Hegel, embodied in the "concrete ethical existence" of the state, a synthesis of legal, religious and aesthetic mores, providing an empirical benchmark for further advancements.26   Nor does the everyday world reveal, as it does for Marx, the current level of development of the antagonism between labor and capital, furnishing empirical evidence for an emerging final conflict between the bourgeoisie and the "universal" class. Heidegger believes that to conceive of nothingness as "determinate" serves merely to reify the historical process itself, lifting it out of its generative origins and objectifying it as a record of man's outward, rational transformation of the environment. For Heidegger, this record can only be a catalogue of the varieties of inauthenticity into which peoples "fall" from their primordial encounters with Being. Those who look to such a "world-historical" record for a solution to human alienation are, instead of reorienting themselves more closely to Being, "floating" further away from it as they rummage among "exotic and alien cultures."27 For Heidegger, rather than a dialectic of historical progress, there is a titanic opposition between the awesome negative "power" of Being - resurging as the people's destiny - and the "rootless" inauthenticity of everyday life. The "power" of destiny is in no way mediated - that is, mitigated or qualified - by existing socio-economic and cultural conditions. Instead, freedom-toward-death "revokes" those conditions and sweeps them away.28

Germany, the West and the Decline of Spirit

Whatever Heidegger's private thoughts may have been in 1927, *Being and Time* cannot strictly be said to anticipate "the language of 1933." *Being and Time* contains only scant references to Germany or to the politics and society of any people, although the "dictatorship of the they" is clearly meant to evoke the conformism and egoism of bourgeois modernity in general. The aim of fundamental ontology is to generalize the ways in which worlds come into being at any given time and place (notwithstanding the fact that the content of each such destiny would be unique). Heidegger later came to regret the "transcendental" quality of fundamental ontology for obscuring the thoroughgoing historicity of its principles.29 The importance of *An Intro-duction to Metaphysics* (originating in a lecture series given in 1935) is that it sets the formal categories of *Being and Time* into the context of what Heidegger took to be the destiny of a particular people - Germany - in his own era. This destiny is, for him, pre-eminent in "the West" as a whole inasmuch as it involves the heritage of Europe stretching back to the ancient Greeks.30 With this work Heidegger's view of historical progress and its implications for twentieth-century politics emerge in a rounder and more concrete way.

Heidegger's initial aim in this work is to demonstrate that "metaphysics" cannot deal with the question, "Why are there beings rather than nothing?" As in *Being and Time*, the problem with traditional metaphysical thinking is that, because it takes objectivity to be "self-evident," it cannot deal with nothingness or Being.31 Metaphysics tries to go "beyond beings" *by way of* beings. Thus, it can conceive of their source only as "another and higher kind of thing" - a supersensible form or ideal.32 According to Heidegger, when we try to interpret experience from a metaphysical viewpoint - for instance, a storm over the mountains - the heart of the experience and our relation with it must always elude us. Having catalogued its objective geo-graphical and meteorological attributes, we pronounce this underlying experiential unity to be an unintelligible "vapor," like Kant's unknowable thing-in-itself or Locke's x-I-know-not-what. This vapor is none other than the "destiny" of Being altogether, damned up by metaphysical thinking in its thralldom to being.33

For Heidegger, the surest historical precedent for understanding an authentic relation to Being is Greece in the age of the great pre-Platonic poets, thinkers and statesmen. In the original Greek experience of *physis* or nature, the relation between man and Being is a reciprocal one. Being, as the literal meaning of *physis* suggests, "grows" out of nothing to reveal itself.34 Statesmen, poets and thinkers make a stand against this "overpowering" force. Through the "creative violence" of their own "power" and "struggle," they enable Being to "presence" as poetry, thought and *polis* or city.35

For Heidegger, therefore, man's relation to Being is not a question of a human subject exerting its will against an objective environment. It is rather a reciprocal interaction by which man assumes the passive role of "letting-be" *(Seinlassen)* - acting as a conduit for Being's revelation - precisely through assuming the active role of "resolve" against the "care" which Being's protean power to generate all things imposes on him.36 Heidegger now plays on the word "resoluteness" to let it suggest "unclosedness" (*Entschlossenheit*).[37] He thereby doubly stresses that resolve is not a kind of subjective willfulness, but rather a simultaneous passive openness to Being and opposition to it - modes by which Being "has" man to accomplish its own "presencing."[38] In founding the *polis*, a stateman "administers" the power of Being by interpreting it for his people as their *nomos* - their laws and mores.[39] The "greatness" of the founding - its spontaneity and vitality - occurs only at the "beginning," when it is closest to Being.[40] Later, laws and mores degenerate into listless routines. At this point, Heidegger says, when they become "ethical" in the sense of being taken to possess a timeless validity, "Being has gone out of them."[41]

For Heidegger, the rise of empiricism and positivism since the seventeenth century is coeval with the steady reduction of Being to metaphysics which began with Plato.[42] The history of the West, not only philosophically but also politically and socially, is the working out of this alienation from Being. The Germans, as the only people beside the Greeks through whom philosophy has "spoken," are today, accordingly, the locus both for the consciousness of the most acute alienation from Being and for harboring the greatest possibility for reopening an authentic relation to Being.[43] The "greatness" of German Idealism, Heidegger suggests, resulted in its partial recognition of, and struggle against, the accelerating process of decline.[44] Seeming to evoke Hegel, he uses the term Spirit (*Geist*) to describe the confrontation of man and Being embodied in the dynamic unity of an historical epoch like that of the Greeks. Indeed, Heidegger's presentation of the reciprocal interaction between man and Being closely resembles the reciprocity of self-consciousness and Spirit found in Hegel, where man, by pursing his own freedom, also accomplishes Spirit's self-actualization. The crucial difference, however, is that for Heidegger, the "greatness" of this interaction lies in its creative origins, not in its subsequent working out. Hegel's error, in Heidegger's view, was to assimilate Spirit into the rationality of a completed historical "system."[45]

As a consequence, he argues that today Spirit has alienated itself from its creative origins and been reduced to the "intelligent" manipulation of beings. The identification of Spirit with intelligence presupposes the reification of the world into what is empirically real and the "vapor" of what is merely logical, ideal or a value. In restricting itself to managing the tasks of, for instance, economic productivity of government bureaucracies, Spirit confesses its contemporary impotence to change the world fundamentally. It allies itself with positivism to organize all experiences, flattening them so that they can be shared by the average man of all countries. In the modern world, thus given over to mediocrity, prize fighters are considered heroes and a symphony concert in Tokyo can be experienced simultaneously with an assassination. Marxism "in its extreme form" is devoted to "the exploitation of the means of production." Philosophy and art become of merely relative worth. Conceding their impotence to shape the lives of peoples, they retreat from the real world into a realm of values pursued "for their own sake."[46]

In *Being and Time*, Heidegger had criticized the idea of world-historical progress as the reification of authentic historical existence into a catalogue of varieties of "inauthentic everydayness" stitched together in a spurious reconciliation. In *An Introduction to Metaphysics*, he develops this critique as he assesses the specific historical situation of Germany. The mention of Spirit and of Marxism as allies of positivism suggests that, for Heidegger, German historical philosophy as a whole has degenerated into a set of methods for pursuing what are, at bottom, the same goals as bourgeois liberalism. The "everyday world" and "dictatorship of the they" are now located predominantly in America and Russia, which take themselves to be the spearhead of historical advancement, but which Heidegger believes have raised the organizing powers of inauthenticity to an unprecedented height. "Metaphyiscally the same" despite their superficially different ideologies, America and Russia oppress Germany not only figuratively but literally, from either side, like "pincers." The "inner truth and greatness" of National Socialism thus emerges from "the encounter between global technology and modern man" - the possibility that, having experienced alienation from Being to its depths and being threatened with destruction by the two super-powers, Germany has no alternative but to recover its destiny and "move" the West out of these pincers.[47]

In *Being and Time*, the finitude from which a people seeks to hide in everyday life finally compels it, through anxiety, to resolve upon the recovery of its destiny. In 1935, Heidegger believed that Germany faced the peril of its literal as well as spiritual finitude or destruction - a peril which, if properly heeded, could expose the groundlessness of bourgeois modernity for itself and the West as a whole. The history of the West, however, begins to assume a prominence which it lacked in *Being and Time* as providing the "determinate" content of man's alienation from Being.[48] In order to recover its destiny, Germany - or at least its thinkers - must rethink this "determinate" history in order to understand exactly how the "fall" from Being came about. Only in this way will Germany's contemporary struggle be able to redeem the West all the way back to its roots in classical antiquity. This history has, indeed, a kind of dialectic - but not in the Hegelian sense discussed earlier of freedom progressing in gradual, "mediated" stages out of its interplay with alienation. On the contrary, the provenance of this history will remain "hidden," according to Heidegger, as long as it is viewed in such a benignly teleological light.[49] It must be seen instead as a dialectic *only* of alienation - as a steady, regressive development *away* from freedom. And yet, the very persistence and strength of this alienation seem to have been necessary, in Heidegger's view, to compel "modern man" to face his period with a clear-sightedness unknown in the West since the "violent ones" who founded the Greek *polis*.50 This negative dialectic, in which man must undergo the extremity of alienation from Being, in the 1930s passes from view.

Technology as the Destiny of the West

Heidegger wrote the *Letter on Humanism* in 1947 in order to clarify the differences between his philosophy and French existentialism, which had drawn heavily on *Being and Time*.51 According to Heidegger, the reduction of Being to beings has meant that throughout the history of philosophy man's reality has characteristically been conceived of as that of a biological "animal." One must then try to explain man's distinctively human qualities by piling a soul, mind or free will upon this empirical being. Existentialism's contribution to this metaphysical catalogue is to affirm the radical freedom of the human subject in the face of empirical contingency. It is thus, in Heidegger's view, part and parcel of "the destiny of Western history and of all history determined by Europe" against which it purports to rebel.52 The existentially free man is in truth the "tyrant of Being" who reacts to his imprisonment within empirical reality by striving to manipulate and exploit it.53

Heidegger also takes this opportunity to provide a retrospective view of German politics. As we shall see, the "encounter between global technology and modern man" is, in his view, at the heart of the crisis of the West every bit as much as it was in 1935. Now, however, he makes a pointed distinction between what he terms "nationalism" and the longing for a "homeland [*Heimat*]...near to Being."54 "Nationalism," as Heidegger uses the word, is a collective subjectivism bent on the "lordly" domination of external reality, thus completing "subjectivity's unconditional self-assertion."55 As such, nationalism is what we might term the reification of the longing for a homeland, or of what was earlier called a "people." "Internationalism" is no better an alternative, since it is a mere yoking together of collective national subjects.

Citing the poet Hölderlin (a contemporary of Hegel), Heidegger now offers a considerably modified view of the German destiny from the one expressed in 1935. The message of Hölderlin's poetry, he argues, is not for Germans to transform the world (as Heidegger himself seemed to expect in 1935), but to return to their "fateful belongingness" to the West. In linking Germany's destiny to that of the West as a whole, Heidegger is consistent with his earlier view. But the belligerent lexicon of "resolve," "violence" and "struggle" now fades from view in favor of a more purely passive openness to Being by "letting-be" one's own people and other peoples.56 At the same time, however, this suggestion of a kind of irreducible pluralism of autonomous peoples is not to be confused with the assumption of universal values. Hölderlin's evocation of the homeland in its uniqueness is favorably contrasted with the "mere cosmopolitanism" of Goethe. This recalls Heidegger's criticism in *Being and Time* of searching among "exotic and alien cultures" for evidence of a universal humanity.57   On the whole, though, the criticism of nationalistic "self-assertion" predominates. We should note here that even in *An Introduction to Metaphysics* there were a few critical allusions to a predilection in Germany for mass political rallies and the heedless pursuit of scientific prowess.58   If we put them together with the forthright critique of nationalism given in 1947, perhaps we can surmise that Heidegger wished to distinguish between the flawed, merely nationalistic (or "everyday") actual outcome of national Socialism and its "inner truth and greatness" - the promise it originally embodied for establishing a "homeland."59

The heightened emphasis on "letting-be" one's own homeland and other homelands - on the passive mode of a people's relation to Being as opposed to the active mode of resolve - is accompanied by a markedly more ambivalent view of America and Russia, the two "pincers" of 1935. Now, as before, "Americanism" and "communism" are presented as the major spearheads of global technology's advance. But whereas they were earlier depicted as enemies of a prospective German "struggle" to redeem the history of the West, now, in the absence of any such prospect, they are given more weight in exposing the "determinate" content of the contemporary historical situation. They are not, we are admonished, to be seen as mere "world-views" erected to defend some arbitrary and superficial value preference. Rather, they contain an "elemental experience" of the destiny of the West which is now working itself out as technology.60 In *An Introduction to Metaphysics*, the rather contemptuous descriptions of America and Russia as promoters of "dreary" mediocrity contrasted with the incipient authenticity of the German mission (though the German people too, of course, would be poisoned by the same inauthentic trends until and if it hearkened to its destiny). With the collapse of the German mission in both its original "inner" promise and its vitiated outcome, Heidegger seems to concede that the course of Western history has ceased to provide an either/or choice between an authentic political community and the triumph of global technology. Instead, the course of Western history has settled more firmly than ever into the development of the technological superpowers. Whatever intimations of an authentic relation to Being are now possible, therefore, will have to be experienced *within* the horizon of a politically already-dominant world system. Accordingly, Marxism, earlier dismissed as an ideology for economic exploitation, is now commended for harboring a "superior" account of modern alienation. This is presumably because, although it conceives of man in the "metaphysical" mode of a subject which objectifies its labor, it also expresses the full historical development and agony of this separation of man from his creative powers. As such, it is, in Heidegger's view, altogether preferable to the ahistorical subjectivism of the existentialists.[61]

The *Letter on Humanism* reveals the evolution of Heidegger's critique of the idea of historical progress in light of the way in which he sees the encounter between man and technology unfolding in the postwar world. Specifically, it signals Heidegger's abandonment of any possibility of overt opposition by a people to the unfolding process of global technology and his de-emphasis of the active, aggressive mode of man's relation to Being in favor of the passive, open one. The two developments are plainly linked, since Germany's defeat was the defeat of what Heidegger had taken in 1935 to be the most promising contemporary manifestation of resolve. Already in *An Introduction to Metaphysics*, we saw the beginning of the emphasis on "letting-be," inasmuch as the transcendental resolve of *Being and Time* had given way to the "unclosedness" of man to Being as revealed in the historical epoch of a people. However, whereas *An Introduction to Metaphysics* had allowed a place along with poetry and thinking for the specifically political role of statesmanship, in the *Letter on Humanism*, only the poet and thinker remain of the original trio.[62] Heidegger now seems to believe that an authentic relation to Being occurs when man is the "shepherd" of revelations carefully husbanded by art and thought.[63] The world may yet be transformed, he intimates, but in an apparently more quietistic way than the "creative violence" of the founders of the *polis* commended in 1935. Poetry and thinking may enable Being to "upsurge" into the beings from which it has drained away, sustaining them once again as a "hale" or "healing" wholeness (*des Heilens*).[64]

The *Letter on Humanism* develops the identification which Heidegger began in *An Introduction to Metaphysics* between global technology, as the working out of Western history, and the "inauthentic everydayness" of *Being and Time*. Hence, bourgeois modernity is depicted, just as in 1927 and 1935, as a "dictatorship" defending "the habitual somnolence of prevailing opinion."[65] Heidegger is as much as ever against the evasion of this dictatorship by retreating into private diversions. Moreover, it is even more the case than in previous works that the contemporary era has, for Heidegger, a privileged place in the history of Being. By nearly obliterating Being, Heidegger argues, technology has revealed more starkly than ever before the absence of Being from beings. Because Being is absent from the modern world, it is nearer and more manifest than ever before as something overwhelmingly lacked. Furthermore, we have been freed from the comforting delusion that the history of our alienation has been, as Hegel believed, a benevolent, teleological process.[66] Thus, precisely because of technology, Being "has made itself known in the present epoch of world history" after lying "hidden so long in oblivion." Hence, although Heidegger no longer speaks of salvation in any recognizably political sense, he believes that "in the future" man may yet emerge into an authentic relation with Being.67

Before discussing that future more fully, there is a final point to note about the *Letter on Humanism*. Heidegger is more sympathetic here than in earlier works to the contemporary yearning for an ethics to "safeguard bonds" in a world where, he believes, virtually all human relationships are coming to serve the imperative of technology.68 He still maintains, however, that no binding ethical standards can be derived from Being. The "healing upsurge" of Being into beings has, it transpires, a destructive counterpart after all - the "malice of rage."69 The interplay of the healing and the malice of rage can be viewed as Heidegger's attempt to ground the phenomena of what are taken, in conventional moral discourse, to be good and evil in the "upsurge" of Being.70 If so, this does not correspond to a distinction between good and evil as between better and worse, more and less free, real or satisfying ways of life. It is impossible, in Heidegger's view, to pass ethical judgments on the destructive dimension of historical change. Being must, as the genesis of history, contain both the malice of rage *and* healing; it must annihilate in order to create.

Technology and the Future of Being

We may complete our analysis by turning to *The Question Concerning Technology*, where Heidegger further develops his view of technology as the "determinate" outcome of the history of man's "fall" from Being. Technology, he argues, is one of the primordial ways - along with art and thinking - through which Being "presences" or reveals itself. Like the poets, statesmen and thinkers described in 1935, the craftsman does not so much produce things *ex nihilo* as he "lets be." The rules by which he fashions his product are modes by which Being achieves presencing through him.71 Modern technology, by contrast, although rooted in the original Greek experience of *physis*, has forgotten its openness to Being in pursuit of one (now historically predominant) way of producing.72 For the very capacity of man to turn against Being in order to let it reveal itself has also enabled him to "block" Being from any further revelations.

Where remnants of the old technology still exist today, Heidegger says, they "take care of" nature as they use it. The windmill, for example, uses the wind but does not "lock it up." Modern technology, on the other hand, drains nature of its heterogeneous powers and organizes them as a "standing reserve" of abstract, undifferentiated energy. Thus, while the old wooden bridge preserves the Rhine by framing it and linking it to its users, the modern power station converts the Rhine into a source of hydroelectricity. Its living presence is siphoned off into an ensemble of techniques in no way dependent on the dense textures of local experience. The river itself is now a dead object "on call for inspection by a tour group ordered there by the vacation industry."73

In evoking the sway of technology over all aspects of modern life, Heidegger uses terms he employed in *Being and Time* to describe man's ensnarement by inauthentic "everyday" existence: We are "fallen" into and "surrendered" to technology.74 Our varying attempts to advance, cope with or evade technology, he claims, only testify to the grip of its power over us. As long as technology is viewed from an "anthropological" perspective - that is, as an objective process standing over against human subjects - we are condemned to veer between the equally fruitless alternatives of trying to convert technology to "human" purposes or regarding it as simply out of control. To the extent that technology "challenges" man to exploit nature, he himself is organized as a part of the standing reserve. People become "human resources," a "supply of patients," and so forth. But because it is man who, as the conduit for Being's presencing as technology, "orders" the natural environment and "drives" its exploitation, he is never wholly reduced to the standing reserve but experiences technology "more primordially" than other beings. The point, therefore, is neither to devise a humanistic code of ethics for the proper use of technology, nor to abandon all hope of resisting it. Rather, we must recognize technology as one pole of a reciprocal relationship between man and the particular "presencing" of Being that has predominated since Plato.75 It is "too late" in Western history to choose either to have technology or to abandon it - rather, it "has" us. Our choice is neither to resist nor to submit, but, in a sense, to submit freely - to "prepare a free relation" to technology.76 As in *Being and Time*, therefore, Heidegger is arguing that we can only "choose to make this choice" - choose to choose technology. By raising our relationship with technology to full historical consciousness, we become aware retrospectively that it is indeed the "destiny" of the West - just as, in *Being and Time*, the people's rechoosing of its destiny established retrospectively the content of its heritage.77

If the origin of modern technology can be thought through, Heidegger suggests, its capacity to "block" man's relation to Being may be dissolved, opening up the possibility that man "might be admitted more and sooner and ever more primarily to Being." As in the *Letter on Humanism*, the over-bearing quality of Being's presencing as technology, closing off new relations to Being, itself sparks the return to Being. In this way, Heidegger fills with the "determinate" history of the West the transcendental relation expressed in *Being and Time*, whereby the anxiety imposed on man by his everyday existence provided a liberating insight into its impermanence and, thus, into the possibility of its regeneration.78 There is, however, no mention of "peoples" or "homelands" in *The Question Concerning Technology*. This may suggest that, just as capitalism had, for Marx, made the unity of mankind a realistic prospect for the first time in history through the scope and intensity of its oppression, "global technology" has had the same effect in Heidegger's eyes. It is likely, however, that - as the *Letter on Humanism* suggests - Heidegger envisions the future free relation to Being as one which will be taken up by autonomous peoples once mankind as a whole has been delivered from its global oppressor. In other words, the universal oppressor does not give way (as in Marx) to the universal class, but to an efflorescence of authentic "homelands."

However this may be, the crisis said to face modern man in Heidegger's postwar works has become ever more international in scope as the role of a specific salvational people has receded. It is worthwhile to summarize this development before making some more general observations.

Conclusion

Being and Time, we recall, elaborated the conditions of a people's historicity at any given time and place in principle. In *An Introduction to Metaphysics*, the "coming back" to destiny appears as a specifically German mission, one that will redeem the West's flawed relation to Being stretching back to the Greeks. In the later works we have analyzed, Germany's mission fades from view along with any mention of the "rulers" whom Heidegger had previously granted a privileged place along with thinkers and poets in opening the relation to Being. But Heidegger now raises the possibility that the "saving power" of Being may yet be released from within the juggernaut of global technology, ushering in a relation to Being which is freer than ever before. Today man is said to face the "danger" of finding his way between alternatives of the absolute of technology and a future in which he may become "more experienced" with Being; a future in which he will assume, permanently and undistractedly, the "guardian's" and "shepherd's" passive role of tending "all that is present on this earth."[79] In this we can detect a final pale residue of the choice which Germany was said to face in 1935 between the West's resurgence and the triumph of "global technology," now drained of any recognizably political outcome because it is no longer identified with the destiny of any one people.

Heidegger's persistent emphasis on man's "thrownness" into a world not of his conscious choosing is meant to repudiate the Hegelian notion of the unity of subject and object - a unity "already actual" or immanent in the modern epoch, awaiting only the Hegelian "science" to raise it to consciousness.[80] As we have seen, however, for Heidegger man achieves a kind of *immediate* unity with history - a self-abandonment to Being as the force of sheer nihilation which sweeps away all mediating conditions. It follows from this, as we observed, that neither the state (as for Hegel) nor a class (as for Marx) offers an empirically demonstrable embodiment of progress toward freedom. In Heidegger's hope for a future liberation from the sway of technology there is, however, a conceptual resemblance to Marxism. Gadamer has described this either/or choice between a new openness to Being and the "oblivion" of Being as a "dialectical reversal" - not in the Hegelian sense of dialectic, but rather of an "eschatological" character. As with Marx, one may say that for Heidegger, a hitherto unprecedented degree of alienation and despair establishes the possibility of a hitherto unprecedented degree of freedom and fulfillment. In their rejection of the notion that freedom is "already actual" in the modern epoch for the notion of an agonizing opposition between a merely prospective freedom and an all-too-firmly established oppression, Marx and Heidegger may both be seen as rebels against Hegelianism.

In this sense, Heidegger's influence flows together with that of Lukács and the Frankfurt School, filling the void left by the failure of a socialist revolution to occur according to what Marx had called the laws of political economy.[81] Heidegger's contribution was to view alienation as separation, not primarily from our labor and its products, but from nothing less than "Being" altogether - from the "temporality" binding man to all that comes into existence and passes away. Thus broadened, the concept of alienation grows to embrace not only reified labor, but (at a minimum) art, culture and psychology. Of course, Heidegger's particular brand of anti-empiricism, with its emphasis on the irreducible autonomy of traditionally-rooted peoples and his strictures on Marxist and liberal "cosmopolitanism," places him on the right end of the ideological spectrum, especially in the context of the 1920s and 1930s.[82] His elaboration of the passive mode of man's relation to Being contradicts, in particular, the unconditional, freely projected futurism of Lukács' Party of creators. Yet the despair over an "evolutionary" solution to modern alienation,[83] and the rejection of any notion of morality that was not time-bound and, therefore, revocable during liberating new historical departures, indicate a ground of far-reaching agreement between Heidegger and his contemporaries on the left.

Notes

1. For a discussion of this episode and its ramifications, see Karsten Harries, "Heidegger as a Political Thinker," in *Heidegger and Modern Philosophy: Critical Essays*, ed. Michael Murray (New Haven: Yale University Press, 1978); Alexander Schwan, *Politische Philosophie im Denken Heideggers* (Koln und Opladen: Westdeutscher Verlag, 1965), pp. 134-137; Stanley Rosen, *Nihilism: A Philosophical Essay* (New Haven: Yale University Press, 1969), pp. 119-124; Fred R. Dallmayr, "Ontology of Freedom," *Political Theory*, 12 (May, 1984), 204-234; George W. Romoser,

"Heidegger and Political Philosophy," *Review of Politics*, 29 (April, 1967), 261-268; Eric Weil, "Le Cas Heidegger," *Les Temps Modernes*, 2, no. 22 (1946); Hannah Arendt, "Martin Heidegger at Eighty," in *Heidegger and Modern Philosophy: Critical Essays*, ed. Michael Murray (New Haven: Yale University Press, 1978); Alphonse de Waehlens, "La Philosophie de Heidegger et le Nazisme," *Les Temps Modernes*, 2, no. 22 (1946); Mark Blitz, *Heidegger's "Being and Time" and the Possibility of Political Philosophy* (Ithaca: Cornell University Press, 1981), p. 217.

2. See David F. Krell, "Analysis," in Martin Heidegger, *Nietzsche: Volume 4, Nihilism*, trans. Frank A. Capuzzi (San Francisco: Harper and Row, 1982), pp. 262-274.

3. See, eg., Werner Marx, *Hegel's Phenomenology of Spirit*, trans. Peter Heath (New York: Harper and Row, 1975), pp. 107- 108; Hans-Georg Gadamer, *Hegel's Dialectic*, trans. P. Christopher Smith (New Haven: Yale University Press, 1976), pp. 107-109. I have omitted any consideration of Nietzsche, whose relation both to German Idealism and to Heidegger is so complex, as being beyond the scope of this paper.

4. I follow Dallmayr's suggestion (p. 209) that Heidegger's works may be periodized as "three successive and only partially discontinuous phases": pre-1930 (eg. *Being and Time*), 1930 to 1945 (eg. *An Introduction to Metaphysics*), and post-1945 (*Letter on Humanism* and *The Question Concerning Technology*).

5. Martin Heidegger, *Sein und Zeit* (Frankfurt am Main: Klostermann, 1983), p. 12; *Being and Time*, trans. John Macquarrie and Edward Robinson (New York: Harper and Row, 1963), p. 32. Henceforth cited as Heidegger, *SZ*. The pagination of the German edition is provided in the margins of Macquarrie's and Robinson's translation, and subsequent references are to those page numbers.

6. Heidegger, *SZ*, pp. 188-189, 307-308.

7. *Ibid.*, pp. 16-17, 178, 266.

8. *Ibid.*, pp. 179, 285, 383-385.

9. *Ibid.*, p. 177.

10. *Ibid.*, p. 168.

11. *Ibid.*, p. 178.

12. *Ibid.*, pp. 125-129, 193.

13. *Ibid.*, pp. 21, 138, 167, 194-195, 385-386.

14. George Steiner, *Heidegger* (Glasgow: Fontana/Collins, 1978), p. 109.

15. Karl Löwith, "Les implications politiques de la philosophie de l'existence chez Heidegger," *Les Temps Modernes*, 2, no. 14 (1946).

16. Theodore W. Adorno, *The Jargon of Authenticity*, trans. Knut Tarnowski and Frederic Will (Evanston: Northwestern University Press, 1973), pp. 2-19, 92-113.

17. David Couzens Hoy, "History, Historicity and Historiography in *Being and Time*," in *Heidegger and Modern Philosophy*, pp. 343-345; Werner Marx, *Heidegger and the Tradition*, trans. Theodore Kisiel and Murray Greene (Evanston: Northwestern University Press, 1971), pp. 247-251.

18. Heidegger, *SZ*, p. 16.

19. *Ibid.*, pp. 25-26, 164-165, 173, 225.

20. *Ibid.*, pp. 2, 21-22.

21. *Ibid.*, pp. 405, 428-430, 434, 436. See also Martin Heidegger, *Hegel's Concept of Experience*, ed. J. Glenn Gray (New York: Harper and Row, 1970), pp. 38-39, 137-138.

22. G.W.F. Hegel, *The Phenomenology of Mind*, trans. J.B. Baillie (New York: Harper and Row, 1967), p. 137.

23. *Ibid.*, pp. 250-267.

24. Karl Marx, *The German Ideology*, ed. and trans. C.J. Arthur (New York: International Publishers, 1978), pp. 41, 47, 59-61; *The Marx-Engels Reader*, ed. Robert C. Tucker (New York: W.W. Norton, 1972), pp. 11-23. See also Gadamer, *Hegel's Dialectic*, pp. 105-115 and Werner Marx, *Hegel's Phenomenology*, pp. 14, 56.

25. Heidegger *SZ*, pp. 283-285.

26. See, eg., Hegel, *Phenomenology of Mind*, pp. 466-467; G.W.F. Hegel, *The Philosophy of History*, trans. J. Sibree (New York: Dover, 1956), pp. 38-50.

27. Heidegger, *SZ*, pp. 20-23, 175-180.

28. *Ibid.*, pp. 383-386.

29. See Gadamer, *Hegel's Dialectic*, p. 104; Michael Allen Gillespie, *Hegel, Heidegger and the Ground of History* (Chicago: University of Chicago Press, 1984), pp. 124-125.

30. Martin Heidegger, *Einfuhrung in die Metaphysik* (Frankfurt am Main: Klostermann), pp. 28-29; *An Introduction to Metaphysics*, trans. Ralph Mannheim (New Haven: Yale University Press, 1975), pp. 37-38. Henceforth cited as Heidegger, *EM*, with the German and English page numbers separated by a semi-colon (eg., Heidegger, *EM*, pp. 28-29; 37-38).

31. Heidegger, *EM*, pp. 22; 29.

32. *Ibid.*, pp. 1-3, 13-15; 1-3, 17-19.

33. *Ibid.*, pp. 26-28, 32; 33-36, 42.

34. *Ibid.*, pp. 10-12; 13-15.

35. *Ibid.*, pp. 46-49, 115-117, 130-131; 60-62, 149-153, 171.

36. *Ibid.*, pp. 22; 28-29.

37. *Ibid.*, pp. 16; 20-21.

38. *Ibid.*, pp. 108; 141.

39. *Ibid.*, pp. 131-132; 172.

40. *Ibid.*, pp. 118-119; 155.

41. *Ibid.*, pp. 48; 63.

42. *Ibid.*, pp. 72; 94-95.   See also Heidegger, *Hegel's Concept of Experience*, p. 33.

43. Heidegger, *EM*, pp. 26-32, 43-45; 37-39, 57-59.

44. *Ibid.*, pp. 34-35; 45.

45. *Ibid.*, pp. 137; 180.

46. *Ibid.*, pp. 35-38; 46-50.

47. *Ibid.*, pp. 152; 199.

48. *Ibid.*, pp. 64, 154; 85, 202.

49. *Ibid.*, pp. 70; 92.

50. *Ibid.*, pp. 120; 157.

51. See, eg., Gadamer, *Hegel's Dialectic*, p. 114.

52. Martin Heidegger, "Brief über den Humanismus," in *Wegmarken* (Frankfurt am Main: Klostermann, 1976), pp. 153-165; "Letter on Humanism," in *Martin Heidegger: Basic Writings*, ed. David F. Krell (New York: Harper and Row, 1977), pp. 202-214. Henceforth cited as Heidegger, *BH*, with the German and English page numbers separated by a semi-colon (eg., *BH*, pp. 153-165; 202-214).

53. Plato, Heidegger recalls, had made "essence" or eternal being the cause of what exists temporally, including man. In asserting that, on the contrary, "existence precedes essence" - that man creates what is taken to be objectively true - Sartre has, in Heidegger's view, merely inverted the older metaphysics while retaining the dichotomy between subject and object which is at the basis of all metaphysical judgments.

54. Heidegger, *BH*, pp. 168-179; 217-218.

55. *Ibid.*, pp. 171; 221.

56. *Ibid.*, pp. 146; 196.

57. *Ibid.*, pp. 170; 219.

58. See, eg., Heidegger, *An Introduction to Metaphysics*, pp. 38, 107.

59. Of great interest in this connection is Heidegger's essay on his rectorate at Freiburg University, written in 1945 but not published until 1983 (Martin Heidegger, "The Self-Assertion of the German University," "The Rectorate 1933/34: Facts and Thoughts," trans. Karsten Harries, *Review of Metaphysics*, vol. 38 (1985), pp. 467-502.) It appears to confirm my interpretation of Heidegger's considered judgment of the significance of National Socialism: "I saw in the movement that had gained power the possibility of an inner recollection and renewal of the people and a path that would allow it to discover its historical vocation in the Western world" (p. 483); "The rectorate was an attempt to see in the 'movement' that had come to power, beyond all its failings and crudities, something that reached much farther and that might some day bring about a gathering of what is German unto the historical essence of the West" (p. 498).

60. Heidegger, *BH*, pp. 171; 220.

61. *Ibid.*, Heidegger, 170; 219-220.

62. *Ibid.*, pp. 145-146; 194.

63. *Ibid.*, pp. 173; 221.

64. *Ibid.*, pp. 189, 194; 237, 242.

65. *Ibid.*, pp. 163, 149, 178; 212, 197, 226.

66. *Ibid.*, pp. 166; 215.

67. *Ibid.*, pp. 160, 167, 184; 209, 216, 232.

68. *Ibid.*, pp. 183-185; 231-233.

69. *Ibid.*, pp. 188-191; 236-239.

70. See, eg., the following passages from the "Letter on Humanism": "The essence of evil does not consist in the mere baseness of human action, but rather in the malice of rage. Both of these, however, healing and raging, can essentially occur only in Being....To healing Being first grants ascent into grace; to raging, its compulsion to malignancy" (pp. 237-238).

71. Martin Heidegger, "Die Frage nach der Technik," in *Vorträge und Aufsätze* (Stuttgart: Neske, 1978), pp. 13-17; "The Question Concerning Technology," In *Martin Heidegger: Basic Writings*, ed. David F. Krell (New York: Harper and Row, 1977), pp. 291-295. Henceforth cited as Heidegger. *FT*, with the German and English page numbers separated by a semi-colon (eg., *FT*, pp. 13-17; 291-295).

72. Heidegger, *FT*, pp. 29, 36; 307, 314.

73. *Ibid.*, pp. 20-26; 298-394.

74. *Ibid.*, pp. 9, 30; 287, 308. Cf. Heidegger, SZ, pp. 144, 178.

75. *Ibid.*, pp. 10-22; 288-300.

76. *Ibid.*, pp. 9, 27-28; 287, 305.

77. *Ibid.*, pp. 28; 306.

78. *Ibid.*, pp. 32; 309.

79. *Ibid.*, pp. 36; 313.

80. See Gadamer, *Hegel's Dialectic*, pp. 107-110; Werner Marx, *Hegel's Phenomenology of Spirit*, pp. 105-108.

81. Marx, *The Marx-Engels Reader*, p. 56. See also Martin Jay, *The Dialectical Imagination*, (Boston: Little, Brown and Company, 1973), pp. 122-123, 272; Lucien Goldmann, *Lukács and Heidegger: Towards a New Philosophy*, trans. William Q. Boelhower (London: Routledge and Kegan Paul, 1977); Alasdair MacIntyre, *After Virtue: A Study in Moral Theory* (London: Duckworth, 1981), p. 244; Leszek Kolakowski, *Main Currents in Marxism*, trans. P.S. Falla (Oxford: Oxford University Press, 1981), III, 357; Steiner, *Heidegger*, pp. 140-143; W.R. Newell, "Heidegger on Freedom and Community: Some Political Implications of His Early Thought," *American Political Science Review*, 78, no. 3 (1984).

82. See, eg., Otto Pöggeler, *Philosophie und Politik bei Heidegger* (Freiburg: Karl Alber, 1974), pp. 25-32.

83. Kolakowski, *Main Currents*, pp. 253-260.

FIRE ALARM: WALTER BENJAMIN'S
CRITIQUE OF TECHNOLOGY

Michael Löwy

The uncritical approach to technical progress has been the dominant trend in Marxism since the end of the nineteenth century. Marx's own views were less one-sided: one can find in his writing an attempt towards a *dialectical* understanding of the antinomies of progress.

It is true that in some of his works the main emphasis is on the historically progressive role of industrial capitalism. For instance, in the *Communist Manifesto* one can find an enthusiastic celebration of bourgeois technological progress: "The bourgeoisie, during its rule of scarce one hundred years, has created more massive and more colossal productive forces than have all preceding generations together. Subjection of nature's forces to man, machinery ... steam navigation, railways, electric telegraphs ... what earlier century had even a presentiment that such production forces slumbered in the lap of social labour?" But even here there are some clear references to the negative consequences of industrial technology: owing to the extensive use of machinery, the work "has lost all individual character, and consequently, all charm for the workman"; the proletarian becomes "an appendage of the machine" and his work becomes increasingly "repulsive" (a term Marx borrows from Fourier).[1]

These two aspects are dealt with extensively in Marx's main economic writings. For instance, in the *Grundrisse* he insists on the "great civilizing influence of capital," but nevertheless recognizes that the machine robs labor "of all independence and attractive character" (another Fourierist category - *travail attrayant*). He has no doubt that capitalist technology means a degradation and intensification of labor: "The most developed machinery thus forces the worker to work longer than the savage does, or than he himself did with the simplest, crudest tools."[2]

In *Capital* the dark side of industrial technology comes very forcefully to the forefront: because of machinery, work in the capitalist factory becomes

"a sort of torture," a "miserable routine of endless drudgery and toil in which
the same mechanical process is gone through over and over again ... like the
labor of Sisyphus" (here Marx quotes from Engels, *The Condition of the
Working Class in England*); the whole labor process is "turned into an organized mode of crushing out the workman's vitality, freedom and independence." In other words: in the present mode of production, the machine, far
from improving the condition of labor, "deprives the work of all interest"
and "confiscates every atom of freedom, both in bodily and intellectual
activity."[3]

Marx seems also to be aware of the *ecological* consequences of capitalist
technology: in the chapter on "Great Industry and Agriculture" in *Capital* he
observes that capitalist production "disturbs (*stört*) the metabolism
(*Stoffwechsel*) between man and the earth" and puts in danger "the eternal
natural conditions for the permanent fertility of the soil." As a result, it
"destroys both the physical health of the urban worker and the spiritual life
of the rural worker." Each step in the progress of capitalist agriculture, each
improvement of fertility in the short run, is at the same time "progress in
ruining the permanent sources of this fertility. The more a country, like the
United States of America for instance, has great industry as the background
of its development, the quicker this process of destruction. Therefore, capitalist production only develops the technique and combination of the social
process of production, while at the same time undermining the springs of all
wealth: the earth and the worker."[4]

Although Marx is far from being romantic, he draws extensively on the
romantic criticism of capitalist industrial civilization and technology.
Among those who are often quoted in his economic writings are not only
utopian communists such as Fourier, but also *petit-bourgeois* socialists such
as Sismondi and even outright Tories like David Urquhart.

However, unlike the romantic economists, Marx does not criticize modern technology itself, but only the way in which *capitalism* uses it. The
contradictions and antinomies of machinery do not grow out of machinery
itself, but "out of its capitalist use (*Anwendung*)." For instance: "Considered
in itself, machinery reduces labor time, while its capitalist use extends the
labor day; in itself it makes work easier, its capitalist use heightens its
intensity; in itself it is a victory of the human being over the natural force, its
capitalist use enslaves man to the natural force; in itself it multiplies the
wealth of the producer, its capitalist use pauperizes him, etc."[5]

How then might we understand a postcapitalist, or a *socialist* use of
machines and industrial technology? The answer, both in *Capital* and
Grundrisse, is that mechanization, by shortening the working day, will
create free time, which is both idle time and time for higher activity. In a
socialist society, technical progress will permit "the general reduction of the
necessary labour of society to a minimum, which then corresponds to the

artistic, scientific, etc. development of the individuals in the time set free, and with the means created, for all of them."6

Does this mean that the modern industrial-technological structure is a *neutral instrument* which can be used either in a capitalist or in a socialist manner? Or is the nature of the present technological system affected by its capitalist origin? This and many other relevant questions are left unanswered by Marx. But much of the *dialectical* quality of his writings on machinery - his attempt to seize the *contradictory* character of its development - has been lost in later Marxist literature, which fell under the spell of technological progress and celebrated its achievements as an unmixed blessing.

Walter Benjamin never dealt systematically with the problems of modern technology, but one can find in his writings remarkable insight which sets him apart as one of the first Marxist thinkers to approach these questions with a critical mind. Rejecting the semipositivist and naively optimistic axioms prevalent in mainstream Marxism (both of the Second and Third Internationals) before World War II, he tried to sound the fire alarm, warning of the dangers inherent in the present pattern of technical progress. His double protest - against technical progress in warfare and against the destruction of nature - has a prophetic ring and an astonishing relevance to our own time.

The roots of Benjamin's attitude towards technology can be found in the romantic tradition. German romantics and neoromantics (at the end of the nineteenth century) criticized *Zivilisation* - soulless material progress linked to technical and scientific development, bureaucratic rationality, quantification of social life - in the name of *Kultur*, the organic body of moral, cultural, religious and social values. They particularly denounced the fateful results of mechanization, division of labor and commodity production, nostalgically harking back to precapitalist and preindustrial ways of life. Although much of this romantic anticapitalism was conservative or reactionary, it also expressed a powerful revolutionary tendency. Romantic revolutionaries criticized the bourgeois industrial order in the name of past values, but their hopes were oriented towards a postcapitalist, socialist and classless utopia. This radical world-view - shared by authors such as William Morris or Georges Sorel, and in Germany by Gustav Landauer and Ernst Bloch - is Walter Benjamin's cultural background and the initial source of his reflections on technology.

In one of his first writings, an essay from 1913 on "The Religiosity of our Times" - wherein he claims that "we all still live very deeply immersed in the discoveries of Romanticism " - Benjamin complained of the reduction of men to working machines and the debasement of all work to its technical form. Directly echoing certain contemporary neoromantic motifs, he believes in the need for a new religion (inspired by Tolstoy and Nietzsche) and rejects the shallow materialism which narrows all social activity to "an affair of *Zivilisation*, like the electric light."7

After 1924, Benjamin becomes increasingly interested in Marxism and sympathetic to the Communist movement. His criticism becomes more political and more specific. In an article published in 1925 - "The Weapons of Tomorrow" - he draws attention to the usage of modern technology in the service of "international militarism." Describing in detail the future battles "with chlorazetophenol, diphenylaminchlorasine and dichlorathysulphide," which are being prepared in chemical and technical laboratories, he argues that the horrors of gas warfare are beyond human imagination: poisonous gas does not distinguish between civilians and soldiers, and it can destroy all human, animal and vegetable life in vast expanses of land.8

But it is in *One-Way Street* (written before 1926 and published in 1928) that Benjamin really tries to confront the problem of technology in Marxist terms, relating it to *class struggle*. In one of his most impressive illuminations, the paragraph entitled "Fire Alarm," he sees the downfall of the bourgeoisie through proletarian revolution as the only way in which to prevent a catastrophic end to "three thousand years of cultural development." In other words: "if the abolition of the bourgeoisie is not completed by an almost calculable moment in economic and technical development (a moment signalled by inflation and poison-gas warfare), all is lost. Before the spark reaches the dynamite, the lighted fuse must be cut."9   This argument - surprisingly similar to ideas advanced today by the antinuclear pacifist movement - focuses once more on the mortal danger of war and military technology; moreover, it does not conceive the proletarian revolution as the "natural" or "inevitable" result of economic and technical "progress" (the vulgar semipositivist axiom shared by many Marxists at the time) but as the critical *interruption* of an evolution leading to catastrophe.

The relation between capitalism and the military manipulation of technology is examined in another passage of *One-Way Street*, entitled "To the Planetarium." Technology could have been an instrument for the "marriage" (*Vermählung*) between humanity and the cosmos; but "because the lust for profit of the ruling class sought satisfaction through it, technology betrayed man and turned the bridal bed into a bloodbath" during the World War. Benjamin links the military use of technical progress to the most general issue of the relationship between mankind and nature: technology should not be the mastery of nature - "an imperialist teaching" - but the mastery of the *relation* between nature and man. Comparing the nights of annihilation of the last war to an epileptic crisis of mankind, he sees in the proletarian power "the measure of its convalescence"and the first attempt to bring technology under human control.10

It is difficult to know how far the Soviet Union (which Benjamin visited in 1926-27) corresponded with his expectations. In some articles published in 1927 concerning the Soviet cinema - which he defended against various critics - he complains that the Soviet public, because of its passionate admiration for technology, cannot accept grotesque Western movies, whose humor is directed against technology. "The Russians cannot grasp an ironic and skeptical attitude towards technical things."[11]

If he had some hopes in relation to the Soviet experiment, he had none whatsover for the development of technology in the capitalist world. Following the (oppositionist-Trotskyist) French Communist writer Pierre Naville, Benjamin calls for an *organization of pessimism* and ironically refers to "unlimited trust only in I.G.Farben and the peaceful perfection of the *Luftwaffe*."[12] Both institutions were soon to show, beyond Benjamin's most pessimistic forecasts, the sinister usage which could be made of modern technology.

Benjamin saw in bourgeois society a "gaping discrepancy between the gigantic power of technology and the minuscule moral illumination it affords," a discrepancy which manifests itself through imperialist wars. The increase in technical artifacts and power sources cannot be absorbed and is channelled toward destruction; therefore "any future war will also be a slave revolt of technology." Nevertheless, Benjamin believes that in a liberated society technology will cease to be "a fetish of doom" in order to become "a key to happiness"; emancipated mankind will use and illuminate the secrets of nature thanks to a technology "mediated by the human scheme of things."[13]

In his well-known essay on "The Work of Art in the Age of Mechanical Reproduction" (1936) he again insists that imperialist war is "a rebellion of technology," by which he means the following : "if the natural utilization of productive forces is impeded by the property system, the increase in technical devices, in speed, and in the sources of energy will press for an unnatural utilization, and this is found in war." The "technological formula" of capitalist society can thus be summarized: "Only war makes it possible to mobilize all of today's technical resources while maintaining the property system."[14]

Walter Benjamin becomes increasingly aware that his critical views on technology are radically opposed to the blissfully optimistic approach so characteristic of the dominant ideology in the labor movement - in particular, the positivist-oriented Marxism adopted by Social-Democracy from the end of the nineteenth century. In his essay "Eduard Fuchs, Collector and Historian" (1937) he criticizes the positivist identification of technology with natural sciences: technology is not a purely scientific fact but also a *historical* one, which, in present society, is to a large extent determined by capitalism. Social-Democratic positivism - which Benjamin traces back to Bebel - seemed to ignore the fact that in bourgeois society technology serves mainly to produce commodities and to make war. This apologetic and uncritical attitude blinded socialist theoreticians to the *destructive side* of technological development and its socially negative consequences.   There is a continuous thread stretching from the Saint-Simonist hymns in glorification of industry to modern Social-Democratic illusions concerning the unmixed blessings of technology.   Benjamin believes that today the power and capacity of machines is well beyond social needs, and "the energies which technology develops beyond this threshold are destructive" - they serve above all for the technical perfection of war.   He opposes his pessimistic-revolutionary perspective to the shallow optimism of the modern Marxist epigones, and links it to Marx's own prognosis concerning the barbaric development of capitalism.[15]

The negative effects of mechanization and modern capitalist technology on the working class is one of the leitmotifs of Marx's *Capital*.   In his essay on Baudelaire (1938), and in his notes for the planned book on the Parisian Arcades, Benjamin articulates Marx's own views with a romantic nightmare: the transformation of human beings into automatons.   According to Marx (quoted by Benjamin), it is a common characteristic of capitalist production that the working conditions make use of the worker and not the reverse; but "it takes machinery to give this reversal a technically concrete form."   By working with machines, workers learn to coordinate "their own movements with the uniformly constant movements of an automaton" (Marx).   While in craftsmanship work required experience and practice, the modern unskilled worker is, writes Benjamin, "sealed off from experience" and "deeply degraded by the drill of the machines."   The industrial work process is an "automatic operation," "devoid of substance," wherein each act is the "exact repetition" of the preceding one.   He compares the behavior of workers in the factory to that of pedestrians in a big-city crowd (as described by Edgar Allen Poe) : both "act as if they had adapted themselves to the machines and could express themselves only automatically"; both "live their lives as automatons ... who have completely liquidated their memories."[16]

Referring to the "futility," "emptiness" and inability to complete something which are "inherent in the activity of a wage slave in a factory," Benjamin compares industrial time to "time in hell" - hell being "the province of those who are not allowed to complete anything they have started."   Like the gambler described by Baudelaire, the worker is forced to "start all over again," performing always the same movements.[17]   This is why Engels, in *The Condition of the Working Class in England* (quoted by Benjamin), compared the interminable torture of the worker, who is forced to repeat again and again the same movements, to the infernal punishment of Sisyphus.[18]   Considering these views on the "hellish" nature of modern industrial work, it is not surprising that in his last writing, the "Theses on the Philosophy of History" (1940), Benjamin sharply criticizes the German Social-Democratic ideology of labor as a new version ("in secularized form") of the old Protestant ethic of work - i.e., factory labor is seen by Social-Democracy not only as a welcome result of technological progress but even as "a political achievement."19

However, Benjamin's criticism of semipositivist "vulgar Marxism" is broader, putting into question its global understanding of technology: "Nothing has corrupted the German working class so much as the notion that it was moving with the current. It regarded technological developments as the fall of the stream with which it thought it was moving."20   What Benjamin rejects in this Panglossian ideology is both the presupposition that technical progress in itself is leading towards socialism, by laying the economic foundations for a new social order, and also the belief that the proletariat has only to take into its hands the existing (capitalist) technical system and develop it further. Blind to all the dangers and socially negative consequences of modern technology, vulgar (i.e.positivist) Marxism "recognizes only the progress in the mastery of nature, not the retrogression of society; it already displays the technocratic features later encountered in Fascism."21

As a matter of fact, Benjamin's critique goes even deeper: it is the very axiom of a "mastery" (*Beherrschung*) over nature, or its "exploitation" (*Ausbeutung*) by technology, which is unacceptable already in his first Marxist writings, as we saw above. For the positivist conception, nature "exists gratis" (a formula used by the Social-Democratic ideologist Joseph Dietzgen) - i.e. is reduced to a commodity and envisaged only from the viewpoint of its exchange value - and is there to be "exploited" by human labor. Searching for an alternative approach to the relation between mankind and its natural environment, Benjamin refers back to the socialist utopias of the nineteenth century and particularly to Fourier.

This issue is discussed in the notes for the book on the Parisian Arcades (1938): in matriarchal societies, as Bachofen showed, the modern "murderous conception of the exploitation of nature" did not exist - nature was conceived as a *giving mother*. This could again be the case in a socialist society, because the moment production ceases to be founded on the exploitation of human labor, "labor will in its turn lose its character of exploitation of nature by humankind. It will then be accomplished according to the model of children's play, which is in Fourier the paradigm for the *travail passionné* of the *harmoniens*.... Such a work instilled with the spirit of play is not oriented to the production of values but to an amelioration of nature."22   Similarly, in the Theses (1940) he celebrates Fourier as the utopian visionary of "a kind of labour which, far from exploiting nature is capable of delivering her of her creations which lie dormant in her womb as potentials." This does not mean that Benjamin wants to replace Marxism by utopian socialism: he considers Fourier to be complementary to Marx, and in the same passage where he so favorably writes of the French socialist, he also contrasts Marx's insights with the utter confusion of the Social-Democratic Gotha Program on the nature of labor.[23]

In his first Marxist work (*One-Way Street*, written in 1923-26) Benjamin sounded the fire alarm: if proletarian revolution does not come in time, economic and technical progress under capitalism may lead to catastrophe. The defeat of revolution in Germany, France and Spain led to one of the greatest catastrophes in the history of humankind: World War II. As the war began, in 1940, it was too late for ringing the bell. Benjamin had not lost his desperate hopes in revolution, but he redefined revolution through a new version of the allegorical image he used in the 1920s: "Marx said that the revolutions are the locomotives of world history. But perhaps they are something quite different. Perhaps the revolutions are the hand of the human species travelling in this train pulling the alarm brakes."[24]

In conclusion, one can (perhaps) criticize Benjamin for offering images, utopias and allegories instead of concrete and scientific analysis of modern technology and of the possible alternatives. But one cannot deny his importance as a visionary pathbreaker and a revolutionary philosopher. With his critical insight into the dangers and damages of industrial capitalist technology, he renewed Marxist thinking in this area and opened the way for the Frankfurt School's future reflections. He may also be considered a fore-runner of the two most important social movements of the end of this century: ecology and antinuclear pacifism. If one reads today his "Fire Alarm" (as well as other writings) it is enough to replace the word "gas" by "nuclear" in order to discover the extraordinary relevance and urgency of his warnings.

Notes

1. Karl Marx, "Manifesto of the Communist Party," in Marx, *The Revolutions of 1848*, ed. David Fernbach (New York: Vintage, 1974), pp. 72-74.

2. Marx, *Grundrisse*, trans. Martin Nicolaus (New York: Vintage, 1973) pp. 708-709.

3. Marx, *Das Kapital*, in Karl Marx-Friedrich Engels, *Werke*, Band 23 (Berlin: Dietz Verlag,1968), pp. 445-446, 528-529.

4. *Ibid.*, pp. 528-530.

5. *Ibid.*, p. 465.

6. Marx, *Grundrisse*, pp. 706, 712.

7. Walter Benjamin, "Dialog über die Religiosität der Gegenwart," in *Gesammelte Schriften* (hereafter *G.S.*), Band II.1 (Frankfurt am Main: Suhrkamp Verlag, 1972-85), pp. 16-35.

8. Benjamin, *G.S.*, IV.1, pp. 473-476.

9. Benjamin, "One-Way Street," in *Reflections*, ed. Peter Demetz, trans. Edmund Jephcott (New York: Harcourt Brace Jovanovich, 1978), p. 84.

10. *Ibid.*, pp. 92-94. Cf. *G.S.*, IV.1, pp. 147-148.

11. Benjamin, "Zur Lage der Russischen Filmkunst" and "Erwilderung an Oscar H.H. Schmitz," in *G.S.*, 11-2, pp. 750, 753.

12. Benjamin, "Surrealism : The Last Snapshot of the European Intelligentsia, " in *Reflections*, p. 191.

13. Benjamin, "Theories of German Fascism," *New German Critique*, 17 (Spring, 1979), 120-121, 126-128.

14. Benjamin, *Illuminations*, ed. Hannah Arendt, trans. Harry Zohn (Fontana, 1973) pp. 243-244.

15. Benjamin, "Eduard Fuchs, Collector and Historian,"*New German Critique*, 5 (Spring, 1975), 33-34, 45.

16. Benjamin, "On Some Motifs in Baudelaire," in *Illuminations*, pp. 177-180. In an article written several years before (1930) on E.T.A. Hoffman, Benjamin referred to the romantic writer's metaphysical dualism between Life and Automat and his horror for the diabolical mechanisms which transform men into an automaton (Benjamin, "E.T.A.Hoffman und Oscar Panizza," in *G.S.*, II.2, pp. 644-647). Some of this romantic fear is present in Benjamin's remarks on the condition of modern workers and city-dwellers.

17. Benjamin, *Illuminations*, pp. 179, 181.

18. See Benjamin, *Das Passagen-Werk*, *G.S.*, V.1, p. 162. Marx also compares the gates of the factory to the gates of hell. Benjamin quotes him in *G.S.*, V.2, p. 813.

19. Benjamin, *Illuminations*, pp. 260-261.

20. *Ibid.*, p. 260.

21. *Ibid.*, p. 261. This definition of fascism as *technocratic* reveals a significant re-evaluation of Benjamin's former views. In an article from 1934, "The Author as Producer" - one of the few of his writings which seems to entertain illusions regarding the benefits of technical progress in itself - he opposes the need for "technical innovations" in cultural production to the call for "spiritual renewal" which he considers typical of fascism - forgetting Marinetti's rapturous hymns to the glory of modern technology (Benjamin, "The Author as Producer," in *Reflections*, p. 228).

22. Benjamin, *Das Passsagen-Werk, G.S.*, V.1, p. 456.

23. Benjamin, *Illuminations*, p. 261.

24. Benjamin, *G.S.*, I.3, p. 1232 (Preparatory notes for the "Theses on the Philosophy of History").

CONSENT TO THE UNIVERSE:

SIMONE WEIL AND THE NATURAL GROUND

FOR TECHNOLOGICAL CHOICE

Gary A. Lewis

In discussing "Some Influences of Simone Weil on George Grant's Silence," Edwin B. Heaven and David R. Heaven ask "To whom or what" George Grant is directing us "when, in those occasional moments in his writings, he turns away from his primary task (which is the destruction of inadequate sources of hope) and points toward a veiled but positive affirmation?"[1]

Grant has confined his speech on modernity largely to bringing the "darkness into light as darkness," while Weil, whose notion of what counts as illumination Grant shares, has written luminously "from within a vision of the whole," of "*all that is* (including modernity)."[2]

The answer to "whom" is clearly Weil. The nature of the "what" is less clear, and is only pursued by Heaven and Heaven as far as it relates to the reasons for Grant's deference. (Among these is Grant's judgment that Weil has greater authority than he to speak on matters of science and love.) We do not learn (for this is beyond the intended scope of the piece) what it is that Weil says about relating the good to technological choice. Yet we want to know this, if for no other reason than that this is precisely the problem on which Grant has been so tantalizingly and publicly "silent."

Grant is silent in the sense that he does not tell us how to enlighten the technological cave. He denies the possibility of "good" uses of technology, since it is technology which "presents us with what we think of the whole, with what we think is good, with what we think good is."[3]

But technology does not tell Grant what he thinks good is. And if Weil understands the good as he does and still speaks out about technological choice, we will want to learn what these choices are and how she makes them.

One of the reasons Heaven and Heaven give for Grant's silence is prudence. Weil makes the supernatural the explicit ground of her analysis.

Grant, who agrees with Weil, but has been influenced almost as much by Leo Strauss, is uneasy about speaking of the supernatural in public.[4]

Grant's uneasiness is shared, to say the least, by political science. If we are going to learn from Weil's speech, we will have to know how her con ception of the supernatural permits her to make proposals for action in the real world, and whether and to what extent it correlates with a conception of nature which will be accessible to us in ways that the supernatural is not. We may then arrive at the point of being able to consider Weil's normative pronouncements as part of a comprehensible theory of political choice and action.

I

Weil is ancient and modern at the same time.[5] This is achieved not by a synthesis - such as that (of Hobbes and Socrates) which Grant derides Hegel-Kojève for attempting and necessarily failing to perform[6] - but by a sustained comprehension of "correlated contraries." On the basis of these she develops a teleology of tension within man's social nature. "The essential contradiction in the human condition is that man[7] is subject to force, and craves for justice. He is subject to necessity, and craves for the good."[8] Her ruling principle is contradiction; her central image is the circle. Her thought about the whole does not lend itself to rectilinear exegesis.

Necessity and the Good

The architectonic pair of contraries in the universe is necessity and the Good. Everything in the manifested world is ruled by necessity, including chance.[9] Good, like geometry, is not for man an accident or an invention, but a discovery. Absolute Good exists outside the world in the same sense that the idea of a circle (which is an image of this Good) exists apart from any approximate circle which appears in the world. A circle which one might draw or imagine participates in the other perfect circle, as the relative good of the world participates in the absolute. The "reality outside the world" is the unique source of all the good within the world; of all beauty, truth, justice, legitimacy, order, and "all human behaviour that is mindful of obligations."[10]

This notion of an absolute does not, however, imply the possibility (much less the imperative) of deducing particular moral action from universal rules. Even a "golden" rule requires reflective judgment:

> To love our neighbour as ourselves does not mean that we should love all people equally, for I do not have an equal love for all the modes of existence of myself. Nor does it mean that we should never make them

suffer, for I do not refuse to make myself suffer. But we should have with each person the relationship of one conception of the universe to another conception of the universe, and not to a part of the universe.[11]

The relation of necessity to the Good is that "necessity in so far as it is absolutely other than Good is Good itself."[12] Free will presupposes resistance. Evil and suffering are a structural condition of the good which is possible in the world. Another world might exist where happiness and freedom could coincide with the absence of tension with their opposites, but we cannot conceive it and can only "imagine" it by an act which amounts to "filling the void" "through which grace must pass."[13] Necessity is thus blind obedience to Good. The movement of the ocean waves, the pull of gravity, the development of species by natural selection, are ineluctable responses to the order of the universe.

The Object of Science

This Good (as invisible light) can be approached by the intellect but experienced only in refraction through a love that is directed toward the beauty of the world. Beauty is both the manifestation and the proof of the existence of Good. "A Greek statue inspires by its beauty a love which cannot have a piece of stone for its object; in the same way the world inspires a love which cannot have matter for its object."[14]

Beauty is "the supreme mystery" in the world of appearance. It attracts us, stimulates desire, yet "feeds only the part of the soul that gazes," because "the one thing we want is that it should not change." If we do not avoid (fill the void of) the "exquisite anguish it afflicts, then desire is gradually transformed into love." And we begin to acquire the faculty of "pure and disinterested attention." Beauty speaks in this way for truth and justice, "like a dog who barks to bring people to his master lying unconscious in the snow." The spirit of justice and truth is nothing else than "a certain kind of attention, which is pure love." To pay no attention to the world's beauty "is, perhaps, so great a crime of ingratitude that it deserves the punishment of affliction." (It does not always get it, but the alternative punishment is a mediocre life, which is in no way preferable.)[15]

Through the beauty of the world even harsh necessity becomes an occasion for love. The sea is not less beautiful because ships are sometimes wrecked. The order of the world is the same as the beauty of the world.[16] And love of the beauty of the world is the precondition of scientific knowledge.

"The spirit of truth can dwell in science on condition that the motive prompting the savant is the love of the object that forms the stuff of his investigations.   That object is the universe in which we live."   No observations other than those arising from love can discover nature. Science is thus "the study of the beauty of the world." And if man loses touch with this beauty and strays outside his "natural scale" (by accumulating experimental data or increasing the range of his telescopes or microscopes), he may "find himself among a complexity of facts in which he can discern no necessity." In order to rediscover reality, he would have to see either much less or much more. And the latter is impossible, partly because technical progress is limited, but also because as technique progresses, man's "mental capacity remains always subject to the same limits." Equilibrium, insofar as it "defines limits," is therefore the "essential idea of science."[17]

Necessity and force cannot produce love (or a circle). Awareness of the existence of the Good which can, is a part of our nature and our "destiny." "At the bottom of the heart of every human being, from earliest infancy until the tomb, there is something that goes on indomitably expecting, in the teeth of all experience of crimes committed, suffered, and witnessed, that good and not evil will be done to him."[18]

The Absence of God

This ultimate Good - which is in unity with truth, beauty, and justice - is what Weil means by God.[19] The most striking thing about this God is its absence from the world. God's absence is for humans the condition of their being. For if God "did not abandon them they would not exist....His presence would annul their existence as a flame kills a butterfly." And what we think we love in a God who gives us "hope, comfort, and consolation" is not God, but hope, comfort, and consolation - from which "atheism"[20] is a kind of "purification." "The world, insofar as it is quite empty of God, is God itself."[21]

Because it expresses the essence of our condition - we are a part of the Good yet embedded in what is altogether other - contradiction is itself the means for approaching the absolute; not the resolution of contradiction but its dialectical transcendence through the contemplation of what Grant says "cannot be adequately thought."[22] Actually, "as Plato knew," "contradiction ... is the sole instrument of developing thought." But there are illegitimate ways of using it. These consist in combining incompatible assertions as if they were compatible. The legitimate way is to try first to resolve the contradiction, then, if this cannot be done, to use both elements as "a two-limbed tool, like a pair of pincers, so that through it direct contact may be made with the transcendental sphere of thought beyond human faculties." This is what Plato called "dialectics": "that movement of the soul which, at each stage, in order to rise to the sphere above, leans for support on the irreducible contradictions of the sphere wherein it finds itself."[23]

Examples of the illegitimate use of contradiction are idealism and materialism. Idealists believe "that the thoughts of man concerning the good possess the highest degree of force here" in the world. Materialists believe that "force" (as invisible hand or history) "is of itself directed towards the good." Both are doubly mistaken: the first, because their thoughts "do not lay hold of the good" and in any case "are without force" (there is "no other force on earth except force"); and the second, because "force is ... indifferent to the good" and is "not always and everywhere the stronger." (Marx "believed in miracles without believing in the supernatural.") The only recourse is the "incomprehensible notion" that the "unity between necessity and the good" lies "outside this world."[24]

Discontinuity and Limit

Reality, like the circle, is a combination of the continuous and the discontinuous. The problem with "classical" (nineteenth-century) science was that it neglected the latter. A problem with quantum theory is that it neglects the former.[25] With regard to Bohr's dictum on measurement of waves and particles, that "the nearer we approach to precision in regard to one of these aspects, the further from it we get in regard to the complementary aspect," Weil remarks: "This complementarity is nothing other than the old correlation of contraries which is basic in the thought of Heraclitus and Plato. From the philosophical point of view it has no novelty, but that does not make it the less interesting, because nothing is so interesting in philosophy as a recent discovery of an eternal idea."[26]

Greek science is exemplary for Weil because of its preoccupation with proportion and relation, a concern which was both aesthetic and, "as historically confirmed for the age of Pythagoras," "philosophico-religious." Greek mathematics was not (as is so much of ours) a game, but an "art," whose "sole aim was to conceive more and more clearly an identity of structure between the human mind and the universe." And their geometry was a science of nature. The discovery of incommensurables was not a shock to the Pythagoreans, Weil believes, because they thought of number not algebraically, as integer, but geometrically, as relation. They were therefore undismayed that certain spatial relationships (such as the diagonal of the square) could not be expressed in rational numbers. It was the Pythagorean philosopher Eudoxus, "inventor of the theory of real numbers and of the concept of limit and the concept of integration," who discovered the "mean proportional," a factor which relates "number and unity." (The mean proportional between 1 and 9, for example, is 3, since $1/3 = 3/9$.) The Greeks identified the mean proportional with mediation between necessity and the Good. Man is to Prometheus as Prometheus is to Zeus. Prometheus gave man technology. Ultimately Prometheus is reconciled with Zeus, but he is punished and suffers as man is punished and suffers. Harmony is defined by the Pythagoreans as the unity of contraries. "The first couple of contraries is God and the creature. The Son is the unity of these contraries, the geometrical mean which establishes a proportion between them: He is the mediator."27

The limited and the limitless provide parameters for all the other contraries.

> Limitation is the law of the manifested world. Only God (or whatever name one may choose) is without limits. Man, who is of the world and who has a part in God, puts the unlimited and the absolute into the world, where they are error....Deliverance consists in reading limit and relation in all sensible phenomena without exception....The significance of a true science is to constitute a preparation for deliverance.28

For the Greeks, "the very principle of the soul's salvation was measure, balance, proportion, harmony...." In relations between men also, "the good consists in abolishing the uncontrolled and unlimited; that is what justice is (so it can only be defined by equality)."29

II

For Weil it is not technology as such but social necessity which gives us our "beliefs concerning good." She keeps returning to Plato's image of a "huge beast which men are forced to serve and whose reflexes they study" in order to derive these beliefs. Her elaboration is a model of operant behaviorist observation: "we may imagine that among those with the task of grooming it, one takes charge of a knee, another of a claw, another of the neck, another of the back. Perhaps it likes being tickled under the jaw and patted on the back. One of its attendants will consequently maintain that it is tickling which constitutes the supreme good; another that it is patting." Such an "inhuman system ... models all those subjected to it - oppressed and oppressors alike - according to its own image." We are "absolutely incapable of having on the subject of good and evil opinions other than those dictated" by the beast's reflexes.30

But to all this she makes a constant qualification: we can be freed from enslavement to the beast by the operation of "a supernatural grace." According to Plato this was possible only for "predestined souls." Weil's discovery about grace is that it can be elicited. We can exercise "a sort of compulsion" [contrainte] "on God" through "mechanisms instituted by God" and which function even in God's absence or practical nonexistence. One mechanism of elicitation is the practice of "attention," which is active consent to and contemplation of the Good (or, more precisely, of the void which separates us from the Good; which is why the absolute is accessible through affliction as well as through beauty). Another mechanism is reason itself. For "force is powerless to overcome thought." The problem is that first "there must be thought."[31] The kind of thought which enables us to transcend our enslavement to the beast is necessarily thought about what we ought to do, or what it is right for us to do as human beings. This is distinguished from thought about what we as persons have a "right" to do or to have, a claim which must be upheld by force against what others claim as a "right" to do or have, since "rights" rhetoric appeals to the person's juridical relation to the beast.[32] This means that the first mechanism, attention, will inform the second: for thought to produce effective action, rather than mere behavior, it must proceed from a notion of good. Thought about collective action must be grounded in a good which people share in common. This is achieved not by collective thought (a collective cannot think) but by a dialectic of individual thinking which is "impersonal." So long as we think in the first person, we are entirely subjected to the mechanical play of forces. But by a "positive act of concentration" we can open our soul to allow the "conceptions of eternal Wisdom" in. Then we carry within us "the very conception to which force is subjected."[33]

The Natural Ground of Obligation

This is the basis for Weil's doctrine of obligation, which is consent to act impersonally, out of the respect due to human being as such on account of the presence in each of a desire for good. But since desire touches the limitless, and this respect cannot be expressed to a reality outside the world, it must find expression in concern for "men's need, the needs of the soul and the body, in this world," which are limited (and in principle determinable). Need is the basis of all obligation. "There is no other kind ... so far as human affairs are concerned." And it is the aim of public life to arrange that power is entrusted, as far as possible, to those who "effectively consent" to be bound by such an obligation.[34]

In her "Draft for a Statement of Human Obligations," Weil lists, in addition to bodily needs, the needs of the soul, expressed as opposites which balance and complete each other. They are: (1) equality and hierarchy; (2) consented obedience and liberty; (3) truth and freedom of expression; (4) solitude and society; (5) personal property and collective property; (6) punishment and honor; (7) "disciplined participation in a common task of public value and ... personal initiative within this participation"; (8) security and risk; and (in Andrew's reformulation) (9) "rootedness in a particular tradition and ... openness to universal standards of truth, beauty and goodness."[35]

Weil gives a somewhat altered list in *The Need for Roots*. It begins with the need for order, which stands above the other needs, and subsumes beauty. Order here refers not to the divine or natural order of the world but to the arrangement of conditions for the compatibility of obligations. We notice that of the thirteen needs which follow (supposedly in antithetical pairs), the one which bears most critically upon ethical choice or obligation is the odd one - "responsibility" - which conflates initiative and self-discipline in her other list. This requirement of human nature implies a politics of participation and self-determination based on habituation to competence.

For the need for responsibility to be satisfied, it is necessary that a man should often have to take decisions "in matters great or small affecting interests that are distinct from his own, but in regard to which he feels a personal concern." The additional stipulation that the person must be "continually called upon to supply fresh efforts" accords with Weil's conception of the human individual as defining himself in tension with necessity. Finally, she says, "he requires to be able to encompass in thought the entire range of activity of the social organism to which he belongs, including branches with which he has never to take a decision or offer any advice." He must be "asked to interest himself in it, be brought to feel its value, its utility, and, where necessary, its greatness, and be made fully aware of the part he plays in it."[36] This is a description of the practice of citizenship in a democratic society. And the primary locus for its appearance is the realm of work.

Work as a Process of Self-Creation

For Weil, "the reality of life is ... activity" which is both mental and physical. "From the moment that I act," she says," I make myself exist." And the action which takes the form of "consent to the order of the universe" is work. This is the crucial aspect of nature which eluded the ancients (the "human value" whose recognition is the one "spiritual conquest achieved by the human mind since the miracle of Greece").[37]

Work is as much man's destiny[38] as is the ceaseless "pressure exerted by necessity." An existence from which work had more or less disappeared "would be delivered over to the play of the passions and perhaps to madness; there is no self-mastery without discipline, and there is no other source of discipline for man than the effort demanded in overcoming external obstacles." Work is thus the means of habituation to virtue. Only out of this tension with necessity do we develop a "clear view of what is possible and what impossible, what is easy and what difficult....[T]his alone does away with insatiable desires and vain fears," leading us toward "moderation and courage, virtues without which life is but a disgraceful frenzy." Through coming "directly to grips with naked necessity, without his being able to expect anything except through his own exertions, [man's] life is a continual creation of himself by himself." If the "material conditions that enable him to exist were exclusively the work of his mind directing the effort of his muscles" - this "would be true liberty."[39]

In his confrontation with nature, man is not a warrior but an artisan who seeks to express his vision through the form implicit in the material. His method is epitomized in Francis Bacon's "veritable charter expressing the relations between man and the world: 'We cannot command Nature except by obeying her.'" This "single pronouncement," she says, "ought to form by itself the Bible of our times. It suffices to define true labour, the kind which forms free men, and that to the very extent to which it is an act of conscious submission to necessity."[40] In this way, man becomes a mediator between necessity and the Good.

Mediation is the point of tangent between the circle and the straight line, the fulcrum between the lever and the earth, an infinitesimally small point which concentrates the direction of energy. The absolute can only be expressed in the manifested world by infinitesimal amounts of good. The resulting "persuasion" is not precisely a force but a *rapport*, a logos, a relation to equilibrium.

Therefore the way of deliverance in the world from blind force or social necessity is not from desire to satisfaction (both of which are shaped by the beast) but from thought to action. And the only ones fit to persuade will be those who have reunited in themselves the relation between thinking and doing. The separation of these in the workplace produces a condition of humiliating dependency which destroys the workers' ability and will to act, leaving them (as Weil learned from her own experience of factory work) with the "resigned docility" of animals. The "only hope" for bringing about change resides in those who have somehow "already brought about in themselves, as far as is possible in the society of today, that union between manual and intellectual labour which characterizes the society we are aiming at."[41]

The full range of Weil's vision of human freedom within necessity emerges in "Reflections concerning the Causes of Liberty and Social Oppression," which became the central section of *Oppression and Liberty*. Oppression is characterized not by the use of power for base ends, but by the limitless race for power itself, which, "owing to its essential incapacity to seize hold of its object, rules out all consideration of an end, and finally comes, through an inevitable reversal, to take the place of all ends." This results in a servitude of both oppressors and oppressed to the "instruments of domination they themselves have manufactured." She sets out to discover an opening in this "sinister mesh of circumstances" through which "an attempt at deliverance might find its way." Man's history suggests that he is "born to be a slave" and that this is his natural condition. Yet man can never accept servitude, for "he is a thinking creature." She therefore proposes, in a manner reminiscent of Rousseau, to

> form an idea of what would constitute the least unhappy position for him to be in, ... the one in which he would be the least enslaved to the twin domination of nature and society; and discern what roads can lead towards such a position, ... and what instruments present-day civilization could place in men's hands if they aspired to transform their lives in this way.

And she proceeds to construct a provisional utopia. She argues that we must strive for a representation of "Perfect Liberty ..., not in the hope of attaining it, but in the hope of attaining a less imperfect liberty than is our present condition; for the better can be conceived only by reference to the perfect." A future that is completely impossible, she says elsewhere, "like the ideal of the Spanish anarchists, degrades us far less and differs far less from the eternal than a possible future. It does not even degrade us at all, except through the illusion of its possibility. If it is conceived of as impossible, it transports us into the eternal."[42]

Social and technological necessity would seem to lead humans into total helplessness, maintained by force. Deliverance consists in discovering a ground for choice within necessity. The ground is the relation of man's needs to his specific natural capacity for satisfying them: his need for responsibility and his capacity to think and choose and learn from the results of choosing. Liberty is a relation between thought and action.

Increasing Consciousness

Ideally, "method" should constitute the "very soul of work." But the relationship of thought to movement is "wrapped in impenetrable obscurity." We "cannot conceive any form of necessity" between mind and body because "we cannot determine what are the intermediate links." Accordingly, the method she prescribes is "a kind of miracle," in which the body is "rendered ... fluid through habit" applied to "difficulties ... so varied that it would never be possible to apply ready-made rules." Such an ideal "can never be fully realized," but will be brought nearer if we "widen bit by bit the sphere of conscious work." And this could be done "if man were no longer to aim at extending his knowledge and power indefinitely, but rather at establishing, both in his research and in his work, a certain balance between the mind and the object to which it is being applied."[43]

Since collectivities can be controlled only by individual thought, we must visualize a form of material existence wherein efforts only exclusively directed by a clear intelligence would take place, which would imply that each worker himself had to control, without referring to any external rule, not only the adaptation of his efforts to the piece of work to be produced, but also their co-ordination with all the other members of the collectivity.

This implies in turn a commensurability of the techniques employed in the various tasks and a generalized technical education which would enable each worker to form a clear idea of specialized procedures. No longer would workers' mutual dependence imply that their fate rested on arbitrary or mysterious forces, since each "would be in a position to verify the activities of all the rest by using his own reason."[44]   These proposals seem less absurdly utopian when we realize that the units she has in mind are quite small - on the same scale, and indeed with much the same intended result, as the autonomous work teams (especially the "matrix" and "network" groups) introduced into Norwegian industry in the 1970s.[45]

In such a setting vanity would be a spur to virtue: the "desire to win the esteem of his fellows" would provide each worker with the "stimulus necessary to overcome fatigue, sufferings and dangers." Wherever any creativity is involved, outward constraint, which is useless in such cases, would be replaced by self-discipline: "the sight of the unfinished task attracts the free man as powerfully as the overseer's whip stimulates the slave." And "output might well increase in proportion with clear thinking."[46]

This would permit a community of freedom and equality. Individuals would be bound by collective ties, but exclusively as human beings: "they would never be treated by each other as things." Each person would see in every work fellow "another self occupying another post."[47]

She gives a Tocquevillean glimpse of such a collectivity in operation:

it is a fine sight to see a handful of workmen in the building trades, checked by some difficulty, ponder the problem, each for himself, make various suggestions for dealing with it, and then apply unanimously the method conceived by one of them, who may or may not have any official authority over the remainder. At such moments the image of a free community appears almost in its purity.[48]

One way in which this differs from the operation of autonomous work groups in Norway is that in the latter the solution would be less likely to come from only "one of them." In her concern for scientific method and her adamance regarding collective thoughtlessness, Weil seems sometimes to underestimate the importance of dialectical interaction between individuals, and of spontaneity - the highly efficient forms of creative cooperation involving improvisation toward consensual goals (as in jazz, for instance) - as method. These will emerge only when Weil's basic condition is met; when each member has been permitted to develop the competence and achieve the freedom necessary to exercise responsibility as an individual.

Her analysis concludes that "the least evil society is that in which the general run of men are most often obliged to think while acting, have the most opportunities for exercising control over their collective life as a whole, and enjoy the greatest amount of independence."[49]

Transforming the Workplace

In *The Need for Roots*, which was written almost a decade later, Weil makes some suggestions for changing the system concerning "concentration of attention" at the workplace. She objects to the means used to motivate workers - "fear and extra pay" (she has had bitter first-hand experience of piece-rate work) - and to the quality of the obedience required: the "far too small amount of initiative, skill, and thought demanded of workmen, their present exclusion from any imaginative share in the work of the enterprise as a whole, their sometimes total ignorance of the value, social utility, and destination of the things they manufacture...."[50]

She proposes that new machines be devised which would neither exhaust the spirit nor lacerate the flesh, and would be easily adaptable to a multiplicity of purposes ("to a certain extent indeterminate ones"). The contribution of machine design to the well-being of the worker should become a principal focus of technological inquiry, its study encouraged by cooperation between trade unions and engineering schools.[51]

The reintegration of mental and material labor would provide that obedience would no longer be a matter of "uninterrupted submissiveness," but would take the form of self-discipline conjoined with initiative. Workers would have a job to do within a given time and be allowed to plan and complete it themselves, taking responsibility for their own product.[52]

"There is," she says, "a certain relation to time which suits inert matter, and another sort of relation which suits thinking beings." And it is "a mistake to confuse the two." We have an obligation to human being not to torture it. The mind is free and sovereign only

> when it is really and truly exercised. To be free and sovereign as a thinking being, for one hour or two, and a slave for the rest of the day is such an agonizing spiritual quartering that it is almost impossible not to renounce, so as to escape it, the highest forms of thought.

It might be objected that renunciation of the highest forms of thought would not be regarded by most workers as a serious deprivation; some would even

question whether most workers (or most of any category except philosophers) are capable of the highest forms of thought. But Weil insists that
each of us has the capacity for the highest form of thought, which is to say,
for detached attention to the good, and that any differential inability workers
may have is a direct consequence of the crippling of their faculties by the
conditions of their employment.[53]

The first step toward the liberation of the workers' capacity to think as
well as move would be the abolition of large factories and the substitution of
assembly shops connected to constellations of small facilities in which
workers would be given space to operate their own multipurpose machines.
Although the decentralization Weil urges evokes the early Marx and G. D.
H. Cole, she did not consider it socialistic; her proposals were intended "to
put an end to the proletarian condition," whereas "what is called socialism
tends ... to force everybody without distinction into that condition." It was to
be an arrangement more in the spirit of the Spanish anarchist collectives, in
which government would be an instrument of balance and limitation. A
"well ordered society" is "one where the State [has only] a negative action,
comparable to that of a rudder: a light pressure at the right moment to
counteract the first suggestion of any loss of equilibrium."[54]

That persuasion of the beast's disciples to a standard of good other than
technical rationality or force is "beyond our power" is "no reason for not
undertaking it." There is "no difficulty ... in maintaining intact, on the level
of action, those very hopes which a critical examination has shown to be
wellnigh unfounded; in that lies the very essence of courage." And we are
not really without hope: "the mere fact that we exist, that we conceive these
things and want something different" - that technology does not in fact tell
us what the good is - "constitutes for us a reason for hoping." If we are to
perish, she says, "let us see to it that we do not perish without having
existed."[55]

III

Weil's orientation and language changed somewhat between the composition of the "Reflections" section of *Oppression and Liberty* and *The Need
for Roots*. She seemed to be turning away from the political toward the
spiritual. She begins to speak as often of the path to the Good which leads
through suffering - pain and affliction - as of that through joy in love of the
world's beauty (although she persuades us that there is beauty in the
necessity of pain). She focuses on the "irreducible servitude" which is
inherent in all labor, on its unyielding and compelling aspect, which is - like
attention to the void presented by the unanswerable question "why?" which
affliction evokes - a means of apprehending the Good. And she begins to
speak of labor in terms of its relation to contemplation, of the need for

attention to the highest things. Frederick Rosen calls this "connection ... between what has been regarded for centuries as the lowest and highest of human activities" the "most striking aspect of Weil's analysis."[56] He gives this example from *Gravity and Grace* (a selection of fragments from Weil's later notebooks) of the opportunities for "spirituality" Weil now finds in work:

> Work makes us experience in the most exhausting manner the phenomenon of finality rebounding like a ball; to work in order to eat, to eat in order to work. If we regard one of the two as an end, or the one and the other taken separately, we are lost. Only the circle contains the truth.
>
> A squirrel turning in its cage and the rotation of the celestial sphere - extreme misery and extreme grandeur.
>
> It is when man sees himself as a squirrel turning round and round in a circular cage that, if he does not lie to himself, he is close to salvation.[57]

She seems to Rosen to be urging "passive acceptance ... as a form of obedience ... to God." And Rees says the "prevailing idea" in these writings "is that salvation comes only through despair."[58]

Yet she keeps on telling us in detail how the conditions of work force workers into mindlessness; into the "narcotics" of violent pleasure or dreams of revolution (the "opium of the people") - into anything but attention to the source of the good. And she continues to propose changes in the relations between people and between people and things which amount to a transformation of the workplace "no less extensive," as Rosen notes, "than that envisioned by Marx."[59]

In "*Condition première d'un travail non servile*" (1941 or 1942), Weil speaks of the affinity between labor and contemplation of the beautiful, then goes on to consider the conditions which might permit such contemplation. Workers "need poetry as they need bread. Not the poetry closed inside words: by itself that is no use to them. They need poetry to be the very substance of daily life." The tasks and materials of the workplace themselves must therefore be imbued with a "reflective property" which could catch the eternal light and spread it throughout the workers' daily lives.[60]

But it is not enough to rediscover the lost source of poetry; "working conditions must themselves favour its continued existence." This means eliminating all physical suffering "except that which the nature of the work makes unavoidable"; banishing all advertising, propaganda, and "anything designed to stimulate the desire for excess"; and excluding from work, as far as possible, not only the "arbitrary," but "all unnecessary authority" - from which it follows that "big is bad" wherever small is possible, and that "parts are better manufactured in a small workshop" than under a factory foreman.

Harm is done by every unnecessary command. The "worst outrage," however, is the violation of the workers' attention by Taylorism or intense heteronomous control, which "drains the soul of all save a preoccupation with speed." Since this mode of organization cannot be transformed it must be supplanted. "This is the most important standard to establish: the whole of society should be first constituted so that work does not demean those who perform it."61

In "Factory Work" (1941), she is ready to accept a certain monotony in work - a natural rhythm which is conducive to attention - but not the synthetic "cadence" which thoughtless mechanization and mismanagement produce. Otherwise her concerns resonate with those expressed in "Reflections" (which in 1943, the year of her death, she is still calling her "great work"). The factory ought to be a "place of joy," where, even though the work is arduous, "the soul can ... taste joy and nourish itself in it." To provide for this, technological choice must consider "the needs of the body and the needs of the soul." Stultifying tasks involving "repeated sequences of a small number of simple movements" should be performed by automatic machines. But these machines should be designed for flexible adaptation to many purposes, so that the worker, in regulating the machines and "contriving the cams appropriate to the various parts to be turned out," would participate in both "intellective" and "manual" activity.62   This accords with theories of workers' control of computerized technology being advanced in the 1980s.63

Just as important, work must be returned to a human dimension of time. "The future must be opened up for the workingman through removal of the blinders that keep him from exercising his sense of foresight," so that he has a sense of moving in time according to a plan, toward some goal. Each worker should be familiar with the function of the enterprise as a whole and the work organized in a way which permits "some kind of autonomy of each shop unit in relation to the whole" and "of each worker in relation to his shop."64

In a letter to Alain, her former professor, she writes that we must make "a thorough study of the instruments of labor, no longer from a technical point of view ... but from the point of view of their relation to the man and to human thought." Comments Pétrement: "She thought in fact that the liberation of the worker must be accomplished in the work itself, and that the work, in order to become that of a free man, must be pervaded by thought, invention, and judgment."65

And in the same notebooks in which the passage cited by Rosen occurs, she writes that "The secret of the human condition is that there is no equilibrium between man and the surrounding forces of nature, which infinitely exceed him when in inaction; there is only equilibrium in action by which man recreates his own life through work."66 Action, intellection, and spirit are so inextricably interwoven in Weil's theory that it may be a mistake to regard the changes in language and emphasis in some of her later writing as anything more than a circling of the object of her thought to illuminate the other side of what she had been calling to our attention all along.

Conclusion

There is a sense, of course, in which Grant is right. Even our estimates of technological depredations (the greenhouse effect, acid rain, ozone layer depletion) are technologically conceived. Technology tells us what "good" air and water would be like. Measurement against a standard is itself technique. And we may be farther from embracing a science of love than we are from being persuaded by the supernatural. But blind necessity seems to be driving us toward consent to a universe in which technological progress is at least in tension with reason.

Weil reminds us (as does Grant) of the consequences of our loss of the ancient sense of fittingness, of what we owe to our nature. And she points beyond this (as Grant does not) toward the single thing that we have gained which might lead us away from or mediate the technological conquest or destruction of that nature: the possibility of freedom within necessity, based on a relation of thought to action.

Notes

1. Edwin B. Heaven and David R. Heaven, "Some Influences of Simone Weil on George Grant's Silence," in *George Grant in Process: Essays and Conversations*, ed. Larry Schmidt (Toronto: Anansi, 1978), p. 68.

2. *Ibid.*, pp. 73, 71.

3. George Grant, "'The computer does not impose on us the ways it should be used'," in *Beyond Industrial Growth*, ed. Abraham Rotstein (Toronto: University of Toronto Press, 1976), p. 129.

4. Heaven and Heaven, p. 73. Cf. George Grant, "Tyranny and Wisdom," *Technology and Empire* (Toronto: Anansi, 1969), p. 109.

5. She would endorse most of what Strauss ascribes to classic natural right - the natural status of hierarchy, the primacy of order, individual excellence or virtue as the aim of political society, the superiority of good over pleasure, and the need for small political units - up to the point where a closed, coercive society is held to be necessary and just if man is to "reach the perfection of his nature." Cf. Leo Strauss, *Natural Right and History* (Chicago: University of Chicago Press, 1953), pp. 120-133, 132.

6. Grant, "Tyranny and Wisdom," pp. 104-105.

7. What strikes us, even after allowing for the innocence of prewar conventions of discourse and translation from an inflected language, as an exaggerated use of masculine signifiers, may be Weil's at least partly ironic literary response to the social vulnerability of women in a world dominated by force; her chosen pen name was Emile Novis. No attempt will be made to resist this. Cf. Simone Pétrement, *Simone Weil: A Life*, trans. Raymond Rosenthal (New York: Random House, 1976), pp. 27-29, 192-93.

8. *Oppression and Liberty*, trans. Arthur Wills and John Petrie (Amherst: University of Massachusetts Press, 1958), p. 159.

9. So that, although the contingencies of chance are theoretically determinable, the possibility of overcoming chance in the world is naturally limited.

10. *The Need for Roots: Prelude to a Declaration of Duties Toward Mankind*, trans. Arthur Wills (New York: Harper & Row, 1952), p. 291-92; *Two Moral Essays*, ed. Ronald Hathaway, trans. Richard Rees (Wallingford, PA: Pendle Hill, 1981), p. 5.

11. *Gravity and Grace*, trans. Emma Craufurd (London: Routledge and Kegan Paul, 1952), p. 129.

12. *Cahiers* (Paris: Plon, 1974), III, p. 39.

13. *Gravity and Grace*, pp. 17, 16.

14. *On Science, Necessity, and the Love of God*, trans. Richard Rees (Toronto: Oxford University Press, 1968), p. 131.

15. *Two Moral Essays*, pp. 31, 32; *On Science*, p. 198.

16. *On Science*, p. 178; *Roots*, p. 295.

17. *Roots*, p. 261; *On Science*, pp. 80, 79.

18. *Roots*, pp. 5-6; *Two Moral Essays*, p. 14.

19. "To believe that there are several distinct and mutually independent forms of good, like truth, beauty, and morality, that is what constitutes the sin of polytheism, and not just simply allowing the imagination to play with the notions of Apollo and Diana." *Roots*, p. 252.

20. Through which we experience one of the "most exquisite pleasures of human love - to serve the loved one without his knowing it." *First and Last Notebooks*, trans. Richard Rees (Toronto: Oxford University Press, 1970), p. 84.

21. *On Science*, pp. 153, 155; *Gravity and Grace*, p. 104; *Cahiers*, p. 39.

22. Grant, *Technology and Empire*, p. 133.

23. *Oppression and Liberty*, pp. 159, 173, 190.

24. *Ibid.*, pp. 159-60; *Roots*, p. 279; *Oppression and Liberty*, p. 160.

25. Weil's brother, the mathematician André Weil, says that "her idea on this specific point was totally mistaken and not worth discussing." Quoted in George Abbott White, "Introduction," Simone *Weil: Interpretations of a Life*, ed. George Abbott White (Amherst: University of Massachusetts Press, 1981), p. 8. Cf., however, Pétrement, p. 448; Simone Weil, *Seventy Letters*,

trans. Richard Rees (Toronto: Oxford University Press, 1965), pp. 112-27, 134-35; and "Reflections on Quantum Theory," *On Science*, pp. 48-64.

26. *On Science*, pp. 69-70.

27. *Seventy Letters* (note 25 above), pp. 116, 117, 118, 119-20, 115; Pétrement, p. 369; *Intimations of Christianity among the Ancient Greeks*, trans. Elisabeth Chase Geissbuhler (London: Routledge and Kegan Paul, 1957), pp. 164, 57-70, 95.

28. *On Science*, p. 79.

29. *Seventy Letters*, p. 125.

30. *Oppression and Liberty*, pp. 180, 181, 117.

31. *Ibid.*, p. 180; *Roots*, pp. 263, 264; *L'Enracinement* (Paris: Gallimard, 1949), p. 332; *Oppression and Liberty*, p. 119.

32. For a full account of Weil's theory of rights and obligation, see Edward Andrew, "Simone Weil on the Injustice of Rights-Based Doctrines," *Review of Politics*, Winter 1986, 60-91. Weil's argument appears in the first pages of *Need for Roots* and in her "Draft for a Statement of Human Obligations" and "Human Personality," in *Two Moral Essays*. Both essays appear also in Sian Miles, ed., *Simone Weil: An Anthology* (London: Virago, 1986).

33. *Roots*, p. 291.

34. *Two Moral Essays*, pp. 6, 7, 8, 9.

35. *Ibid.*, pp. 10-12; Andrew (note 32 above), p. 81.

36. *Roots*, p. 15.

37. *Seventy Letters*, p. 12; Pétrement, p. 64; *Notebooks*, p. 358; *Oppression and Liberty*, p. 106.

38. A "continuous and unlimited increase in productivity is, strictly speaking, inconceivable." Only "the frenzy produced by the speed of technical progress" has brought about "the mad idea that work might one day become unnecessary." *Oppression and Liberty*, p. 54.

39. *Oppression and Liberty*, pp. 84, 87, 154.

40. *Ibid.*, pp. 106-107. Cf. Bacon, *The New Organon*, ed. Fulton H. Anderson, trans. James Spedding, Robert Leslie Ellis, and Douglas Denon Heath (New York: Liberal Arts Press, 1960), Aphorism 129, p. 119.

41. Pétrement, p. 245; "Prospects" ["*Revolution Proletarienne*"], *Oppression and Liberty*, pp. 23.

42. *Oppression and Liberty*, pp. 69, 78, 83, 80, 84; *Gravity and Grace*, p. 154.

43. *Oppression and Liberty*, pp. 89, 90, 91, 95-96.

44. *Ibid.*, pp. 98, 99.

45. Largely by the workers, with researcher-consultants (who had already united mental and material labor within themselves) acting as catalysts, and with guarded support from centralized trade-union and employer organizations, which were ready to sacrifice a portion of control for increased productivity. See Bjorn Gustavsen and Gerry Hunnius, *New*

Patterns of Work Reform: The Case of Norway (Oslo: Universitetsforlaget, 1981); Ph. G. Herbst, *Alternatives to Hierarchies* (Leiden: Martinus Nijhoff, 1976). Also my *News from Somewhere* (Westport, CT: Greenwood Press, 1986), Part Three.

46. *Oppression and Liberty*, pp. 99, 105.
47. *Ibid.*, p. 100.
48. *Ibid.*, p. 101.
49. *Ibid.*, p, 103.
50. *Roots*, pp. 54-55.
51. *Ibid.*, pp. 57, 58.
52. *Ibid.*, p. 60.
53. *Ibid.*, pp. 60, 71.
54. *Ibid.*, p. 78; *Gravity and Grace*, p. 151. Cole would agree but insist she was opposing not (true) socialism but "collectivism"; see G. D. H. Cole, *Self-Government in Industry*, 5th ed. (London: G. Bell and Sons, 1920). For Marx see "The Civil War in France," in *The Marx-Engels Reader*, 2d ed., ed. Robert C. Tucker (New York: W. W. Norton, 1978), pp. 618-652; for the Spanish anarchists, Gaston Laval, *Collectives in the Spanish Revolution*, trans. Vernon Richards (London: Freedom Press, 1975). Also the discussion of these in my *News from Somewhere*, Parts One and Two.
55. *Gravity and Grace*, p. 140; *Oppression and Liberty*, pp. 22-23.
56. Fred Rosen, "Labour and Liberty: Simone Weil and the Human Condition," *Theoria to Theory*, 7, 4 (October 1973), 40.
57. *Gravity and Grace*, p. 158.
58. Rosen, p. 43; Richard Rees, *Simone Weil: A Sketch for a Portrait* (Carbondale, ILL: Southern Illinois University Press, 1966), p. 173.
59. "*Condition première d'un travail non servile,*" *La condition ouvrière* (Paris: Gallimard, 1951), pp. 357-58; Rosen, p. 45.
60. "Prerequisite to Dignity of Labour," in Miles (note 32 above), pp. 268, 269-70, 272.
61. *Ibid.*, pp. 274, 275-76.
62. "*Expérience de la vie d'usine,*" *La condition ouvrière*, pp. 337, 344; "Factory Work," in *The Simone Weil Reader*. ed. George A. Panichas (Mt. Kisco, NY: Moyer Bell, 1977), pp. 68-69.
63. See, for example, Harry C. Katz, *Shifting Gears: Changing Labor Relations in the U. S. Automobile Industry* (Cambridge: M.I.T. Press, 1985), pp. 134-37; Robert Howard, *Brave New Workplace* (New York: Viking, 1985), pp. 107, 198-213; Steven Deutsch, "New Technology, Union Strategies and Worker Participation," *Economic and Industrial Democracy*, 7, 4 (November 1986), 534-37.
64. "Factory Work," p. 70.
65. Pétrement, p. 240.
66. *Gravity and Grace*, p. 157.

GEORGE GRANT ON TECHNOLOGICAL IMPERATIVES

Edward Andrew

Philosophy, Technology and Democracy

George Grant has been called the only major philosopher accessible to a reading public.[1] Indeed, Grant's style of writing - the crystalline purity of his prose (polished by his wife, Sheila), the absence of "philosophic" jargon, of footnotes, pedantic scholarship and needless erudition - is exoteric, not esoteric. The clarity of his thoughtful prose is not merely the form of his political philosophy, but is a manifestation of its substance. For Grant, humans have a composite nature: they are political animals or beings destined to discuss the meaning or purpose of life in public forums; they are essentially contemplative beings, with the unique possibility of being open or receptive to Being (the totality of what is, in and above nature); they are above all beings fitted for love and charity, whose care for others limits otherwise limitless egoism or childish desire. For reasons we shall come to analyze, modern technological societies, according to Grant, do not provide nourishment for political, philosophic and caring beings. Politics has been supplanted by administration, philosophy by cybernetics, and charity by professional care. On behalf of his view of what human beings are, Grant, armed with his pen, tilts at dark satanic mills. Charity directs his pen to communication on the highest matters with his fellow citizens. Grant is not esteemed by "professional philosophers" for originality or creative breakthroughs but is justly admired by his wide readership as Canada's public philosopher.

Philosophy, like technology, has an ambiguous relationship to democracy. In calling Grant a public philosopher, I do not mean that he is a popular or people's philosopher in the sense of one who provides a world-view or an ideology for the Canadian people. Although Grant appeals to popular traditions and prejudices in his most partisan works, *Lament for a*

Nation and *Technology and Empire* (where he attacks the continental drift at the time of the Vietnam war), he provides no ready-made answers but provokes the thoughtless with thought-provoking questions. *Lament for a Nation* taught Grant's fellow Canadians that underlying the appearance of a scramble of the ins and outs to administer the consensual goal of an ever-expanding economy, partisan politics is about principles. However, Grant leaves his readers to decide whether the liberal principle of welcoming ever more expansive and homogeneous societies is more choiceworthy than the conservative principle of preserving natural and cultural differences. Only in his recent writings on abortion, genetic engineering, artificial reproduction and euthanasia does Grant, in conjunction with his wife, depart from the philosophic task of posing thoughtful questions. The technological assault on the sanctity of life provoked the Grants to make a firm practical stand on these matters and to replace theoretical inquiry with thoughtful and systematic doctrine.[2]

In referring to Grant as a public philosopher, I do not mean that he is an ideologist or one who systematizes popular beliefs. Nor do I mean that he is a popularizer of philosophy in the sense of one who distorts a philosophy in simplifying it for a mass audience. Grant's *Time as History* presented Heidegger's Nietzsche to the listeners of the Canadian Broadcasting Corporation with consummate clarity: the simplification necessary to make a difficult teaching accessible and relevant to his audience did not, in my view, bastardize Nietzsche but presented his philosophy with greater depth and precision than more opaque scholarly commentaries.   Grant is democratic in the sense that he believes that all humans can "have a philosophy" or entertain general ideas that give meaning to their lives, but he does not think many people can be philosophers or have the sustained attention to dwell on and with Being (as distinct from specific beings or classes of beings).

As Gad Horowitz has pointed out, the egalitarian dimensions in Grant's thought derive from his Christianity.[3] Not the capacity for philosophy (that only a few can realize) but the universal capacity for love is the highest, and definitive, quality of human beings. To be sure, Grant does not think the claims of philosophic reason and Christian love to be necessarily opposed. For Grant, the faith of philosophers (such as Plato and Simone Weil) is the faith of Christians, namely, that intelligence is illuminated, not blinded, by love. But universal love is prior to the particular gift for philosophy.

In his earlier writings, such as *Philosophy in the Mass Age* and "An Ethic of Community," written when he was a democratic socialist, Grant emphasized that we are all equal in terms of our moral choices. Although some are more clever than others, better at calculation, more skillful or technically adept, we are all equal with respect to what fundamentally matters, our ability to choose good rather than evil. Grant appeared to follow Kant and Hegel with their Protestant insistence on the rights of conscience, on our right to assent or dissent to the laws and conventions handed on to us. Will or choice, rather than reason, appeared, at this stage of Grant's intellectual voyage, to be that which is definitive of human beings.

At the same time, Grant strongly emphasized the liberating effects of modern technology. Technology is the harnessing of reason in the service of the human will to subdue nature in order to alleviate suffering from hunger, disease, overwork and conflict arising from scarcity. Reason is no longer to contemplate and interpret an unchanging order; reason is set to work to comprehend the laws of nature so that men can intervene and change nature to suit human purposes. The technological mastery of nature was an expression of (Protestant) Christian spirituality. Any depreciation of the "materialism" or "worldliness" of modern welfare states by those who have never experienced the poverty and other afflictions of premodern men and women is shallow and callous. For Grant, any real spirituality must attend to the material needs of the deprived. State-capitalist and socialist regimes are the mechanized and bureaucratized offspring of a genuinely spiritual impulse. Even after Leo Strauss helped to lead Grant back from Hegel to Plato, and to see the threat to liberty and plurality posed by technique, the technical control of human nature, the danger of ecological or nuclear disaster, the decline of nurturing traditions, the banality of education, the deprivation of purpose and meaning to an increasing number of modern men and women, Grant continued to emphasize the irreducible good of the modern technological project.[4]

Grant's rethinking the destiny of technological societies led him to de-emphasize choice or will as the essential feature of humans. The will, not graced by love, will gravitate towards evil. Secularized Protestantism, based on will or free choice, engenders a society where one can choose to abort a fetus at will, where one can purchase on the open market a surrogate mother or father as easily as one can purchase a gun, where one can choose to terminate one's life or that of others deficient in "quality of life," where choice or will triumphs over the natural (or unchosen) processes of life and death. Curiously, the Grants' opposition to eugenic engineering, abortion, and euthanasia is posed in the language of rights that presupposes the primacy of choice.[5] (Rights permit, while duties prescribe and laws proscribe. Rights secure choices or options; they do not direct us to what is choiceworthy. One who possesses rights has the option of exercising or waiving them.) Since the unborn and the severely handicapped are incapable of deciding to exercise or waive their rights, one might disagree with the Grants that fetuses and imbeciles have rights and, at the same time, agree with the Grants that we have duties to them, that the weak need legal protection, and that a society which does not care about the old and suicidal or infants with Downs' syndrome would be a hell on earth. Grant states that he employs the language of rights for strategic purposes - because a liberal language is the only one comprehensible to contemporaries - but he never indicates that the language of rights is as intimately bound up with the concept of the autonomous will as is the language of values, while he unceasingly points out the inextricable connection between the language of values and the concept of the autonomous will.

Grant repeatedly points out that Nietzsche was the creator of the language of values. The language of values is the necessary expression of the opposition between will and nature. There are no natural laws or moral facts; there is no natural order we can discover; everything of value is a construction of the subjective or autonomous will. The atheist Nietzsche unfolds what is contained in the philosophies of Kant and Hegel (parallel to the externalization of Protestant interiority into godless capitalism). Nietzsche is the philosopher of technological civilization *par excellence*.[6] Nietzsche champions the will to power, mastery of the earth, control of nature as an end in itself. This view is implicitly upheld by modern men who "make history," whose science aims at the control of chance and the conquest of internal and external nature. The earlier view of liberals and socialists was that technology was to serve human purposes; it was thought to be an instrument or means rather than an end in itself, a means to welfare, leisure and civic participation. However, Grant came to see in the Vietnam war, in genetic engineering and the psycho-social sciences, and in the technological control of life and death, that technological advance was imperial and irresistible. If a weapon or genetic advance is technically feasible, its production and deployment is imperative, whatever the cost to welfare or virtue. The Nietzschean will to power, or willing with no end beyond willing or mastery, is the fitting doctrine of our age; it is liberalism with its eyes open. The undemocratic Nietzsche best captures the spirit of our age.

To sum up: the inspiration of the technological conquest of the earth was, in a sense, democratic; technical mastery was "for the people" but not "by the people." The means to overcome natural scarcity and to provide abundance and leisure for all produced a hierarchy of specialists, competent in the sciences of control, whether in capitalist corporations or socialist bureaucracies. The masses, purportedly served by state-capitalist or socialist regimes, have to be adjusted to the goal of ever-expanding technical mastery by the proliferating disciplines of penology, sociology, psychology and genetics. Human beings come to be resources to be employed in our ever-expanding economy. The domination of nature requires the domination of those men who work on nature, and those elements in human nature that resist routinized work and pleasure, that rebel against standardized outlets for our instincts. As the means to human fulfillment - technique - becomes an end in itself, technological societies become dehumanizing; those who hold themselves to be superhuman debase themselves by lording it over those they consider subhuman (the weak, those with a low quality of life).

Grant's philosophy, after *Philosophy in the Mass Age* and "An Ethic of Community," is pessimistic about the possibilities of either decency or excellence in a technological civilization. Grant thinks Nietzsche and Heidegger, and secondarily Strauss and Ellul, have laid bare our civilization. Grant's criticism of technological societies seems to strike a note of lament or despair (leavened by his faith in an eternal order untouched by impending doom for the temporal order). However Grant's lament for the death of Canada must be considered in the light of his unflagging attempts to revivify the corpse of the Canadian body politic. His apparent certainty that no political or moral restraints can impede the development of technology must be assessed in conjunction with his commitment to pacifism and the right to life movements (which are precisely attempts to provide moral-political limits to technical mastery). Grant has thrown his soul into the gear wheels of the machine rather than contemplating the unstoppable mechanism at a respectable theoretical distance. Is this response a futile gesture or an enduring hope for a more humane technological society?

To answer this question, we must first consider in greater detail what Grant means by technology, why he thinks liberalism is the appropriate ideology to justify an expansive technological society, in what respects essential human possibilities are denied through the structures of modern society, and, finally, why he believes that alternative industrial, educational and political goals and methods of organization are impracticable in our epoch.

Technology, Liberalism and Illiberalism

By technique, Grant, following Jacques Ellul, means the systematic utilization of the most efficient methods of producing and distributing desired goods. Technique homogenizes the world; it prescribes the "one best way" of doing things; it establishes uniform standards, routines, procedures. Grant does not attend sufficiently to the positive side of standardization, to the possibility, for example, that McDonald's has raised the level of cuisine and nutrition for a large number of Canadians, and other beneficiaries of American knowhow. Nor, on a more lofty plane, does Grant consider the undeniable boon that jet-setting scholars can crawl to motel rooms, identical from Bangkok to Oslo, and find the toilet bowl, even if they lack the power to reach up to the familiarly placed light switches. Technique refers to the systematized, standardized, "mechanized" character of our deeds and works.

Grant prefers the North American "neologism," "technology," to the European word "technique."[7] Technology brings together *techne* and *logos*, our making and our knowing. This fusion of our practice and our thought in the word "technology" means, for Grant, that we are unable to do or make anything which is not prescribed by the imperatives of technological mastery, and we are unable to think about our doings other than through the categories prescribed by the technological project of opposing will and nature. The fact-value opposition, or the view that there are no natural facts that have a bearing on moral conduct, inheres in the Baconian-Cartesian antithesis of will and nature (subject versus object, man versus obstacles to satisfaction).

Liberal pluralism, according to Grant, is the fitting ideology of our technological age. The public world is a world of fact (systematized by research, business and military bureaucracies and coordinated cybernetically by public "administration" or "management") unassailable by mere values. The realm of values or personal choices is limited to that which does not obtrude on the public world. Grant writes:

> As for pluralism, differences in the technological state are able to exist only in private activities: how we eat; how we mate; how we practise ceremonies. Some like pizza, some like steaks; some like girls, some like boys; some like synagogues, some like the mass. But we all do it in churches, motels, restaurants indistinguishable from the Atlantic to the Pacific.[8]

The public world is a world of beings conceived as objects, staffed by laughless and lifeless actors and lesser *apparatchiks*; the private world is one of "hectic subjectivity," titillated and controlled by the entertainment and drug industry, and supported by sex therapists, psychologists and ethicists. "The vaunted freedom of the individual to choose becomes either the necessity of finding one's role in the public engineering or the necessity of retreating into the privacy of pleasure."[9] The fact-value distinction produces a "monism of technological values," a false pluralism that masks the uniformity, the structured and confined choices available in the factory, the supermarket, the home and the school.

The liberal state is purportedly neutral; it is an honest broker with no moral objectives of its own but responds to, and balances, the values or claims placed upon it by its subjects. The liberal state is a neutral instrument that provides a framework for the satisfaction of individual objectives, insofar as these may be fulfilled without fraud or coercion of others. The educational system of a liberal state is not supposed to direct youth to any moral or political objective; it is to provide factual information and technical competence to handle that information. The information includes a knowledge of other cultures so that we do not uncritically accept our own ways as the only or best way of living. "The mark of education is claimed to be scepticism about the highest human purposes, but in fact there is no scepticism in the public realm about what is important to do."[10] Underlying pluralism, there is technological monism; underlying skepticism, an uncritical certitude about the desirability of an expanding Gross National Product or increasing control over natural forces. Education serving a mass technological society provokes no thought about the meaning of life, engenders no reflection upon itself, no meditation, introspection, contemplation, dwelling on the question of life.   Anglo-Saxon liberal societies do not directly teach moral philosophy in the schools but, by means of the fact-value distinction, indirectly inculcate the dogmas of technological mastery or control, and bar serious questioning of any alternative to the "orgasm at home...napalm abroad"[11] and the iron cage of technological rationality in between.

Liberalism, as Grant understands it, is the doctrine that the human essence is freedom. Humans are free to make themselves as they will; no natural or supernatural restraints limit human history. Human nature is human history; our essence is not fixed by nature, or created by God, but is indeterminate, malleable, plastic. Humans do not suffer history but make it; human will is the definite attribute of man. Will is that which asserts itself vis-à-vis nature and human nature; it is self-overcoming, the conquest of the nature within as without.   Will is the personalization of soul and the mechanization of body. Body and soul become at the disposition of the will, or possessed by the moral-juridical person (the will dressed up for the market and the law courts). Liberalism then is, for Grant, the fitting doctrine of an expansive technological society because it denies that there are any given restraints to the imperial dynamic of technology. According to this view, man is not subject to any heteronomous (God-given or natural) rules; not a creature of a given moral order, man creates his values, his own moral order, by his autonomous (self-legislating) will. Man makes himself by his own free choices. Grant's conception of liberalism may well be dismissed as too sweeping in that many modern thinkers who hold themselves, and are held by others, to be conservatives or socialists base their thought on the proposition that the human essence is freedom.[12]

Conservatism and socialism are less successful ideologies for a technological society, according to Grant, because they cannot conceive of technology as an end in itself. Both conservatives and socialists maintain doctrines of virtue (excellence) or of good (happiness) that do not serve the goal of the technical mastery of (human) nature.[13]   On the contrary, conservatives and socialists believe that technique is a means to human excellence and happiness, and thus the means is to be limited by conservative or socialist goals that supersede pure mastery. While Grant favors limits to technological expansion, he thinks that both conservatives and socialists are naive if they think humans can easily invert the means-end relationship. Man, the minder of the machine and the servant of technology, cannot, through a sudden political transformation, become the master of technique. For the technological world is not "out there"; it has penetrated us without active resistance. We are technique.[14] Technology is no more "out there" than language or religion. Technology is our religion. The celebration of space probes provides us with meaning and a sense of belonging, as does our mourning for the "lucified" astronauts. Our hearts, minds, bodies - our persons - are as shaped by technology as the minerals composing our automobiles and the milk from our contented cows.

Liberalism is then unfettered by the socialist aspiration to subordinate economic life to the purpose of perfecting human nature or creating the new socialist man or woman or by the conservative aspiration of creating virtuous patriots and reverent men and women. Even the social-democratic aspiration of using technology for human welfare or to alleviate suffering conceives of technical mastery or power as a means not an end. Socialism restricts technological development to the extent that the introduction of new technology is conditional upon, or subject to, its function of developing virtuous socialist citizens. More efficient ways of producing and distributing goods do not necessarily produce more active citizens or even more technically competent producers. Moreover, scientific research would be severely hampered if a case for its beneficent technical application had to be demonstrated prior to its funding. Research and development would be severely restrained if socialists and conservatives were to live up to Grant's conception of their calling; namely, to subordinate technique to some good beyond technical mastery. Knowledge as power has become an end in itself. The view of man as freedom, will, power finds its consummation in a technological society with no limits, restraints or taboos to the control and mastery of natural processes.

Socialists and conservatives are distinct from liberals in that they postulate the primacy of social order over individual freedom.[15] Socialists may question their allegiance to the conservative priority of order to freedom but, Grant says, they have not sufficiently considered the effects of original sin. Greed is innate in all the unredeemed offspring of Adam and Eve.[16] The liberation of the passions, a product of the liberal primacy of freedom, liberated greed, acquisitiveness or "the spirit of capitalism." In practice, socialists, in suppressing capitalist acquisitiveness, have espoused the conservative principle of social order rather than the liberal idea of individual freedom. However, lacking access to conservative ideas of honor, piety, loyalty, and tradition, and with only a half-hearted love of country, socialists have had to rely more heavily on coercion to implement the conservative principle of social order.

Grant does not discuss authoritarian regimes in Latin America or Khomeinist Iran, which have used unconstitutional methods and extra-legal coercion but which would seem to conform more to Grant's model of conservatism than to liberalism or socialism. Grant's model of conservative statesmen are, firstly, Charles de Gaulle and, secondly, Réné Lévesque. Grant's conservatism is the antithesis of most of that which goes by the name today. American conservatives, who appeal to free enterprise and limited government, are merely old-fashioned or nineteenth-century liberals.[17] Genuine conservatives are willing to use the state to prevent the commercial dissolution of cherished customs, to initiate or coordinate industrial development like Otto von Bismarck and Charles de Gaulle, or to protect ways of living (economies and cultures) from the threat of more powerful economies and cultures, like the Canadian conservatives who used the government to establish an economic infrastructure, and a national system of transportation and communications. While Grant thinks the threat of centralized bureaucratic government is very real, he thinks it superficial, particularly for citizens of smaller states, to overlook the power of the multinational corporations, and the impersonality of corporate bureaucracies, in a one-sided attack on big government.

Grant, "the Red Tory," has often been accused of being too soft on communist (Russian) imperialism and too hard on capitalist (American) imperialism. Doubtless, if Grant were a Polish, Czech or Afghan conservative, he would think differently. But, like other prominent Canadian conservatives, such as Donald Creighton and William Morton, Grant thinks the American *imperium* a greater threat to the Canadian nation and conservative traditions than the Russian empire. Like the crusty reactionary, Donald Creighton, Grant has advocated that Canada withdraw from NATO and NORAD and has blessed the socialist form of economic nationalism proposed by the Waffle group within the NDP.[18]

The more general point is that, since conservatives and socialists are committed to some goal beyond technological mastery, American liberalism embodies the most progressive and dynamic force for the homogenizing of the world. Following Alexandre Kojève's reading of Hegel, Grant thinks that the end of history is the creation of a universal homogeneous state.[19] Like Leo Strauss, Grant thinks that a world state would be a monstrous tyranny, suppressing all natural, national, class and cultural differences, eliminating all differences of religion and tradition.[20] However, unlike Strauss, Grant thinks international capitalism, spearheaded by the Pentagon, to be a more effective agent of the end of history than international communism, controlled by the Kremlin.

Why Cannot Technology Be Used for Democratic Purposes?

Grant does not write very much about democracy. Clearly, he does not think democracy a bad thing, as does Nietzsche. However, Grant seems to share Nietzsche's view that most of the talk about democracy is shallow and spurious. Grant, unlike Nietzsche, has a strong allegiance to the rule of law and constitutional government but does not seem to think that universal suffrage is the only means to limit governmental power and even seems to adopt the Marxist position that elected representatives cannot check the combined power of the nonelected elites (the bankers, industrialists, civil service and military).

The monolithic control of state-capitalist societies is not to be understood as a conspiracy. Not only a powerful elite but also a large number of the electorate has a stake in an ever-expanding Gross National Product. If elected representatives were to pass laws (with respect to unionization, safety measures, environmental controls and the like) that made the country or region a less hospitable environment for capital investment, the multinational corporations would withdraw and reinvest in areas less finicky about human and natural resources. If more drastic measures, such as nationalization of foreign-owned natural resources or control over foreign exchange or money supply were attempted, the resulting shortage of foreign capital would probably engender sufficient domestic unrest that domestic elites, strengthened by international capital, would be able to topple the elected governments. (Counterexamples are Cuba and Nicaragua but neither country had a liberal past to compete with a socialist present. Moreover, the military pressure placed upon Cuba and Nicaragua has perpetuated a seige mentality; such garrison states are unlikely to become beacons of socialist democracy in the near future.) Thus stringent limits to political intervention in technological societies are set by the necessity (internalized by most people) of maximum capital accumulation. The engineering of consent, in bad times as well as in good, is more efficiently performed in capitalist societies than in communist societies, more because of the greater accessibility of consumer goods than because of the apparatus of legitimation (two parties, periodic elections, a commercial press and so forth).

If Grant has a semi-Marxist conception of "bourgeois democracy," he does not offer Marxist solutions of extending the elective principle to nonelected spheres of government and of submitting industry to public ownership and control. Even in his socialist period, Grant advocates, in "An Ethic of Community," that unionists should attempt to woo educated professionals to the cause of social democracy. The possibility that workers could run industry by themselves or select their own managers and political representatives does not seem to be entertained by Grant. Socialism, for Grant, must repress greed and self-assertion presumably because he thinks individuals can never be equal in power. Without the poor imbalance generated by division of owners and workers, the individual pursuit of power and wealth might complement, as much as compete with, the pursuits of one's fellows. Powerful self-assertion becomes domination only against the powerless. Grant, in denying the possibility of a libertarian socialism, appears to adhere to the law of oligarchy. Whether as a socialist or a conservative, he seems to call for a more humane and reverent aristocracy to replace inhumane and unrestrained capitalist or communist oligarchies.

Curiously, although Grant considers Simone Weil to be the greatest influence on his thinking,[21] he never entertains her profound and novel suggestions about how to transform the workplace, to construct machines that expand, not cripple, human faculties and to enlarge vocational education.   Unlike Grant, Weil provided concrete guidelines about the methods to promote workers' understanding of the role of their specific function in the wider industrial process, to endow meaning in work, and to facilitate workers' control over a mechanized working environment. Hegel dismissed Plato's detailed proposals in *Laws* as beneath the dignity of philosophy. Whether Grant's neglect of Weil's proposals for an altered industrial division of labor, which Gary Lewis investigates in this volume, is to be taken as Hegelian arrogance, an inability to share Weil's faith in the capacities of working people, or as an expression of complete pessimism about the possibility of humanizing a technological civilization is unclear.

In an important essay, "Thinking About Technology," Grant asserts that technology is not a set of instruments at the disposal of individuals, not like the tools purchased at a hardware store and stored in a handicraftsman's basement. Rather modern technology is somewhat like a package tour where we have chosen two weeks in Europe or China and, in doing so, have ceded to the tour company the disposition of every unforgiving minute on the tour.[22] We are an integral part of one of the package tours departing from our place of birth. Nor are we to see technology as a world of things (of material means of production, reproduction, communications, "defense," etc.) but as a world-view, present in our attitudes to things and other people, and embodied in an integrated system of procedures, language and purposes. We are used by technology in our use of it; our minds and bodies are attuned to, and exploited by, our systematic control of human and nonhuman nature. Technology is not neutral about the ends it serves: it prescribes our ends as well as it expands our means. The expanded methods to achieve our moral, epistemic or aesthetic goals limit, condition or shape our apprehension of what is good, true or beautiful.

Grant is sensitive to the changing language of a technological world. The age-old pursuit of knowledge has become research, as the love of truth has become professional competence in research. Research is an ongoing (endless, or without an end other than keeping on) activity that requires a fragmentation of what is to be known into ever-dissolving and reforming disciplines, an explosion of philosophy into specialized sciences that secure new frontiers of knowledge without embarking on the perilous journey home (to the place where the researcher's specialized discipline is differentiated from other specialized disciplines). Indeed, the home-coming (called philosophy) is actively discouraged in the modern multiversity. Grant cites Lord Rutherford as saying: "Don't let me catch anyone talking about the universe in my department."[23] The university has become a multiverse of ongoing research projects, staffed by technical experts in grantsmanship.

Research is objective knowledge, knowledge of things conceived (held at a distance) as objects. The subject-object split is given in technological research. The model of knowing is provided by modern physics. Nature (*physis*) is beheld as objects (or particles in motion) to which numbers can be applied. Our experience of nature as objective (or nonsubjective) is a mode of designating quantity rather than quality as real. Quantification rather than qualification, or homogeneity rather than heterogeneity, characterizes the world of the scientific researcher, whether she be a physicist, sociologist or classicist.

The world conceived as objects is a chaos to be controlled and changed, not a cosmos to be loved and trusted. Knowledge of those chance occurrences or random relationships constituting a world of objects (abstracted from the "subjectivity" of the scientific researcher) becomes the ability to control the world experienced as objects, an ability optimized in a "controlled" or laboratory environment. The human or nonhuman guinea pigs, subjected to scientific apprehension as objects, are not loved for what they are, or trusted to be good enough as they are, or desired to remain as they are. Objectives exist for the purpose of control, not because the research scientist is a Machiavellian manipulator or a Hollywood Baron Frankenstein. The "subjectless" cognition of objects is subjected to the general objective of science, not the particular subjectivity of the scientist. The technological world is not neutral but aims at the total control of human and nonhuman nature (conceived as the raw material for the integrated procedures and processes of scientific technique). Technique is not the application of science, for pure and applied science are not separate activities. Not only does pure science depend upon the latest technology for methods of observation and experimentation but also, and more fundamentally, pure science dismisses as "subjective" any objective other than the control of "objective" processes, any apprehension of the world other than of quantifiable objects.

As "subjects" exist in inextricable relationships to "objects," so "values" are necessarily related to "fact." As "subjectivity" is submerged in "subjectless" scientific cognition to re-emerge as the generalized subjectivity of scientific experience, so "values" are denied cognitive status in a technological world only to return as the consumer preferences required by expanding technology (or the public value on which all private values depend). Values are precisely the "goods" of the technological world, not heteronomous goods desired by human creatures but those produced by human creativity, by autonomous human will. (Will stands in the same relation to desire or passion, as scientific control stands to philosophic love.) Grant shows how the values created by autonomous human willing seem as standardized and "ready-made" as anything produced by automatic machinery, as adaptable to, and integrated in, our system as any other components of our technological world. Thus to criticize our age in terms of the language of values - "Nuclear energy must be subordinated to humane values" or "Existing reproductive technology displays the dominance of male values" - is to assess it in technological terms or within the conceptual horizons of a technological world. To employ the language of values is to assert that the problems created by technology are to be resolved by technology.

Grant examines our technological destiny by means of an examination of the proposition that the computer is a neutral instrument or that it "does not impose upon us the ways it should be used." Grant points out that computers did not drop from the sky, but arose from determinate ways of knowing, producing and communicating. "Their existence has required generations of sustained effort by chemists, metallurgists and workers in mines and factories."[24] This systematic productive effort was called into being by the necessity of integrating ever-expanding productive and consumer requirements. Cybernetics presupposes the epistemological foundation of mathematical physics, which, wedded to the fecund science of economics, fathered our homogenizing world. Grant writes:

> To take a simple example from the modern institutions of learning and training: in most jurisdictions there are cards on which children are assessed as to their "skills" and "behavior," and this information is retained by computers. It may be granted that such information adds little to the homogenising vision inculcated throughout society by such means as centrally controlled curricula or teacher training. It may also be granted that as computers and their programming become more sophisticated the information stored therein may be able to take account of differences. Nevertheless, it is clear that the ways that computers can be used for storing and transmitting information can only be ways that increase the tempo of the homogenising processes. Abstracting facts so that they can be stored as information is achieved by classification, and it is the very nature of any classifying to homogenise. *Where classification rules, identities and differences can appear only in its terms. Indeed the word "information" is itself perfectly attuned to the account of knowledge which is homogenising.* "Information" is about objects, and comes forth as part of that science which summons objects to give us their reasons.[25]

Moreover, Grant asserts, computers can only be built for large corporate institutions, multiversities, corporations run for profit or for state service, for civilian or military purposes. To state the obvious, computers have less place in local farmers' markets than in modern supermarkets, less place in guerrilla armies than in highly mechanized armies, less place in scattered pockets of resistance to government than in the forces of centralized control, less place in a village church or neighborhood synagogue than in a nationally televised evangelical corporation, less place in a traditional than a yuppie household, less place in a fishermen's or artisans' cooperative than Chrysler or Lada automobile plants. "In this sense computers are not neutral instruments, but instruments which exclude certain forms of community and permit others."26

One might even go farther than Grant and say that no genuine community - that is, an association bound by feeling and communication, not by external management and one-way transmissions - is possible in any corporation dependent upon a computer. Just as all the skill and variety has to be eliminated from manual work before manual labor can be replaced by automatic machinery, so thinking must be reduced to responsive calculating (or the functions of the white-collar lackeys of the chief executives) before the computer can replace mental labor. A hierarchy of command, or a division of labor between thinking and doing, is the precondition of the automatization of production and calculation.

Humane forms of socialism and conservatism are bound to fail in that modern societies must commit themselves to dynamic technology in order to survive. Social-democratic Quebec nationalism was caught in the dilemma of having to eliminate everything (but language) that kept Quebec unique in North America - the public status of the Church, family-centeredness, classical education - in order to avoid being engulfed by imperial technology. Grant writes:

> the most brilliant conservative of our era has only been able to preserve what he loves (the power and culture of France) by gaining support for nationalism from the most advanced technocrats. De Gaulle has had immediate success, but in the long run he will have helped to build a Europe in which the peculiarities of France cannot hope to exist.27

Do the above reflections constitute a black night of despair in which all technological societies, whether communist, social-democratic or capitalist, are alike? Do electoral processes and constitutional forms not differentiate substantially technologically advanced countries? Would North America remain substantially the same if, for example, feminist and ecological movements were wiped out or were to increase in strength? Does Grant's diagnosis of technological society constitute a counsel of despair, an advocacy of the vanity of worldly aspirations, a throwing up one's hands before the advance of technology?

In my opinion, Grant does not think technological societies unalterable or that technology cannot be subordinated to moral-political purposes. The appearance in Grant's writings of irresistible technological imperialism serves, I think, to impress upon North Americans the gravity of the issue. Technology is not simply a problem soluble to a problem-solving mentality. North Americans, Grant says, lack a tradition of reflection, contemplation, introspection, or a receptive dwelling on earth.[28] We would rather take the broad highway of progressing through the world than the narrow mountain paths of seeing it: we are practical rather than theoretical; we want to get on with the easier task of changing our environment by practical-technical means rather than sink into ourselves, find out who we are and what is really worth doing; we instinctively flee the difficult task of ordering our souls. Technology is the entropic flow of energy from the "inner" to the "outer."

However, transformative practice may flow from charity or philosophy, as well as from inner impoverishment or spiritual fear. Grant, while failing to provide concrete proposals for humanizing our technological age as Simone Weil did, shared her view that a socio-political order rests on a moral order that is not of man's making. Grant then is not saying that a technological world cannot be changed but that substantive change must begin with a recognition of an unchanging order, which changes us in that recognition. The fundamental insight that Grant commends to his readers is that we are not our own and thus are not morally free to alter the world to suit our convenience. Neither our lives, nor those of others, are our property to be disposed of at will. As creatures, not self-created, as instruments of supernatural love and divine reason, we shall become more effective guardians of life, of what is unique and irreplaceable in all human life, and will be able to actualize the human potential for politics, philosophy and love.

Perhaps it is not given to carnivores to ruminate. The resolute few in professional or executive positions, who find meaning from their careers or positions of command, would do well to reject decisively Grant's ruminations. For the rest of us, who depend upon "canned" entertainments and distractions to supplement the competitive pursuit of income, status and sex-objects, the product of Grant's ruminations appears more refreshing than Carnation's milk from contented cows, or canned tiger's milk for contented cows.

Notes

1. J.E. O'Donovan, *George Grant and the Twilight of Justice* (Toronto: University of Toronto Press, 1984), p. 3.
2. See G.P. Grant, "The Language of Euthanasia" and "Abortion and Rights," in *Technology and Justice* (Toronto: House of Anansi, 1987).
3. The ideas program on the Canadian Broadcasting Corporation, February 3, 1986, published as *The Moving Image of Eternity* (Montreal: CBC Transcripts, 1986), pp. 14-15.
4. G.P. Grant, *Lament for a Nation* (Toronto, McClelland and Stewart, 1965), p. 94; *Technology and Empire* (Toronto: House of Anansi, 1969); *Technology and Justice*, p. 15.
5. G.P. Grant, *English-Speaking Justice* (Sackville, N.B.: Mount Allison University, 1974), part 4; *Technology and Justice*, pp. 103-30. In *George Grant in Process: Essays and Conversations*, ed. L. Schmidt (Toronto: House of Anansi, 1978), p. 18, Grant says his use of the language of rights is "strategic," that is, designed to appeal to the contemporary idiom.
6. G.P. Grant, *Time as History* (Toronto: Canadian Broadcasting Corporation, 1969); *Technology and Justice*, pp. 93-5; *English-Speaking Justice*, pp. 82-90.
7. Grant, *English-Speaking Justice*, pp. 1, 78; *Technology and Justice*, p. 12.
8. Grant, *Technology and Empire*, p. 26.
9. Grant, *Lament for a Nation*, p. 57.
10. Grant, *Technology and Empire*, p. 129.
11. *Ibid.*, p. 126.
12. Michael Oakeshott, Hannah Arendt, Jean-Paul Sartre, Maurice Merleau-Ponty and Jürgen Habermas would all be liberals, by Grant's sweeping definition.
13. Grant, *Lament for a Nation*, pp. 56, 69-72, 75-7.
14. Grant, *Technology and Empire*, p. 138.
15. Grant, *Lament for a Nation*, p. 59.
16. *Ibid*; "An Ethic of Community," in *Social Purpose for Canada*, ed. M. Oliver (Toronto: University of Toronto Press, 1961), p. 26.
17. Grant, *Lament for a Nation*, p. 64
18. The affinity of Grant's and Creighton's ideas can perhaps best be seen in D.G. Creighton, *Towards the Discovery of Canada* (Toronto: MacMillan, 1972) where the influence of Grant is clear. I have called Creighton, but not Grant, a reactionary in that Grant's conservatism is not tinged with Creighton's anti-Semitism and phobic reaction to French-Canadian nationalism.
19. Grant, *Technology and Empire*, pp. 81-109.
20. *Ibid.*

21. E.B. Heaven and D.R. Heaven, "Some Influences of Simone Weil on George Grant's Silence," in *George Grant in Process: Essays and Conversations*, ed. L. Schmidt, pp. 68-78.

22. Grant, *Technology and Justice*, p. 32.

23. *Ibid.*, p. 35.

24. *Ibid.*, p. 21.

25. *Ibid.*, p. 23 (emphasis added).

26. *Ibid.*, p. 26.

27. Grant, *Lament for a Nation*, p. 67.

28. Grant, *Technology and Empire*, p. 34.

ACTION INTO NATURE:
HANNAH ARENDT'S REFLECTIONS
ON TECHNOLOGY

Barry Cooper

It is part of Hannah Arendt's rhetorical style to declare one or another topic to be superlatively important. Considering the number of crises in the modern world about which she has written, this is perhaps not surprising. What Arendt has said directly about technology does not lend itself to a summary presentation. The overall context within which her reflections may be understood is indicated by arguments developed in *The Human Condition* regarding modern worldlessness. The loss of a sense of worldliness is identical with a sense that all things are in movement, that all is process and change. The perplexing aspect of modern change is that it is not understood as taking place within a stable framework. We cannot step into the same river twice because we, unlike Heraclitus, are convinced that both the river *and men* change. It is as if we were travellers through a landscape that is altered as a landscape by the fact of our passage.

The Prologue to *The Human Condition* began with a comment upon our first little travelling companion, Sputnik. "This event, second in importance to no other, not even to the splitting of the atom" was greeted with a "strange statement" and an "extraordinary line," namely that the earth was a place to escape from, that it was a place where humans were bound, a house of bondage. Heretofore such sentiments belonged to science fiction; now they were commonplace. Using an older language, she asked: "Should the emancipation and secularization of the modern age, which began with a turning-away, not necessarily from God, but from a god who was the Father of men in heaven, end with an even more fateful repudiation of an Earth who was the Mother of all living creatures under the sky?"[1] The earth is the "very quintessence" of the human condition because it provides a habitat where humans can move and breathe without effort and without artifice. True, the artifice of the world is what distinguishes men from other living things, but the fact remains that life, human and non-human alike, is freely at home on earth.

Moreover, our repudiation of the earth as a habitat for life has been accompanied by a rebellion against life as it has been given to us. Instead of accepting the naturalness of life, a gift, secularly speaking, from nowhere, we have been working hard to exchange it for one we have made. Like Nietzsche's superman we seem to be trying to extend grace to ourselves. Arendt did not doubt that the appropriate technologies to fabricate life or extend it beyond the span of three score and ten would be developed soon enough; and indeed, twenty-five years after her book was published recombinant-DNA technologies flourish. What these new technologies mean, she said, is that man has begun "a rebellion against the very factuality of the human condition."[2] This rebellion, moreover, is not an imaginative *Sturm und Drang*, a metaphorical storming the heavens, but an active reality, or a real activity. This is significant, as Sputnik was significant, because, Arendt tirelessly insisted, events not ideas change the world.

The most immediate and pressing aspect of the question concerning technology, however, deals with atomic weapons, devices that have changed the meaning of war from victory to deterrence and thereby have altered the traditional military virtues of courage and obedience. Considered theoretically, the most significant characteristic about nuclear weapons is not that they are very destructive but that the explosive force is carried out by physical processes that do not occur naturally on earth but on the sun, even though we measure the strength of the devices in terms of the explosive force of TNT. Indeed, the processes of some of our newer weapons apparently occur only in outer space.

The first thing to bear in mind about technology, then, is that "the release of natural forces is more characteristic of recent developments in technology than the constant improvement of methods of production."[3] Arendt had in mind chiefly the natural forces associated with nuclear physics. As late as 1969 she remarked that the ability to release such forces decisively shifted the emphasis of technology from production to destruction.[4] The implications of releasing biological processes are perhaps even more puzzling.

The ultimate pragmatic consequences of technology are still unknown. The more immediate ones have made themselves known "in a crisis within the natural sciences themselves."[5] This crisis is twofold. First, the truths of modern science can be proved only by technical activity. Second, they can be demonstrated only by mathematics and not by "normal expression in speech and thought." Arendt's immediate concern was with the second problem. She attributed the paradoxical "speech" concerning subatomic physics, for example, to our ability to act as if we were dwellers in the universe. Arendt assumed reasonably enough that normal expression in speech and thought reflected the very quintessence of the human condition, that we dwell upon the earth where the sun rises and sets. If nevertheless we act as if we were not at home on the earth but "in" the universe, the speech we use to articulate that experience is, by normal standards, nonsense. Or, to be more precise, it is meaningless. The reason for formulating the topic this way is that when we adopt the imaginative position of an observer freely poised in space, then all human activities appear as external behavior, all historical and technical changes appear as large-scale biological metamorphoses. From such a perspective, Werner Heisenberg once said, the development of the automobile appears as if humans grew metallic exoskeletons.

From this perspective, speech and everyday language would indeed no longer be meaningful. Mathematical signs would in fact do the job much better.[6] What science and technology have done, to speak most broadly, has been to force open the ground of appearance "so that man, a creature fitted for appearances, can catch hold of it. But the results have been rather perplexing. No man, it has turned out, can live among 'causes' or give full account in normal human language of a Being whose truth can be scientifically demonstrated in the laboratory and tested practically in the real world through technology."[7] If this is so, it would seem that we "will forever be unable to understand, that is, to think and speak about things which nevertheless we are able to do."[8] What we might expect is that computers monitor our behavior. But monitoring is no more thought than knowhow is knowledge. An alternative formulation of the problem could be restated as follows: if knowledge and thought have parted company for good, "then we would indeed become the helpless slaves, not so much of our machines as of our know-how, thoughtless creatures at the mercy of every gadget which is technically possible, no matter how murderous it is."[9] This understanding of technology, I submit, is essentially that of Jacques Ellul, one of the few men who have thought through what technology means.

The presentation of this typical Arendtian thought-train is taken from about a page and a half of *The Human Condition*. In a short and somewhat speculative piece such as this, we cannot critically differentiate the terms central to her analysis. What has been gained so far may be summarized as follows: whether viewed as was done by Ellul or, for that matter, by Heidegger, and whatever its final consequences, technology remains a political question of the first order.

Technology is political not simply because, as many say, it may be "used" for different purposes, which is a pious hope that is in no way self-evident, but because speech is involved. "Wherever the relevance of speech is at stake, matters become political by definition, for speech is what makes man a political being."[10] Accordingly, if we adjust our speech and "culture" to the achievements of technology, it will become meaningless. Mathematical "speech," which initially was developed as an abbreviation for spoken statements, now contains statements that cannot be "translated" back into speech. The political problem involved is akin to that faced by St. Paul when dealing with glossolalia: there may be truths beyond ordinary speech and they may be highly significant to individual men, but they are utterly irrelevant to men as political beings. That is why, if holy gibberish cannot be interpreted into ordinary speech, the community can ignore it (I *Cor.* 14). In Arendt's words, "men in the plural, that is, men in so far as they live and move and act in this world, can experience meaningfulness only because they can talk with and make sense to each other and to themselves."[11] For that reason, and not because of their character or naivete, the political judgment of technicians cannot be trusted. To be blunt: we cannot trust their political judgment because they do not talk sense. They do not talk sense because they cannot; they cannot because they cannot understand what they do.

An equally decisive and perhaps threatening event is the advent of automation. Technology again has been central in modifying "a fundamental aspect of the human condition,"[12] namely the toil and trouble of labor. Freedom from labor, which automation may provide for the many, has previously been accorded only the few. It might appear that all that automation promises is to achieve for all what, in the past, was the privilege of a small minority. The problem, however, is that in the past labor was despised as meaningless, whereas "the modern age has carried with it a theoretical glorification of labor" the factual result of which is that the whole society, both the many and the few, however they are distinguished, has been transformed into a laboring society, or rather, a society of jobholders. Accordingly, if a laboring society is freed from the toil and trouble of labor by technology, and, lacking members who know of more meaningful activities than labor, "surely nothing could be worse."[13] Factually, a laboring society freed from labor's toil and lacking anything more meaningful than a job to do (whether that job be king or plumber or cop on the beat), has largely relied on technology to fill up the empty time when one is not actually on the job. Arendt's question again was: What does this mean?

The Human Condition did not provide an answer to the questions of technology since such "answers" would be the very substance of practical politics and matters of agreement for the many. Her task, she said, was to reconsider the human condition in light of recent experiences. "This, obviously, is a matter of thought, and thoughtlessness ... seems to me among the outstanding characteristics of our time. What I propose, therefore, is very simple: it is nothing more than to think what we are doing." What we are doing, our activities, are within the capacities of all men alive or dead or yet unborn. For this reason Arendt called them "the most elementary articulations of the human condition."[14] Thinking, in contrast, is able to transcend the conditions of human existence, but only mentally, never in the reality of the existing world or, for that matter, in cognition and knowledge by which human beings are able to explore the real world and their own reality as well.15

The reality to which the word "world" referred was the experience of a space of appearance that separates and relates men as a dining table separates and relates those seated around it. Maintaining the distinction between public and private is essential to the maintenance of the world. Politically speaking, the two are connected and distinguished by law. Law establishes boundaries and limits and thereby provides a measure of stability to a regime. Indeed, Arendt has said that the political spirit of modernity is to found a political world that would last.16 But by this token, a great deal of the modern spirit is worldless and antipolitical. Historically, the change can be described "in its most tragic aspect as the slow but steady transformation of the *citoyen* of the French Revolution into the *bourgeois* of the pre-war period."17 Precisely because the nineteenth-century bourgeois was neither ready nor willing to assume responsibility for public affairs, political issues decomposed "into their dazzling, fascinating reflections in society."18 For the bourgeoisie, the consequence was that eventually they "were turned into mere beasts who could be used for anything before being led to the slaughter."19 Technological societies in the west have not turned into criminal regimes. Nevertheless, there still exist difficulties in maintaining the boundaries of the world.

The main characteristic of the world with respect to the individuals who share it is that it is more permanent than they. "There is an intrinsic conflict between the interests of individual mortals and the interest of the common world which they inhabit, and the source of this conflict lies in the overwhelming urgency of individual interests." One's self-interests always seem more urgent than the common good for the simple reason that "such urgency protects that which is most private, the interests of the life process itself."20 A modest amount of persecution is all it takes to ensure that individuals will be incapable of forming a public space. Persecution puts pressure on individuals and constricts the inner space of their world. It produces a warm glow in the dark, heat from huddled bodies, but no light by which to see and care for the world. It even produces a natural compassion in outsiders, but "the humanity of the insulted and injured has never yet survived the hour of liberation by so much as a minute." The significance of this fact is that it makes insult and injury endurable; by the same token, politically speaking, "it is absolutely irrelevant."21 Politics, the public realm, the world, become distorted when used as a theater for spiritual or psychological activities. And correspondingly, "the souls of men are strangely transformed when politics is converted into an inner experience and the reality of public affairs into private emotion."22 Let loose on the world, compassion devours every structure. Social revolutionaries beginning with Robespierre have demonstrated the fact time and again.

Modern technological societies are not threatened by outbursts of revolutionary compassion. Nor are great economic sacrifices and corresponding acts of courage required to liberate citizens from the care for mere life.[23] Rather, the boundary between public and private, and thereby the world, is challenged in a different way by a lack of privacy. "The primary condition of privacy is ownership, which is not the same as property."[24] Neither capitalist nor socialist economies respect ownership, though both respect the fundamental Machiavellian activity of acquisition. Not just poverty, persecution, and misery pose a threat to the world. An affluent society without ownership does as well.

Antique and medieval Latin sometimes rendered Aristotle's *zoon politikon* as *animal socialis*. Modern social reality, which is neither public nor private, strictly speaking, added greatly to the linguistic difficulties we have in sorting out various meanings and in describing the historical realities to which they refer. What for Aristotle was a clear and obvious distinction in reality is for us a question of great conceptual subtlety. Many of Arendt's critics consider her distinction between public and private to be wholly arbitrary. Ernest Barker once remarked that, for Aristotle, "political economy" was a contradiction in terms; for us, that term best describes the scientific discourse involved. What we call society is "the collective of families economically organized into the facsimile of one super-family" whose "political form of organization is called 'nation'."[25] Society, one might say, is housekeeping carried on in public. As was the ancient *oikia*, it is ordered by the sting of necessity.

That it corrodes political life is indicated by the commonplace observation that, whatever else it might be, the *tableau vivant* of conspicuous consumption is not politics. On the contrary, "economic growth may one day turn out to be a curse rather than a good, and under no conditions can it either lead into freedom or constitute a proof for its existence."[26] This is not to say that affluence is, by itself, a political evil, which would be absurd, but that the activities necessary for life in an affluent society may undermine the continued existence of freedom.

The most obvious danger is mass conformity. In the *polis*, one-man rule was the organizational device of the household; in early modern society, one-man rule was repeated, this time on the grander scale of the "national family." In both instances, the opinion of a single man governed all, and so, in a way, there existed a kind of unanimity. North-American societies, because they are immigrant societies, could not possibly be national societies in the European mode. This has meant that social conformity is not based on nationality, not that it does not exist.

One reason why conformity is a danger is that, in the end, it destroys the world. In order for there to be a world, things and individuals appear in a variety of ways without changing their identity. Sameness appears in diversity. The common world can be destroyed, then, either by dissolving it into sheer diversity or by congealing it into sameness. Politically speaking, dissolution into diversity is the objective of tyranny, a regime where no one can agree with anyone else because they have nothing in common, trusting neither the world nor one another. But the public world may equally be destroyed if sameness no longer appears in several aspects. If everyone prolongs and reinforces the view of everyone else, the result is a singular experience innumerably multiplied, not plurality. Without a world to separate and relate them, men are turned into members of a "lonely crowd" (Riesman) or they are compounded into the intensified isolation of a huddled mass. These are equivalent social forms inasmuch as neither contains a public or private space. Accordingly, no exchange of views is possible; the world is invariably degraded. Moreover, with the application of the appropriate techniques of propaganda, the two forms of lonely crowd and huddled mass can be easily changed into one another.

Early modern societies may be conceived as national housekeeping under the supervision of one man, the monarch; late modern societies, in contrast, are supervised by nobody. This "no-man rule," the rule of interconnected bureaux, is the contrary to no-rule. In a fully developed bureaucracy there is no one with whom one can argue or dispute, no one upon whom the pressures of power can be exerted. Rules are rules, period. It is, Arendt said, "a tyranny without a tyrant,"[27] the chief drawback of which is that it is a form of tyranny for which the desperate remedy of tyrannicide is necessarily excluded. Any particular bureaucrat is simply a functionary. Functionaries function, they do not act and so are in no respect irreplaceable. Just the opposite: the whole purpose of functional organization is that anyone, good or bad, stupid or intelligent, could make it go.

So far as opinion is concerned, the same assumption applies to bureaucracy as applied in the ancient household or to national monarchy: society has a single opinion and a single interest. This opinion is expressed by being processed through the correct channels; the corresponding interest is guarded, fostered, and implemented by administrative decisions, which are invariably rendered in the imperative mood. Action is completely excluded from bureaucratically regulated society, just as it was excluded from the ancient household. Instead of action, society expects normal behavior, behavior that conforms to the rules, whatever they may be. In the early days of "high" society, behavior was regulated by rules that reflected social rank; in the bourgeois society of the last century behavior conformed to class expectations; in today's mass society behavior reflects job and function. Society is greatly aided in its search for smooth functioning by the transformation of political parties from representative bodies that enabled citizens to participate in political life into bureaucracies representing nobody except the members of the party machines that staff them.[28] Even those who do not behave, delinquents, for example, perform a function: they keep the police and social workers busy and so, in a sense, they do behave. The absence of action, one hardly needs add, means an end to excellence as well.

The normal social self is a being whose behavior is predictable. That is, it conforms to expected patterns and regular statistical frequency-distributions. Now statistical laws are valid only for large numbers of items and long periods of time. Meaning, however, is disclosed only in those rare events and acts that light up, usually quite briefly, our everyday, normal existence. The statistical analysis of politics, therefore, obliterates its own subject matter by turning rare and significant events into error variance. The ridiculousness of the behavioral persuasion in politics has a grimmer side. "Statistical uniformity is by no means a harmless scientific ideal; it is the no longer secret political ideal of a society which, entirely submerged in the routine of everyday living, is at peace with the scientific outlook inherent in its very existence."[29] An anonymous and uniform society is the perfection of administrative striving.

Though it might have horrified him, Marx's old dream, that the governance of man be replaced with the administration of things, has partially been realized in modern technological job-holding society. Moreover, "the constant increase in leisure for the masses is a fact in all industrialized countries."[30] But it is also true that modern free time is not the Greek *skole*, which also had the form of an active verb meaning "to do leisure" or "to leisure," a notion that is nearly unimaginable in modern languages. Modern "leisure" is just left-over time, vacant time, time available after the job is done, the meals are down and you have had enough sleep.

Society is concerned with public housekeeping, and housekeeping with the affairs of biological life. Life, by a kind of internal drive, has an irresistible tendency to grow and multiply. With the admission of house-keeping activities to the public realm, society has likewise grown, devouring first the older realms of public and private, initially by eroding the border, the difference, between them. More recently, the sphere of intimacy has also been invaded by society. Any bookstore, for example, is filled with technical manuals on self-manipulation, the object of which is to adjust the manipulee, the "heart," to the social norms of the day. Society, the public domain of the life process, apparently has an irresistible tendency to be fruitful and multiply, like life itself.

The expansion of society in advanced technological societies is simply an intense and concentrated form of an ecumenic phenomenon. Mankind, which used to be a symbol of humanist aspirations, has become "an urgent reality"[31] owing to the technological development of the Western world. Europe and North America did not simply unite the world through technical cleverness, they exported at the same time the processes of their own internal disintegration.

The danger inherent in the new reality of mankind, an ecumenic society based on technologies of administration, communication, and violence, is that it "destroys all national traditions and buries the authentic origins of all human existence."[32] Even if it were true that these transformations are necessary for the mutual understanding of all men, an oft-voiced justification that seems unlikely in the extreme, the result would also be "a shallowness that would transform man, as we have known him in five thousand years of recorded history, beyond recognition. It would be more than mere superficiality; it would be as though the whole dimension of depth, without which human thought, even on the mere level of technical invention, would simply disappear."[33] Such an outcome, the global affluent society, would have the effect of transforming all the historical pasts of all nations, tribes, and hordes, in their vast disparity, diversity, variety and bewildering strangeness for one another, into temporary obstacles to a unity at the lowest common denominator. How low, how common, is difficult to imagine. We may suggest some of the dimensions of the question concerning technology with a few brief remarks on Arendt's famous triad, labor, work, and action. Her discussion of the series of "reversals" of the relationship of labor, work and action may be read as an account of the internal disintegration to which we have just adverted.

Earlier we quoted Arendt to the effect that it was hard to conceive of anything worse than a society of laborers that had virtually no labor to perform. The reason for this remark seems plain enough: the triumph of the modern age over necessity and the apparently eternal curse of toil, hardship and poverty was achieved by the emancipation of labor, "as though we had forced open the distinguishing boundaries which protected the world, the human artifice, from nature, the biological process that goes on in its very midst as well as the natural cyclical processes which surround it, delivering and abandoning to them the always threatened stability of the human world."[34] On his own, *animal laborans* knows only the life processes, the endless cycle of exhaustion and regeneration, the pain of toil followed by the pleasure of relief. It seems, moreover, that a life of pleasure without the experience of painful effort is boring. A laboring society that has reduced to the vanishing point the experiences of pain and effort has thereby also reduced what had served to compensate pain, namely pleasure. The widespread, if not universal, unhappiness of modern society can in part at least be traced to the joyless quest for joy that seems inevitably to be a consequence of the emancipation of labor from necessity.

The activity of work fabricates the things of the world, the totality of which constitutes the human artifice. Using things the way they were intended does not cause them to disappear, though the durability of things is not absolute: use uses up. Even so, destruction of use-objects is incidental to use, but inherent in consumption. The increase in durability, particularly of the highest products of *homo faber*, gives the latter a greater dignity than *animal laborans*.

Considered from the perspective of the world, beauty is connected to durability. Without the power of endurance, things cannot be beautiful or ugly. But by appearing as beautiful or ugly, things thereby transcend their sheer usefulness. A thing is never judged simply in terms of its utility but also in terms of its adequacy or inadequacy to what it should look like, to how closely it conforms to the image or idea that is visible to the inner eye and that preceded the genesis of the thing and survives its degeneration. In general the human artifice becomes a home for mortal men only because it transcends the functionalism of things produced for consumption and the sheer utility of use-objects, and becomes a place of beauty.

The stages of technological development can be distinguished in terms of their degree of impact upon the world and upon the activities of *homo faber*. The first stage, so far as the modern age is concerned, is characterized by the imitation of natural processes and the use of natural forces for human purposes. It is typified by such machines as the steam engine. A second stage, characterized chiefly by the use of electricity, cannot be described as an enlargement of the old arts and crafts. Here men no longer interrupt natural processes but change them radically for their own ends. Nature and the human artifice have become distinct and separate. Third, men "create" by unchaining natural processes and "instead of carefully surrounding the human artifice with defenses against nature's elementary forces, keeping them as far as possible outside the man-made world, we have channeled these forces, along with their elementary power, into the world itself."[35] Here the symbolic example is the assembly line, which has transformed the manufacturing process from a series of discrete steps into a continuous process. The application of automation and robotics to assembly-line manufacturing, by removing the need for human muscle, perfects this stage. Last, instead of channeling natural forces into the world of the human artifice, "the universal forces of the cosmos around us" are channeled "into the nature of the earth."[36] Here the great examples, as we indicated, are the atomic bomb and the atomic reactor. Nowadays we may add particle-beam weapons to the list.

It nearly goes without saying that questions of beauty cannot arise when discussing either the processes or the devices. When natural forces, which come into being by themselves, are channeled into the world, they destroy its purpose, which is to keep natural forces outside the world. Technology, it seems, has reversed the fundamental purpose of *homo faber*: fabrication has come to destabilize the human artifice. Increasingly products are designed not to be useful or beautiful, which are worldly standards, but to fulfill certain functions in accord with the capacity of the machine to produce them. In this situation the distinction between end and means no longer makes sense because it is the means, the capacity of the machine, and not the end, that determines the shape of the product. That is, the product is no longer distinct from the process that created it. The result, again, is an increase in worldlessness even though it is accompanied by more of the good things of life.

Life in its biographical not biological sense, life as the time-line of appearance between birth and death, manifests itself in action and speech. Without *homo faber* in his highest capacity, as poet and monument-builder, historian and artist, the stories men enact and tell would not survive after the moment of action and speech. *Animal laborans* needs *homo faber* to ease his labor and remove his pain; mortals need him to erect a home on earth. Consequently, when men no longer care for immortality in the sense of remembrance, they no longer care for the world. This could be stated the other way around as well: if men believe that the world, a product of mortal hands, is as mortal as its makers, they will no longer care about being remembered by the yet unborn. This may reflect the sentiment that "all is vanity." But equally it may be a device to enhance the enjoyment of consumption: eat, drink and be merry for tomorrow not only do we die, which is not news, but the world comes to an end, which is. Arendt captured the vulgarity, stupidity and thoughtlessness of the sentiment with aphoristic pungency: "Worldlessness, alas, is always a form of barbarism."[37]

Kant once made a joke - or perhaps he borrowed it from Hume. He said: war is like two drunks fighting in a china shop. The serious implication is that the world (the china shop) is not taken into account during a war by the warriors. Even when the drunks are sober they may be unable to put the pieces back together. This is even more true when war would have the effect not simply of dismantling the world but of destroying it. Prior to its most recent phase, modern technology was the slow destruction of the world, the deliberate smashing of the plates and cups and saucers one by one. Nuclear and bio-medical technologies, in contrast, are more like loose bulls. To see why, we look at the third mode of activity, action.

Plurality, the condition of action and speech, has the twofold character of equality and distinction. Distinction is more than otherness or alterity because it expresses itself, whereas alterity universally exists in sheer multiplicity. In men, distinction is expressed in speech and in this way is transformed into uniqueness. There is, therefore, a kind of hierarchy of appearance: all things possess alterity; all living things possess distinction; all humans possess uniqueness. In terms of communications all organisms can communicate something - fear, hostility, attraction to the light - but humans can communicate themselves. Unlike labor and work, speech and action are not optional: the impulse to begin, to initiate and so to disclose arises from our being born.[38] Because it is the "nature" of a man to be a beginning, each man is something new and, from the point of view of the world, quite unexpected, a "miracle." Moreover, man knows that he is a beginning, that he can act, and that he will have an end. He knows that his beginning is the beginning of his end. By analogy with Homer's term, men are "natals" as much as men are "mortals." Action is the actualization of this condition of natality and the fact of birth; speech is the actualization of the condition of plurality and the fact of uniqueness and death. From the perspective of the world, the death of an individual means more than just a disappearance: an irreplaceable voice has been stilled.

Taken together, speech and action reveal a "who," the actual individual that has appeared in the world before others and with them, not on their behalf or against them. In contrast to production (for example, the production of art), action without a named actor is meaningless. Anonymous art is not meaningless; a thing of beauty remains a joy even if its author is unknown. Or, consider the contrast, an extreme one, to be sure, between Homeric and modern warfare. Homer's heroes were not simply opposed to one another and did not employ violence to the work of generating a grand body-count. Before fighting, they made speeches; the audience was not only the enemy but the gods and the allies. In this way they disclosed the who that was prepared to die. The opposite to all this self-disclosure is found in the appearance of unknown soldiers whose tombs were first built after World War I. Recollection of what has been lost may account for the cinematic careers of Clint Eastwood or Sylvester Stallone.

The conviction that the greatest human achievement is to appear before others is by no means uncontested. *Homo faber* believes it to be the creation of a beautiful and useful world; *animal laborans* says it is a long and comfortable life. From the point of view of action and the world, these other modes of activity do not fully disclose the individual; the stories told are not very interesting. The death of a salesman lights up much less of the human landscape than the death of a Caesar or of a Macbeth. Work, undertaken in isolation, can never produce an autonomous public realm but only a marketplace, a collection of boutiques, not a plurality of initiators. Even so, *homo faber* is still connected to a space of appearance and to the world by tangible things he has produced, which are, if not unique, at least stylish and highly individual. "Workmanship, therefore, may be an unpolitical way of life, but it certainly is not an antipolitical one."39 *Animal laborans* is both alone and worldless, alone with his body and taxed only with keeping it alive. He is with others, of course, but they are just other examples of an organism like himself. He may be distinct, like a dog or a butterfly, but chiefly he is a specimen, a radically equal example that, at the extreme, loses even the quality of otherness.

So far as *homo faber* is concerned, the great defect of action is its boundless unpredictability. It has no goal or specific aim and it never attains any end. This is a drawback, however, only for the activity of fabrication.

Power and action are not justified by what they achieve, since they achieve nothing and at most can serve as the source of stories. They are, instead, legitimated by the initial act that brings a plurality of people together.[40]

Men have always been tempted to overcome the general haphazardness of political acting by substituting doing for it. Doing, like fabrication, starts with the assumption that the author of an "act" cognitively knows what is to be done, knows what the objective is, so that the sole problem is to find the appropriate means to achieve the sought-for ends. The difficulty with really doing something, that is, with acting in the mode of making, is that it combines the boundlessness of action with the violence of fabrication. Making means using violence to do whatever one has in mind, and if things do not work out, violence is used to undo as well. An unsuccessful work - a cracked clay pot, for example - is simply destroyed. Men have always been able to destroy what they have made. Left to themselves the things of the world eventually decay on their own anyhow. In addition, thanks to technology, men can even destroy what they did not make, the habitat of the earth. Far more important in this connection than the arresting imagery of apocalyptic annihilation is the ordinary and prosaic fact that men have never been able to undo the processes they have begun by action nor even to control them with any reliability. There are many ways to hide the origin of an act - by lying, for example - but there is no way to prevent its consequences. By the same token, we can never reliably foretell the consequences of action even if we know what moves the actor. The great strength of the process of action is that it is both irreversible and unpredictable. And that is also its great burden, for it makes actors responsible for consequences that never were intended.

Arendt has argued that there exists a sort of natural hierarchy among the human capacities of labor, work and action such that the higher redeems the lower from futility and meaninglessness. As was indicated above regarding durability, the dignity of *homo faber* is inherently greater than that of *animal laborans*. Alternatively, the pain and trouble of labor, the imprisonment of man in the cycle of laboring and consuming, is relieved by tools and by the making of a durable world. Likewise, *homo faber* is saved from meaninglessness by the capacities of action and speech that are the source of meaningful stories. In each case what saves and redeems comes from outside (or above, but in any case, beyond) the activity itself. But how to relieve the predicaments of action? How to wash away the guilt the actor acquires simply by acting and thereby becoming responsible for consequences unseen and unintended? How to control the chaotic uncertainty of the future that action commences, to say nothing of sheer human unreliability? Theologically, the predicament is overcome by God's promise of forgiveness to the faithful. On earth, politically, the same two capacities are involved.

The means-end category of doing and making excludes the capacity to forgive as a matter of course and alters the meaning of promise from mutual agreement to imposed plan. Even more significant is the technological variation of the final reversal: acting into nature, an activity that carries irreversibility and unpredictability into a realm where no possible remedy exists to forgive or to undo. Modern technology can do in the realm of nature what Vico thought could be done only in the realm of history. This activity has the inevitable consequence of carrying human unpredictability "into that realm which we used to think of as ruled by inexorable laws."[41] The final and puzzling consequence of acting into nature is that we have succeeded in "making" nature. By reproducing universal or cosmic processes, the habitat of which is beyond even the household of earth-bound nature, these processes "have become part of what is going on on earth, so that it is as though we now 'make nature.'"[42] Where recombinant-DNA technologies are involved, even the qualifying "as though" is unnecessary.

In contrast to the other schematic definitions of man as rational animal, or as *homo faber* or even as *animal laborans*, modern technology seems to have shown that man is pre-eminently a being capable of action. Yet, both modern "history-making" and contemporary "nature-making," both of which are in fact ways of acting, are initiations that exclude plurality. In both instances, the greatness of the human power to initiate begins to destroy the conditions under which life was originally granted to man. If man could "make" history all further action would be impossible; indeed, such experimental "makings," which in fact constituted the activity of concentration camps, simply destroy men. Second, "making" nature has the effect of undermining the stability of the world, the human artifice, and eventually the habitat of the earth itself.

In the Prologue to *The Human Condition*, Arendt distinguished between the modern age, that began with Galileo's inventing and using the telescope and ended early in this century with modern "post-classical" physics, and the modern world. The modern world "was born with the first atomic explosions,"[43] which themselves were made possible only on the basis of the new speculation. The "true meaning" of the modern age did not come to light until our own times.[44] During the last few decades we have come to live not merely in a world determined by science and technology, but one whose truths and knowhow are derived from standpoints outside the earth. The distinction between the modern age and the modern world, we have already seen, is found in the difference between what was still called a natural science, even though it looked upon nature from the perspective of the universe, and a technology that introduced cosmic processes into nature, "even at the obvious risk of destroying her and, with her, man's mastership over her."[45] As mentioned, this same technology is not simply destructive, though that is its most immediately impressive characteristic, but is also enormously creative. Men have populated the heavens with new stars, created new elements and new forms of life. Man's acting into nature, especially his creative activities regarding life, seems more blasphemous than the development of atomic weapons because it seems as if we are arrogating to ourselves a task heretofore reserved only to divinity. But the possibility of destroying the earth was also traditionally in divine hands. So the obvious question is: How is this possible?

We are not dealing here with any Nietzschean questions of murder or of drinking up the sea. Nor are we concerned with such recondite matters as alchemy and hermeticism. Rather, we need only to follow out the implications of Archimides' quest for a universal standpoint. If men assumed that location, they could initiate processes that were decisive in the genesis of matter and life but that played no part in maintaining the stability of matter and life on earth.

The attitude that men have taken to all this, which we know from everyday experience, was anticipated, at least partially, by the philosophers and poets who reflected upon what the busy scientists were doing. Only recently, when "they began to appear in their own work and to interfere with their own inquiries,"[46] have scientists too begun to wonder about these things. Modern experimental science, seeking to test natural processes under prescribed conditions, now must take into account, as one of those conditions, the observer. In fact, "the answers of science will always remain replies to questions asked by men; the confusion in the issue of 'objectivity' was to assume that there could be answers without questions and results independent of a question-asking being."[47] Behind the confusion of the issue of objectivity and subjectivity lay the central experience of modern philosophy, doubt.

Doubt may have brought an end to the Christian belief in the certainty of immortal life so that man again became a mortal. But unlike the mortals of antiquity, the world for modern mortals was no longer their immortal home. Having lost hope in a world to come, modern mortals have not fallen back upon "this" world. (To speak of this world without tacitly assuming there is an other world makes no sense.) On the contrary, modern mortals are unsure the world is real since they have the ability to view it from anywhere. Having doubted the other world, man lost this one too. What is worse, he did not gain life even though he considered it the highest good. Rather he was "thrown into the closed inwardness of introspection, where the highest he could experience were the empty processes of reckoning of the mind, its play with itself."[48] The sole contents of introspection were bodily urges, biological processes; the sole hope for immortality was the life of socialized man, man the species-being. The thought of an absolute mortality apparently no longer troubles us; the old alternatives of individual immortality in a mortal world or mortal life in an immortal world are no longer meaningful.

With so many modern vulgarians searching for "meaning," it sounds like a piece of cheap moralizing to observe that modern society is pervaded with an absence of meaning. It follows directly, however, from the modern connection that we can know only what we have made, on the one hand, and the confusion of ends and meanings on the other. It is certain that we undertake projects and produce things and that these things are the end for which the project was begun. But once they are made, the project itself ends and the things, which we say gave meaning to the project, simply become means to further projects. What is even more discouraging is the fact that, in our present circumstances, we can take almost any hypothetical end, declare it to be meaningful, and proceed to act in such a way that the sequence of results not only makes sense logically but in fact actually works. In this way, for example, walking around on the moon is supposed to be meaningful - a "giant leap for mankind." Such a way of thinking, however, "means quite literally that everything is possible not only in the realm of ideas but in the field of reality itself."[49] Our modern conviction that truth and meaning are made, are products of the human mind, seems to ensure only that meanings will never reveal themselves.

The most striking feature about life in the modern world, by this account, is not simply the loss of contemplation but the sheer impoverishment of human experience. First, we are surrounded with a veritable avalanche of fabulous instruments, which means that it is increasingly unlikely that we encounter anything in the world that is not man-made and hence, in the last analysis, is not man in a different disguise.[50] The great symbol here is the moon-walker whose words were just quoted: he cannot encounter his actual environment without instantly dying. Moreover his practice, the hours logged in the simulator, were so much more rigorous than the actual flight that one observer, Tom Wolfe, has called it all a prepackaged experience. Second, however, the apparent necessity and automony of the process of technological innovation, which has effectively transformed the human artifice from a stable home for man into a kind of liquid movement, has had an effect on man not dissimilar to the old fears of ruin at the hands of nature. If man decides to become a part of nature he turns himself into a blind tool of natural laws whose course is set beforehand. By so doing he has renounced the capacity to prescribe his own laws to nature, to call a halt to her eternal rhythms. But if the world is abandoned and left to the play of nature, if nature is uninfluenced by human world-building even while it exists as a field into which man's active capacity empties itself, we are left only with the melancholy wisdom of *Ecclesiastes*. "If man recognizes the enforced course of events as his own supreme law and places himself at its disposal, then all he can do is prepare for the downfall of the human race."[51] Technology is akin to the old fears of nature insofar as it seems to follow its own law, swallowing more and more of the world and inducing a futile and melancholic search for meaning.

A final aspect of our impoverishment, then, is that the one mental faculty that is suited for the search for meaning, namely thought, has been excluded almost entirely from the modern technological world. In place of thought we have substituted logical reckoning, at which computers are far better than humans, or we have substituted cognition, the highest criterion of which is scientific and technical truth. We said at the beginning of this paper that Arendt sought "to think what we are doing." One conclusion at least seems clear, neither reckoning nor cognition can replace thought.

Technological cleverness, moreover, has altered the nature of the most highly celebrated capacity of modern man, labor. In some parts of the world, the abolition of labor itself is not a wild impossibility. Indeed, laboring is too lofty a term to describe the jobholding that has become characteristic of the contemporary world. We have reached the last phase of a laboring society when, in a society of jobholders, nothing more is demanded than a kind of automatic functioning, as if "the only active decision still required of the individual were to let go, so to speak, to abandon his individuality, the still individually sensed pain and trouble of living and acquiesce in a dazed, 'tranquillized,' functional type of behaviour."[52] This does not mean, however, that man has lost his capacities for work and action and thought simply because social scientists tell tales of a social animal.

Work is still done; men still fabricate. But the faculty is exercised increasingly only by artists. Accordingly, the experiences of worldliness and of beauty are confined to diminishing numbers of people. Men still act, in the sense of releasing processes. But this faculty is exercised increasingly only by scientists and technicians. Unfortunately, their actions are meaningless because they generate no stories. By acting into nature rather than into the web of human relationships, nothing is revealed. Only thought, it would seem, is still possible. But thought requires neither the presence of others nor a common world for its actualization. In fact its most characteristic feature is that it withdraws from the world. This does not mean, however, that it is indifferent to political freedom. "Unfortunately, and contrary to what is currently assumed about the proverbial ivory tower independence of thinkers, no other human capacity is so vulnerable, and it is in fact far easier to act under conditions of tyranny than it is to think."[53] If the widespread sense of meaninglessness in technological society and its accompanying moods of melancholia and regret are connected to thoughtlessness, the technology, even if not assimilated to tyranny, at least displays an elective affinity with it.   The result of both technology and tyranny is worldlessness, though the means used to achieve it differ.   There is no comfort to be found in the observation that traditional tyrants did not have modern technologies at their disposal.   All it means is that modern, technological "tyranny" wears an impenetrable disguise: the bars of Weber's iron cage have been replaced, so to speak, with more up-to-date invisible synthetics.

According to Arendt the distinguishing feature of totalitarianism is not that, like tyranny, it destroys political freedom, but that it seeks to annihilate the human capacity for spontaneity. That there may exist an inner affinity and even a partial equivalence of meaning between technological society and totalitarian domination is suggested by two facts. First, there is the coincidence of the modern population explosion, which to a significant degree was made possible by technology, with the discovery of technical devices that, through automation, will make large sections of the populations "superfluous" even in terms of labor; moreover, through nuclear energy, it is possible to deal with this twofold "difficulty" by the use of devices the destructive capacity of which is enormously greater than the comparatively inefficient organizations of state-directed mass murder used by the totalitarian regimes of fifty years ago. Second, scientific and technical progress has been essentially automatic: "The progresses made by science have nothing to do with the I-will; they follow their own inexorable laws, compelling us to do whatever we can, regardless of consequences."[54] If power is connected to the we-will-and-we-can, and is not simply a function of the we-can, then the vast increase in our technological capacities has been accompanied by a vast increase in impotence. Like totalitarianism, the technological order constitutes a new regime.

Notes

1. Hannah Arendt, *The Human Condition* (Chicago: University of Chicago Press, 1958), p. 2.

2. Arendt, *On Violence* (New York: Harcourt, Brace and World, 1970), p. 13.

3. Arendt, "Europe and the Atom Bomb," *The Commonweal*, 60, 24 (September 17, 1954), 578.

4. Arendt, Letter, *The New York Review of Books*, (June 19, 1969), 38.

5. Arendt, *The Human Condition*, p. 3.

6. Arendt, *Between Past and Future*, revised ed. (New York: Viking, 1968), pp. 279-80.

7. Arendt, *Life of the Mind*, Volume I: *Thinking*, (New York: Harcourt, Brace, Jovanovich, 1978), pp. 25-6.

8. Arendt, *The Human Condition*, p. 3.

9. *Ibid.*

10. *Ibid.*

11. *Ibid.*, p. 4.

12. *Ibid.*

13. *Ibid.* p. 5.

14. *Ibid.*

15. Arendt, *Thinking*, pp. 70-1.

16. Arendt, *On Revolution*, (New York: Viking, 1963), p. 226.

17. Arendt, "Privileged Jews," *Jewish Social Studies*, 8 (1946), 6; "pre-war" meant prior to 1914.

18. Arendt, *The Origins of Totalitarianism*, 3rd ed., (New York: Harcourt, Brace and World, 1966), p. 80.

19. Arendt, "Privileged Jews," 6.

20. Arendt, "Public Rights and Private Interests," in *Small Comforts for Hard Times: Humanists on Public Policy*, eds., Michael Mooney and Florian Stuber (New York: Columbia University Press, 1977), p. 106.

21. Arendt, *Men in Dark Times*, (New York: Harcourt, Brace and World, 1968), pp. 16-17.

22. Arendt, "Privileged Jews," 30.

23. Arendt, *Between Past and Future*, p. 156.

24. Arendt, "Public Rights and Private Interests," p. 108.

25. Arendt, *The Human Condition*, p. 29.

26. Arendt, *On Revolution*, pp. 219-20.

27. Arendt, *On Violence*, p. 81.

28. Arendt, *Crisis of The Republic*, (New York: Harcourt, Brace, Jovanovich, 1972), p. 89; *On Violence*, pp. 81-2.

29. Arendt, *The Human Condition*, p. 43.

30. Arendt, *Between Past and Future*, p. 20.

31. Arendt, *Men in Dark Times*, p. 82.

32. *Ibid.,* p. 87.

33. *Ibid.*

34. Arendt, *The Human Condition*, p. 126.

35. *Ibid.,* p. 149.

36. *Ibid.,* p. 150.

37. Arendt, *Men in Dark Times*, p. 13.

38. Arendt, *The Human Condition*, p. 177.

39. *Ibid.,* p. 212.

40. Arendt, *On Revolution*, p. 52.

41. Arendt, *Between Past and Future*, p. 61.

42. Arendt, Letter, *The New York Review of Books*, (Jan. 1, 1970), p. 36. Arendt was responding to the puzzlement of J.M. Cameron, "Bad Times," *NYRB*, (Nov. 6, 1969), 6, to which he replied: "Her views on nature and natural processes I find even more difficult to grasp than I did before .... Miss Arendt doesn't seem to me to be maintaining anything intelligible." *NYRB*, (Jan 14, 1970).

43. Arendt, *The Human Condition*, p. 6.

44. *Ibid.*, p. 268.

45. *Ibid.*

46. *Ibid.*, p. 273.

47. Arendt, *Between Past and Future*, p. 49.

48. Arendt, *The Human Condition*, p. 320.

49. Arendt, "History and Immortality," *Partisan Review*, 24 (1957), p. 32.

50. Arendt, *Between Past and Future*, p. 277.

51. Arendt, "Imperialism: The Road to Suicide," *Commentary*, (Feb. 1, 1946), p. 32.

52. Arendt, *The Human Condition*, p. 322.

53. *Ibid.*, p. 324.

54. Arendt, *On Violence*, p. 86.

ETHICS AND TECHNOLOGY:
HANS JONAS' THEORY OF RESPONSIBILITY

Ronald Beiner

Biblical wisdom and ancient thought provided, in the American past, a language for those who were discontented with the terms, as well as the practices, of the dominant liberal tradition. That genuine counter-culture recognizes the multi-dimensionality of the human soul, and among its first principles is the proposition that there are limits to what human beings can and should attempt to do.[1]

George Grant, in his essay *English-Speaking Justice*, remarks that American Protestantism, while less congenial to modernity than the Calvinism that preceded it, possessed less intellectual force than the latter and therefore "its direct practical effect on the control of technology (the central political question) is generally minimal."[2] What is surely most striking in this passage is the statement that the control of technology is the supreme political question of our epoch. Today, it appears, we are all at least in agreement (whatever our other political disagreements) that political progress is premised upon higher technological achievements. Whether we seek to maximize the growth potential of unfettered capitalism, or to redistribute the resources of society to the welfare of the needy; whether we seek to promote the new high-tech industries on behalf of the already well-off, or to siphon off the surplus riches of these industries for the benefit of "the least advantaged," we can all at least agree in assuming that technology is the indispensable condition of realizing our political goals, whatever they may be. It therefore comes as a surprise indeed to be told that the limitation of technology is an object of political deliberation at all, let alone being situated at the top of the agenda.

What are the ethical and political implications of modern technology? Is it the case that our technological enterprises today "are having an impact on the total dispensation of things," that "willy-nilly we are embarking on courses which affect the total condition of things on earth and the total future condition of man?"[3] If so, how are we to orient ourselves theoretically to these new dimensions of responsibility and obligation? How can we establish objectively known principles by which to set strict limits upon our tampering not just with our own future but with that of later generations? How big can we allow the stakes to grow before we must call a halt to our intrepid dice-throwing? These are the questions to which Hans Jonas attempts to offer a systematic answer in his major work, *The Imperative of Responsibility*.[4]

Jonas' starting point is the fact that traditional ethics no longer suffices. The scope of human action has expanded so enormously that the very nature of agency, and the nature of ethics applicable to human agency, have undergone radical transformations.   Traditional ethics presupposed that nature remained more or less constant and that man's own nature, likewise, remained more or less constant.   Traditional ethics also assumed that the sphere of human action did not reach beyond the present and immediate - specifically, relationships with other human beings who were one's contemporaries, and with whom one had to deal in the role of friend, neighbor, relation, etc. "All this has decisively changed. Modern technology has introduced actions of such novel scale, objects, and consequences that the framework of former ethics can no longer contain them."[5] Jonas states that "responsibility is a correlate of power and must be commensurate with the latter's scope and that of its exercise ."[6] Today, there is no doubt that we have the power to affect or to disrupt the entire ecological balance of our planet. It follows that we also assume ethical responsibility for our new powers. In expanding our powers to reshape nature, including the fate of the earth as a whole, we simultaneously acquire the capacity to reshape our own nature as ethical agents. We are no longer the beings we were previously, for we carry a burden and exercise a responsibility of which earlier generations were happily oblivious.

Jonas declares that our novel technological capacities create entirely new and unprecedented problems for ethics. For instance, traditional ethics either dismissed the need for knowledge altogether (Kant), or at least specified the need for a kind of moral knowledge very different from any sort of theoretical competence (Aristotle). Post-technological ethics, however, demands so much in the way of knowledge concerning the possible eventual outcomes of our actions that we cannot even hope that our achieved knowledge will be equal to this demand, and therefore we must place cautionary restrictions on our action on account of the shortfall of our knowledge. Ignorance places definite limits on the ethical validity of our deeds, where we are forbidden to act in the absence of secure knowledge of what we are doing (or what will be the full consequences of what we are doing). Ethics thus changes from a sphere of action where the demands of knowledge are minimal,[7] to one where knowledge is absolutely requisite for ethically sanctioned action.[8] As Jonas says, our "knowledge must be commensurate with the causal scale of our action," and "the fact that it cannot really be thus commensurate ... creates a novel moral problem."[9]

According to Jonas, "The changed nature of human action changes the very nature of politics."[10] Jonas' aim is to outline an ethics that corresponds to this newly transformed nature of politics. Politics on a new scale means at the same time novel dimensions of ethical responsibility and new kinds of obligation. A set of moral imperatives must be formulated for which, previously, no need existed. Consequently, modern technology has wrought decisive changes, not merely in the extent of political responsibility, but in the very character of ethics. Jonas assumes that any ethical claims must ultimately be underwritten by a metaphysics. Putting these two conditions together, it follows that we must come up with a new metaphysics capable of addressing the new kinds of ethical demands posed by our current technology. In regard to the new ethics that is sought, Jonas thus states "its ultimate grounding can only be metaphysical."[11]

To illustrate the insufficiency of traditional ethics, Jonas begins by discussing Kant's notion of practical reason. Kant's categorical imperative, based on the logical self-consistency of the willing self, is insufficient. To imagine the termination of the human species at some point in the future involves no logical contradiction at all with respect to my present self, or the maxims of my immediate will. Therefore the categorical imperative does nothing to constrain the scope of my action in relation to future generations. At most, Kantian practical reason serves to regulate one's relationships with one's own contemporaries. In fact, *every* previous ethics turns out to be "an ethics of contemporaneity and immediacy"[12]; all premodern ethics, according to Jonas, are "present-oriented."[13] But the scope of present-day action reaches far beyond our own contemporaries. We assume obligations to future generations that are untouched by Kantian (or any other) ethics. Thus Jonas proposes a new imperative, entirely unlike the categorical imperative of Kant, which does not merely derive from principles of logical consistency, but instead requires independent metaphysical grounding. As Jonas puts it, "An imperative responding to the new type of human action and addressed to the new type of agency that operates it might run thus: 'Act so that the effects of your actions are compatible with the permanence of genuine human life'."[14]

The first radical difference, then, between Jonas' post-technological ethics and all earlier ethics is that Jonas breaks with "the orientation of all previous ethics to the present."[15] Jonas does, however, exclude one previous ethic from this general characterization - namely Marxism. Marxist eschatology, like Jonas' own post-technological ethic, assumes responsibility towards the future, and ascribes to this historical responsibility a scope and depth commensurate with the most far-reaching technological capacities of modernity. Marxism, then, stands in a privileged relation to Jonas' post-traditional ethics. As he says, his position and that of Marxism, "as answers to the unprecedented modern situation and especially to its technology, have so much in common over against premodern ethics."[16] What they have in common is the colossal dimensions of the responsibility they invoke. The *difference* between the two positions is summed up in the injunction formulated by Jonas as follows: "that the prophecy of doom is to be given greater heed than the prophecy of bliss."[17] Marxism, indeed, is of such importance as a foil to Jonas' project[18] that he reserves the last chapter of his book to a critique of Marxism and implies that *only* Marxism "stands comparison with the ethic for which we want to plead here."[19] As Jonas perceives the issue between himself and Marxism, the decisive point of distinction is that, in contrast to the ethic implicit in Marxism, "the ethic we are looking for is *not* eschatological."[20] At the same time Jonas hints at a more profound difference in the two respective estimations of the status of technology. Marxism (in common with liberalism or capitalism) assumes that technology is something that can be *put to use*, as an instrument of human agency. Jonas, by implication, denies this. Contemporary technology, on the contrary, has begun to make a mockery of human agency. He writes: "technology's power over human destiny has overtaken even that of communism, which no less than capitalism thought merely to make use of it."[21] This directly echoes Heidegger's dictum that capitalism and communism are both predicates of the subject technology.[22]

Hannah Arendt's book *The Human Condition* begins with an account of how human power has begun to modify (or to acquire the capacity to modify) the basic conditions of human life. One of these conditions is the fact that humans inhabit the Earth. But beginning with Sputnik, humans have acquired the capacity (at least in principle) potentially to alter or disrupt our earthly condition.[23] Jonas considers how other fundamental conditions of human life are now potentially malleable. Obviously, our powers of technology have extended, and continue to extend, the bounds of our control over our own mortality. Death is seen increasingly not as an immovable destiny but as a condition to be treated, or even a malady to be cured. (Jonas refers to advances in cell biology that aim to arrest or control the very process of aging.)[24]

Technology plainly works upon external nature, but it *may* also be turned (and *is* actually being turned) inwards, towards our own nature, towards ourselves. The technological subject gains the possibility of altering his own being, or the very nature of his own subjectivity. The subject of technology is no longer a stable given who directs his power outward, to shape and reshape a malleable external nature. Rather, the subject of technology is itself capable of becoming the object of his own powers, so that the exercise of technological capabilities is indistinguishable from the act of self-transformation.

What is distinctive about the current projects of technology is that "they concern the total condition of nature on our globe and the very kind of creatures that shall, or shall not, populate it."25 But for projects on this kind of global scale, wisdom in the absolute sense would be needed. As Jonas points out, however, far from possessing today the wisdom that has always eluded man, the moral skepticism of contemporary man renders the possibility of wisdom even *more* remote than it has been perennially. "We need wisdom most when we believe in it least."26 In the absence of wisdom, we require humility and restraint. Western philosophy in the tradition of Socrates has always taught wisdom as knowledge of ignorance. It is above all precisely this form of Socratic wisdom that we need today, when we are tempted to embark on projects that only the most all-seeing wisdom could legitimately sanction.

Jonas ventures a new ethics in a situation that he sees as approaching nihilism: a situation in which "near-omnipotence is paired with near-emptiness, greatest capacity with knowing least for what ends to use it."27 Jonas' thought is that if we cannot have a systematic reflection on ethics that tells us comprehensively what ends we should pursue, perhaps we can at least formulate a negative ethics that delimits what ends we categorically ought *not* to pursue.

But even a negative ethics implies a theoretical ordering of activities within society, and this, in turn, assumes that the ends of our various human endeavors are subject to critical reflection. It is just this assumption, however, that is put in question by the self-propelling dynamism of modernity. Jonas argues in his essay, "The Practical Uses of Theory," that according to the classical conception of theory, theory's role was to reflect on the ends for the sake of which we develop our technical capacities. According to the modern conception of theory, on the other hand, the relationship between theory and practice is far too intimate for theory to obtain the critical distance by which to judge the ends of our various *technai*. In Jonas' telling image, modern theory is chained to the chariot of unceasing dynamism, "in harness before it or dragged in its tracks - which, it is hard to tell in the dust of the race, and sure it is only that not theory is the charioteer."28 Because we conceive of science as serving us and therefore at our disposal, we are content to assume that we retain the prerogative of judging freely to what ends or purposes we put our technical powers. But this assumption of the neutrality of technical means is illusory: "science, with its application governed solely by its own logic, does not really leave the meaning of happiness open: it has prejudged the issue, in spite of its own value-freedom. The automatism of its use ... has set the goal of happiness in principle: indulgence in the use of things." Thus, "the direction of all effort and thereby the issue of the good tends to be predecided."29 It follows that the classical function of theory, the judging of ultimate ends, is rendered totally redundant: "Science is ... theory and art at once. But whereas in other arts having the skill and using it are different, so that its possessor is free to use it or not, and to decide when, the skill of science as a collective property begets its use by its own momentum, and so the hiatus between two stages, where judgment, wisdom, freedom can have their play, is here dangerously shrinking: the skill possesses its possessor."30 To open up once again this shrinking space of "judgment, wisdom, freedom" is Jonas' task in his theory of responsibility.

Jonas' "ethics of futurity" is intended to apply not to any kind of human action, but just to "matters of a certain magnitude - those with apocalyptic potential."31 The point, however, is that the scope of potentially apocalyptic action is today expanding alarmingly. Jonas' basic premise is that "both today and in the future we will have to deal with actions of just that magnitude, which is itself a *novum* in human affairs. This *novum* renders obsolete the tacit standpoint of all earlier ethics that, given the impossibility of long-term calculation, one should consider what is close at hand only and let the distant future take care of itself."32 The old ethics will continue to apply in the private sphere of action, but will no longer suffice for "the new action-sphere of planetary technological planning."33

Jonas begins to develop his actual argument in Chapter 2. He starts from the fact that all human action involves an element of wager or gambling. The question is: How much am I entitled to wager of what is not my own but belongs properly to others? (Owing to "the inextricable interweaving of human affairs," I cannot help drawing others into my own wager.) Jonas' analysis depends crucially on the decisive difference between personal actions which put the interests of other individuals at stake, and collective actions which put at stake "the whole existence or whole being of man in the future."34 Where the stakes include the "nonexistence or dehumanization" of future humanity, Jonas argues that not the promise of a supreme good but only the avoidance of a supreme evil can suffice to render defensible the wager. Pointing to the "asymmetry between goods desired and evils shunned" (for "one can live without the supreme good but not with the supreme evil"), Jonas seeks to establish that only the threat of a terrible future, never the enticement of a wonderful future, can permit us to wager on stakes of this kind.35

One aspect of Jonas' argument is that our present scientific and technical (as well as other) capacities are deliverances of human nature *as given*, and that it would be both illogical and unseemly to place in jeopardy the very givenness of human being that has put us in our present position. These capacities illustrate the "essential sufficiency of our nature such as it has evolved within this world."36 In particular, our aptitude for "truth, valuation, and freedom" proves that there is "something infinite" that we stand to lose if we make ill-considered wagers and wrong decisions. But it is just this "share of transcendence" that we put at risk when we cast our existing nature into "the crucible of bio-technological alchemy."[37] Under such conditions, caution "becomes the core of moral actions."[38]

Another dimension of Jonas' argument is the infinite difference between being and nothingness, and the imperative to preserve human being at all costs if the alternative may be human nothingness (we are commanded "to opt for being and against nothingness").[39] The preservation of "the given" must have absolute priority if we confront even the *possibility* of the disappearance of all that we know as human. According to Jonas, not only is there an absolute difference between an individual's decision to terminate his own existence and collective suicide, but there is also an absolute ("infinite") difference between collective suicide of a people or nation and the collective suicide of man as such. It is the difference between "being" and "nothingness," or between the givenness of human nature (with its "innate sufficiency"),[40] and the complete abrogation of this givenness. These arguments yield Jonas' supreme principle: "Never must the existence or the essence of man as a whole be made a stake in the hazards of action."[41]

Jonas points out that the familiar language of rights and duties is inappropriate to the ethic of responsibility that concerns him. Generations that do not yet exist obviously cannot be the bearers of rights. Rather, their very existence is a crucial part of the responsibility itself. Moreover, there is an obvious nonreciprocity between those who are responsible and those to whom they are responsible (and we tend to assume that reciprocity is the mark of standard rights and duties, at least according to the liberal-contractualist paradigm). Jonas argues that there is a precedent for this nonreciprocal moral relationship in the relation of parent to child. The decisive difference in the case of the latter relation, however, is that the object of the responsibility is a being that already exists. Can we be said to bear a duty towards beings whose very existence is the outcome of the responsibility we are supposed to exercise? Let us point out another interesting feature of this nonreciprocity. The duty, if there is one, to procreate future humanity must be borne by us *collectively*. It would be odd to demand that every individual, as an individual, has a duty to procreate, yet *as a society* we are clearly responsible for whatever posterity there may be.[42] It seems to follow, then, that as members of society we assume collective obligations that do not apply to us individually, or are not the mere sum of individual duties.

But physical procreation of a future humanity is clearly insufficient. It is quite imaginable that we could bring forth a future generation that, on account of what we have wrought with "the alchemy of our 'utopian' technology,"[43] has no idea of what it is to be human. Jonas points out that such a generation would not assert its claims against us, in the sense of holding us culpable for violating its rights, simply because it has no conception of that of which it has been deprived as heirs of the human legacy. In this case, we are answerable not to the particular generation that is the object of our responsibility (for they are oblivious of the injury), but to our own sense of transcendent obligation.[44] This clarifies why it is not a matter of *rights* exercised by this future progeny (and therefore why the language of rights is out of place in this whole inquiry). Assuming these beings to have a right to exist, it would be a right that they might well disown. It is conceivable that they would judge the responsibility of carrying on the human vocation to be too onerous for them, and one they would rather forgo (even at the price of never being brought into existence). However, the fact that these hypothetical beings would disown their right to exist would in no way lessen the strength of our obligation to perpetuate the future of humanity. As Jonas says, to give life to future generations may be not to bestow a gift upon them but to tax them with a burden - a burden they may be reluctant to assume.[45] This just proves that our obligation is grounded not in rights held by those who are yet to be (our successors), but rather in "the 'ought' that stands above both of us."[46] The first principle of Jonas' ethic of responsibility is, then, an "imperative of existence" that stands independent of the wishes or the entitlements of those whose existence it enjoins. "With this imperative we are, strictly speaking, not responsible to the future human individuals but to the *idea* of Man."[47]

The question, "Why ought we to commit ourselves unconditionally to the future existence of mankind?" devolves in turn upon the question, "Why ought there to be Man?," which is a form of the question, "Why ought there to be something rather than nothing?" This is an *ontological* question, and as Jonas makes clear, it puts us under an obligation to recur to metaphysical inquiry. This idea that ethics should proceed from ontology and metaphysics is today a deeply unfashionable one, but it is, Jonas says, unavoidable nonetheless. The question of why we should be duty-bound to ensure the continued existence of Man presupposes an answer to the question of whether and why the idea of Man has value, and this requires that we probe the *ontological* status of Man. Jonas' whole enterprise would be hopeless unless one were willing to allow "the *possibility* of a rational metaphysics, despite Kant's contrary verdict."[48]

In Chapter 3 Jonas argues that we are purposive beings through and through, and much more ambitiously, that in fact nature *as a whole* is purposive through and through. In other words, he is committed to a teleological view of nature and appeals for a restoration of something like Aristotelian ontology (thus: "purpose in general is indigenous to nature").[49] As is well known, modern science has founded its claims to progress on a deep and comprehensive repudiation of teleology. However, Jonas attempts to demonstrate that the antiteleological position leads to logical perplexities and aporias no less serious than those that befall the teleologist. Although there is no doubt that the *methodological* assumption that there are no "final causes" in nature has been tremendously fruitful in the advancement of science and of scientific mastery of nature, this is not in itself any proof of metaphysical adequacy. As Jonas puts it: "methodological advantage must not be confused with ontological judgment."[50] The fact that we can abstract from a holistic understanding of nature with great advantage in no way establishes that these methodological abstractions exhaust the truth of nature (and even Kant, who was wholeheartedly committed to modern science, maintained that it was extremely difficult to avoid a teleological way of thinking in our reflective judgments upon nature).[51] Moreover, we would not be compelled to repudiate "the modern causal explanation of nature" simply because we allow that there are aspects of nature that modern natural science does not touch. Jonas maintains that we can embrace "an 'Aristotelian' understanding of being" without contradicting modern science as a method of causal explanation or forgoing its advantages for causal explanation.[52] The point, rather, is that we can *explain* nature to the limit of our needs without thereby fully comprehending her.[53] In other words, the validity of objections to the *explanatory role* of teleology does not thereby invalidate the very concept of teleology altogether.[54] Nature presents us with undeniable instances of teleological phenomena (e.g., consciousness, subjectivity, etc.), and their existence is in no way compromised by the fact that they (quite legitimately) have no place in the methodology of modern science.

Jonas' strategy is to deploy the ontological argument that there are ends or purposes in (and throughout) nature in the service of the normative claim that nature, and ultimately human life, is valuable in itself - a "value" that makes binding claims upon us. That is to say, he hopes to establish ethical imperatives with respect to our relationship to nature and to the perpetuation of our own form of natural life "by grounding the good in being."[55] He thereby seeks to derive from an ontological thesis (namely "the immanence of purpose in nature") important conclusions for ethics. This step from ontology to ethics commences in Chapter 4, with the assertion of "the superiority of purpose as such over purposelessness."[56] Jonas has previously argued that being, as we encounter it, is suffused with purposiveness through and through. Jonas now attempts to derive norms and imperatives (at least negative ones) from this ontological claim. If it is absolutely better for there to be purposes in general than for there not to be purposes, then being (as purposive) is preferable to nothingness. If this is true, then of course practical injunctions of one kind or another ineluctably follow, for it is within our (growing) power to obliterate being and replace it with not-being (or put otherwise: to eliminate the very capacity for purposive goal-striving).

From these general reflections on the relationship between ontology and ethics, Jonas now turns specifically to his theory of responsibility. Although he seeks to ground his theory upon a rational principle, this rational principle would be merely abstract and without any force unless it could gain a purchase on human sentiment. In fact the principle of responsibility *does* engage concrete human sensibility: we speak of *feeling* a sense of responsibility towards others, or feeling responsible *for* them. Without the disposition of human agents to be gripped by such moral feelings, a mere theory of moral or political responsibility, however rationally compelling, would remain without effect, and therefore irrelevant to the moral situation of those it is supposed to address. Therefore Jonas, quite rightly, launches his theory with a discussion of the role of sentiment: "the gap between abstract validation and concrete motivation must be bridged by the arc of sentiment."[57] Once again, Jonas turns to Kant as the point of reference for highlighting his own distinctive position. Kant, for all the rigorism of his moral theory, also concedes the unavoidable role of moral feeling or sentiment in ethics.[58] But for Kant this takes the form of "reverence" directed at the law itself, or the formal character of practical reason, rather than at the actual objects of our practical interest (the beneficiaries of our action). For Jonas, by contrast, "the content of the aim reigns supreme"[59]; that is, we exercise responsibility because we perceive worth in certain objects, and this perception moves us to act on their behalf. It is the *content* of the *objects* (people and things *in the world*) that elicits our moral sentiment, not (as Kant held) the mere form of our willing.[60] Jonas insists that it is *Being* alone that is entitled to our "reverence," whereas Kant of course would reject as heteronomous any moral feeling that would confer a sense of reverence upon anything other than our own capacity to legislate a moral law for ourselves.[61]

Jonas focuses on two exemplary models of responsibility: parental responsibility, and the political responsibility of the statesman. Notwithstanding all the dissimilarities between the parent's responsibility for his child, and the stateman's responsibility for his fellow citizens, Jonas identifies three main traits that are shared by his models of responsibility: both are "total," that is, comprehensive in scope, unlike the physician's responsibility for his patients or the ship captain's responsibility for his passengers; both are continuous, meaning that "its exercise dare not stop," that such responsibility can allow itself neither vacation nor pause;[62] finally, both are directed to the future, extending in the reach of their concern and commitment beyond the boundaries of their own power or foresight. It is the incalculability of such total responsibility that especially concerns Jonas. As he says, we may "extract a practical knowledge from ignorance itself."[63]

But here a significant disanalogy arises between the two models, for parental responsibility is not so incalculable. In educating a child we know at least that nature assures a preordained evolution from infancy to maturity; there is a definite destination. But with political responsibility there is no such knowledge of the goal. In fact, Jonas insists, against the historicist doctrines of Hegel and Marx, that there is no mature epoch of mankind that is the goal of history; and he asserts, against the utopian fantasies of Marx and Nietzsche, that man is not an "unfinished" project that awaits completion.[64] Jonas states that his position can expect contradiction "from the political eschatologies of history and from the non-political belief in endless progress."[65] Against all such progressivist and eschatological teachings, Jonas cites Ranke's dictum: "Every epoch is immediate to God."[66] It is in this sense, too, that Jonas insists upon a practical knowledge drawn from ignorance (namely, ignorance concerning the character of future generations).

At this point, Jonas introduces a more concrete discussion of the contemporary features of political responsibility (which easily dwarf the responsibilities of traditional statecraft).[67] Although modern politics engages far greater dimensions of responsibility, and places much greater demands upon the capabilities of statecraft, our actual power to anticipate the future is, however, far less, for modern politics is based on a condition of continual (and accelerating) flux: "Dynamism is the signature of modernity."[68] In premodern politics, not only were the stakes much smaller, but the rules of the game were more or less constant. In our circumstances, by contrast, "we must always figure on novelty without ever being able to figure it out."[69] Just when knowledge of the future is most urgently required, to support the newly expanded breadth of our responsibilities, precisely then is it least likely to be available. To bank on unbroken progress, for purposes of planning, is to enter a kind of "twilight zone" of unknown vistas.[70] That statesmen should feel compelled to cross into this uncharted region is virtually inevitable in an age characterized by "the great wager that the human enterprise as a whole has become."[71] What is absolutely forbidden to the responsible statesman, however, is "the expectation of miracles." Yet it is just this promise to perform miracles which seems to captivate the political imagination of the present. The fact that the so-called "Strategic Defense Initiative" is the major long-term policy commitment of the Reagan Presidency should be quite sufficient to confirm that our politicians today are carried away by "a superstitious faith in the omnipotence of science."[72]

Jonas calls himself a "post-Marxist."[73] By this he means that he shares with Marxism a concern (to be found in *no other* previous ethics)[74] with assuming responsibility for the historical future,[75] but that he no longer gives credence to any notion of a "reason in history."[76] Whereas Marxism still conceives of history as conferring upon man the possibility of free agency, Jonas tells us that "with technology's having seized power" (and moreover, threatening catastrophe "from the very progress of history itself"), we are forced to view differently the dynamism of history.[77] The fact that our ethics today is "post-Marxist," and not, say, pre-Marxist, is not a matter of choice but rather a historical fatality. In this sense, Jonas' "ethics of responsibility" is a kind of second-best or *faute de mieux*, given our historical situation, in an epoch where power far outpaces insight. Jonas' thought is that, while it may be the case that an ethics, like Plato's, addressed to a transcendent good is intrinsically superior, we must put aside all such higher ethics on account of the more pressing obligation to take responsibility "for what has been set afoot." Our "vulgar causality in the world" accords precedence to "vulgar duties," such as mere perpetuation of the conditions of existence, when these are menaced by our own powers. In modernity man's "exorbitant capacity is already at work," and therefore, for the time being at least, our highest ethical aspirations must take a back seat to "mere" responsibility.[78] It is, as Jonas says, "an ethics of preservation and prevention, not of progress and perfection" - "an emergency ethics of the endangered future" - and all further inquiry into a full "theory of the human good and the 'best life' " must await an easing of the immediate peril.[79]

According to Jonas, his theory of responsibility is fully encapsulated in our experience of the infant whose very being *commands* (not merely entreats) that we care for it.[80] The archetype of the infant allows us to understand what it means to feel total responsibility for a creature of nature *simply because it is given*, and because it requires our care and attention to sustain its perilous existence. Just as we feel *obliged* to protect and preserve the infant when we are actually presented with it, in its absolute dependence upon us, so we are, Jonas urges, no less obliged, collectively, to preserve and protect the future as a reservoir of human possibilities. Just as we dedicate ourselves to the particular infant, as the guardian of an open future, without knowing how the child will turn out, so too we ought to labor on behalf of coming generations without any assurance as to what use they will make of their inheritance or what content they will give to their humanity. Parental responsibility thus offers a "primal paradigm" of what political responsibility might become.[81] Indeed, if we are to avert the prospect of self-inflicted global catastrophe, we *must* come to feel the same weight of responsibility in the relations between whole generations that we naturally do in the concrete immediacy of the parent-child relationship. This calls to mind the following motto of the German "Greens": "We do not inherit the earth from our parents; we borrow it from our children."[82]

In his two concluding chapters, Jonas pursues the sought-after dialogue with Marxism. In the penultimate chapter he offers a comparison between socialism and capitalism with regard to their respective capacities for measuring up to the now-looming tasks of responsible statesmanship. Jonas concedes that Marxism, in principle, possesses some definite advantages over liberal capitalism. However, these advantages are largely cancelled out by the utopian aspects of Marxism and by the "cult of technology" that communist regimes fully share with the nations of the West. It turns out that the potential of communist states to elicit sacrifices and renunciations from their citizens (which is the basis of their theoretical advantage) depends on the utopian promise of the Marxist ideal - which is certainly part of the malady, not the cure. Far from *elevating* our ambitions as a civilization, we must learn to restrain and retract our material expectations. Obviously, this task of global renunciation cannot be delegated to a doctrine which "is a fruit of Baconianism and in its basic self-understanding regards itself as its chosen executor."[83]

In the final chapter Jonas completes the critique of Marxism that is prefigured in Chapter 5. In our times, the harboring of utopian hopes is not merely an extravagance, but a real hazard. To postulate the overcoming of scarcity exposes us to the dire threat of the "greenhouse effect." To postulate universal leisure is to countenance universal redundancy. To postulate the eventual arrival of the realm of freedom causes us to overlook the population explosion. To postulate the infinite advance of technology is to be oblivious to the second law of thermodynamics. In short, to each utopian yearning corresponds a blindness or a forgetfulness of potentially catastrophic proportions. Thus Jonas directs the full force of his cautionary morality at the utopian fancies of Ernst Bloch, who typifies the Promethean aspects, the hubris, of Marxism. As Jonas says, "In Marxist utopianism, technology is put to its most ambitious test," and therefore, seeing its reflection in Marxism, we are able to discern "what the worldwide technological impetus of our civilization is moving toward anyway."[84] Utopia, which in ancient thought served as an indispensable guide to reflection, now merely casts into grim relief the most dangerous tendencies of modernity.[85]

Although Jonas offers radical criticisms of Kant's moral thinking and takes care to distinguish his own position from Kant's ("what matters are things rather than states of my will"),[86] in regard to the guiding ambition of his theory, Jonas' project is basically Kantian. He does not, for instance, offer (like Aristotle) a descriptive account of the virtues that alone are capable of realizing the good, yet which cannot be specified concretely apart from their embodiment in a character habituated to virtue. Rather, he seeks a foundational account of *principles* that are meant to constrain our judgment and *imperatives* that are meant to regulate our action. In the face of the demands of the present, one cannot rely on ordinary practical wisdom (Aristotelian *phronesis*); one requires binding *rules* that set strict limits upon what is permissible and impermissible in the realm of action. Jonas himself states that the need for an objectively binding ethics that rests not on mere sentiment but on intelligible principle renders urgent "the quest for foundations."[87] The emphasis on "principles" (which are rule-bound - as opposed to an emphasis on virtue, prudence, and character, which cannot be specified by rules) is unmistakably Kantian.[88] Jonas speaks of "a heuristic casuistry that is to help in the spotting of ethical principles," "a casuistry of the imagination which ... assists in the tracking and discovering of principles."[89] Although Jonas has been described (by Habermas)[90] as a "neo-Aristotelian," his basic approach to ethics (with its emphasis on "foundations," "principles," and "casuistry") is anything but Aristotelian. In fact, Jonas expressly embraces Kant's repudiation of classical ethics when he casts his supreme principle in the form of Kantian morality: "not just as an advice of moral prudence but as an unqualified command."[91]

In the end, I remain skeptical that the theoretical deduction of binding principles can do much to restrain the most dangerous impulses of our technological civilization. As is always the case in the ethical sphere, and as Aristotle established so compellingly in his ethics, what ultimately determines whether we make the right choices and whether we commit ourselves to the right course of action is the *ethos* by which we are habituated to living the proper kind of life. And it is just this *ethos* of a society that mere theory or philosophy has the least power to affect, as Jonas himself surely knows as well as anyone.[92]

It seems highly fanciful that any endeavor (even a successful one) in quest of philosophical foundations could, as Jonas seems to suggest, make its influence felt in "the battle of opinions."[93] There is indeed a kind of "unity of theory and practice" that achieves efficacy, and an awesome one at that. This consists of the application in practice of that specific kind of theory formulated first of all by Bacon (a new meaning of theory characterized by Jonas in "The Practical Uses of Theory"). It is the very same concept of theory that Marx presupposes when he speaks of theory "gripping the masses," where theory can hardly signify more than an instrument of ideological manipulation.[94] It would certainly be a considerable achievement of theory today if it could merely arrest or repulse this Baconian "unity of theory and practice" (that is, restore to theory its former modesty).[95] Seen in the light of this modern conception of theory, the purpose of Jonas' ethic is to annul the latter by reversing the Baconian injunction: not to act upon nature with a fearless "will to experiment," but to abstain from gratuitous action out of a fearful anticipation of the worst (not the optimal) consequences of knowledge.

The theme of the hubris of the knowledge seeker has haunted the literary imagination of the West, from the *Book of Genesis* and Aeschylus, to the Faust legend, to *Frankenstein*. Jonas' claim, however, is that the "Frankenstein" problem now extends to the whole of our civilization as it is actually constituted in the present. That is, we have not yet even begun to reflect seriously on the unforeseen consequences of what we are setting in motion and are blithely oblivious to the possible long-term effects of the projects in which we are already implicated.

Today we believe that the cure for technology is more technology. Thus Ronald Reagan believes that the threat of nuclear war can be remedied by a trillion-dollar supertechnology suspended in the heavens above us. What technology causes, technology can heal.96 The idea that technology is never out of our control is, for us, a virtual tautology. Technology is the means for controlling our own destiny, therefore (it follows) technology is always at our disposal. We have thought like this since the seventeenth century, when Bacon formulated the "new organon" for our civilization. Perhaps delusions such as that of Reagan concerning "Star Wars" are what we require to shield ourselves against, and fend off, a recognition of the groundlessness of this way of thinking. Possessed with the Promethean dream of unlimited means, we have meanwhile forgotten the humble question of ends.

Notes

1. Wilson Carey McWilliams and Marc K. Landry, "On Political Education, Eloquence and Memory," *PS*, 18, No. 2 (Spring, 1984), 210.

2. George Parkin Grant, *English-Speaking Justice* (Notre Dame, Ind.: University of Notre Dame Press, 1985), p. 61.

3. *Hannah Arendt: The Recovery of the Public World*, ed. Melvyn A. Hill (New York: St. Martin's Press, 1979), p. 312. (The quotations are taken from remarks by Hans Jonas in the context of an exchange with Hannah Arendt.)

4. Hans Jonas, *The Imperative of Responsibility: In Search of an Ethics for the Technological Age* (Chicago: University of Chicago Press, 1984).

5. *Ibid.*, p. 9.

6. *Ibid.*, p. x.

7. *Ibid.*, pp. 5-6.

8. *Ibid.*, pp. 7-8.

9. *Ibid.*

10. *Ibid.*, p. 9.

11. *Ibid.*, p. 11.

12. *Ibid.*, p. 13.

13. *Ibid.*, p. 15.

14. *Ibid.*, p. 11.

15. *Ibid.*, p. 14.

16. *Ibid.*, p. 17.

17. *Ibid.*, p. 31; cf. pp. x, 34, 37.

18. See *ibid.*, p. 241, note 6, where Jonas mentions that the original (German) title of the work was chosen "in conscious antithesis" to Ernst Bloch's famous book, *The Principle of Hope.* Cf. p. 127: "Marxism must be again and again our partner in dialogue, as we pursue our theoretical effort at an ethics of historical responsibility."

19. *Ibid.*, p. 17.

20. *Ibid.*

21. *Ibid.*

22. Cf. Grant, *English-Speaking Justice*, p. 82.

23. Hannah Arendt, *The Human Condition* (Chicago: University of Chicago Press, 1958), Prologue: pp. 1-6; cf. Arendt, "The Conquest of Space and the Stature of Man," in *Between Past and Future: Eight Exercises in Political Thought*, enl. ed. (New York: Viking Press, 1968), pp. 265-280. For commentary, see George Kateb, *Hannah Arendt: Politics, Conscience, Evil* (Totowa, N.J.: Rowman & Allanheld, 1984), pp. 163-172.

24. Jonas, *The Imperative of Responsibility*, pp. 18-19. Cf. Arendt, *The Human Condition*, p. 2.

25. Jonas, *The Imperative of Responsibility*, p. 21.

26. *Ibid.*

27. *Ibid.*, p. 23.

28. Hans Jonas, *The Phenomenon of Life: Toward a Philosophical Biology* (Chicago: University of Chicago Press, 1982), Eighth Essay, p. 208.

29. *Ibid.*, pp. 208-209.

30. *Ibid.*, p. 209.

31. Jonas, *The Imperative of Responsibility*, p. 34.

32. *Ibid.*

33. *Ibid.*

34. *Ibid.*, pp. 35-37.

35. *Ibid.*, p. 36.

36. *Ibid.*, p. 33.

37. *Ibid.*

38. *Ibid.*, p. 38.

39. *Ibid.* In his essay "Socio-Economic Knowledge and Ignorance of Goals," Jonas writes: "No argument can establish that being is better than not-being" (*Philosophical Essays: From Ancient Creed to Technological Man* (Chicago: University of Chicago Press, 1980), p. 87 n.). Yet this is precisely what the argument of *The Imperative of Responsibility* requires Jonas to demonstrate.

40. Jonas, *The Imperative of Responsibility*, p. 33.

41. *Ibid.*, p. 37.

42. *Ibid.*, p. 40.

43. *Ibid.*, p. 42.

44. *Ibid.*, pp. 41-42.

45. *Ibid.*, p. 42.
46. *Ibid.*, p. 41.
47. *Ibid.*, p. 43.
48. *Ibid.*, p. 45.
49. *Ibid.*, p. 74.
50. *Ibid.*, p. 70.
51. See Kant, *Critique of Judgment*, Second Part: "Critique of Teleological Judgment." On teleology, cf. Jonas, *The Phenomenon of Life*, pp. 33-37; the book as a whole is an unrelenting critique of the modern repudiation of teleology.
52. Jonas, *The Imperative of Responsibility*, p. 71.
53. *Ibid.*, p. 72.
54. *Ibid.* Cf. Kant, *Critique of Judgment*, sects. 61, 68, 70, 78, 80, where Kant argues that while the ascription of final ends to nature would be illegitimate for the *explanation* of natural causality, it is indispensable as a heuristic aid to our *reflection*, which furnishes insights and guidance for our investigation of nature (hence the distinction between "reflective" judgment and "determinant" judgment). Kant's treatment of teleology is clearly a very important source of Jonas' discussion of natural ends. But while Jonas agrees with Kant that "finality" should not be appealed to for explanatory purposes (which implies rejection of Aristotle), he goes well beyond Kant in the claims to cognitive validity that he allows to such reflective or speculative judgment (in Kantian terminology: teleology as a "regulative" idea is turned into a "constitutive" idea).
55. Jonas, *The Imperative of Responsibility*, p. 78.
56. *Ibid.*, p. 80.
57. *Ibid.*, p. 86.
58. *Ibid.*, pp. 86-87.
59. *Ibid.*, p. 87.
60. *Ibid.*, pp. 85, 89.
61. *Ibid.*, pp. 89-90.
62. *Ibid.*, p. 105.
63. *Ibid.*, p. 107.
64. *Ibid.*, pp. 109-110.
65. *Ibid.*, p. 109.
66. *Ibid.*, p. 237, n. 15.
67. On p. 124 of *The Imperative of Responsibility*, Jonas suggests that, relative to the norms of premodern politics, *all* political responsibility today appears hubristic. (He adduces this fact to help explain why previous ethics had no need to contend with the concept of responsibility.)
68. *Ibid.*, p. 119.
69. *Ibid.*
70. *Ibid.*, p. 120.

71. *Ibid.*, p. 121.

72. *Ibid.*

73. *Ibid.*, p. 127.

74. In this respect (as in other respects) Nietzsche's philosophy offers a counterpart to Marxism, for Nietzsche too is preoccupied with bearing responsibility towards the future - e.g., *Genealogy of Morals*, Essay III, section 14, on liability for "the future of man."

75. Jonas' typical formulation is that "the concept of responsibility nowhere plays a conspicuous role in the moral systems of the past or in the philosophical theories of ethics" (*The Imperative of Responsibility*, p. 123). This seems to presuppose, though, that the concept of responsibility is centrally defined by "responsibility for the coming" (p. 124). However, Jonas does qualify somewhat his general view that a theory of responsibility, as such, is directed specifically to the future, for on p. 149 he mentions that responsibility will have to be borne simultaneously towards our *contemporaries* in the Third World, who already suffer the deprivations postulated for our descendents. Indeed, it is not at all clear why the stateman's concern for our indigent contemporaries should count any the less as a manifestation of responsibility than that on behalf of our indigent descendents. For Jonas' discussion of the plight of our necessitous contemporaries, see *The Imperative of Responsibility*, pp. 180-186.

76. *Ibid.*, pp. 127-128.

77. *Ibid.*

78. *Ibid.*, pp. 128-129.

79. *Ibid.*, pp. 139-140.

80. *Ibid.*, p. 131.

81. *Ibid.*, p. 135.

82. Cf. Marx: "Even an entire society, a nation, or all simultaneously existing societies taken together, are not the owners of the earth. They are simply its possessors, its beneficiaries, and have to bequeath it in an improved state to succeeding generations, as *boni patres familias* [good heads of the household]" (*Capital*, trans. David Fernbach (New York: Vintage, 1981), III, 911).

83. Jonas, *The Imperative of Responsibility*, p. 154.

84. *Ibid.*, pp. 178, 201.

85. Cf. *ibid.*, pp. 176-77.

86. *Ibid.*, pp. 10-12, 85, 88-90; quotation is on p. 89.

87. *Ibid.*, p. 25.

88. Cf. Alasdair MacIntyre, *After Virtue* (Notre Dame, Ind.: University of Notre Dame Press, 1981), pp. 112, 141, 143-144, 216-219, 239.

89. Jonas, *The Imperative of Responsibility*, pp. 29, 30; cf. p. 35.

90. Jürgen Habermas, "Modernity versus Postmodernity," *New German Critique*, 22 (Winter, 1981), 13. The label "neo-Aristotelian" is of course a

fairly accurate characterization of Jonas' ontology. (Yet even with respect to ontology, this description of Jonas requires some qualification: cf. Jonas, *The Phenomenon of Life*, p.2.)

91. Jonas, *The Imperative of Responsibility*, p. 38; cf. p. 83.

92. On the limits of theory in instructing practical judgment, see Jonas' mention of Aristotle in *The Phenomenon of Life*, p. 199. Also, consider the description of the current predicament of theory in the passage from the same essay discussed earlier (see p. 340 above).

93. Jonas, *The Imperative of Responsibility*, p. 25.

94. Karl Marx, *Early Writings*, ed. Quintin Hoare, trans. Rodney Livingstone and Gregor Benton (New York: Vintage, 1975), p. 251. For an account of Marx's and Nietzsche's adherence to the Baconian understanding of theory, see Edward Andrew, "The Unity of Theory and Practice: The Science of Marx and Nietzsche," in *Political Theory and Praxis: New Perspectives*, ed. Terence Ball (Minneapolis: University of Minnesota Press, 1977), pp. 117-137. Also: Jonas, *The Imperative of Responsibility*, pp. 142-144, 154-156.

95. For further discussion of these issues, see my article "On the Disunity of Theory and Practice," *Praxis International*, 7, No. 1 (April 1987), 25-34.

96. Cf. Jonas, *The Imperative of Responsibility*, p. 239, n. 26. Jonas tends to play down the relative urgency of the nuclear menace (*Philosophical Essays*, pp. xv-xvi; *The Imperative of Responsibility*, pp. ix, 202-203). For an extension of Jonas' "heuristics of fear" to the question of nuclear war, see George Kateb, "Nuclear Weapons and Individual Rights," *Dissent*, 33, No. 2 (Spring, 1986), 161-172.

NOTES ON CONTRIBUTORS

Edward Andrew teaches political philosophy at the University of Toronto. His publications include *Closing the Iron Cage: The Scientific Management of Leisure (1981) and Shylock's Rights: A Grammar of Lockian Claims* (1988).

Ronald Beiner is Associate Professor of Political Science at the University of Toronto. He has edited Hannah Arendt's *Lectures on Kant's Political Philosophy* (1982) and is the author of *Political Judgment* (1983).

Barry Cooper is Professor of Political Science at the University of Calgary. He is the author of books on Maurice Merleau-Ponty, Michel Foucault, Eric Voegelin and Alexander Kennedy Isbister. In addition, he has written *The End of History* and recently completed a book on technology and tyranny.

Richard B. Day is Professor of Political Economy at the Erindale Campus of the University of Toronto. His publications include *Leon Trotsky and the Politics of Economic Isolation* (1973); *The 'Crisis' and the 'Crash': Soviet Studies of the West, 1917-1939* (1981); N.I. Bukharin, *Selected Writings on the State and the Transition to Socialism* (1983); E.A. Preobrazhensky, *The Decline of Capitalism* (1985) - the latter two edited and translated by R.B. Day with introductions and notes.

Marie Fleming is Associate Professor of Political Science at the University of Western Ontario. She is the author of *The Anarchist Way to Socialism: Elisée Reclus and Nineteenth-Century European Anarchism* and is currently working on a book entitled *Force and Consent: Deconstructive Readings of Habermas' Theory of Communicative Action.*

H.D. Forbes is Associate Professor of Political Science at the University of Toronto. He is the author of *Nationalism, Ethnocentrism and Personality: Social Science and Critical Theory* (1985) and editor of *Canadian Political Thought* (1985).

Frank Harrison is Professor of Political Science at St. Francis Xavier University in Antigonish, Nova Scotia. He is the author of *The Modern State: An Anarchist Analysis* (1983) and is editor of Michael Bakunin's *Statism and Anarchy*, published in English in 1976.

László G. Jobbágy taught political science at Karl Marx University of Economics in Budapest from 1976 to 1981 and is currently completing a Ph.D. thesis on "The Concept of Market in Socialist Thinking."

Frank J. Kurtz is Executive Director of Leadership Greater Chicago. He teaches political theory at Loyola University of Chicago and has been on the faculties of the University of Toronto and Shimer College. He holds a Ph.D. in Political Science from the University of Toronto.

Gary A. Lewis is a writer on political theory and practice and has been a recent Post-Doctoral Fellow of the Department of Political Science at the University of Toronto. His current book, *News from Somewhere: Connecting Health and Freedom at the Workplace*, was published in 1986.

Michael Löwy is research director in sociology at the CNRS (Centre National de la Recherche Scientifique) in Paris. Publications available in English include *From Romanticism to Bolshevism: Lukács' Political Evolution 1909-1929* (1979; published also in French, Spanish, Italian and Portuguese) and *The Politics of Uneven and Combined Development* (1981).

Joseph Masciulli has taught political philosophy at the University of Toronto and at St. Francis Xavier University. Currently he is a Jesuit novice at Ignatius College in Guelph, Ontario. He has recently published "The Armed Founder versus the Catonic Hero: Machiavelli and Rousseau on Popular Leadership" in *Interpretation*.

W.R. Newell is Associate Professor of Political Science at the University of Nebraska at Lincoln. He received the B.A. and M.A. degrees from the University of Toronto and the Ph.D. from Yale University. His articles have appeared in the *American Political Science Review*, *Political Theory* and *History of European Ideas*.

Dusan Pokorny is Professor Emeritus of Economics and Political Science at the University of Toronto. He has written on the epistemological character of modern economic models and on philosophy and method in Smith and Marx.

Willem H. Vanderburg, after completing a doctorate in engineering, spent nearly five years with Jacques Ellul examining the relationship between technology and contemporary society. The first part of this study has been published as *The Growth of Minds and Cultures* (1985). Professor Vanderburg is Director of the Center for Technology and Social Development at the University of Toronto.

Jerry Weinberger is Professor of Political Science at Michigan State University. He is editor of Francis Bacon's *The Great Instauration* and *New Atlantis* (1980) and the author of *Science, Faith and Politics: Francis Bacon and the Utopian Roots of the Modern Age* (1985).